KU-514-344

# Raspberry Pi® Projects

Dr. Andrew Robinson

Mike Cook

Jonathan Evans

Sean McManus

ST HELENS
COLLEGE

LIBRARY

This edition first published 2014

© 2014 John Wiley & Sons, Ltd.

*Registered office*

John Wiley & Sons Ltd, The Atrium, Southern Gate, Chichester, West Sussex, PO19 8SQ, United Kingdom

For details of our global editorial offices, for customer services and for information about how to apply for permission to reuse the copyright material in this book please see our website at www.wiley.com.

The right of the authors to be identified as the authors of this work has been asserted in accordance with the Copyright, Designs and Patents Act 1988.

All rights reserved. No part of this publication may be reproduced, stored in a retrieval system, or transmitted, in any form or by any means, electronic, mechanical, photocopying, recording or otherwise, except as permitted by the U.K. Copyright, Designs and Patents Act 1988, without the prior permission of the publisher.

Wiley also publishes its books in a variety of electronic formats. Some content that appears in print may not be available in electronic books.

Designations used by companies to distinguish their products are often claimed as trademarks. All brand names and product names used in this book are trade names, service marks, trademarks or registered trademarks of their respective owners. The publisher is not associated with any product or vendor mentioned in this book. This publication is designed to provide accurate and authoritative information in regard to the subject matter covered. It is sold on the understanding that the publisher is not engaged in rendering professional services. If professional advice or other expert assistance is required, the services of a competent professional should be sought.

**Trademarks:** Wiley and the John Wiley & Sons, Ltd. logo are trademarks or registered trademarks of John Wiley and Sons, Ltd. and/ or its affiliates in the United States and/or other countries, and may not be used without written permission. Raspberry Pi is a trademark of the Raspberry Pi Foundation. All other trademarks are the property of their respective owners. John Wiley & Sons, Ltd. is not associated with any product or vendor mentioned in the book.

A catalogue record for this book is available from the British Library.

ISBN 978-1-118-55543-9 (paperback); ISBN 978-1-118-55556-9 (ePub); ISBN 978-1-118-55553-8 (ePDF)

Set in Chaparral Pro Regular 10/12.5 by Indianapolis Composition Services

Printed simultaneously in Great Britain and the United States.

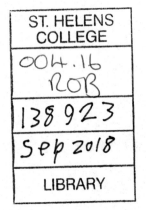

ST. HELENS
COLLEGE

004.16
ROB

138 923

Sep 2018

LIBRARY

*To the kitchen table inventors, and their long-suffering families that have to live with them.*
*–Andrew Robinson*

*To Mike Bibby, who was the first editor to give me the opportunity to write regularly about computers and hardware. His unfailing enthusiasm about all things and his inability to take anything just on trust are an example to us all. A continuing and valued friend.*
*–Mike Cook*

# Publisher's Acknowledgements

Some of the people who helped bring this book to market include the following:

## Editorial and Production

**VP Consumer and Technology Publishing Director**
Michelle Leete

**Associate Director–Book Content Management**
Martin Tribe

**Associate Publisher**
Chris Webb

**Executive Commissioning Editor**
Craig Smith

**Project Editor**
Dana Lesh

**Copy Editors**
Dana Lesh, Kathryn Duggan

**Technical Editor**
Genevieve Smith-Nunes

**Editorial Manager**
Jodi Jensen

**Senior Project Editor**
Sara Shlaer

**Editorial Assistant**
Annie Sullivan

## Marketing

**Associate Marketing Director**
Louise Breinholt

**Marketing Manager**
Lorna Mein

**Senior Marketing Executive**
Kate Parrett

**Marketing Assistant**
Polly Thomas

# About the Authors

**Andrew Robinson** is the founder of a successful embedded computing design consultancy firm based in Manchester. Passionate about education, he runs workshops and training sessions for all levels of experience, from design engineers to teachers and school children. His projects with the Raspberry Pi have appeared in the national press and on ITV, Channel 5 and BBC television. He is an Honorary Research Fellow of the University of Manchester, where previously he completed his Ph.D. in low power-embedded processors.

Andrew can trace his enthusiasm for electronics and computers back to building a working model lighthouse at the age of five.

**Mike Cook,** veteran technical author and electronics maker from the U.K., was born in Manchester and still lives close by. He is best known to the public for a series of over 300 articles which appeared in *The Micro User, Acorn Computing* and *Acorn User* from 1983 to 2000. These were called the "Body Building Course" and "Run the Risc" and covered the design and build of new gadgets, interfaces and peripherals for the old (vintage) BBC computer and the RISC PC. He also wrote numerous reviews, software articles and the readers' problem page in these magazines.

Mike started work in the late sixties at an industrial electronics company in Oldham. He went on to take a degree in physical electronics at Newcastle, including a year spent working at the Admiralty Underwater Weapons establishment at Portland. His post-graduate research was in sound compression at the University of Salford. He spent over 20 years at Manchester Metropolitan University (initially Manchester Polytechnic) lecturing in physics, specialising in computer instrumentation, astronomy and image processing. Later he moved back into industry where he headed the hardware design team for the pioneering digital terrestrial set top box, and has been a development manager for security and RFID products.

He now works freelance as an embedded electronics consultant and author. His last book was *The Raspberry Pi For Dummies* published by Wiley.

Recently he has been designing even more things in the arena of physical computing, exhibiting at the U.K. Maker Fairs, Mini Maker Fairs and the prestigious New York World Maker fair. Mike was the recipient of a Maker of Merit Blue Ribbon at the 2013 Rome Maker Faire.

**Jonathan Evans** has had a life-long interest in computers and electronics. At the tender age of 10, he taught himself how to program a computer, and he quickly learned how computers and electronics could be married for a functionality to keep his siblings out of his room. He has gone on to become a distinguished IT professional with over 20 years of experience. His passion for creation and innovation combines perfectly with the Raspberry Pi phenomenon, and in his spare time he enjoys exploring projects to make the Raspberry Pi relevant to everyday life. He enjoys sharing his ideas at www.projects.privateeyepi.com where he continues to explore the endless possibilities of this computing platform.

**Sean McManus** writes inspiring books and articles about computing. He contributed the chapter on Minecraft to *Raspberry Pi Projects,* and his previous books include *Raspberry Pi For Dummies* (written with Mike Cook), *Scratch Programming in Easy Steps, iPad for the Older and Wiser, Microsoft Office for the Older and Wiser,* and *Web Design in Easy Steps.* Visit his website at www.sean.co.uk.

# Contents

# Introduction

**WHEN WE'RE YOUNG,** making things is second nature – painting a picture, inventing a game, telling a story, building a rocket from a washing-up liquid bottle that we're convinced will fly all the way to the moon. Childhood is all about adventure, discovery – the quest for something new.

Although these joys don't fade with age, it can become harder to find space and time for play and discovery as "real life" takes over. But yet, some of the greatest inventions and discoveries of history were the result of curious people not being afraid to "have a go", often tinkering away in their own homes or garden sheds rather than high-tech well-funded engineering companies.

What's this got to do with a book on things to do with a Raspberry Pi?

Well, after reading and having a go at some of the projects in this book you might discover the pleasure of making something with a computer can bring. Computing offers a fantastic world of new and untapped opportunities for adventure and creativity. It touches so many areas of our lives (game consoles, set top boxes and smartphones are all computers) that you can combine it with almost any other passion or hobby.

You'll see why a sprinkling of computing is beneficial for everyone, and that a moment of personal creativity on the kitchen table can have a much bigger impact. You'll also discover the story behind a particular credit-card sized computer.

## A History of Making

World-changing inventions can come from unconventional places.

Orville and Wilbur Wright were two ordinary brothers from Ohio who owned a bicycle shop. Fascinated with the workings of these simple machines, they became convinced that they could build a flying machine. And they did. In 1903, they launched the world's first aeroplane. Nearly a century later, as HIV/AIDS swept through Africa, Trevor Baylis, an ex-stuntman, became convinced he could help. He sat in his suburban garden shed and invented an inexpensive and durable wind-up radio for use across Africa to spread simple health messages and undoubtedly prevented many, many deaths. Steve Jobs and Steve Wozniak, the founders of Apple, both learned about electronics and computers from experimenting in their bedrooms and family garages. These are just three examples that show the worldwide impact on millions tinkering at home can have.

Many inventors can clearly imagine what they want to make, but might not know how to build it. But, spurred on by the joy of creativity, they teach themselves the skills needed to build what they could imagine. Wozniak and Jobs developed their skills this way, taking apart existing appliances, figuring out how they work and putting them back together. Sometimes the appliances would be enhanced by tinkering, and sometimes they'd no longer work at all! But they weren't put off; sometimes it was just about discovering how something worked, or the journey to overcome technical adversity, rather than producing a polished product.

## Consumer Computing

It is ironic that the birth of Apple computers was a result of poking around in the innards of appliances. Nowadays, computers are sold as sleek, refined aluminium caskets of magic, sealing in opportunities to experiment and discover how they actually work. In a continual quest to add value to their products, manufacturers lure customers with the promise of easy-to-use products and an effortless user experience with your every need taken care of.

Unfortunately it's not been a smooth journey. Rarely do modern computer systems do exactly what users want. How often are we left frustrated by a computer system failing, consoled by the manufacturer's line that "that will be fixed in the next update" or "you need to buy the next version if you want it to do that"? For the technologically fearless, these statements are more like rallying cries, an excuse to tinker until the computer does what they really want. But these days, there are few people brave or skilled enough to roll their sleeves up and get inside.

## Why Everyone Should Learn About Computing

Computers really are everywhere, pervading every aspect of our lives. As well as the laptop, desktop and smartphone, just think about the computers behind life support systems and medical records in our hospitals, in banking and shopping keeping the economy going, in manufacturing and our food-supply chain. They are key for our communications, powering digital TV and radio and mobile phone networks, as well as the Internet. With computers so integral to the functioning of our media, commerce and government, it seems odd that so many of us are ignorant of how they work.

Given how widespread the reliance on computers is, think how much we could all benefit from a little bit more understanding. Business leaders and politicians could make more informed decisions on projects involving computers, and the man-on-the-street would be less likely to fall prey to online scams or be duped by overimpressive advertising claims about products. They'd have the skills to make computers work for them to improve their lives.

I see similarities between computing and cooking. Cooking has recipes, which is about following steps. It is about making meals, consisting of sets of dishes. To make an apple pie, you need to break down the task into manageable elements (making the pastry, coring the apples, baking for just the right amount of time), all of which add to a complete (and hopefully tasty) apple pie. This is an example of *abstraction*, and is key to mastering computing. The problem-solving and logical-thinking techniques, such as managing abstraction, that are developed in computing are valuable to other aspects of life.

We teach our children how to cook, not because we want to train them to become professional chefs, but because we view it as an essential life skill. Without it, we condemn our children to a lifetime of preheating ready meals, often unfulfilling and expensive. For many people, learning the basic skills is the start of a lifelong love of cooking. They see it as an outlet for their creativity, perhaps starting with a recipe and adapting it to make it their own. It's a social occupation, a chance to show achievements and discuss techniques, challenges and adventures around a lively dinner table.

I'd argue that learning to use computers has parallels with learning to cook. Everyone needs the basic skills. Some may use those skills to go on to become professional programmers, but I'd hope that for most people it is an opportunity for creativity, as well as a survival skill in today's modern environment.

However, given the need for more people to learn more about how computers work and the reliance on them, it's also ironic that getting into computing has become more difficult with modern computers. That is, until a certain credit-card–sized computer came along. . . .

## Enter the Raspberry Pi

For most people, beginning to experiment on a £1000 laptop, putting precious data at risk is a daunting prospect. I'd think twice before putting all my digital photos, my music collection and my online banking at risk! Games consoles and some phones actively prevent people from creating their own games and apps, presumably to protect revenue by forcing consumer to buy manufacturer's products.

With the desire to share the fun of computing and the need for more people to know how computers worked, Eben Upton created a small, cheap computer on his kitchen table. With the help of Dr. Rob Mullins, Professor Alan Mycroft and Jack Lang from Cambridge University; Pete Lomas, an expert in hardware; and David Braben, the Raspberry Pi Foundation was born, a charity that set out to promote the study of computer science and related topics, especially at the school level, and to put the fun back into learning computing.

The Raspberry Pi Foundation aimed to open up the world of computing by creating a hardware device that was pocket-money affordable, so it was accessible to everyone, and there'd be no need to worry about experimenting with it. It was unboxed to make it easy to tinker with.

In 2011, after five years' intense kitchen-table engineering, the first prototype Raspberry Pi computers were produced. After a feature about the Raspberry Pi on technology journalist Rory Cellan-Jones's blog went viral the Foundation wondered if they were at the early stages of something bigger than they were expecting.

After some clever engineering to allow the Raspberry Pi to be built cheaply enough to be sold for $25, an initial batch of 10,000 went on sale on 29th February 2012 at 6 a.m. A few minutes later, they had sold out. Eighteen months later, 1.75 million had been sold worldwide.

## About This Book

During the development of the Raspberry Pi I'd been working on public engagement projects at the University of Manchester to encourage more people into computing.

I'd been following the Raspberry Pi from an early stage, and thought it had great potential. Like thousands of other engineers, I was also very excited by the technology crammed in this tiny PCB of components. I was also aware that for most people less familiar with computers, the same PCB wouldn't be particularly exciting, and perhaps a scary mass of wires, components and metal. Like the Foundation, I wanted to share the wonder and joy computing could bring.

The big advantage of the Raspberry Pi was that it could be put it in places you couldn't put a PC. I wanted the Raspberry Pi to be relevant to what people are interested in. To make it easy to connect to the Raspberry Pi, I came up with the PiFace Digital interface, developed at home on the kitchen table in my free evenings and weekends. I'm still amazed when I see people all over the world posting videos online showing what they're doing with the Raspberry Pi and PiFace. I've seen children building robots, door-entry systems for the elderly, games and industrial applications in banks and railway stations.

## How to Use This Book

This book aims to answer the question "You've got a Raspberry Pi – now what?" and is packed full of fun Raspberry Pi projects to inspire you.

This book is divided into three parts. There is some progression, but after you've got your Raspberry Pi up and running it should be fairly easy to dip into any of the other chapters. You can just follow the step-by-step instructions to get results quickly, but don't be afraid to experiment and make them your own. That's where the real fun lies! Background information is provided that will help you learn the skills you will need if you want to extend the projects.

At the end of each chapter, there are ideas and suggestions for extensions, but you will probably have your own too. We want to see what you create, so share your work with social media such as Facebook, Twitter and YouTube and tag them with RaspberryPiProjects.

Some code listings are available to download from the companion website at www.wiley. com/go/raspberrypiprojects if you get really stuck, but part of learning to program is about typing code in, so not all the code is provided!

Much of the background information is relevant to the classroom, and the book can be used to supplement teaching the new U.K. computing qualifications. If you're a teacher, look out for supporting information that can help students learn through Raspberry Pi projects.

## Part I: Getting Started with the Raspberry Pi

This part will take you through plugging together your Raspberry Pi and installing the software, plus introduces you to Python:

- ○ Chapter 1, "Getting Your Raspberry Pi Up and Running", covers your first basic steps in getting your Raspberry Pi running.
- ○ Chapter 2, "Introductory Software Project: The Insult Generator", gets you started programming in Python.

## Part II: Software Projects

This contains some fun software projects:

- ○ Chapter 3, "Tic-Tac-Toe", has you programming a game of tic-tac-toe, particularly covering lists and artificial intelligence.
- ○ Chapter 4, "Here's the News", shows you how to program your own teleprompter.
- ○ Chapter 5, "Ping", covers how to program your own computer Ping-Pong game, describe movement to a computer, detect collisions and handle the physics of reflection.
- ○ Chapter 6, "Pie Man", shows you how to program your own version of Pac-Man using animated sprites, layers and transparent pixels.
- ○ Chapter 7, "Minecraft Maze Maker", uses a Python program to build a maze in Minecraft.

## Part III: Hardware Projects

This contains some exciting and challenging hardware projects:

- ○ Chapter 8, "Colour Snap", is an introductory hardware project that implements the game of Snap using different coloured lights and shows you how to safely power LEDs and use surface mount components.
- ○ Chapter 9, "Test Your Reactions", gets you wiring up simple computer-controlled circuits.

○ Chapter 10, "The Twittering Toy", shows you how to make your code talk to Twitter and gets you hacking household items.

○ Chapter 11, "Disco Lights", shows you how to control LED strips and make them dance in time to music.

○ Chapter 12, "Door Lock", covers how to build a computer-controlled door lock controlled by RFID tags and explains computer authentication.

○ Chapter 13, "Home Automation", shows you how to create home-automation projects to make your home environment more intelligent, implementing door switches, motion sensors, a webcam and e-mail alerts.

○ Chapter 14, "Computer-Controlled Slot Car Racing", gets you wiring up a slot car game and using it to keep score in a two-player multiple choice quiz.

○ Chapter 15, "Facebook-Enabled Roto-Sketch", shows you how to use rotary controls to draw elaborate designs and automatically post them to Flickr and on to Facebook.

○ Chapter 16, "The Pendulum Pi, a Harmonograph", shows you how to create a harmonograph for producing intricate patterns using an Arduino to help the Pi with real-time data gathering.

○ Chapter 17, "The Techno–Bird Box, a Wildlife Monitor", covers how to build a "techno–bird box" that will monitor the bird activity in your garden.

## The Future

Computers are set to be an ever-bigger part of our lives and touch more areas. Systems will be more complex with more connectivity. In the future your washing machine and other appliances in your home will likely talk to your smartphone. And we'll all need more computing skills to master them. New ways of using computers will mean that there will be new areas for adventure and opportunities to change people's lives and solve problems in the world.

One word of warning before you begin your adventure: After you start you might never stop! Electronics and coding can be addictive; who knows what you might go on to make with the skills you learn from this book.

Building and making is incredibly rewarding and satisfying. We want to get more people of the world to become producers of technology rather than consumers. The projects in this book are starting points – but then the real rewards come from making the project your own and seeing your own ideas become reality.

Welcome to the world of digital making. Are you ready to invent the future?

Part I

# Getting Started with the Raspberry Pi

# Chapter 1
# Getting Your Raspberry Pi Up and Running

**by Dr. Andrew Robinson**

## In This Chapter

- ○ What the operating system is for
- ○ How to put the operating system on an SD card for the Raspberry Pi
- ○ How to connect up your Raspberry Pi
- ○ A bit about the boot process
- ○ Basic troubleshooting if your Raspberry Pi doesn't start

**THIS CHAPTER IS** a beginner's guide to your first steps with the Raspberry Pi. It goes from getting it out of the box to getting something on the screen. Even if you already have your Raspberry Pi up and running, it's worth a quick skim as you'll discover how a 21-year-old student changed the world and a bit about how the operating system for your Raspberry Pi works. After this chapter, you'll get into the real fun of creating projects!

# The Operating System

The Raspberry Pi primarily uses Linux for its operating system (OS) rather than Microsoft Windows or OS X (for Apple). An *operating system* is a program that makes it easier for the end user to use the underlying hardware. For example, although the processor (the chip at the centre of the Raspberry Pi that does the work) can do only one thing at a time, the operating system gives the impression the computer is doing lots of things by rapidly switching between different tasks. Furthermore, the operating system controls the hardware and hides the complexity that allows the Raspberry Pi to talk to networks or SD cards.

# Linux

Part of the success of the Raspberry Pi is thanks to the enthusiastic community that is behind it. Linux is a testament to what can be achieved with the support of volunteers around the world. In 1991, Linus Torvalds began work on an operating system as a hobby while he was a 21-year-old student at the University of Helsinki. A year later, his hobby operating system for desktop PCs (80386) was available online under the name *Linux*. Crucially, the code for the operating system was available as well. This allowed volunteers around the world to contribute; to check and correct bugs; to submit additional features; and to adapt and reuse other's work for their own projects. If you master the projects in this book and learn more about computing, then who knows – one of your hobby projects could be as successful as Linus Torvalds's is.

The popularity of Linux grew, and in addition to its use as a desktop operating system, it is now used for the majority of web servers, in Android devices and in the majority of the world's supercomputers. Most importantly for us, it is used on the Raspberry Pi.

# Linux Distributions

Because Linux code is publically available, different organisations have made slight changes to it and distributed it. This has led to different *distributions* (versions), including Red Hat, Fedora, Debian, Arch, Ubuntu and openSUSE. Some companies sell their distributions and provide paid-for support, whereas others are completely free. Raspbian is based on the Debian distribution with some customisations for the Raspberry Pi and is what is used in this book.

The most popular operating system for the Raspberry Pi is Linux. The widescale use of Linux (just think how many Raspberry Pis there are, not to mention Android phones, web servers, and so on) shows how much an idea can grow. After you start tinkering with the Raspberry Pi, one of your ideas might grow to be as big (or bigger) than Torvalds's or those of the founders of the Raspberry Pi, and you too will make a real impact on the world. So let's get started!

## Getting the OS on an SD Card

The Raspberry Pi doesn't know how to coordinate its hardware without an OS. When it is powered up, it looks on the SD card to start loading the OS. As such, you're going to need an SD card with an OS on it.

You can either buy an SD card that already has an OS on it, or you can copy an OS to your own SD card with a PC. A premade card is simplest, but more expensive. Creating your own isn't too difficult, but it is slightly more involved than just copying a file.

### Premade Cards

Premade cards are bundled in kits or available to purchase from element14, RS or other online stores. A 4GB card should be big enough for getting started and cost less than £10.

## Filesystems

Computer storage like SD cards, USB memory sticks and hard disks essentially contain millions of separate compartments that store small amounts of data in large grids. The individual compartments, called *blocks*, are addressed by a coordinate system – you can think of them as a piece of squared paper the size of a sports field. The sports field is partitioned into areas of blocks that are handled by the operating system to provide *filesystems*. It is the OS's job to manage how data is written to this massive storage area, so that when a user refers to a file by name, all the tiny blocks of data are fetched and combined in the correct order. There are different ways in which the blocks are formatted, with different features. As such, an identical file will be stored differently on the underlying grid by different filesystems.

Typically, Microsoft Windows uses FAT or NTFS, OS X uses HFS Plus and Linux uses ext. Most blank SD cards are formatted as FAT by default. Because the Raspberry Pi runs Linux, it uses the ext filesystem, which must be set up and populated with files.

# Images

When talking about downloading the OS for the Raspberry Pi, you may hear it called an *image,* which may be slightly confusing. It is an image of the underlying storage. (Imagine an aerial photo of the entire sports field of storage blocks, even the blank ones, rather than separate files! If you were to print this photo at the same size on another sports field, you'd have an exact copy of all the files stored on the original one.)

It is possible to store an image as a single file in another filesystem, but this arrangement is not suitable for a running Raspberry Pi. As such, a Raspberry Pi will not work if you just copy an image onto a FAT-formatted card. Instead, you must tell your OS that you want to transfer it at the block level, so that every block on your card matches those of the person who made the image. That way, Linux interprets these underlying blocks on the disk to provide a filesystem that is identical to the person who made the image.

In summary, filesystem images provide an easy way of cloning an entire filesystem such that all the files, their permissions, attributes, dates, and so on are identical.

### Creating Your Own SD Card

There are two ways to create your own SD card for the Raspberry Pi, using NOOBS or by transferring an image yourself.

### Using NOOBS

New Out Of Box Software (NOOBS) was created for the Raspberry Pi to automate transferring SD card images. NOOBS boots your Raspberry Pi from a FAT-formatted card and then repartitions and clones the filesystem for you. Using NOOBS should be as simple as formatting a card on your desktop PC and unzipping NOOBs downloaded from `www.raspberrypi.org/downloads`. Some operating systems do not format cards properly, so it is sometimes necessary to download a program to format the card. Although NOOBS can be simple, it doesn't always work, and it can be slower. Anyway, it's more satisfying to use the do-it-yourself approach.

### Transferring an Image Yourself

You need an SD card larger than 2GB to fit the OS on it. A 4GB card is ideal.

Visit `www.raspberrypi.org/downloads` and follow the links to download the latest version of Raspbian. You are looking for a filename containing the word `raspbian` and a date, and that ends in `.zip`. Make a note of the letters and numbers that are shown as SHA-1 checksum. Because of the speed of development, new versions are released frequently, so the exact name will differ from the one that's used in the following instructions. The location you download the file to may also be slightly different, so you should use your location accordingly when completing the instructions.

The download page has links to other distributions and other operating systems that you can try later, but for now it's best to stick with Raspbian because it is reliable, has a good selection of software for beginners and is consistent with the examples in this book.

# Checksums

A *checksum* is an easy way to check whether data has been corrupted. A checksum is a mathematical sum that is performed by the supplier of the data. When you receive the data, you perform the same sum and, in most cases, if the answer is the same, you can be almost certain that the data is the same, without comparing it bit by bit. Checksums are used extensively in computing – in network communications, when processing credit cards and even in barcodes. Although they are not infallible, they make it much easier to be fairly confident data is correct.

The instructions for creating an SD card are different depending on which OS you're using. Refer to the appropriate section for Windows, Linux and OS X.

### Creating an SD Card with Windows

It is hard to check checksums in Windows, so the following instructions assume that the downloaded image file is correct. After the download is complete, follow these steps to uncompress it and transfer the data to the SD card:

1. Unzip the downloaded file `2013-07-26-wheezy-raspbian.zip`.

2. Insert an SD card and make a note of the corresponding drive letter (for example, E:). Make sure that the card does not contain any data you want to save because it will be completely overwritten.

3. Go to `https://launchpad.net/win32-image-writer` and download the binary version of `Win32DiskImager` from the Downloads section on the right side of the web page. Unzip the program.

4. Start `Win32DiskImager.exe` as Administrator. Depending on how your system is set up, this may require you to double-click the program name, or require you to hold down the Shift key, right-click the program icon and select Run As.

5. In the Win32DiskImager window, select `2013-07-26-wheezy-raspbian.img`.

6. In the Device drop-down on the right, select the drive letter you noted in step 2 (see Figure 1-1).

FIGURE 1-1:<br/>The Win32<br/>DiskImager<br/>window.

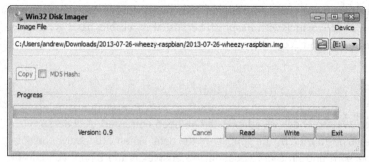

7. Click Write and wait for the imaging process to complete. (This step could take about 15–30 minutes, so be patient.)

8. Exit Win32DiskImager and eject the SD card that should now contain your OS.

### Creating an SD Card with Linux

With Linux, it's easiest to create the SD card image from the command line, as detailed in the following steps.

## Linux Permissions and sudo

Linux restricts some actions that might cause damage to other users. As such, some commands will not work unless you have the appropriate privileges. On some distributions, you need to switch to being the user *root* (the administrator account) before running the command requiring more privileged access. Other distributions will allow selected users to prefix the command with sudo. The following instructions assume that your user account has been set up to use sudo. If not, type su in the terminal first to become root.

1. Start a terminal and use the cd command to change to the directory containing the file you downloaded (for example, cd Downloads).

2. Unzip the downloaded file by typing unzip followed by the downloaded filename (for example, unzip 2013-07-26-wheezy-raspbian.zip).

3. List the image files in the current directory by typing ls *.img and make sure that the extracted image file is listed.

4. Calculate the checksum to ensure that the downloaded file is not corrupt or hasn't been tampered with. To do this, type the following:

```
sha1sum 2013-07-26-wheezy-raspbian.zip
```

Make sure that the result matches with the SHA-1 checksum given on the `http://raspberrypi.org/download` page. Although it is unlikely that they will differ, if they do, try downloading and unzipping again.

5. Insert an SD card. Make sure there's no data on it that you want to save, because it will be completely overwritten.

6. Type `dmesg` and find the device name that Linux uses to refer to the newly inserted card. It will usually be named `sdd`, `sde`, `sdf` or something similar. Alternatively, it may be in the form `mmcblk0`. Use this name wherever you see `sdX` in the following steps.

7. If Linux has automounted the card, you need to unmount it first by typing `sudo umount /dev/sdX`.

8. Double-check that you have the correct device by typing `sudo fdisk -l /dev/sdX`. Check that the size displayed matches the size of the card that you inserted.

9. When you are absolutely sure you are referring to the correct card, type the following (replacing `sdX` with the name you found in step 6) to copy the image across to the card. (This step could take about 15–30 minutes, so be patient.)

```
dd if=2013-07-26-wheezy-raspbian.img of=/dev/sdX
```

10. Type `sudo sync` before removing the card to ensure all the data is written to the card and is not still being buffered.

## Creating an SD Card with OS X

With OS X, it's easiest to create the SD card image from the command line.

Although the Macintosh normally uses drag and drop for many operations, there is a way to get "under the hood" to perform unusual operations. Your gateway to doing this is an application called *Terminal*. This is usually found in the Utilities folder, within the Applications folder. A quick way to find it is to hold down the ⌘ key and press the spacebar. This will open the Spotlight search window. Type `terminal` and then press Enter to open the Terminal application.

To create an SD card, follow these steps:

1. Start a terminal.

2. Use the `cd` command to change to the directory containing the file you downloaded. A quick way to do this is to type `cd` followed by a space and then drag the folder containing the file into the Terminal window. This will automatically fill in the rest of the command with the pathname of that folder. Then press Enter to perform the command.

3. Unzip the downloaded file by typing `unzip` followed by the downloaded filename (for example, `unzip 2013-07-26-wheezy-raspbian.zip`).

    You won't see a progress bar during this process, so you might think the computer has frozen – but don't worry. It could take a minute or two before all of the files are unzipped.

4. List the image files in the current directory by typing `ls *.img` and make sure that the extracted image file is listed.

5. To make sure everything is fine, you can calculate the checksum for the file; however, you can omit this step if you want. Calculating the checksum ensures that the downloaded file is not corrupt. To do this, type the following:

    ```
    shasum
    2013-07-26-wheezy-raspbian.zip
    ```

    Make sure that the result matches with the SHA-1 checksum on the `http://raspberrypi.org/download` page. It is unlikely that they will differ, but if they do, try downloading and unzipping again.

6. Type `diskutil list` to display a list of disks.

7. Insert an SD card. Make sure that it doesn't contain any data that you want to save because it will be completely overwritten.

8. Run `diskutil list` again and note the identifier of the new disk that appears (for example, `/dev/disk1`). Ignore the entries that end with s followed by a number. Use the disk identifier wherever `diskX` appears in the following steps.

9. Type `sudo diskutil unmountdisk /dev/diskX`.

10. Type `sudo dd bs=1m if=2013-07-26-wheezy-raspbian.img of=/dev/diskX`. (This step could take about 15–60 minutes, so be patient.)

11. Type `sudo diskutil eject /dev/diskX` before removing the card.

## Connecting Your Raspberry Pi

Now that you have your OS for your Raspberry Pi, it's time to plug it together.

Remove the Raspberry Pi from the box and, to make it easier to follow these instructions, position it the same way around as shown in Figure 1-2 (so the words *Raspberry Pi* appear the correct way up).

Plug the USB keyboard into one of the USB sockets, as shown in Figure 1-3.

FIGURE 1-2:
The Raspberry
Pi, the size of a
credit card and a
miniature
marvel of
engineering.

FIGURE 1-3:
Inserting the
USB keyboard.

**TIP** Older PS/2 keyboards will not work. You'll have to buy (or borrow) a USB keyboard, but they're not expensive.

Plug the mouse in next to the keyboard, as shown in Figure 1-4.

FIGURE 1-4:
Inserting the
USB mouse.

## Connecting a Display

The Raspberry Pi can be connected by HDMI or composite video directly. With the use of an adapter you can connect it by DVI or VGA. You should use HDMI or DVI whenever possible because they give a better picture.

Look at the sockets on your display to determine how to connect your Raspberry Pi.

### Connecting via HDMI

If your display has an HDMI input, as shown in Figure 1-5, then connect your Pi with an HDMI-HDMI cable. This is the only type of video connection that can also be used to carry audio from the Pi to your display. The HDMI socket on the Pi is at the bottom as shown in Figure 1-5.

FIGURE 1-5:
HDMI
connection
on the
Raspberry Pi.

### Connecting via DVI

If your display has a DVI input as shown in Figure 1-6, you will need an adapter. HDMI and DVI have very similar electrical signals, so adapters are *passive* – that is, they don't contain any electronics, just two sockets with wires in between. You can buy cables with an HDMI and DVI connector or adapters as shown in Figure 1-6 for less than £5.

### Connecting via VGA

DVI and HDMI both work with *digital* signals and are only found on newer monitors. Older monitors with VGA use *analogue* signals and as such need some sort of electronic circuit to convert between them. You can buy adapters that convert between HDMI and VGA for about £20 online. The Pi-View device shown in Figure 1-7 is designed specifically for the Raspberry Pi and is available through element14.

FIGURE 1-6:
HDMI-DVI
adapter.

FIGURE 1-7:
HDMI-VGA
adapter,
Pi-View.

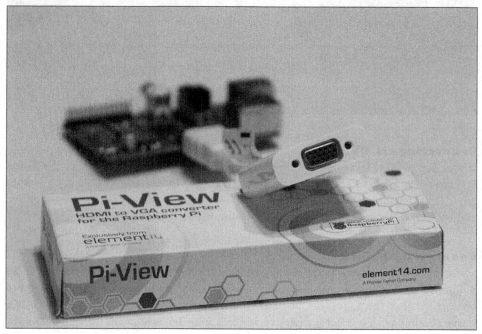

## Analogue and Digital

Inside most computers you will find digital signals – that is, signals where it only matters if they are on or off. Usually there is a difference of a few volts between a signal being on or off. Data is sent by a code of ons and offs, typically referred to as 1s and 0s. A small change in voltage due to radio or magnetic interference is usually not large enough to change the meaning.

Analogue signals tend to only be used in modern computers where they have to connect with something physical such as a monitor or speakers. An analogue signal typically represents data as a continuous range of voltages. As such, a small change in voltage means a different value will be read. This means the data can be changed by electrical interference.

VGA monitors represent different colours with different voltages. Consequently, any interference will affect what is shown on the screen, and the image is degraded! Small amounts of interference will have no effect on digital data for HDMI. However, if the interference is strong enough, then all data will be corrupted and no image will be transmitted.

### Connecting via Composite

If your display only has a connector for composite video, you need a phono-to-phono cable that plugs in to the yellow connector on the top of the Raspberry Pi as shown in Figure 1-8. Be aware that composite is an old technology and may produce a poor quality display.

## Connecting to a Network

The Raspberry Pi has an Ethernet socket that allows your Pi to connect to the Internet or your home network. You can download new software and updates, or browse the web. You could even run your own web server!

FIGURE 1-8:
Phono
connector for
composite video.

If you will be using a network, connect a network cable on the right side as shown in Figure 1-9. Although the Raspberry Pi uses the network to set its clock and to download updates and new programs, it will work without a network connection.

## Booting the Operating System

You will need an SD card with the OS already installed on it. You can either buy one pre-installed or follow the instructions earlier in this chapter to make your own.

Insert the SD card in the slot on the underside of the Raspberry Pi, on the left, as shown in Figure 1-10. Take care to keep the card parallel with the Raspberry Pi when you slide it in or out so as not to break the edge of the retaining slots (shown in Figure 1-11).

FIGURE 1-9:
Network
connection.

FIGURE 1-10:
Insert the SD
card carefully.

FIGURE 1-11: Take care not to snap off the plastic that keeps the SD card from falling out.

## Powering Up!

**WARNING** Before connecting power, get into the habit of checking that there is nothing conductive in contact that could cause a short circuit with your Raspberry Pi. A quick check that there's nothing metallic nearby could save you from damaging your Pi!

Plug in the power supply to the bottom left of the Raspberry Pi as shown in Figure 1-12. On the top-right corner, you should see a green light (labelled *PWR*) come on and another one (labelled *ACT*) flash.

The Raspberry Pi needs a power supply that can supply 5V 700mA (3.5W). Most decent-quality mobile phone chargers will work fine – many have the output marked on them, so it's easy to check. If your power supply can't deliver enough power, your Raspberry Pi may not start, or it may freeze when it does something computationally more demanding. For more information, see the "Troubleshooting" section later in this chapter.

FIGURE 1-12:
Insert a micro
USB for power.

## The Boot Process

After you've connected everything, have a correctly imaged SD card and powered up your Raspberry Pi, it will quickly flash a colourful square to test the graphics. After a few seconds, the Raspberry Pi logo will appear in the top-left corner of the screen, and many lines of text will scroll past.

The text reveals some of the work the OS is doing. You may see messages as the various drivers are loading, such as the keyboard driver, sound driver and network driver. After the drivers have loaded, the OS runs any startup programs and displays the login prompt.

By default, the username is pi, and the password is raspberry.

Type pi and press Enter.

Now type raspberry and press Enter. Linux doesn't display anything when you type passwords, which can be a bit unfamiliar if you are used to other OSes.

You should see the command-line prompt, where you can type commands and run programs. In the next section, you're going to start the program that allows you to use the Raspberry Pi graphically.

## Starting the Graphical Desktop

If you are familiar with Windows or OS X, you are used to a friendly graphical desktop that is loaded automatically with icons you can click. On the Raspberry Pi, however, in order to show that a graphical desktop doesn't have to be integral to a computer, it isn't loaded automatically.

## The X Server

The design of Linux means that the graphical desktop runs on top of the OS as a separate program called the *X server*. This opens up additional possibilities, such as controlling one computer with the display being shown on another computer over a network connection. This means that you can control the Raspberry Pi without having a monitor plugged into it, which is useful if you put it in a remote location (see Chapter 13, "Home Automation").

To start the graphical display on the Raspberry Pi, type `startx`.

After a few seconds the X server will start, and you will be able to use a graphical desktop. If you can see the Raspberry Pi logo in the background, then congratulations – you have successfully connected your Raspberry Pi! The projects in this book assume that you're starting from here, with the desktop displayed.

## Starting a Terminal under X

Linux makes greater use of the text-based command line, often known as a *terminal*. This can be very powerful and quicker for some tasks than using a mouse. To start a terminal in a window under X, double-click the LXTerminal icon on the desktop, or select it from the menu by clicking Accessories and then clicking LXTerminal.

## Troubleshooting

Hopefully, you'll never need this section, but even if you think you've followed all the instructions, you might discover that something doesn't work. Finding and debugging problems are important aspects of computing. The general approach is to be logical and eliminate parts until you can isolate where the problem is. You'll see the same principles apply to finding faults in your programs later in the book. It's a good idea to simplify to the simplest possible configuration first – unplug the keyboard, mouse and/or display to see if the Pi shows signs of life – and then add things one by one. When you are suspicious of what might be at fault, try borrowing a known working replacement from a friend or try the suspected faulty part in theirs. This way, you can eliminate parts until the fault is found.

## Common Problems

The majority of problems in getting the Raspberry Pi to work are easy to fix. The following subsections describe some of the issues that you might encounter with the Raspberry Pi and how to troubleshoot them.

### No Lights Come On

If none of the lights come on when you power up your Raspberry Pi, the power supply may not be providing the required 5V. If you have a meter, you can measure the output as detailed in the subsection "Power Problems"; if not, try borrowing a friend's that you know works.

### Only the Red Light Comes On

If just the red light comes on, then the Raspberry Pi is getting some power, but it isn't booting the OS. Make sure that the SD card is correctly inserted, and then check that it is correctly imaged. Even if the card is correctly imaged, it may be that the card isn't compatible with the Raspberry Pi. If possible, try another card that is known to work, either from a friend or by buying a premade card. Also check that the power supply is providing enough power.

### No Monitor Output

Check that the connector to the monitor hasn't come loose and that if your monitor has a choice of inputs that the correct one is selected. Normally, there is a switch on the front that cycles through the input sources. With some monitors it is necessary to have connected the monitor to the Raspberry Pi before powering it up. If you are still having trouble, try a different monitor and cable.

### Intermittent Problems

If the Raspberry Pi freezes or resets, particularly when you do something that demands more power (such as graphics-intensive work or adding a peripheral), then it's likely the power supply isn't providing enough power.

### Power Problems

The Raspberry Pi needs more power than some micro USB power adapters can provide. It is certainly more than what's provided by the output of most computer USB ports. As the

Raspberry Pi does different tasks, the amount of power it needs varies. Consequently, with some adapters, it may work some of the time, but then stop when it needs more power. Your power supply should provide a minimum of 700mA at 5V or at least 3.5W. Most power supplies will have a label that details the output power or current it can provide. However, some power supplies don't deliver what they claim! If your Raspberry Pi partly works and suddenly stops working, particularly when you ask it to do something more intensive such as graphics, then the power supply is probably not up for the job. In some cases it is not the power supply itself that is at fault, but the cable connecting it to the Raspberry Pi. Some cables can have a relatively high resistance and so can drop the voltage getting to the computer.

The power adapter also has to supply any peripherals plugged into the Raspberry Pi. If a peripheral takes too much power, then your Raspberry Pi will stop working. If you know how to use a multimeter, you can check the voltage supplied by the power supply under load. You can find information about how to do this in the *Raspberry Pi User Guide* (Wiley, 2012). If you measure less than 4.3V at the test points, then it might be worth changing the cable before you change the power supply. Or you can try using a different adapter.

## If You Need More Help

If you're still struggling with your Raspberry Pi, then you may need other sources of assistance. A major benefit of the huge popularity of the Raspberry Pi is the support offered from an enthusiastic, helpful community. See if you can find a solution at `http://elinux. org/R-Pi_Troubleshooting`, or check the Raspberry Pi forums at `www.raspberrypi. org/forum`.

You can often get help in person by attending a user group or local meeting, commonly referred to as a *Raspberry Jam*. It's a worldwide network, so just check `http://raspberry jam.org.uk` to find the nearest location.

The *Raspberry Pi User Guide* also provides suggestions for troubleshooting and configurations to work with specific hardware.

## Let the Fun Begin!

Now that you've got your Raspberry Pi powered up, it's time to start having fun with the projects. The Insult Generator project in Chapter 2 is a good one to start with because it introduces how to program the Raspberry Pi in Python – and more importantly, it can be used to insult your friends and family!

# Chapter 2

# Introductory Software Project: The Insult Generator

## by Dr. Andrew Robinson

## In This Chapter

- ○ Writing and running your first Python program
- ○ Storing data to variables
- ○ Holding text in strings
- ○ Printing messages on the screen
- ○ Creating functions
- ○ Getting input from the user
- ○ Conditional behaviour with `if` statements
- ○ Repetition with loops

**THIS PROJECT IS** just a bit of fun for you to get going with your first program. The program generates a comedy insult by combining a verb, an adjective and a noun at random. In other words, you'll make your highly sophisticated Raspberry Pi display something like "Your brother is a big old turnip!"

By beginning with something simple, you can start having fun without having to write too much code, and after you've got something running, you can change it to make it more sophisticated. In fact, professional computer programmers often take a similar approach: They write something simple and test it, and then add more and more features, testing as they go.

It's also useful to look at sample code, work out what it is doing and then change it to suit your requirements. Most professional programmers work this way too. Feel free to experiment and customise the projects in the book. Just remember to keep a copy of the original program so that you can go back to it if your modifications don't work.

This chapter helps to get you started programming the Raspberry Pi and, as such, it has the most theory. Do stick with it, and at the end of the chapter, you'll have the knowledge to make the program your own. There's a lot in this chapter, but you needn't do it all in one go; sometimes it's better to come back after a break. Programming is no less creative than painting a picture or knitting, and like these hobbies, you need to spend an hour or two covering the basics before you can produce a masterpiece!

In this chapter, you will learn how to enter a Python program and run it. You'll also learn about various aspects of the Python language.

## Running Your First Python Program

Many people use a word processor to produce documents with a computer because it provides features such as spelling and grammar checkers. However, there is nothing to stop you from using a simple text editor like Notepad in Windows, TextEdit on an Apple Mac or LeafPad on the Raspberry Pi. Similarly, when writing code, you can just type it in a text editor, or you can use an Integrated Development Environment (IDE). Similar to a spell checker in a word processor, an IDE checks the syntax (to ensure that it will make sense to the computer) and has other helpful features to make writing code a pleasure!

Just as there are lots of different word processors, there are a number of IDEs for Python. For the simple example in this chapter, you are going to type your first Python program into IDLE. IDLE is good for beginners because it is simple and can often be found wherever Python is installed, including on the Raspberry Pi.

To start IDLE, click the menu in the bottom-left corner of the screen (where the Start button is in Microsoft Windows), choose Programming, and then click IDLE, as shown in Figure 2-1.

FIGURE 2-1:
Starting IDLE.

---

The Raspberry Pi comes with two versions of IDLE. IDLE 3 uses Python version 3.0, which contains more functionality and has subtle changes to parts of the language. The examples in this chapter are written for Python 2 (that is, IDLE). If you use the examples in the book without changing them you'll receive errors.

**TIP**

---

You will see the IDLE window appear in interactive mode. In this mode, what you type is interpreted as soon as you press Return, which is a great way to try out your Python code. To see how this works, follow these steps:

1.  Type the following code:

    ```
    print ("Hello World")
    ```

---

Computers are less forgiving of mistakes than humans, so make sure that you type the code exactly as it appears in this and other examples in this book.

**NOTE**

2. Press Return. You should see Python run your first line of code and display the greeting shown in Figure 2-2.

FIGURE 2-2:
Python says
"Hello World".

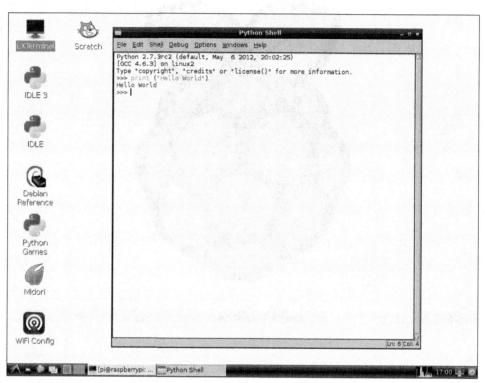

NOTE
Many programmers write a "Hello World" program whenever they learn a new language. It is about the simplest program and is a good way to check that it is possible to write some code and then run it. It dates back to the first tutorials of how to program in the 1970s. There's even an equivalent in hardware to "Hello World" that you'll see in Chapter 9, "Test Your Reactions".

If you got the result shown in Figure 2-2, then welcome to the club – you're now a computer programmer! If not, go back and make sure that you typed the code *exactly* as shown in the example (sometimes even the number of spaces matter in Python), because computers need to be told precisely what to do. This strict rule means that unlike English, a statement can only be interpreted with one meaning.

# Saving Your Program

IDLE allows you to save your code so that you don't have to re-enter it each time you want to run it. Just follow these steps:

1. Create a blank file for your program by selecting New Window from the File menu, as shown in Figure 2-3.

FIGURE 2-3:
Creating a new file.

2. Enter the following code and then click the Run menu and choose Run Module, or press F5.

```
message = "hello world from a saved file"
print (message)
```

3. Python displays a message that says, "Source Must Be Saved", as shown in Figure 2-4. Click OK.

---

*Source* is an abbreviation for *source code*, which is another way of saying the program you've entered.

NOTE

FIGURE 2-4:
Python
prompts,
"Source Must Be
Saved".

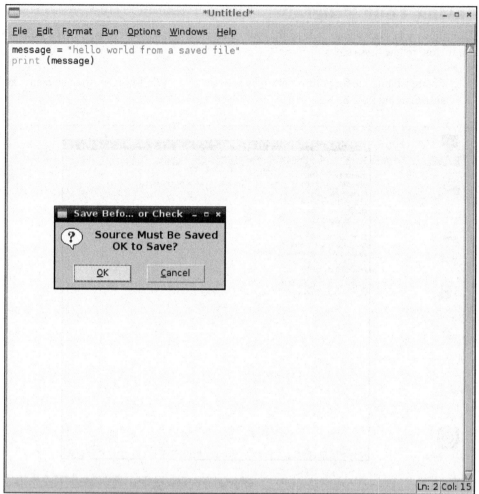

4. Type in a filename (for this example, you can just call it `hello.py`), and then click Save as shown in Figure 2-5.

5. After IDLE has saved your code, you will see a message saying RESTART (Python does this so you know you're always starting from the same consistent point), and then your code will run in the Python Shell window, as shown in Figure 2-6. If you've made a mistake, you'll see an error – correct it and then choose Run Module again.

**TIP**  When you save your code, IDLE adds `.py` to the end of the filename. This is the file extension for Python source files (just as Word adds `.doc` to documents).

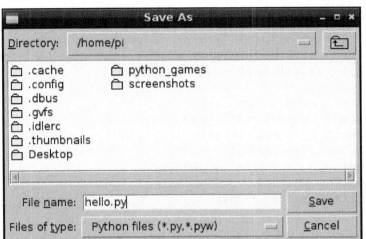

FIGURE 2-5:
The Save As
dialogue box in
IDLE.

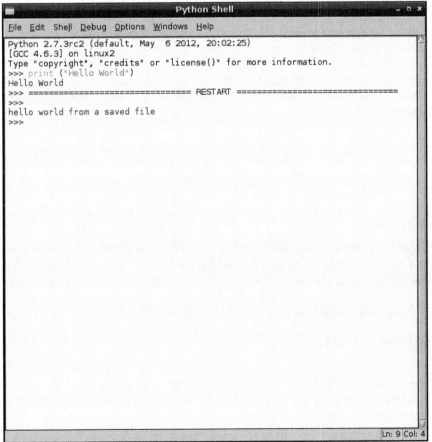

FIGURE 2-6:
IDLE running
Python code
from a file.

# Generating an Insult

Now that you've successfully run your first program, it's time to write something more interesting – in this case, the computer will generate its own message to print. Type the following code in a new file, save it and then run it:

```
from random import choice
adjectives = ["wet", "big"]
nouns = ["turnip", "dog"]
print  ("You are a")
adjective = choice (adjectives)
print (adjective)
print (choice (nouns))
```

When you run this program, you should see a message similar to "You are a big turnip" displayed. Run the program a few times, and you should see a variety of insults, built at random!

You can use the keyboard shortcut F5 to run the program. However, ensure the editor window containing your program has focus (is active) by clicking it before pressing F5 so IDLE knows the correct code to run.

You'll be changing the program to display a personalised message later in this chapter, but before you do, it's worth examining the code more closely. The following subsections describe what the different lines of the program do.

| TIP | Looking at how other people's code works is useful when you're learning to program, and the World Wide Web is a good source of many examples. |
| --- | --- |

# Variables

Variables are used to store data. Creating a variable is like getting a cardboard box to reserve some storage space and writing a unique label on it. You put things in the box for storage and then get them out again later. Whenever you access the box you use its unique label.

Let's start with something simple to illustrate variables:

```
message = "hello"
```

The equals sign means *assignment*, and tells Python to assign (or store) what is on the right-hand side in the variable named on the left – in this case, the characters h, e, l, l and o are stored in the variable named `message`.

## Strings

The " speech marks (also known as quotation marks in some parts of the world) tell Python to treat the enclosed characters as a *string* of letters rather than try to understand the word as an instruction.

To display text on the screen, you use the `print` command followed by what you want displayed after it – for example:

```
message = "hello"
print (message)
```

This will display the contents of the variable `message` on the screen, which in this case is `hello`.

If, on the other hand, you enter the following code:

```
print ("message")
```

The word `message` will be displayed on the screen, because the speech marks tell Python to treat text within them as a string of characters and not a variable name.

---

`print` is slightly confusing in that it displays characters on the screen and has nothing to do with sending it to a printer to appear on paper.    **TIP**

---

## Lists

To store multiple pieces of data in Python together, you can use lists. Lists are specified as items separated by commas within square brackets. Reconsidering the example of the cardboard box, a list can be considered as a named box with internal dividers to store separate items.

---

Looking back at the insult generator code, lists of strings are used to store multiple adjectives and nouns. Because you now know about strings and lists, you can try adding some more words of your own. Remember to enclose them in quotes (" ") and separate them with a comma.    **YOUR TURN!**

---

## Functions

A *function* can be thought of as a little machine that may take an input, perform some sort of processing on it and then produce an output (called its return value) as shown in Figure 2-7.

You can create your own functions, or you can use functions that are included in Python or written by other people. To use a function, you *call* it by entering its name followed by (). 

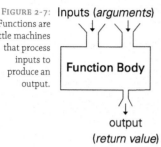

FIGURE 2-7: Functions are little machines that process inputs to produce an output.

Inputs (*arguments*)

**Function Body**

output
(*return value*)

Functions may take *arguments* (sometimes called *parameters*), which are a way of supplying data to them. Think of them as the raw materials into, or the controls that adjust, the function machine. Imagine a machine that makes different pasta shapes; its arguments might be raw pasta and a setting that determines what shape it produces. Arguments can be a variable (which may change as a program runs) or something *hard-coded* (written directly into the program by the programmer and never changed) in the program itself.

You can think of the `print` command that you used in the preceding code as a function that displays its parameter on the screen. The arguments to a function are contained in brackets after the function name.

## Structuring Your Programs

*Functions* are a way to structure programs. Computers and computer programs can quickly become very complicated. The best way to deal with this is to break things down into simple, manageable chunks. It's something we do in everyday life: If you ask someone to make you a cup of tea, you don't give them a long list of instructions about filling the kettle with water, turning it on, waiting for it to boil, adding a tea bag to the teapot, and so on. We don't think about all the details – after someone has been told how to make a cup of tea, they don't need to be told all the steps each time. It's the equivalent of calling the `makeTea()` function – you need to define the steps only once. If you want to pass information like the number of sugars or milk to add to the tea, you might use arguments – for example, to specify tea with three sugars and milk, `makeTea(3, True)`.

If we broke every task down to the simplest steps every time, things would become unmanageable. Programming computers is just the same – tasks are broken down into manageable chunks. Knowing exactly how and where to break a program into chunks comes with experience, but with this approach, it becomes possible to program a computer to make it do just about anything.

choice is another function that you have been using, perhaps without realising it. Its argument is a list of items, and the processing it does is to select one at random. Its output is an item from the list, which it returns.

---

If you find yourself writing the same code in multiple parts of a program, or using copy and paste, you should think about putting the repeated code into your own function.          **TIP**

---

There are so many functions that if all of them were available at once, it would be overwhelming to the programmer. Instead, Python contains only a few essential functions by default, and others have to be *imported* from packages of functions before they can be used. choice is an example of a function that needs to be imported from the random package. In the earlier example, the line import choice from random performs this role. You only need to import a function once in a program, but you can use it multiple times.

## Insult Your Friends by Name!

The programs so far have produced an output, but when run, have not taken any input from the user. The next example asks the user for a name and then prints a personalised greeting. To try this out, enter the following code:

```
name = raw_input("What is your name?")
print ("Hello " + name)
```

---

raw_input became the input function in Python 3. If you're using IDLE 3, remember to type input wherever you see raw_input in the examples in this book.          **TIP**

---

The raw_input function (renamed to input in Python 3) takes a message to print as its argument and returns the data the user entered. In this example, the variable name is assigned the result of the raw_input function, which is what the user types when the program is run.

This example also introduces how to join strings together. Strings are joined together, or *concatenated* as a programmer may say, by placing + between the strings. It's important to note that because the computer treats strings as just characters and not words, when strings are concatenated, it does not automatically insert spaces. Therefore it is up to the programmer to add any spaces needed. In the preceding example, there is a space after Hello in the quotes – without this, the computer would print something like HelloFred.

# Help with Functions

When you type a function like choice in IDLE, a tooltip pops up telling you what arguments the function takes and what it returns. This is a useful quick reference so you don't have to remember exactly what parameters a function takes, and it's easier than looking up the full reference online.

If you press the Ctrl key and the spacebar simultaneously, IDLE will attempt to autocomplete what you've typed thus far, which is useful if you can't remember exactly what a function is called. To try this out, type pri and then press Ctrl + spacebar. You should see a list of functions with print highlighted, as shown in Figure 2-8. Press the spacebar again to have IDLE finish off the typing for you.

FIGURE 2-8:
Autocomplete of
the print
function in
IDLE.

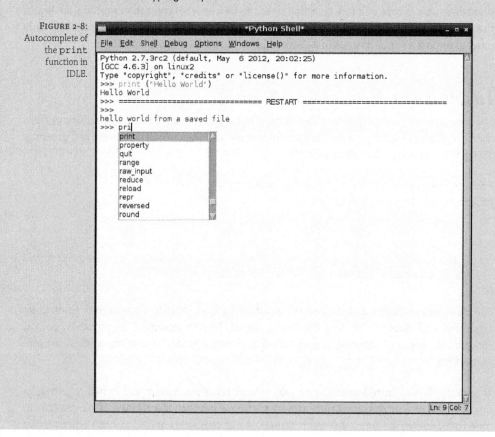

# Conditional Behaviour

Computer programs would be very dull if they always executed the same statements. Luckily, programs can do different things depending on these conditional tests: equal (==), not equal (!=), less than (<), greater than (>), less than or equal (<=) and greater than or equal (>=).

In this example, you'll make your insult generator change what it prints depending on the age of the user. To achieve this conditional behaviour, you'll tell the program to do one thing if something is true, or if not true, do something else. As a quick test of conditional behaviour enter the following code in an empty file:

```
age = 12
if (age < 16):
    print ("young")
else:
    print ("old")
```

Run the program and you should find it prints young. Change the age variable to be larger than 15 and run the program again. This time it should print old.

---

Note that these print statements are indented by typically four spaces or a tab from the beginning of the line. Unlike some other languages, indentation matters in Python. If you don't get spaces in the right place, either Python gets confused and raises an error, or your program won't do what you expect! You should always indent code properly. **WARNING**

---

# Create a Stream of Insults!

In the next part of this project, you're going to change the program to produce multiple insults, which is a good example of the use of functions. You're going to define your own function that you can call whenever you want an insult, and then create a loop that calls the function multiple times.

## Making Your Own Functions

You define functions in Python by writing def (for definition) followed by the name of the function and the parameters it takes and a colon (:), followed by the indented *body* of the function.

As a simple example, enter the following in an interactive Python window to define a simple function that will print a personalised greeting:

```
def printHelloUser (username):
    print ("Hello " + username)
```

Note that the body of the code is indented. This shows that it is still part of the function on the previous line. Also note that there are no spaces in the function names. Including spaces would confuse the computer, so programmers separate words by using capitals in the middle (like printHelloUser in the example). Some programmers call this *camel case* because the capital letters in the middle of a word are like humps on the back of a camel.

---

**TIP**     Python doesn't care what you call your functions, but other programmers will! So if you want other people to use your code, you should follow conventions.

---

Now enter the following to call the function you just defined:

```
printHelloUser("Fred")
```

You're now ready to use what you've learned in this chapter to write a printInsult function. To begin, enter the following code in an interactive Python window, remembering the indentation:

```
from random import choice
def printInsult (username, age):
    adjectives = ["wet", "big"]
    nouns = ["turnip", "dog"]
    if (age < 16):
        ageAdjective = "young "
    else:
        ageAdjective = "old "
    print  (username + ", you are a " +
            ageAdjective + choice(adjectives) +
            " " + choice(nouns))
```

Now, whenever you need a personalised insult you can just call printInsult, with your victim's name and their age, and it will produce one on demand! So, to insult 10-year-old Fred, you would write the following code line:

```
printInsult("Fred",10)
```

And Python would print something like this:

```
Fred, you are a young wet turnip
```

Call the `printInsult` function with the names and ages of some of your friends and **YOUR TURN!**
family!

## Creating Loops

Loops are great when there's repetition in a task. To try this out, you're going to create a
program that loops around a few times, each one producing another insult. You'll look at two
variations of loops: a `for` loop and `while` loop. Both have a test that determines if the code
in the loop body should be run again, or if the program should skip the loop body and continue. A `for` loop is typically used as a counting loop, where code needs to be run *for* a particular number of times – for example, for six times. A `while` loop tends to be used *while* a
condition is true – for example, while a user wants to continue running the program.

### for Loop

Type the following code to loop for each item in the `adjectives` list and print it out:

```
adjectives = ["wet", "big"]
for item in adjectives:
    print (item)
```

The indented code, `print (item)`, is the body of the loop that is repeated on each *iteration*
(loop). `for item in adjectives:` sets up the loop and tells Python to loop for each item
in the `adjectives` variable. On each iteration, the next value from the list is placed in the
`item` variable.

So, to print "hello world" three times you write this:

```
for count in [1, 2, 3]:
    print ("loop number ",count)
    print ("hello world")
```

You can use commas to separate multiple items for printing.          **TIP**

You can use `range` instead of typing every number in a list. Type

```
list(range (10))
```

**TIP** In Python 2 `range` returns a list. In Python 3 you need to tell it specifically when you want it to return a list – this is not necessary within a `for` statement.

Python returns the list of numbers from 0 to 9:

```
[0, 1, 2, 3, 4, 5, 6, 7, 8, 9]
```

You can also give `range` two arguments – a start and an end – like this:

```
range (5,15)
```

You will use a `for` loop with a range to test the `printInsult` function. In the same interactive Python window where you defined `printInsult()`, enter the following code:

```
for testAge in range (14,18):
    print ("age: " + str(testAge)

printInsult("Monty",testAge)
```

Python prints the following:

```
age: 14
Monty, you are a young big turnip
age: 15
Monty, you are a young big dog
age: 16
Monty, you are a old big dog
age: 17
Monty, you are a old wet dog
```

### while Statement

Let's look at an example `while` loop. Type the following code and run it. It will loop and keep printing an insult until you type no.

```
userAnswer=""
while (userAnswer!="no"):
    printInsult("Eric",20)
    userAnswer = raw_input("can you take any more?")
```

`!=` means not equal, so the `while` loop repeats whilst the variable `userAnswer` is not equal to no. After printing an insult the code gets input from the user and updates the `userAnswer` variable ready for the test before the start of the next loop.

---

`raw_input` was renamed `input` in Python 3. **TIP**

---

Consider what the loop would look like if you didn't create a function – you'd have to include all the code inside the loop body. This makes the code harder to read, and means you'd have to retype it in each of these examples!

---

If your program gets stuck in an *infinite loop*, a loop that never ends, you can stop your program by pressing Ctrl + C. **TIP**

---

## Putting It All Together

You should now have a program that generates a torrent of insults! This chapter has covered the basics of programming in Python. Look at each line in the examples and see if you understand what each part does. Then, to personalise your program, you could make it produce different insults depending on the user's name. For example, you could make it say something nice only if your name is entered, or you could change the number of insults it generates depending on the user or their age (such as a younger brother). You could print "really old" for people over a certain age, or if you're clever, you could use a loop to print an additional "really" for every decade someone has been alive.

The main thing is to not be afraid of changing things to see what happens. Just as you can't learn to paint without practising, you won't learn how to program without experimenting. Throughout this book, there are ideas to change the projects to make them your own and to make the computer do what you want it to do.

# Part II
# Software Projects

# Chapter 3
## Tic-Tac-Toe

**by Mike Cook**

## In This Chapter

- ○ Learn more about lists
- ○ Make a list of lists
- ○ Understand what a test harness is
- ○ Get robust user input
- ○ Implement increasingly sophisticated levels of artificial intelligence

TIC-TAC-TOE IS BETTER known as *noughts and crosses* in Europe. So when the 1956 American TV show *Tic Tac Dough,* which had a theme tune that followed the rhythm of those words, was transferred to the U.K., they changed the name to *Criss Cross Quiz* to keep the same rhythm and because no one in the U.K. knew the game as *tic-tac-toe.* On U.S. TV the show was revived in 1978 and in 1980 became one of the first TV shows to have its graphics generated by a computer. Each square was controlled by one Apple II computer, with the whole array being controlled by an Altair 8800 computer system. So it is perhaps fitting that tic-tac-toe should be the subject of this book's first software project. In fact, I made a noughts and crosses automatic playing machine simply out of multipole switches and flashlight bulbs way back in the mid-60s for a school open day.

I am sure that you know how to play tic-tac-toe, but just in case this book reaches places where it is not a familiar game, I'll go over how it is played. The game is played on a 3 X 3 grid formed by drawing two horizontal lines and two vertical lines. Two players in turn mark an empty square with a cross or a zero. The first player to have three of their marks in a line is the winner. The line can be horizontal, vertical or diagonal.

Tic-tac-toe is an ideal game for learning how to program because it uses so many concepts that are useful in computer programming, as well as having the virtue that it can be built up gradually in a step-by-step manner. This is the way that all projects should be developed, one small step at a time. Nobody writes a large program and then runs it for the first time, except perhaps beginners. This is because by writing small and testing, you drastically reduce where any errors can be. If your first bit has no errors, when you write the next bit, and suddenly there is an error, then it is almost certain that your error lies in the code you have just written.

# Errors

When you write code you can make two sorts of errors: The first sort, known as a *syntax error,* is when the computer can't make sense of the instructions you have given it. Examples of these types of errors are spelling variable names incorrectly, not adhering to the same uppercase and lowercase mix in variables and not getting the format of a command correct, such as forgetting to add a colon. The second sort, known as a *logical error,* is much harder to spot. These errors are when the computer does exactly what you told it to do, but what you *told* it to do was not exactly what you *wanted* it to do. Logical errors can be the hardest to find. This often fools beginners because, when the computer is finished complaining about errors, they expect a program to run like they *thought* they wrote it. In this case logical errors are caused by the programmer's thinking more like a human and not enough like a computer. The more experienced you get, the better you will become at avoiding these errors, but it is human nature that you will never be entirely free of them; you will just get better at spotting them and tracking them down.

It is important to realise that there is no one correct way to write a program, despite what some programmers might want to think. The forums are full of raging arguments as to the best style and technique to use, but do not be intimidated by this. Good code is code that does what you want it to. Better code is code that does this in a concise, easy-to-understand way. After that you get some code that is more memory efficient, some that is more efficient in the number of code lines it uses and others that execute faster. Do not get bogged down by this; code that takes a 0.25 second to run between user inputs is totally indistinguishable from code that takes 0.25uS to run. However, context is everything, so code that takes 25 seconds to run will win a lot less friends than 0.25 second code.

## Making a Start

In the preceding chapter, "Introductory Software Project: The Insult Generator", you can see how you could make a list of words, such as nouns and verbs, for the insult generator. Lists are very useful, and you will use them many times in programming. In this chapter you will use a list to represent the tic-tac-toe playing board. Each position in the list represents a square, and the contents of each position represents the contents of the square. This is shown in Figure 3-1.

## Contents

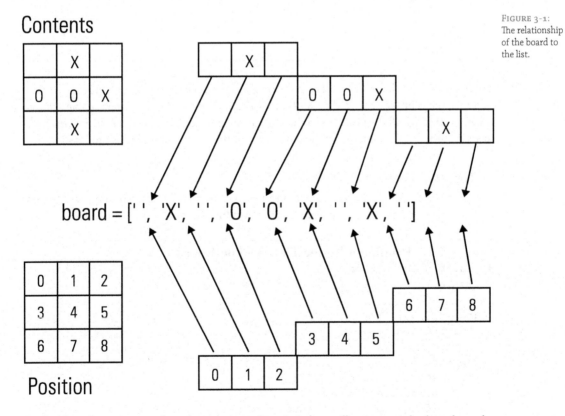

board = [' ', 'X', ' ', 'O', 'O', 'X', ' ', 'X', ' ']

## Position

FIGURE 3-1:
The relationship of the board to the list.

So the first thing you need to do is write a function that will print out the board on the Python text console. This is the sort of thing that was done before the widespread use of graphics windows, and is a lot simpler to cope with. Basically, you need to output each square on the board but print on a new line when you have outputted squares 2 or 5. This first program is shown in Listing 3-1. Remember, all the code listings for the book can be found at www.wiley.com/go/raspberrypiprojects.

---

**Listing 3-1**    **Printing the Simple Tic-Tac-Toe Board**

```python
#!/usr/bin/env python
# Tic-Tac-Toe 1 - print board

board = [ 'O', 'X', ' ', 'O', ' ', 'X', 'O', 'X', 'X' ]
def printBoard():
    print
    for square in range(0,9):
        print board[square],
        if square == 2 or square == 5 :
            print
    print


if __name__ == '__main__':
    printBoard()
```

---

This is a simple for loop that prints out the contents of the board list one at a time. The print statement ends in a comma that means that it will not go onto a new line. The variable square will range through all the positions in the list and when it reaches 2 or 5 an extra print statement is executed. This time it is without a comma at the end, so a new line is produced.

## A Better Board

Although Listing 3-1 fulfills the desire of printing out the board, it could be improved by adding a grid using some text characters. This is shown in Listing 3-2.

---

**Listing 3-2**    **Printing a Better Tic-Tac-Toe Board**

```python
#!/usr/bin/env python
# Tic-Tac-Toe 2 - print a better board

board = [ 'O', 'X', ' ', 'O', ' ', 'X', 'O', 'X', 'X' ]
def printBoard():
    print
    print '|',
    for square in range(0,9):
        print board[square],'|',
        if square == 2 or square == 5 :
            print
            print '- - - - - - -'
            print '|',
```

```
    print
    print

if __name__ == '__main__':
    printBoard()
```

This makes the board look a whole lot better by emphasising the blank squares.

## Checking for a Win

Next you need a function that checks if the board shows a win for a player. With an eye on what is needed later on, you need to write it so that you pass into the function the player's symbol that you want to test for. Also you need a list of the squares that constitute a win. In fact there are eight ways to win, so you need a new concept – a list of lists. To see how this works, look at Listing 3-3.

**Listing 3-3    Checking the Tic-Tac-Toe Board for a Win**

```
#!/usr/bin/env python
# Tic-Tac-Toe 3 - check for win

board = [ 'O', 'X', ' ', 'O', ' ', 'X', 'O', 'X', 'X' ]
wins = [ [0, 1, 2], [3, 4, 5], [6, 7, 8], [0, 3, 6], [1, ⮐
4, 7], [2, 5, 8], [0, 4, 8], [2, 4, 6] ]

def checkWin(player):
    win = False
    for test in wins :
        print test
        count = 0
        for squares in test :
            if board[squares] == player :
                count +=1
        if count == 3 :
            win = True
    return win

if __name__ == '__main__':
    print 'Checking board for X'
    if checkWin('X'):
        print 'Game over X wins'
    print 'Checking board for O'
    if checkWin('O'):
        print 'Game over O wins'
```

The list called wins consists of eight items, and each item is a list of three of the square numbers that constitute a win. The way you drive this is with the loop variables in the for statements. The first statement

```
for test in wins :
```

makes the variable called test take on the value of each of the sublists in turn. Then, when it comes to the for statement

```
for squares in test :
```

which is nested inside the first one, the variable squares will take on the values, in turn, of the squares that you need to fill with one symbol to get a win. What happens now is that if the board's symbol matches the one you are looking for, a count is incremented. If that count reaches a value of three, the board has a win for that player. The logic variable win is set initially to false, but if a win is detected, it is changed to true. It is this variable that is returned to the calling program. The last part of the listing simply exercises the checkWin() function by calling it to check for each playing symbol in turn. For the way the board list is set up, there is a win for the O player. You can change the board list to have a win for the X player if you like.

## More Infrastructure

The last pieces of infrastructure you need are a function to clear the board for a fresh game and one that checks if any new moves can be made. These are quite simple and are shown in Listing 3-4.

---

Listing 3-4　**Utility Functions**

```
def wipeBoard() :
    global board
    for square in range(0, len(board) ) :
        board[square] = ' '
def canMove(): # see if move can be made
    move = False
    for square in range(0, len(board) ) :
      if board[square] == ' ':
        move = True
    return move
```

---

This just shows the function itself without any test harness. *Test harness* is the software term used by software engineers to describe temporary code that exists only to test functions in isolation. It is an important part of the process of developing a project to be able to test functions in isolation from the rest of the code. This is because you can then feed the function with all sorts of conditions that might not happen very often when the function is run as part of the normal code.

The `wipeBoard` function simply puts spaces in every position in the board. Here the statement

```
for square in range(0, len(board) ) :
```

generates the loop variable `square` as just a sequence of numbers. Rather than just put the last number in the range as 16, you have used the `len()` function, which works out the length of the list. This means that it will work with any size board and hence any length list.

You might think the `canMove()` function is not necessary, but one situation that `checkWin()` cannot cope with is when there are no more spaces left on the board – which is why you need `canMove()`. Initially the move variable is set to be false. Then it visits each square on the board; if it sees a blank space, it sets the move variable to true. It doesn't matter if this variable is set to be true once or fifteen times, and it is often simpler in programming to let things run on like this rather than try to stop when you find the first instance of a blank square.

# A Two-Player Game

Now it is time to put the code pieces together and make a program that can run a two-player game. That is, there are two human players, each taking a turn to enter his or her move. The computer keeps track of the moves, prints out the board after each move and checks if one player has won or if it is a draw. There is, however, just one more thing you need to consider before proceeding.

When representing the board as a list, the elements of the list, as always, start off with the first item position number of zero. Most noncomputer people are not happy with a number zero, so as a sop to them you shall be representing the positions on the board as numbers 1 to 9. Therefore, whenever a number is input from a player, the program has to adjust this number to match the internal representation of the position. True, this involves only adding or subtracting one from the number, but you need to remember to do this each time a number is presented to a player. As a reminder of the numbering system the board list is initialised to represent the number of each square before being wiped prior to beginning the game. This is shown in the two-player version of the game, shown in Listing 3-5.

---

**Listing 3-5**    **Two-Player Tic-Tac-Toe Game**

```python
#!/usr/bin/env python
# Tic-Tac-Toe 5 - 2 player game

board = [ '1', '2', '3', '4', '5', '6', '7', '8', '9' ]
wins = [ [0, 1, 2], [3, 4, 5], [6, 7, 8], [0, 3, 6],⤸
 [1, 4, 7], [2, 5, 8], [0, 4, 8], [2, 4, 6] ]

def play() :
    printBoard()
    print 'Tic-Tac-Toe'
    print 'two players'
    while True :
      wipeBoard()
      player_turn = 'X'
      while checkWin(swapPlayer(player_turn)) == False ⤸
 and canMove() == True :
          getMove(player_turn)
          printBoard()
          player_turn = swapPlayer(player_turn)
      if checkWin(swapPlayer(player_turn)):
          print 'Player',swapPlayer(player_turn),'wins ⤸
... New Game'
      else:
          print 'A draw. ... New game'

def swapPlayer(player):
    if player == 'X' :
      player = 'O'
    else:
      player = 'X'
    return player

def getMove(player):
    global board
    correct_number = False
    while correct_number == False :
        square = raw_input('Square to place the '+ player + ' ')
        try:
            square = int(square)
        except:
            square = -2
        square -= 1 # make input number match internal numbers
        if square >= 0 and square < 10 : # number in range
            if board[square] == ' ' : # if it is blank
```

```python
                board[square] = player
                correct_number = True
            else:
                print 'Square already occupied'
        else :
            print 'incorrect square try again'

def wipeBoard() :
    global board
    for square in range(0, len(board) ) :
        board[square] = ' '

def printBoard():
    print
    print '|',
    for square in range(0,9):
        print board[square],'|',
        if square == 2 or square == 5 :
            print
            print '- - - - - - -'
            print '|',
    print
    print

def canMove(): # see if move can be made
    move = False
    for square in range(0, len(board) ) :
      if board[square] == ' ':
        move = True
    return move

def checkWin(player):
    win = False
    for test in wins :
        count = 0
        for squares in test :
            if board[squares] == player :
                count +=1
        if count == 3 :
            win = True
    return win

if __name__ == '__main__':
    play()
```

This contains three functions you have not seen before – play(), swapPlayer() and getMove(). Look at the simplest one first, swapPlayer(): All this does is return a player's symbol, which is not the symbol passed into it. Although this might seem like a trivial thing to do, this action is required at many different parts of the code, which is why it warrants being built into a function.

The getMove() function might look more complex than you might expect. This is because there is a lot of code designed to make sure that a valid number is entered by the user. If you could trust the user to enter a valid square number, this would all be unnecessary – but you can't, so it is necessary.

Chapter 2 uses the raw_input function but only to input a name; here you want to input a number. So first you have to check that it is a number that has been entered and then that the number represents a square that doesn't already have a symbol in it. Therefore the structure used in this function is a while loop that keeps repeating until a valid number has been entered. After getting something from the user you must check that it is a number; this can be done with the int() function, which turns a text input into a number (an integer in this case). If this can't be done because the user has typed in some alphabetical or punctuation characters, the program will crash and print out an error message, and you don't want that to happen. Therefore you use a new function structure try, which allows the program to check if the code is going to throw an error; if so, the program jumps to the except label, where you set the variable to an out-of-range number so that it can be rejected later on in the function. Then you test if the variable is within the range of the board. Finally, you check to see if that space is actually free to take a symbol. Only when this final test is passed do you actually make the move on the board and set the variable correct_number to true, which stops the while loop from repeating. Otherwise, a hopefully helpful error message is relayed to the user.

The play() function orchestrates the whole game. First the board is printed out, which, as mentioned before, contains the square numbering identification information. Then you enter an endless loop which repeatedly plays a game. It starts off by wiping the board and setting the first player as X. The individual game is contained in the while loop that keeps on going until there is a winner or there are no more blank squares to use. The player's move is then made and the board printed again, and then you swap the player for the next move. The code then loops around to the while function, but as you have already swapped the player in anticipation of the next round, when you call the checkWin() function as part of the while tests you must call it for the player who has just gone – hence the use of the swap_player() function in the calling parameter of the checkWin() function. When one player has won or the free squares have run out, the while loop stops, and the code tests for a win; if a win is found, the winning player is printed. However, if there is not a win, the game must have been a draw, so that is printed out. Then a new game is started. When the users want to quit the game they should press the Ctrl and C keys together.

# Getting the Computer to Play

While you now have the computer keeping track of the game, it is not much more than a glorified piece of paper. The fun starts when you get the computer to generate moves in place of one of the players. There are many levels you can do this at, ranging from the computer giving you a poor playing opponent to one of the computer being invincible. Of course, playing a computer at each end of this range is not as much fun as playing one somewhere in the middle. In this section you will look at several ways you can make the computer an increasingly skillful opponent. Because the behaviour that programs like this exhibit often looks like there is some intelligence at play, this sort of programming is often known as *artificial intelligence,* or AI for short. Although I regularly maintain that *artificial intelligence* is the ability some students have of passing exams without actually understanding very much.

## The Computer As a Five Year Old

In the first level of AI, the computer knows the rules but not much else. It can play the game but has no strategy and can only make a winning move by chance. To do this, the computer must gather a list of valid moves and choose one at random. Functions to do this are shown in Listing 3-6.

**Listing 3-6  A Computer Opponent Tic-Tac-Toe Game**

```python
#!/usr/bin/env python
# Tic-Tac-Toe 6 - play against the computer random move
from random import shuffle

def play() :
    global board
    print 'Tic-Tac-Toe'
    print 'play against the computer AI level 0'
    printBoard()
    while True :
      wipeBoard()
      player_turn = 'X'
      while checkWin(swapPlayer(player_turn),board) == False
  and canMove() == True :
          if player_turn == 'X':
              getMove(player_turn)
          else:
              generateMove()
          printBoard()
        player_turn = swapPlayer(player_turn)
      if checkWin(swapPlayer(player_turn),board) :
```

*continued*

Listing 3-6   **continued**

```
        print 'Player',swapPlayer(player_turn),'wins ⊃
... New Game'
    else:
        print 'A draw. ... New game'

def generateMove():
    global board
    moves = list()
    for squares in range(0, len(board) ):
        if board[squares] == ' ' :
            moves.append(squares)
    shuffle(moves)
    board[moves[0]] = 'O'
    print 'My move is ',moves[0] +1
```

Note here that I have only shown the first three functions as all the other functions remain the same. The first thing to spot is the use of the random library

```
from random import shuffle
```

This imports the random function shuffle, which you will use to rearrange a list of valid moves into a random order so that the game played by the computer varies. The play function is much as before, but where it differs is when it is player O's move – then the generateMove() function is called. This function starts off by defining a list called moves, which at first is empty. Then a for loop visits every square on the board, and if a square is blank it appends the square's number to the moves list. The shuffle function is used on the list to get it into a random order, and, as you are only interested in using one move you select the first number in that list, the one at position zero. Next, the move is actually made, and the board is changed. Finally the move number is printed out. Note here that the number printed out is one more than the square's number because, as mentioned before, you are representing the squares for the user as 1 to 9 whereas the computer sees them as 0 to 8.

## Teaching the Computer to Recognize a Winning Move

So whereas Listing 3-6 plays an entertaining game, it is all very hit and miss; when you play it it feels more like miss than hit. Therefore what you want to do is add a bit of strategy to the computer's play. It would be good if the computer could spot a move that would cause it to win. This is quite easily achieved by looking at the results of making the move in each blank square in turn, and seeing if a win results. As you already have a function that checks for a win this is not too difficult. Similarly, it would be good if the computer could spot that its opponent is able to make a winning move and if so then move in that place to block them.

After that you can just let the computer pick a random move like before. The new and changed functions to do this are shown in Listing 3-7.

**Listing 3-7   Computer Opponent Level 1 Tic-Tac-Toe Game**

```python
#!/usr/bin/env python
# Tic-Tac-Toe 7 - play against the computer AI level 1
def generateMove():
    if canIwin():
        pass
    elif canYouWin():
        pass
    else:
        randomMove()


def randomMove():
    global board
    moves = list()
    for squares in range(0, len(board) ):
        if board[squares] == ' ' :
            moves.append(squares)
    shuffle(moves)
    board[moves[0]] = 'O'
    print 'My move is ',moves[0] + 1


def canIwin():
    global board
    testBoard = board
    moveMade = False
    for square in range(0, len(board) ) :
        if testBoard[square] == ' ' and moveMade == False:
            testBoard[square] = 'O'
            if checkWin('O',testBoard):
                board[square] = 'O'
                moveMade = True
                print 'My move is ',square + 1
            else:
                testBoard[square] = ' ' # retract move
    return moveMade


def canYouWin():
    global board
    testBoard = board
    moveMade = False
```

*continued*

**Listing 3-7   continued**

```
    for square in range(0, len(board) ) :
        if testBoard[square] == ' ' and moveMade == False:
            testBoard[square] = 'X'
            if checkWin('X',testBoard):
                board[square] = 'O'
                moveMade = True
                print 'My move is ',square + 1
            else:
                testBoard[square] = ' ' # retract move
    return moveMade
```

Again, I am just showing the functions that have changed. This time the `generateMove()` function is a little more structured. It first calls the `canIwin()` function as part of an `if` statement; when this returns true there is nothing else you want to do. However, Python will throw an error if there is no line there, so you must use the dummy statement `pass`. As its name implies `pass` does nothing but tells the computer specifically you want to do nothing and that you haven't just made a mistake. However, if the function returns false – that is, it cannot win – it then calls the `canYouWin()` function. Note here the `elif` keyword, a concatenation of `else if`, which means it is an `if` statement that controls whether the line following it gets executed. In the event of none of these two functions producing a true value, the final `else` calls the `randomMove()` function, which contains the code you used last time for generating a valid, but random, move.

The `canIwin()` function itself first makes a copy of the board, and then visits every square and puts the O symbol in it. After that, it checks for a win. If this returns as true, that move is made to the real board, and the `moveMade` variable is set to true to stop it from making any more moves. Finally, the move that has just been made is printed out. If the trial move returns false, the move is retracted by placing a blank in the place where the O was just tried. If you look now at the `canYouWin()` function, this is just the opposite; it scans the board, placing an X in each blank square. If it finds that one of these trial moves will result in a win for the human opponent, it uses this position to place its O, thus blocking the winning move. If you examine the code you wrote for those two functions, you will see that they are nearly identical. When you find this happening it is good to shorten the code by consolidating the two functions into one. You will see that the main difference is the symbol being used. When this happens, as a general rule you make the symbol into a variable, enclose one of the functions in a `for` loop and use the loop index to switch over the variable. This is shown in Listing 3-8; give it a new, more descriptive name of `win_block()`.

**Listing 3-8   Consolidating the Two Win Check Functions**

```
def generateMove():
    if win_block():
        pass
```

```
    else:
        randomMove()

def win_block():  #move to win or block
    global board
    testBoard = board
    players = ['O','X']
    moveMade = False
    for moveTry in players:
      for square in range(0, len(board) ) :
        if testBoard[square] == ' ' and moveMade == False:
            testBoard[square] = moveTry
            if checkWin(moveTry,testBoard):
                board[square] = 'O'
                moveMade = True
                print 'My move is ',square + 1
            else:
                testBoard[square] = ' ' # retract move
    return moveMade
```

You will see that the name is changed, as is the code in the generateMove() function. All the other functions remain unchanged. The main addition to the function is the extra list named players, which contains the two symbols to use. Then the extra for loop selects one of these symbols on each pass by the variable moveTry.

The section "Errors" at the start of this chapter discusses logical errors; developing the win_block function initially produced one of these errors. When I wrote the first draft of this function, the loop that changed what symbol was being used was placed on the other side of the next for loop. This actually appeared to work until I spotted that sometimes the program would ignore a winning move in favor of blocking the opponent. It turned out that this was because each square was being tested first – for the computer's symbol and then for the opponent's. This meant that if the computer found a blocking move first it would choose that. Therefore, I needed to move the for  moveTry statement to its current position so that all the winning moves were scanned before the blocking moves were looked at.

## Adding Some Strategy

At this point the game is being played with a modicum of intelligence but still no strategy. You need to devise a playing strategy to use. A strong one but by no means the only one is shown in Figure 3-2, which shows the sort of choices that are made when picking a move. Basically after checking for a winning or blocking move, if there are corners free, then pick one, or if the centre is free, pick it; finally, if none of the previous conditions applies, pick one of the sides.

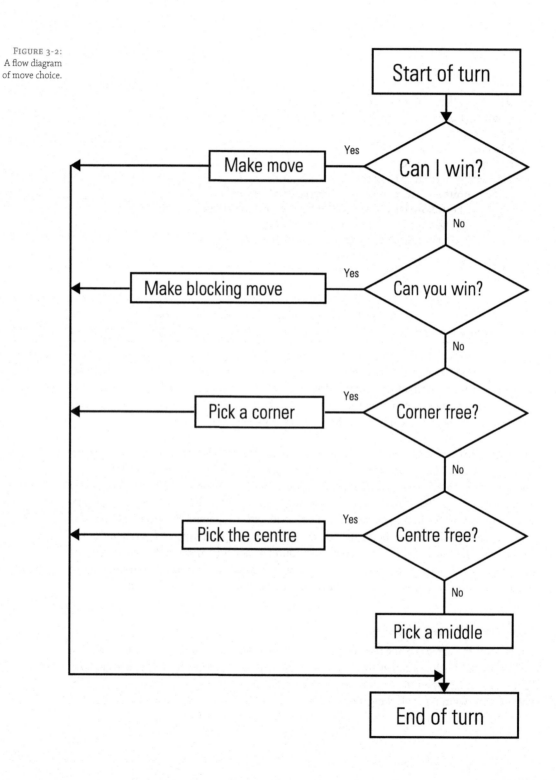

FIGURE 3-2:
A flow diagram
of move choice.

Flow diagrams are a bit out of favor nowadays, but as their name implies, they are good for showing the flow of an algorithm and the decisions that have to be made. One problem is that it can be much harder, with today's programming languages and structures, to translate the flow directly into code. However, for beginners I still feel there is great merit in these diagrams, especially relatively short flow diagrams. Anything in a diamond requires a decision, and there are two or more possible changes in the flow depending on that decision. Now these sorts of statements are fine when you are describing the strategy to another human being, but when you write code you have to be more specific. The way I have decided to implement this is to write a function that is given a list of possible moves; the function will check this list to see if the board is free to take one or more of these moves, and pick a random move from the list if it is. Most of the logic to do this was used in the randomMove() function. The new functions to do this are shown in Listing 3-9.

**Listing 3-9    An Intelligent Move Strategy**

```
def generateMove():
    if win_block():
        pass
    elif prefMove([0,2,6,8]): # corners
        pass
    elif prefMove([5]): # centre
        pass
    else:
        prefMove([1,3,5,7]) # middle row

def prefMove(moves):
    global board
    moved = False
    move = list()
    for potential in moves:
        if board[potential] == ' ':
            move.append(potential)
    if len(move) != 0:
        shuffle(move)
        board[move[0]] = 'O'
        print 'My move is ',move[0] + 1
        moved = True
    return moved
```

Again I have only shown the functions that have changed. The big change this time is the prefMove() function. This is passed a list of preferred moves from the generateMoves() function; notice this is a list, and it is given in square brackets inside the curved brackets. After the win_block() function is called, a list of all the corners is passed. If that does not result in a move, a list of all the centre squares is passed. Of course, there is only one centre square, so it is a short list, but the important thing is that it *is* a list, and the same logic can operate on it all the same. Finally a list of squares in the middle of each row is passed to the `prefMove()` function. This works just like the `randomMove()` function, which is no longer needed, in that it examines the state of the board for each square in the list, and compiles a list of free squares – that is, ones without symbols already in them. Then `prefMove` shuffles the list and chooses the first element. This produces a good game but one that is possible to beat if the random moves chosen are not the right ones. Nevertheless, it is fun to play and good practice in developing the playing strategy even further.

## Refining the Computer's Strategy

Because the game of tic-tac-toe is relatively short, it turns out that the first move the computer makes is vital in its success, so in this next version you refine the move choice for the first move only. Basically, if the human player opened by playing a corner, the computer must respond with the opposite corner if it is to prevent the human from winning. As it is, sometimes this happens by the random choice of corner, but not always. Also, if the human opens with a middle row square, the response should be an adjacent corner square. The whole listing, with all the functions in it this time, is shown in Listing 3-10.

**Listing 3-10   An Improved Computer Playing Strategy**

```python
#!/usr/bin/env python
# Tic-Tac-Toe 10 - play against the computer AI level 3
from random import shuffle

board = [ '1', '2', '3', '4', '5', '6', '7', '8', '9' ]
wins = [ [0, 1, 2], [3, 4, 5], [6, 7, 8], [0, 3, 6], ⏎
[1, 4, 7], [2, 5, 8], [0, 4, 8], [2, 4, 6] ]

def play() :
    global board
    print 'Tic-Tac-Toe'
    print 'play against the computer AI level 3'
    printBoard()
    while True :
      wipeBoard()
      move = 0
      player_turn = 'X'
      while checkWin(swapPlayer(player_turn),board) == ⏎
False and canMove() == True :
          if player_turn == 'X':
              getMove(player_turn)
              move +=1
```

```
        else:
            generateMove(move)
        printBoard()
        player_turn = swapPlayer(player_turn)
      if checkWin(swapPlayer(player_turn),board):
        print 'Player',swapPlayer(player_turn),'wins ⤶
... New Game'
    else:
        print 'A draw. ... New game'


def generateMove(move):
    corners = [0, 2, 6, 8]
    opposite = [8, 6, 2, 0]
    side = [1, 3, 5, 7]
    adjacent = [0, 6, 2, 8]
    if move == 1:
        moved = False
        for square in range(0,4):
            if board[corners[square]] == 'X':
                moved = prefMove([opposite[square]])
        for square in range(0,4):
            if board[side[square]] == 'X':
                moved = prefMove([adjacent[square]])
        if not moved :
            prefMove([0,2,6,8]) # corners
    else:
      if win_block():
          pass
      elif prefMove([0,2,6,8]): # corners
          pass
      elif prefMove([5]): # centre
          pass
      else:
          prefMove([1,3,5,7]) # middle row


def prefMove(moves):
    global board
    moved = False
    move = list()
    for potential in moves:
        if board[potential] == ' ':
            move.append(potential)
    if len(move) != 0:
        shuffle(move)
```

*continued*

**Listing 3-10   continued**

```
        board[move[0]] = 'O'
        print 'My move is ',move[0] + 1
        moved = True
    return moved

def win_block(): #move to win or block
    global board
    testBoard = board
    players = ['O','X']
    moveMade = False
    for moveTry in players:
      for square in range(0, len(board) ) :
        if testBoard[square] == ' ' and moveMade == False:
            testBoard[square] = moveTry
            if checkWin(moveTry,testBoard):
                board[square] = 'O'
                moveMade = True
                print 'My move is ',square + 1
            else:
                testBoard[square] = ' ' # retract move
    return moveMade

def swapPlayer(player):
    if player == 'X' :
       player = 'O'
    else:
       player = 'X'
    return player

def getMove(player):
    global board
    correct_number = False
    while correct_number == False :
        square = raw_input('Square to place the '+ player + ' ')
        try:
            square = int(square)
        except:
            square = -2
        square -= 1 # make input number ⮌
match internal representation
        if square >= 0 and square < 10 : # number in range
            if board[square] == ' ' : # if it is blank
                board[square] = player
```

```python
            correct_number = True
        else:
            print 'Square already occupied'
    else :
        print 'incorrect square try again'

def wipeBoard() :
    global board
    for square in range(0, len(board) ) :
        board[square] = ' '

def printBoard():
    print
    print '|',
    for square in range(0,9):
        print board[square],'|',
        if square == 2 or square == 5 :
            print
            print '- - - - - - -'
            print '|',
    print
    print

def canMove(): # see if move can be made
    move = False
    for square in range(0, len(board) ) :
      if board[square] == ' ':
        move = True
    return move

def checkWin(player,board):
    win = False
    for test in wins :
        count = 0
        for squares in test :
            if board[squares] == player :
                count +=1
        if count == 3 :
            win = True
    return win

if __name__ == '__main__':
    play()
```

Here, the only changes from the earlier listings are to the play() and generateMove() functions, but the program is shown in its entirety. The play() function is changed to keep a count of the number of moves that have been made, and this number is passed to the generate Move() function. If the move number is anything other than one, the move-picking strategy is the same as before. However, if it is the first move the computer has made, it responds in a different way. There are four lists containing the corners and the corresponding opposite corners, along with the side squares and the corresponding adjacent squares to play in response. Note that these adjacent squares are also corners, but this is of no importance here. Also, every side square has two adjacent corner squares, but it doesn't matter which one is picked. Finally, if the human player opens with the centre square, the computer just picks one of the corners.

The way this works is that for each move and its response, a list is generated. Then the move list is stepped through one square at a time, looking for the human player's symbol in each square. If it is found, the corresponding element of the response list is passed to the prefMove() function. As this element is a list whose length is only one, it gets picked. There is no point writing a new function when an existing function will suffice. The same is done for the side moves. Note as this only is performed on the first move, there is only one X symbol to find. This plays a pretty mean game that I think can't be beaten.

## Over to You

Well, it is now over to you; it's time to add your own improvements and embellishments. You might want to improve on how the board looks by printing more characters and giving it more space. On the other hand, you might want it to print quickly and revert to the simpler board you started with. You might not want to print out the board after each move, but only when both you and the computer have moved. The numbering of the board is conventional, but perhaps you want to change this to match the locations of the numbers on the numeric keypad on your keyboard – that is, if you have one. That would mean the top-left square would be 7, and lower-right one would be 3. You can change it in the input section simply by using a list as a lookup table; don't forget to also use another lookup table to translate when the computer prints out its move. (A *lookup table* is a predefined conversion between one number and another. It is simply a list where the input value is the index of the list and the output value; the one you want to associate with the input value is the contents of that list element.)

You will notice that the computer is polite, and it always allows you to go first. Look into making changes to allow the computer to play first. I feel that X should always go first, but you might look into offering a choice of symbols to the opening player as well. You can try and change the playing strategy into giving other classes of squares first priority in place of the corners. If you are more experienced, you might like to look up the minimax algorithm that computes all possible moves. To do that, you have to use a *recursive algorithm,* which involves a function that calls itself. These sorts of things can be very powerful but difficult to get your head around. Perhaps that is too much at this stage; you might be better off leaving that until you have finished the book.

# Chapter 4
# Here's the News

by Mike Cook

## In This Chapter

- ○ Learn about text rendering
- ○ Make text scrolling smooth
- ○ Test the size of text before it is displayed
- ○ Generate mirror writing

**HAVE YOU EVER** tried looking into a camera and delivering a presentation to it? It's not easy. The eye movement has to be totally different from giving a live talk to an audience. With a large audience you can make eye contact with many people around the room to show that you are addressing them all, but on camera this is different. If you try the same trick, it looks quite creepy, with your eyes swiveling about all over the place. With a camera you have to keep your eyes still and look straight into it. Also, you might have to repeat a piece of your presentation to the camera, so you want to be consistent. This was the problem faced by early TV shows – getting newsreaders and actors to learn their lines at a much higher rate than they did back in the theater. The solution they came up with in the 50s was the *teleprompter* – or *autocue*, depending on what side of the Atlantic you live.

## Early Teleprompters

In 1950, there were paper versions of an auto prompter devised by Hubert Schlafly. He used a paper roll of cues, or prompts, that were placed next to the camera. The technique of using a through-the-lens system was first devised by Jess Oppenheimer three years later. Jess was a writer, producer and director on the TV show *I Love Lucy*, popular worldwide, and it quickly gained popularity with newsreaders, soap actors and sitcom comedians. The English comedian Tony Hancock was one of the first in the U.K. to discover the system. After a night of heavy drinking, a fall gave him a concussion that made it impossible to learn his lines. He used an autocue, or as he called it an *idiot's board*, and never learned a line again. Sadly, this led to a demise in his performances, even heavier drinking sessions and eventual suicide. This is a problem I don't think is attached to this project.

The first teleprompter used rolls of paper with the words handwritten on them. They would be wound by hand and put to one side of the lens. Then the strip was placed in front of a closed-circuit TV camera; a monitor and diagonal piece of glass was used, allowing the camera to shoot straight through the glass without seeing the words. This enabled the actor to read the words reflected in the glass while looking directly into the camera. The monitor was modified to give a compensating mirror image so the reflection looked the right way around. This trick relied on the fact that whenever light passes through glass not all of it gets through; a small amount is reflected from the surface. This is known as the *reflective loss* of the glass and is normally about 4%.

With the advent of personal computers in the early 80s, teleprompters entered the digital age. The first personal computer to be used for this was the Atari 900 in 1982. It was called the *Compu=Prompt* and was invented and marketed by Courtney M. Goodin and Laurence B. Abrams, who continued selling systems for 28 years.

## The Pi Prompter

You could spend a small fortune on a teleprompter; however, it is quite easy to make one yourself using nothing more than the Raspberry Pi, a sheet of glass and a few fixings. A rather simplified diagram of what is needed is shown in Figure 4-1.

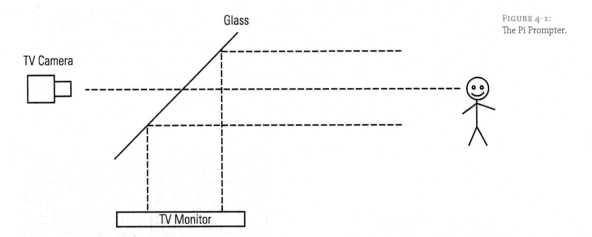

FIGURE 4-1:
The Pi Prompter.

In somewhat of a reverse of the normal procedure, I will discuss the practicalities of this setup last, after you have the Pi producing something to display.

In essence the requirements sound simple: You need to produce large words scrolling slowly and smoothly up the screen. You need to be able to control the speed of the scroll, and pause it if required. The final twist is that you have to include an option to turn the words into mirror writing to compensate for any reflection from the glass, if you have that sort of a physical setup.

So here is an outline of what you need to do: Read words from a file, show them in a window in large type and scroll them up. Then if you think about it a bit more in-depth, you need to make sure that the words can fit on one line without overflowing it and breaking in the middle of a word. This is not quite as easy as you might think.

Like all projects, you don't tackle this whole task head on all at once; instead, you get bits of it going first and build up what you want to do slowly. That is what development is all about. So tackle this in a number of stages.

## What You Need to Do

First off, you need to understand how graphics are shown on a screen. Basically what you see on a TV monitor is a visual representation of an area of computer memory. Each pixel is a memory location; the address of that memory corresponds to the position of the pixel on the screen. The contents of that memory location correspond to the brightness and colour of the pixel. That computer memory is called the *display memory*. If you have a program that is producing something in a window, that window has its own working memory associated with it, known here as *screen memory*. You can then do all your drawing, or setting of memory locations, in that memory area, and when you are finished, you can transfer the whole of that into the display memory in one go. Copying blocks of memory from one place to another is quite efficient in computer-processing terms. This means that the window appears to update instantly. Another step in sophistication is that you can use a separate piece of memory to work in, and then transfer that to your working memory in any position in the screen memory you choose. This is sometimes called a *sprite system*, but in Pygame software this is known as a *surface*. This is illustrated in Figure 4-2.

FIGURE 4-2:
Pygame's
graphic memory
model.

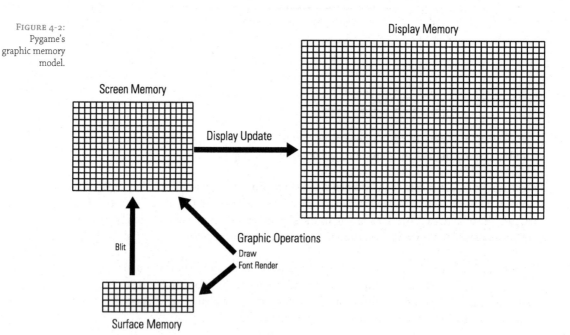

You can see that the display memory is the largest, as it is the whole output seen on the TV monitor. The screen memory corresponds to the window area you have defined for Pygame to use. Transferring data from the screen memory to the display memory is what is done with the display update call. You can do many operations to this screen memory, such as drawing lines, circles and rectangles. If you want to draw some text, however, it is best to do this in the separate area of memory called a *surface*. In that memory you can *render* text, which means to convert the text into a bitmap or graphic representation of letters. This is done in the depths of the computer and can involve several different techniques, the easiest of which is to use a lookup table that contains a bitmap for each letter in the font you want to render. If you render into a separate area of memory, you can transfer that memory to any location in the screen memory by a process Pygame calls *blitting*.

So armed with this knowledge you can work out a strategy for scrolling words. Render each line of the display into its own surface memory, and then blit each surface into the screen memory, one line above the next. The Y coordinate for each line is simply incremented in steps of the window height divided by the number of lines. Then all the lines fit completely within the window. If you have another number, a vertical offset, that you subtract from the calculated Y position, then the display will have each line shown in a slightly different place. If that offset is changed slightly and the screen redrawn repeatedly, the words will appear to scroll up the screen. Figure 4-3 shows what is happening.

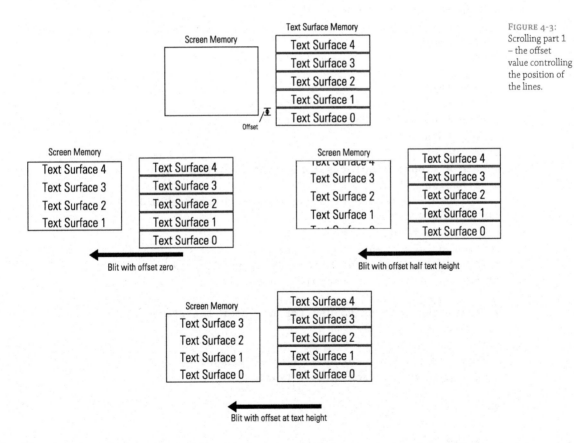

FIGURE 4-3:
Scrolling part 1
– the offset
value controlling
the position of
the lines.

You can see the surface memory for each line and how it lines up with the screen. Surface 0 is entirely below the screen and so gets lost or clipped from the final display. As the offset increases to half the height of the text surfaces, the top half of Surface 4 and the bottom part of Surface 0 are clipped, showing only half of the two lines. Finally when the offset is equal to the height of the text surface, Surface 0 is fully visible, and Surface 4 is totally clipped. So the words have scrolled one line simply by changing the offset variable at a different value in successive frames.

Okay, that is enough theory for the moment; it's time to actually implement this in code. This is not by any means a full, working system, but it allows us to work on this function and get it right before going on to get closer to what you want. Listing 4-1 contains the initial scrolling code.

---

**Listing 4-1    Scrolling 1**

```python
#!/usr/bin/env python
"""
Here is the News
A Raspberry Pi Auto Cue Test 1
"""
import time                           # for delays
import os, pygame, sys

pygame.init()                         # initialise graphics interface
os.environ['SDL_VIDEO_WINDOW_POS'] = 'center'
pygame.display.set_caption("Auto Cue test 1")
screenWidth = 980
screenHeight =610
screen = pygame.display.set_mode([screenWidth, ⊃
screenHeight],0,32)
background = pygame.Surface((screenWidth,screenHeight))
segments = 4
segment = 0 # initial start place
textHeight = screenHeight / segments
textSurface = [ pygame.Surface((screenWidth, ⊃
textHeight)) for s in range(0,segments+1)]

# define the colours to use for the user interface
cBackground =(0,0,0)
cText = (255,255,255)
background.fill(cBackground) # make background colour
font = pygame.font.Font(None, textHeight)

def main():
    lines = 5
    while True :
        for i in range(0,5):
            setWords("This is line "+str(lines-i),i)
```

```
        lines += 1
        for offset in range(0, textHeight,4):
            checkForEvent()
            #time.sleep(0.1)
            drawScreen(offset)

def drawScreen(offset) : # draw to the screen
    global segment
    screen.blit(background,[0,0]) # set background colour
    for index in range(0,segments+1):
      segment +=1
      if(segment > segments): # wraparound segment number
          segment = 0
      drawWords(segment,offset)
    pygame.display.update()

def setWords(words,index) :
        textSurface[index] = font.render(words, ⏎
True, cText, cBackground )

def drawWords(index,offset) :
        textRect = textSurface[index].get_rect()
        textRect.centerx = screenWidth / 2
        textRect.top = screenHeight - (textHeight * ⏎
index) - offset
        screen.blit(textSurface[index], textRect)

def terminate(): # close down the program
    print ("Closing down please wait")
    pygame.quit() # close pygame
    sys.exit()

def checkForEvent(): # see if you need to quit
    event = pygame.event.poll()
    if event.type == pygame.QUIT :
          terminate()
    if event.type == pygame.KEYDOWN and ⏎
event.key == pygame.K_ESCAPE :
          terminate()


if __name__ == '__main__':
    main()
```

Although Listing 4-1 is only a partial implementation of what you need, it is a fully working program, so let's look more closely at what it does and how it does it. The code starts by loading in modules you need and then initialising the Pygame's window, which needs to be large and is going to be where the action takes place. The size is determined by variables, and although the raw numbers could be typed into the commands where needed, this provides a one stop shop for any changes in size you might want to make. The variable `segments` determines how many lines to have on the display; as a lot of the time there will be lines clipped, this variable is one less than the total number of surfaces you need to use. The `textSurface` list is defined initially as just some blank areas of memory. Then the numbers determining the colours of the text and the background are defined, which for now are white text on a black background.

Moving on to the functions `terminate()` and `checkForEvent()` – these are what I call *housekeeping functions*. They provide an easy way to quit an application using the window's close icon or by pressing Esc. Later these functions will be developed to control the application. The simplest function is `setWords()`, which simply renders a line of words in a specified text surface. Again, later this will be greatly expanded as you cope with real text.

The `drawWords()` function takes in an index or number to identify what text surface to use, and an offset. It then gets the rectangle associated with that surface and centers it horizontally, and blits it to the screen memory in a position that depends on the index and the offset values. This function is used exclusively by the `drawScreen()` function that places each text segment, or line, on the screen. This is controlled by the `segment` variable, which is constricted to the values between zero and the maximum number of text surfaces you have; we say this number is "wrapped around". Note here that `segment` and `segments` are two different variables; `segments` defines how many you have, and `segment` defines the first one to use.

The `main()` function simply writes five lines of text to each segment and then scrolls a line's worth by changing the offset each time. The `for` loop that does this has an increment of 4 to give it some decent scroll speed; change that number, and you change the speed of the scroll. I found that this loop didn't need slowing down, so the sleep time was commented out. The result is that this program will scroll forever with the line numbers getting larger. The smaller the offset increment is, the smoother the scroll, but it is also slower. With a large value here, the scroll is a lot faster, but it's more jerky. Fortunately, the Raspberry Pi is just about fast enough for your purposes here.

## A Step Closer to a Usable Program

So now it is time to get a lot closer to what you want to do. First off, you want to make the scrolling a lot more efficient by not rendering all the text every time you want to scroll a whole line. This also makes the selection for the words used on a line easier as you only have to do it for each line once. The new method of line scrolling is shown in Figure 4-4.

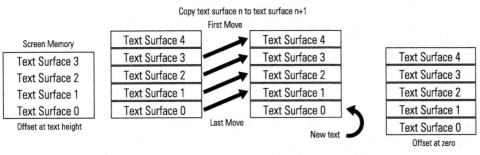

FIGURE 4-4:
Scrolling
part 2 – how
the lines scroll.

This involves copying the memory in the text surface from one location in the list to the next up, when the offset has reached the same height as the text surface. However, you have to do this from the top down, or else you end up with all the text reading the same one line. Then, new text is rendered into text surface 0. When the copying is complete the offset is set to zero, and the screen looks exactly as it did before – only a new line is hidden, clipped at the bottom of the screen, waiting to scroll into view.

The next major improvement in this version is the placing of words onto a line of text so that they will fit. This is a bit more tricky than it at first sounds because the font used is not a monospaced font. In a monospaced font all characters occupy the same size box, so it is easy to know how wide a string of characters will be from the number of them in the string. However, when you are using a proportional font, as you are here, each character's width is variable, depending on the character. That means, for example, a letter *I* is much narrower than a letter *W*. The only way you can see how wide a bunch of words is going to be is if you render them, and then measure the size. This makes the rendering process a bit more tricky than before. Basically what you do is to build up the line one word at a time and measure the resulting text width. If it is less that the width you need, you add another word and measure again. This continues until you exceed the allotted width, at which point you go with a line that is one word short of this. In this way you ensure that the maximum number of words get used to fill the line and no word is split. This process is complicated by the fact that if you run out of words for one line, you just have to go with the remaining words in the line.

Finally, the words for your news story have to come from somewhere, and in this case it is a file called, appropriately enough, `news.txt`. This is just a simple text file you can make with the Leafpad text processor that is bundled with the Pi's operating system. The text I used for testing was the scrolling text used at the start of the first *Star Wars* film, which I thought was suitably geeky. You can find the text with a simple Google search if you want to do the same. The `news.txt` file should be stored in the same folder as the program.

To see how these ideas pan out, look at Listing 4-2. This program is a bit more of a test than the previous one with some debug printout. This results in some rather jerky scrolling, but that will be fixed when you remove the printout.

---

**Listing 4-2   Scrolling Words**

```python
#!/usr/bin/env python
"""

Here is the News
A Raspberry Pi Auto Cue Test 2
"""

import time                          # for delays
import os, pygame, sys

pygame.init()                            # initialise graphics interface
os.environ['SDL_VIDEO_WINDOW_POS'] = 'center'
pygame.display.set_caption("Auto Cue Test 2")
screenWidth = 980
screenHeight =610
screen = pygame.display.set_mode([screenWidth, ⤶
screenHeight],0,32)
background = pygame.Surface((screenWidth,screenHeight))
segments = 4
segment = 0 # initial start place
textHeight = screenHeight / segments
textSurface = [ pygame.Surface((screenWidth,textHeight))⤶
for s in range(0,segments+1)]

# define the colours to use for the user interface
cBackground =(0,0,0)
cText = (255,255,255)
scrollSize = 30
background.fill(cBackground) # make background colour
font = pygame.font.Font(None, textHeight)
numberOfLines = 0
newsLines = list()

def main():
    print"Here is the news"
    getNews()
    lines = 0
    while lines < numberOfLines :
        for i in range(segments, 0, -1): ⤶
```

```
# shuffle up the text boxes
            textSurface[i] = textSurface[i-1]
        lines = setWords(lines,0)
        offset = 0
        while offset < textHeight:
            checkForEvent()
            drawScreen(offset)
            offset += scrollSize
    time.sleep(3.0)
    terminate()

def getNews():  # open news file
    global numberOfLines, newsLines
    nfile = open("news.txt","r")
    for line in nfile.readlines():
        newsLines.append(line)
        numberOfLines +=1
    nfile.close()

def drawScreen(offset) : # draw to the screen
    global segment
    screen.blit(background,[0,0]) # set background colour
    for index in range(0,segments+1):
      segment +=1
      if(segment > segments): # wraparound segment number
        segment = 0
      drawWords(segment,offset)
    pygame.display.update()

def setWords(index,segment) :
        endOfLine = False
        margin = 30 # total gap for the two sides
        words = newsLines[index].split() ⤶
# get an array of words from the line
        wordsAvailable = len(words)
        wordsToUse = 0
        wordsWidth = 0
        tryLine = ""
        while wordsWidth < screenWidth - ⤶
margin and wordsAvailable >= wordsToUse + 1:
            tryLine = ""
            wordsToUse += 1
            for test in range(0, wordsToUse):
```

*continued*

Listing 4-2   **continued**

```
                tryLine = tryLine + words[test] + " "
            textSurface[segment] = font.render(tryLine, ⮌
True, cText, cBackground )
            tryWidth = textSurface[segment].get_rect()
            wordsWidth = tryWidth.right
            print tryLine ," -> is ",wordsWidth," pixels wide"
        useLine = ""
        if wordsWidth > screenWidth - margin :⮌
# for the end of a line
            wordsToUse -= 1 # use one less word
        else :
            endOfLine = True
        for test in range(0, wordsToUse): ⮌
# build up the line you want
            useLine = useLine + words[test] + " "
        textSurface[segment] = font.render(useLine,⮌
True, cText, cBackground )
        print "Using the line :- ", useLine
        print
        newsLines[index] = newsLines[index][len(useLine) :]
        if endOfLine : # work on the next line next time
            index += 1
        return index

def drawWords(index,offset) :
        textRect = textSurface[index].get_rect()
        textRect.centerx = screenWidth / 2
        textRect.top = screenHeight - (textHeight ⮌
* index) - offset
        screen.blit(textSurface[index], textRect)

def terminate(): # close down the program
    print ("Closing down please wait")
    pygame.quit() # close pygame
    sys.exit()

def checkForEvent(): # see if you need to quit
    global scrollSize
    event = pygame.event.poll()
    if event.type == pygame.QUIT :
            terminate()
    if event.type == pygame.KEYDOWN :
```

```
    if event.key == pygame.K_ESCAPE :
        terminate()
    if event.key == pygame.K_DOWN :
        scrollSize -= 1
        if scrollSize == 0:
            scrollsize = 1
    if event.key == pygame.K_UP :
        scrollSize += 1


if __name__ == '__main__':
    main()
```

Most of the initialisation is the same as before, but now there is a new list defined called newsLines, which is set to be initially just an empty list. The getNews() function opens up the news.txt file and copies each line into the newsLines list before closing the file. As it does this it counts the number of lines in the global variable called, appropriately enough, numberOfLines.

The main() function is much as before, but it performs the scroll copying described earlier. Also, the for loop that controlled the offset has been replaced by a while loop, which is to allow the offset increment scrollSize to be altered on the fly by using the up and down arrow keys on the keyboard. This is done with a few extra lines in the checkForEvents() function. The main function is run only as long as there are lines to read from the text file. When it is finished there is a three-second delay, and the program shuts down.

What has changed substantially is the setWords() function, which previously consisted of just a single line. Now it is by far the longest function in the program. It starts off by defining some variables and using the split attribute to decompose the current line of news into a list of words called, with staggering imagination, words. It is this list that is used to build up, one word at a time, a trial line. This is done with the while loop defined by the line

```
while wordsWidth < screenWidth - margin and ⮐
wordsAvailable >= wordsToUse + 1:
```

This keeps on adding words to a string and measuring the width of the resulting text surface. At each stage the line built up so far and its width is printed out so that you can see the progress. This while loop also keeps tabs on if the words list has actually run out of words. This loop can finish when you have run out of words or when the width is too wide by one word. When this loops exits the next line,

```
if wordsWidth > screenWidth - margin : # for the end of a line
```

determines which exit condition caused it to finish. If it was because the resulting text was too wide, you remove one word from the list; otherwise, you set a variable to indicate that the end of the line has been reached. Next, you gather the words into the string you will finally use, and render it, printing it out again so that you can check it. Then those words need to be removed from the news line so that you don't use them again. The line

```
newsLines[index] = newsLines[index][len(useLine) :]
```

does this. Finally, you check if the line has had all the words extracted from it by looking at the wordsAvailable variable you set earlier. If it has, the index variable is incremented, and finally the index variable is returned from the function.

The large initial size of the scrollSize variable, coupled with the printing out of each test string in the setWords function, ensures that the results look very bad on the screen – due to rapid scrolling and a pause while the next line is worked out. However, all that will disappear when you remove the test prints in the final version.

## Your Final Pi Prompter Code

All that remains to do is add in some controls. These are basically keyboard controls, so code is added to the checkForEvents() function to set variables in response to key presses. The controls to add are for pausing/resuming the display, controlling the speed, adjusting the display to a mirror image and changing the file to use to read in more news. You also need to make some tweaks to the code to allow these variables to do their work. The final code is shown in Listing 4-3.

---

Listing 4-3   **The Autocue Listing**

```python
#!/usr/bin/env python
"""

Here is the News
A Raspberry Pi Auto Cue
"""

import os, pygame, sys

pygame.init()                         # initialise graphics interface
os.environ['SDL_VIDEO_WINDOW_POS'] = 'center'
pygame.display.set_caption("Auto Cue")
screenWidth = 980
screenHeight =610
screen = pygame.display.set_mode([screenWidth, ⤶
screenHeight],0,32)
```

```
background = pygame.Surface((screenWidth,screenHeight))
segments = 4
segment = 0 # initial start place
textHeight = screenHeight / segments
textSurface = [ pygame.Surface((screenWidth,textHeight)) ⤶
for s in range(0,segments+1)]

# define the colours to use for the user interface
cBackground =(0,0,0)
cText = (255,255,255)
scrollSize = 6
background.fill(cBackground) # make background colour
font = pygame.font.Font(None, textHeight)
numberOfLines = 0
newsLines = list()
fName = "news.txt" # name of file to use
mirror = False
pause = False
anymore = False

def main():
    global anymore
    while True :
      getNews()
      lines = 0
      while lines < numberOfLines :
          for i in range(segments, 0, -1): ⤶
# shuffle up the text boxes
              textSurface[i] = textSurface[i-1]
          lines = setWords(lines,0)
          offset = 0
          while offset < textHeight:
            checkForEvent()
            if not pause :
                drawScreen(offset)
                offset += scrollSize
      anymore = False
      while not anymore :
        checkForEvent()

def getNews():  # open news file
    global numberOfLines, newsLines
```

*continued*

**Listing 4-3  continued**

```
    numberOfLines = 0
    newsLines = list()
    nfile = open(fName,"r")
    for line in nfile.readlines():
        newsLines.append(line)
        numberOfLines +=1
    nfile.close()

def drawScreen(offset) : # draw to the screen
    global segment
    screen.blit(background,[0,0]) # set background colour
    for index in range(0,segments+1):
      segment +=1
      if(segment > segments): # wraparound segment number
          segment = 0
      drawWords(segment,offset)
    pygame.display.update()

def setWords(index,segment) :
        endOfLine = False
        margin = 30 # total gap for the two sides
        words = newsLines[index].split() ⤶
# get an array of words from the line
        wordsAvailable = len(words)
        wordsToUse = 0
        wordsWidth = 0
        tryLine = ""
        while wordsWidth < screenWidth - margin ⤶
and wordsAvailable >= wordsToUse + 1:
            tryLine = ""
            wordsToUse += 1
            for test in range(0, wordsToUse):
                tryLine = tryLine + words[test] + " "
            textSurface[segment] = font.render(tryLine, ⤶
True, cText, cBackground )
            tryWidth = textSurface[segment].get_rect()
            wordsWidth = tryWidth.right
        useLine = ""
        if wordsWidth > screenWidth - margin : ⤶
# for the end of a line
            wordsToUse -= 1 # use one less word
        else :
```

```
            endOfLine = True
        for test in range(0, wordsToUse): ⤵
# build up the line you want
                useLine = useLine + words[test] + " "
        textSurface[segment] = font.render(useLine, ⤵
True, cText, cBackground )
        newsLines[index] = newsLines[index][len(useLine) :]
        if endOfLine : # work on the next line next time
            index += 1
        return index


def drawWords(index,offset) :
        textRect = textSurface[index].get_rect()
        textRect.centerx = screenWidth / 2
        textRect.top = screenHeight - (textHeight * ⤵
index) - offset
        if mirror :
            screen.blit(pygame.transform.flip( ⤵
textSurface[index], True, False), textRect)
        else :
            screen.blit(textSurface[index], textRect)


def terminate(): # close down the program
    print ("Closing down please wait")
    pygame.quit() # close pygame
    sys.exit()


def checkForEvent(): # see if you need to quit
    global scrollSize, pause, anymore, fName, mirror
    event = pygame.event.poll()
    if event.type == pygame.QUIT :
        terminate()
    if event.type == pygame.KEYDOWN :
        if event.key == pygame.K_ESCAPE :
            terminate()
        if event.key == pygame.K_DOWN :
            scrollSize -= 1
            if scrollSize == 0:
                scrollsize = 1
        if event.key == pygame.K_UP :
            scrollSize += 1
        if event.key == pygame.K_SPACE :
          pause = not pause
```

*continued*

Listing 4-3   **continued**

```
        if event.key == pygame.K_m :
           mirror = not mirror
        if event.key == pygame.K_0 :
           anymore = True
           fName = "news.txt"
        if event.key == pygame.K_1 :
           anymore = True
           fName = "news1.txt"
        if event.key == pygame.K_2 :
           anymore = True
           fName = "news2.txt"
        if event.key == pygame.K_3 :
           anymore = True
           fName = "news3.txt"


if __name__ == '__main__':
    main()
```

Looking at the last thing first, you will see that the checkForEvents() function has been extended to react to the spacebar, which toggles a variable for pausing the scrolling, and the *M* key, which toggles the mirror display. The numeric keys set a variable called anymore to true and a variable fName to one of four filenames. You can see how this can easily be extended to cover all the numbers, allowing some degree of keyboard control over what news file is displayed.

In the main() function the updating of the screen and increment of the offset variable are now dependent on the value of the pause variable, which is controlled by the spacebar. The whole function is not an infinite loop; when a file has finished being output the code is held in a while loop until the anymore variable is set to true with perhaps a change in filename as controlled by the number keys. The getNews() function now zeros the count of the number of lines and the list of lines themselves. The rest of the function is unchanged.

The setWords() function has the printing removed, which makes it much faster. The drawWords() function will render the text either normally or flipped around according to the value of the mirror variable. Note this will only be seen to take effect when the screen is actively scrolling; if it is paused or the end of the text has been reached, you will not see the reverse effect until it starts again.

That is about it for the code.

When running Listing 4-3 it is best to have the desktop background set to black and all the other windows minimised to reduce stray light.

## The Physical Setup for Your Prompter

Now turn your attention to the practical setup. You saw in Figure 4-1 that the basic requirement is to have a sheet of glass at 45° to the camera, along with the Raspberry Pi's monitor being flat on its back pointing upwards. It helps here to have a small monitor; although you might think the ideal would be a 13-inch screen, I quite successfully used a 19-inch TV set for this. This can be physically arranged in many different ways, but perhaps the simplest way is to utilise a large cardboard box and that old standby, duct tape. You can remove one side of the box with a sharp hobby knife, but you should leave the corners in for strength. I used three pieces of 1/4″ × 1/2″ strip pine duct taped to the sides and base of the box to act as the holder for the glass, as shown in Figure 4-5.

FIGURE 4-5:
The first stage in building the autocue.

After that, I slipped a piece of 9 1/4″ × 7″ glass from a photo frame behind the wooden strips and held it on with two small strips of duct tape at the end. Cut a hole in the far end of the box for the camera lens to poke through. Make sure that there is enough zoom on the camera so that it doesn't see the edges of the box. I used some plastic IC tubes to reenforce the corners although you can use 1/2″ square strip pine, again with liberal amounts of duct tape. Figure 4-6 shows this.

FIGURE 4-6:
The finished
autocue.

Now it's time to place the box open side down over the monitor and run the program. The results are shown in Figure 4-7.

You can use normal picture frame glass, and it will give no problems with the size of letters shown here in Figure 4-7. However, there is a small bit of fuzziness or ghosting due to some reflections from the other side of the glass. You can see this in a closeup of the autocue, as shown in Figure 4-8; this was taken with a longer exposure than the photograph in Figure 4-7. You can minimise this double reflection by using as thin a piece of glass as you can get. Another way to cut it down, and to increase the brightness of the prompt in the bargain, is to use some half silvered glass, which is sometimes called a *two-way mirror*. The cheapest way to get this is to apply some laminate film to the glass – the type used for tinting windows. It cuts down the light reaching the camera, but you can compensate for that by using stronger lighting on the subject or a longer exposure/larger aperture on the camera. Make sure that you get the neutral tinted type; otherwise you will get a colour cast over what you film. You can get glass like this in various degrees of partial reflectivity. It would have been better if the inside of the box was sprayed black, but it works acceptably without this.

FIGURE 4-7:
The autocue in
action.

FIGURE 4-8:
A closeup of the
autocue,
showing double
reflections.

# Over to You

It is now over to you to make your own additions and improvements to this project. A simple improvement would be to make the `mirror` function work even when the display is not scrolling. This can easily be done by testing the variables that determine if the display is scrolling and if not calling the `drawScreen` function.

One feature not included in the software is an indication of what word or line should be being said at any time. You can do this in many ways, but the simplest is to make all the text a slightly less bright shade of grey with the middle line in the display being full white. You could also experiment with alternative colours or highlighting individual words.

On the system I made, the text would have fitted better on the TV if the display were turned around by 90°, so you could change the code to do this. Can you think how this would be done? Hint: There is a `pygame.transform.rotate()` function in the box.

If you don't like the system I used to physically make the project, have a look online. There are numerous suggestions for alternative methods of construction.

On the control side you can use some of the hardware input techniques covered in later chapters to build your own handheld controller to pause and change the speed of the scrolling. Whatever you do you can say with confidence, "Good evening. Here's the news".

# Chapter 5
# Ping

**by Mike Cook**

## In This Chapter

- ❍ Describe movement to a computer
- ❍ Display a dynamic game
- ❍ Discover one way to detect collisions between on-screen objects
- ❍ Handle the physics of reflection
- ❍ Make single-player and two-player versions of the game

A VERSION OF Ping-Pong, or table tennis, was one of the early electronic games; it was first produced by Willy Higginbotham in 1958 and used an oscilloscope as a display. This was long before the advent of microcomputers. You could make a version of the game by using just logic gates, with no processors involved. I made one back in 1970 that generated its own TV signal. It was, by today's standards, a weird hybrid of an analogue and digital circuit – with the path of the ball being driven by two analogue integrators, and those voltages triggering comparators against an analogue sawtooth TV time base. By 1975 all the logic had been combined into one chip, the AY-3-8500, making it a much easier circuit to build. It even had a choice of games which were simple variants on the same theme. This chip appeared in hundreds of products and was the first low-cost home TV console. I even built a console using this chip as well. A few years after that, home microcomputer systems came along, and table tennis was one of the first graphics games to be implemented.

## Early Commercial Products

On the commercial side, the Magnavox Odyssey, designed by Ralph Baer, was the first game console to go on sale to the general public. This was first demonstrated in 1968, but was not commercially available until 1972. It was seen before its launch by Nolan Bushnell, who cofounded Atari, so he assigned the newly appointed engineer Allan Alcorn to implement the game as a training exercise. The results were so impressive that Bushnell decided to launch it as an video arcade game using the name *Pong*. This name sounded odd to U.K. ears, as it is a slang word for a very bad smell. Just a few days into the testing of the first prototype in a bar, the owner rang up to say that the game had stopped working. On investigation they found that the money had backed up and jammed the mechanism. So the first upgrade was to fit a bigger coin box – something Bushnell later said he was "happy to live with". Inevitably Magnavox and Atari ended up in court, but out-of-court settlements were reached. Pong then went on to be released as a home TV console.

So the game has a honored place in the history of computing and serves as an interesting introduction into arcade type games on the Raspberry Pi. You might think that being a game from the early days of computing it will be simple, and it is, but it is not as simple as you might hope. The early games were written in Assembler language; with today's computing power you can write a table tennis game in a high-level language like Python.

## The Ping Game

Basically, what I am calling *Ping* is a copy of the bat-and-ball game which spawned a whole generation of computer games. What you are going to implement here are two games, a one-player game and a two-player game. Figure 5-1 shows the screen display of the two-player game, but they look very similar. As with all projects, it is best to start implementing features one at a time and building up the sophistication and complication as you go. However, first you need a bit of theory.

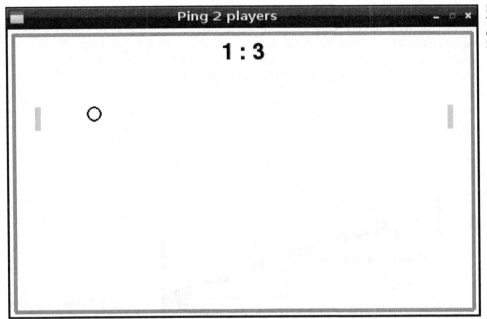

FIGURE 5-1:
The screen
display of the
Ping game.

## On-screen Movement

Movement on the computer screen is created by drawing a number of separate pictures in quick succession with one or more elements moving between each frame. In the case of a ball moving across the screen, there are two components to the movement: a change in the X coordinate and a change in the Y coordinate. Whenever you are dealing with changes there is a special word scientists use – *delta*, which is represented by the Greek letter delta ($\Delta$) and just means "change". So to describe the path of an object moving in a straight line, all you need is two quantities – $\Delta X$ and $\Delta Y$. On each successive frame $\Delta X$ and $\Delta Y$ are added to the X and Y coordinates to get the new position to plot the object. This defines the angle of movement as shown in Figure 5-2.

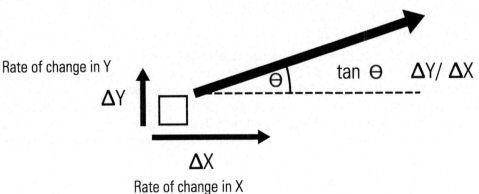

FIGURE 5-2:
The movement
angle defined by
the two values
$\Delta X$ and $\Delta Y$.

Rate of change in Y

$\Delta Y$

$\tan \theta$    $\Delta Y/ \Delta X$

$\Delta X$

Rate of change in X

If you want to define the exact angle Θ (angles are always called *theta*), you can apply the formula shown in Figure 5-2. However, for this project there is no need to work in terms of angles, basically because all reflections are from orthogonal surfaces. This means that you are considering only horizontal or vertical surfaces to reflect from. Take a look at Figure 5-3; here you see a block bouncing off, or being reflected from, a vertical surface. The angle it is reflected at is equal to the incoming angle or incident angle. But the point is that you don't have to know the actual angle – in fact, you don't care. All that you need to do is reverse the sign of ΔX – that is, make it negative. The same goes if the block is approaching the reflecting surface from the other direction. ΔX will be negative in that case, and all you need to do is to reverse the sign. If you make a negative number negative, you end up with a positive.

FIGURE 5-3:
The reflection
from a vertical
surface by
negating ΔX.

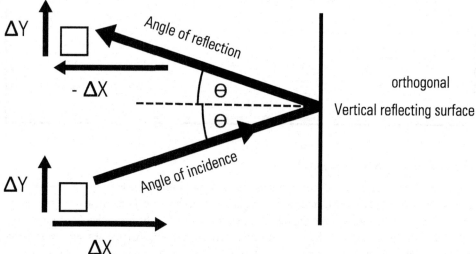

I think you can see that exactly the same applies for reflections off a horizontal surface – only this time it is ΔY that is negated. So when the time comes to bounce off a surface all that you need to do is to invert the appropriate delta value.

## Detecting Collisions

Now all you need to get some bouncy action is to work out when things collide. This is easy for humans to spot but can be a bit tricky for a computer. Every object you draw on the screen will be put there by specifying one or more coordinates. However, that describes only one point on the object. Take a rectangle, for example: You specify the X and Y coordinates of the top-left corner and the width and height, as well as the line thickness. When you draw a line, you specify the X and Y coordinates of the start of the line, and the coordinates of where you want it to finish, along with the line thickness. There are two ways of detecting if these overlap: The first is to look at what is already drawn on the screen to see if anything is in the place you are going to draw the next block. The second, and the one you shall use here, is to compute the extent of the objects and see if there is an overlap. Figure 5-4 shows this calculation for a rectangle and a line. Note the difference in how the line thickness is handled. For a line the thickness is built up by drawing in pixels either side of the required line, whereas for a rectangle the thickness is built up by drawing in pixels inside the rectangle. This is the way that Pygame handles the graphic coordinates; other systems such as Apple's QuickTime take a different approach, with the defined line being in between the pixels and any line thickness being below and to the right of the line. There are many ways to implement graphics drawing routines.

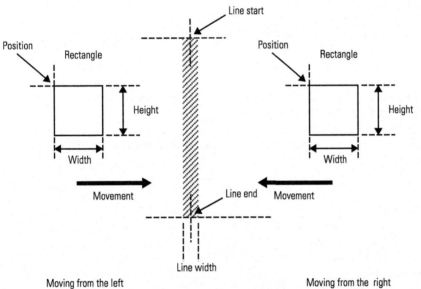

FIGURE 5-4: Calculating limits for a collision.

You will see from Figure 5-4 that the limits set depend on the direction of approach the object has, so when going from left to right it is different than going from right to left.

## The Test Bounce

Armed with this information, you can now get some coding done and set the framework for your game. Type in the code in Listing 5-1, and it will bounce a square around a window at high speed.

---

**Listing 5-1 Bounce Test 1**

```python
#!/usr/bin/env python
"""
Bounce
A Raspberry Pi test
"""
import time                         # for delays
import os, pygame, sys

pygame.init()                       # initialise graphics interface
os.environ['SDL_VIDEO_WINDOW_POS'] = 'center'
pygame.display.set_caption("Bounce")
screenWidth = 400
screenHeight =400
screen = pygame.display.set_mode([screenWidth,⤸
screenHeight],0,32)
background = pygame.Surface((screenWidth,screenHeight))

# define the colours to use for the user interface
cBackground =(255,255,255)
cBlock = (0,0,0)
background.fill(cBackground) # make background colour
dx = 5
dy = 10

def main():
    X = screenWidth / 2
    Y = screenHeight /2
    screen.blit(background,[0,0])
    while True :
            checkForEvent()
            #time.sleep(0.05)
            drawScreen(X,Y)
            X += dx
            Y += dy
            checkBounds(X,Y)
def checkBounds(px,py):
    global dx,dy
    if px > screenWidth-10 or px <0:
        dx = -dx
    if py > screenHeight-10 or py < 0:
        dy = - dy

def drawScreen(px,py) : # draw to the screen
```

```
    screen.blit(background,[0,0]) # set background colour
    pygame.draw.rect(screen,cBlock, (px, py, 10 ,10), 0)
    pygame.display.update()

def terminate(): # close down the program
    print ("Closing down please wait")
    pygame.quit() # close pygame
    sys.exit()

def checkForEvent(): # see if you need to quit
    event = pygame.event.poll()
    if event.type == pygame.QUIT :
            terminate()
    if event.type == pygame.KEYDOWN and ⏎
event.key == pygame.K_ESCAPE :
            terminate()


if __name__ == '__main__':
    main()
```

You will see that the direction of the block is defined by the two variables dx and dy (for delta X and delta Y) and is fixed at five pixels in the X direction and ten in the Y direction per frame. The square is drawn in solid black on a white background.

The main function first of all defines the square in the center of the screen, and goes into an endless loop in which it checks the keyboard for a quit and draws the screen. Then it updates the square's position and checks for any collision between the square and the sides of the window. Note as the sides of the window are not a drawn line, there is no need to account for the line thickness here.

In the main loop there is a sleep command, but this is commented out with a #, which means that it is ignored. Try removing the # and see how much slower the block will move around. Also experiment with changing the values of dx and dy and see how this changes both the speed and the angle of trajectory of the block. Finally, have a play with adjusting the screenWidth and screenHeight variables.

## Improving the Ping Game

Well, Listing 5-1 is a good start, but a number of things are not quite right in it. First of all, the object bouncing about is a square, and although that is true to the original game, you can do much better these days. So let's make the object a circle instead of a square. This will change the collision calculations because a circle is drawn by defining its center point. Also, if you rely on simply detecting when the position of the ball is greater than the collision limits you calculated, you will most times draw the ball actually overlapping the line. This will look like the ball has penetrated into the reflecting object. It would be much better if, when you detect a collision, the position of the ball is adjusted to sit on the colliding surface. This is shown in Figure 5-5; the ball's position is shown in successive frames, and when the collision occurs the position of the ball would normally be behind the reflecting object. This does not look good, so it is hauled back to sit on the line. This has the effect of slowing down the ball at the point of collision, but you do not perceive this as you are expecting a collision to occur at the surface and the brain's expectation overrules anything else.

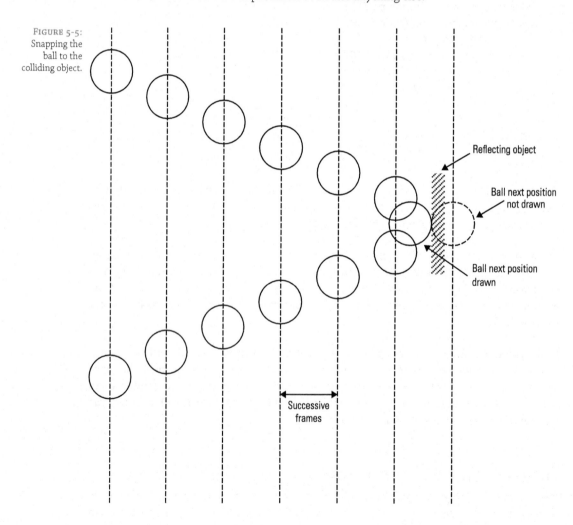

FIGURE 5-5:
Snapping the
ball to the
colliding object.

Reflecting object

Ball next position
not drawn

Ball next position
drawn

Successive
frames

To make the bouncing a bit more interesting, a sound should be produced at the moment of impact, something that did not occur in the first incarnations of the game. Finally, the code makes the bounding rectangle (the rectangle containing the ball) adjustable from the cursor keys of the keyboard. All this is added to produce the code in Listing 5-2.

**Listing 5-2  The Improved Bounce Code**

```python
#!/usr/bin/env python
"""
Bounce with sound
A Raspberry Pi test
"""
import time                      # for delays
import os, pygame, sys

pygame.init()                    # initialise graphics interface
pygame.mixer.quit()
pygame.mixer.init(frequency=22050, size=-16, ↩
channels=2, buffer=512)
bounceSound = pygame.mixer.Sound("sounds/bounce.ogg")
os.environ['SDL_VIDEO_WINDOW_POS'] = 'center'
pygame.display.set_caption("Bounce2")
screenWidth = 400
screenHeight =400
screen = pygame.display.set_mode([screenWidth,↩
screenHeight],0,32)
background = pygame.Surface((screenWidth,screenHeight))

# define the colours to use for the user interface
cBackground =(255,255,255)
cBlock = (0,0,0)
background.fill(cBackground) # make background colour
box = [screenWidth-80,screenHeight-80]
delta = [5,10]
hw = screenWidth / 2
hh = screenHeight /2
position = [hw,hh] # position of the ball
limit = [0, 0, 0, 0] #wall limits
ballRad = 8 # size of the ball

def main():
    global position
    updateBox(0,0) # set up wall limits
```

*continued*

**Listing 5-2** **continued**

```
    screen.blit(background,[0,0])
    while True :
            checkForEvent()
            time.sleep(0.05)
            drawScreen(position)
            position = moveBall(position)

def moveBall(p):
    global delta
    p[0] += delta[0]
    p[1] += delta[1]
    if p[0] <= limit[0] :
       bounceSound.play()
       delta[0] = -delta[0]
       p[0] = limit[0]
    if p[0] >= limit[1] :
       bounceSound.play()
       delta[0] = -delta[0]
       p[0] = limit[1]
    if p[1] <= limit[2] :
       bounceSound.play()
       delta[1] = - delta[1]
       p[1] = limit[2]
    if p[1] >= limit[3] :
       bounceSound.play()
       delta[1] = - delta[1]
       p[1] = limit[3]
    return p

def drawScreen(p) : # draw to the screen
    screen.blit(background,[0,0]) # set background colour
    pygame.draw.rect(screen,(255,0,0), (hw - ⤶
(box[0]/2),hh - (box[1]/2),box[0],box[1]), 2)
    pygame.draw.circle(screen,cBlock, (p[0], p[1]),ballRad, 2)
    pygame.display.update()

def updateBox(d,amount):
    global box, limit
    box[d] += amount
    limit[0] = hw - (box[0]/2) +ballRad #leftLimit
    limit[1] = hw + (box[0]/2) -ballRad #rightLimit
    limit[2] = hh - (box[1]/2) + ballRad #topLimit
```

```
        limit[3] = (hh + (box[1]/2))-ballRad #bottomLimit

def terminate(): # close down the program
    print ("Closing down please wait")
    pygame.quit() # close pygame
    sys.exit()

def checkForEvent(): # see if you need to quit
    event = pygame.event.poll()
    if event.type == pygame.QUIT :
            terminate()
    if event.type == pygame.KEYDOWN :
        if event.key == pygame.K_ESCAPE :
            terminate()
        if event.key == pygame.K_DOWN : ⏎
# expand / contract the box
            updateBox(1,-2)
        if event.key == pygame.K_UP :
            updateBox(1,2)
        if event.key == pygame.K_LEFT :
            updateBox(0,-2)
        if event.key == pygame.K_RIGHT :
            updateBox(0,2)


if __name__ == '__main__':
    main()
```

You can see here that not only have the functions' names changed but the variables defining the movement and some other parameters also have changed from being separate named variables to being items in a list. This makes it easer to pass them into and out of functions. A function is restricted to returning only one item, but by packing lots of variables into a list you get to return many under the one name. Note that in this code checking for a collision involves only checking the position of the ball against predefined limits. This eliminates the need to do calculations such as adjusting for the ball radius every time you want to do a collision check. Precalculating these limits helps to speed up the overall program and gets the ball moving faster and smoother.

The sound is handled by loading in a bounce sound. Note here though that the initialisation of the sound does not use the default values but uses

```
pygame.mixer.init(frequency=22050, size=-16, ⏎
channels=2, buffer=512)
```

This ensures that the sound is produced as soon as possible after the software command is given. Without this there is an unacceptable delay, which is sometimes called *latency*. You need to create a sound file in the .ogg format with a sample rate of 22.05 KHz; call it bounce.ogg and place it inside a folder called sounds. This sounds folder should be placed in the same folder as the Python code. A short blip sound will do for now. If you like, you can look inside the Python games folder at some of the sound files that are there; you can copy and rename beep.ogg, for example, here. I use the application Audacity for creating sound files. It is free, and there are versions that run on Windows machines or Macs.

## A Single-Player Game

The next step produces a usable single-player game, complete with scoring. The point of a single-player game is to see how many times you can return the ball from a perfect computer player. You get three balls, and the number of returns you make from those balls is your score. If it is the highest one of the session, it is transferred to the left number, and that is the one to beat next time. There are a few steps in going from the simple bounce around a box to the single player, but space in the book restricts me from going through all the intermediate stages.

The chief change is that you no longer need to look at just a single value to detect a collision because a bat also has a limited length; you need to see if the ball is sailing over the top or underneath it. The top and bottom collisions are still the same, though. There are a few shortcuts I have taken to simplify the detection of a collision with a ball as opposed to a rectangle. Figure 5-6 shows the dimensions of the bat and ball. For the detection of a collision, you can consider just the bounding box of the circular ball and not worry about the actual geometry of the circle.

FIGURE 5-6:
Measurements
for the bat
and ball.

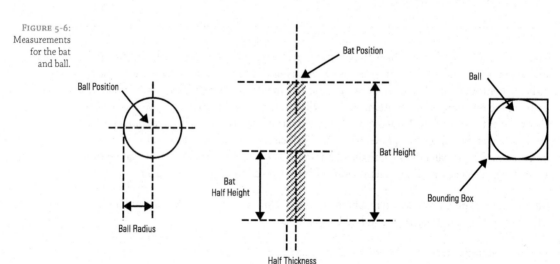

Now when you consider bat-and-ball collisions you must look at both the X and Y elements of the coordinates of the bat and ball. Figure 5-7 summarises this by showing both sets of conditions that have to be met. This is complicated by the fact that whereas the X coordinate of the bat is fixed, the Y coordinate is going to change with input from the player. Note here that unlike conventional coordinates, Pygame has the Y-axis numbers increase as you move down the screen.

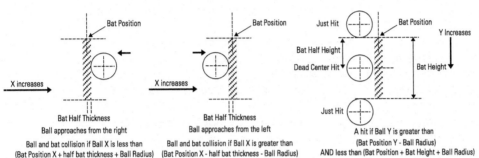

FIGURE 5-7: The collision geometry of the bat and ball.

The overall structure of the game also needs to be defined. Previously there was just a ball bouncing around the screen. Now you have to have more code to define the various stages of the game. Each game consists of three balls, and a *rally* is the time one ball spends in play. The score advances each time you hit the ball, and a ball is lost when it collides against the far-right bounding box. After each ball is lost, the automatic left-hand player serves a new ball at a randomly chosen speed and direction. This structure needs to be imposed on the simple game mechanics. Let's see how all this comes together in Listing 5-3.

Listing 5-3    **The Single-Player Ping Game**

```python
#!/usr/bin/env python
"""
Ping - Tennis game one player
with score
For the Raspberry Pi
"""

import time                       # for delays
import os, pygame, sys
import random


pygame.init()                         # initialise graphics interface
pygame.mixer.quit()
pygame.mixer.init(frequency=22050, size=-16, ⤶
channels=2, buffer=512)
bounceSound = pygame.mixer.Sound("sounds/bounce.ogg")
os.environ['SDL_VIDEO_WINDOW_POS'] = 'center'
```

*continued*

Listing 5-3 **continued**

```
pygame.display.set_caption("Ping 1 player")
screenWidth = 500
screenHeight =300
screen = pygame.display.set_mode([screenWidth, ⤵
screenHeight],0,32)
background = pygame.Surface((screenWidth,screenHeight))
textSize = 36
scoreSurface = pygame.Surface((textSize,textSize))
font = pygame.font.Font(None, textSize)
pygame.event.set_allowed(None)
pygame.event.set_allowed([pygame.KEYDOWN,pygame.QUIT])

# define the colours to use for the user interface
cBackground =(255,255,255)
cBall = (0,0,0)
background.fill(cBackground) # make background colour
cText = (0,0,0)
box = [screenWidth-10,screenHeight-10]
deltaChoice = [ [15,1], [14,1], [13,1], [12,1], ⤵
[11,1], [10,1], [15,2], [14,2], [13,2], [12,2], [11,2], [10,2] ]
maxDelta = 11
delta = deltaChoice[random.randint(0,maxDelta)]
hw = screenWidth / 2
hh = screenHeight /2
ballPosition = [-hw,hh] # position of the ball off-screen
batMargin = 30 # how far in from the wall is the bat
batHeight = 24
batThick = 6
batInc = 20 # bat / key movement
batX = [batMargin, screenWidth - batMargin]
batY = [hh, hh] # initial bat position
limit = [0, 0, 0, 0, 0, 0] #wall limits & bat limits
ballRad = 8 # size of the ball
rally = True
pause = True
score = 0
best = 0  # high score
balls = 3 # number of balls in a turn
ballsLeft = balls

def main():
    global ballPosition, rally, balls, pause, score, best
    updateBox(0,0) # set up wall limits
```

```
    updateScore()
    screen.blit(background,[0,0])
    while True :
      ballsLeft = balls
      if score > best:
         best = score
      score = 0
      updateScore()
      while ballsLeft > 0:
       ballPosition = waitForServe(ballPosition)
       while rally :
            checkForEvent()
            time.sleep(0.05)
            drawScreen(ballPosition)
            ballPosition = moveBall(ballPosition)
       ballsLeft -= 1
      print "press space for",balls,"more balls"
      pause = True
      while pause :
        checkForEvent()


def waitForServe(p) :
    global batY, rally, delta
    computerBatDelta = 2
    serveTime = time.time() + 2.0 #automatically serve again
    while time.time() < serveTime :
            checkForEvent()
            drawScreen(p)
            batY[0] += computerBatDelta ⏎
# move bat up and down when waiting
            if batY[0] > limit[3] or batY[0] < limit[2]:
                computerBatDelta = -computerBatDelta
    p[0] = batX[0]
    p[1] = batY[0]
    delta = deltaChoice[random.randint(0,maxDelta)]
    rally = True
    return p

def moveBall(p):
    global delta, batY, rally, score, batThick
    p[0] += delta[0]
    p[1] += delta[1]
```

*continued*

**Listing 5-3**   **continued**

```
        # now test to any interaction
        if p[1] <= limit[2] : # test top
            bounceSound.play()
            delta[1] = - delta[1]
            p[1] = limit[2]
        elif p[1] >= limit[3] : # test bottom
            bounceSound.play()
            delta[1] = - delta[1]
            p[1] = limit[3]
        elif p[0] <= limit[0] : # test missed ball player 1
            p[0] = limit[0]
            rally = False
            print " missed ball"
        elif p[0] >= limit[1] : # test missed ball player 2
            p[0] = limit[1]
            rally = False
            print " missed ball"
        # now test left bat limit
        elif p[0] <= limit[4] and p[1] >= batY[0] - ballRad ⮐
and p[1] <= batY[0] + ballRad + batHeight:
            bounceSound.play()
            p[0] = limit[4]
            delta[0] = random.randint(5,15)
            if random.randint(1,4) > 2 : ⮐
# random change in y direction
                delta[1] = 16 - delta[0]
            else :
                delta[1] = -(16 - delta[0])
        # Test right bat collision
        elif p[0] >= limit[5] and p[1] >= batY[1] - ballRad ⮐
and p[1] <= batY[1] + ballRad + batHeight:
            bounceSound.play()
            delta[0] = - delta[0]
            p[0] = limit[5]
            score+= 1
            updateScore()
    batY[0] = p[1] - ballRad # make auto opponent follow bat
    #batY[1] = p[1]- ballRad # temporary test for auto player
    return p

def updateScore():
    global score, best, scoreRect, scoreSurface
    scoreSurface = font.render(str(best)+" : "+str(score),⮐
```

```
True, cText, cBackground)
    scoreRect = scoreSurface.get_rect()
    scoreRect.centerx = hw
    scoreRect.centery = 24

def drawScreen(p) : # draw to the screen
    global rally
    screen.blit(background,[0,0]) # set background colour
    pygame.draw.rect(screen,(255,0,0), (hw - (box[0]/2),⊃
hh - (box[1]/2),box[0],box[1]), 4)
    pygame.draw.line(screen,(0,255,0), (batX[0], batY[0]),⊃
(batX[0], batY[0]+batHeight),batThick)
    pygame.draw.line(screen,(0,255,0), (batX[1], batY[1]),⊃
(batX[1], batY[1]+batHeight),batThick)
    screen.blit(scoreSurface, scoreRect)
    if rally :
        pygame.draw.circle(screen,cBall, (p[0], p[1]),⊃
ballRad, 2)
    pygame.display.update()

def updateBox(d,amount):
    global box, limit
    box[d] += amount
    limit[0] = hw - (box[0]/2) +ballRad #leftLimit
    limit[1] = hw + (box[0]/2) -ballRad #rightLimit
    limit[2] = hh - (box[1]/2) + ballRad #topLimit
    limit[3] = (hh + (box[1]/2))-ballRad #bottomLimit
    limit[4] = batX[0] + ballRad + batThick/2 ⊃
#x Limit ball approaching from the right
    limit[5] = batX[1] - ballRad - batThick/2 ⊃
#x Limit ball approaching from the left

def terminate(): # close down the program
    print ("Closing down please wait")
    pygame.quit() # close pygame
    sys.exit()

def checkForEvent(): # see if you need to quit
    global batY, rally, pause
    event = pygame.event.poll()
    if event.type == pygame.QUIT :
            terminate()
    if event.type == pygame.KEYDOWN :
```

*continued*

Listing 5-3   **continued**

```
        if event.key == pygame.K_ESCAPE :
            terminate()
        if event.key == pygame.K_DOWN : ⤵
# expand / contract the box
            updateBox(1,-2)
        if event.key == pygame.K_UP :
            updateBox(1,2)
        if event.key == pygame.K_LEFT :
            updateBox(0,-2)
        if event.key == pygame.K_RIGHT :
            updateBox(0,2)
        if event.key == pygame.K_s :
            rally = True
        if event.key == pygame.K_SPACE :
            pause = False
        if event.key == pygame.K_PAGEDOWN :
            if batY[1] < screenHeight - batInc :
            batY[1] += batInc
        if event.key == pygame.K_PAGEUP :
            if batY[1] > batInc :
            batY[1] -= batInc


if __name__ == '__main__':
    main()
```

There are a lot more changes this time, but hopefully this code is recognisable in structure from Listing 5-2. The various phases of the program are defined by the Boolean variables rally and pause, which can be changed from the keyboard, in the checkForEvent() function, along with the Y position of the bat. I chose to use the Page Up and Page Down keys for the movement of the bat as they are on the far right of my keyboard.

The updateBox() function has two more limits added to it, that of the ball approaching the bat from the left or right. The drawScreen() function now draws the two bats and only draws the ball if the rally variable is true. It also draws a surface bitmap containing the score. updateScore() is a new function that, as its name implies, changes the surface containing the score and positions the score rectangle. This works just like you saw in Chapter 4, "Here's the News", with the teleprompter.

The moveBall() function has grown some. The list of if statements is now replaced by a string of elif clauses based on the original if statement. This means that only one of the sections of code will be executed in each pass. This is because the positional condition for a ball to be off the right side of the screen would also trigger the right ball bat collision, so you must carefully test for collisions in the correct order to avoid a misidentification of what is colliding with what. The function takes the first case that is true from the following list:

○ A collision with the top of the box

○ A collision with the bottom of the box

○ A collision with the left edge of the box (missed ball, computer player)

○ A collision with the right edge of the box (missed ball, human player)

○ A collision with the left bat

○ A collision with the right bat

In the event of any of those conditions being met, the code will take the appropriate action. In the case of the top or bottom walls, the ball's direction will change appropriately as you have seen before. If the active player hits the ball, the score will be incremented along with an elastic collision. If the computer's bat hits it, a new value of the two delta variables will be chosen from the list defined at the start of the program. All collisions also cause a bounce sound to be played. Basically, this function controls the action on the screen. The last line keeps the computer's bat in line with the ball. You can also make the player's bat follow the ball for testing, but then the game element disappears altogether.

The `waitForServe()` function is used to restart the rally when the ball has been missed. Here the computer's bat moves up and down the screen for two seconds before being served with a new random set of delta values. In the two-player game described in the next section of this chapter, this will be expanded.

That leaves us with `main()` as the only function you have not looked at. As usual, this function orchestrates the whole program. After a bit of initialisation it enters a `while True` endless loop, which initialises the number of balls and score for a game, before entering a `while` loop that basically counts down the number of balls in a game. Finally, the third `while` loop controls the rally and keeps the screen action going until a ball is missed. When it is `moveBall()` sets the `rally` variable to `False`, and that loop terminates. When all the balls have been played the final `while` loop in this function just checks for any events, one of which could be the spacebar, which sets the `pause` variable to `False` and allows another game to be played.

# A Two-Player Game

It doesn't take much to turn this into a two-player game, but there is a subtle change in what the object of the game is, and that has a few ramifications in the code. In the one-player game the point was to simply return the ball to the perfect opponent. So there was no need to do anything about altering the flight of the ball when the player hit it back. In a two-player game, however, you not only have to return the ball, but you also have the opportunity of changing the flight of the ball to make it more difficult for your opponent to return. In a real game of Ping-Pong, this is done by adding top spin to the ball. In your Ping game you can simulate the same sort of effect by having more delta movement in the Y direction, the further from the center of the bat the collision occurs. This involves a further calculation once the collision has been detected. The other thing that needs changing is the method of serving. The serve goes to the player who has just lost the point, and there needs to be a bit of an element of surprise for the opposing player. Therefore, the serve can be played early by pressing a key, but if the player waits too long, the serve will happen automatically. All these changes can be seen in Listing 5-4, the two-player game.

### Listing 5-4　The Two-Player Game of Ping

```python
#!/usr/bin/env python
"""

Ping - Tennis game two player
with score
For the Raspberry Pi
"""

import time                        # for delays
import os, pygame, sys
import random


pygame.init()                            # initialise graphics interface
pygame.mixer.quit()
pygame.mixer.init(frequency=22050, size=-16, ⤶
channels=2, buffer=512)
bounceSound = pygame.mixer.Sound("sounds/bounce.ogg")
outSound = pygame.mixer.Sound("sounds/out.ogg")
p0hitSound = pygame.mixer.Sound("sounds/hit0.ogg")
p1hitSound = pygame.mixer.Sound("sounds/hit1.ogg")
os.environ['SDL_VIDEO_WINDOW_POS'] = 'center'
pygame.display.set_caption("Ping 2 players")
screenWidth = 500
screenHeight =300
screen = pygame.display.set_mode([screenWidth, ⤶
screenHeight],0,32)
background = pygame.Surface((screenWidth,screenHeight))
textSize = 36
scoreSurface = pygame.Surface((textSize,textSize))
font = pygame.font.Font(None, textSize)
pygame.event.set_allowed(None)
pygame.event.set_allowed([pygame.KEYDOWN,pygame.QUIT])

# define the colours to use for the user interface
```

```
cBackground =(255,255,255)
cBall = (0,0,0)
background.fill(cBackground) # make background colour
cText = (0,0,0)
box = [screenWidth-10,screenHeight-10]
deltaChoice = [ [15,1], [14,1], [13,1], [12,1], [11,1],⤷
[10,1], [15,2], [14,2], [13,2], [12,2], [11,2], [10,2] ]
maxDelta = 11
delta = deltaChoice[random.randint(0,maxDelta)]
hw = screenWidth / 2
hh = screenHeight /2
ballPosition = [-hw,hh] # position of the ball off-screen
batMargin = 30 # how far in from the wall is the bat
batHeight = 24
batThick = 6
batInc = 20 # bat / key movement
batX = [batMargin, screenWidth - batMargin]
batY = [hh, hh] # initial bat position
limit = [0, 0, 0, 0, 0, 0] #wall limits & bat limits
ballRad = 8 # size of the ball
rally = True
pause = True
server = 0 # player to serve
serve =[False,False]
score = [0,0]  # players score
balls = 5 # number of balls in a turn
ballsLeft = balls
batMiddle = (ballRad - (batHeight + ballRad))/2

def main():
   global ballPosition, rally, balls, pause, score, server
   updateBox(0,0) # set up wall limits
   updateScore()
   screen.blit(background,[0,0])
   while True :
     ballsLeft = balls
     score = [0,0]
     updateScore()
     while ballsLeft > 0:
      ballPosition = waitForServe(ballPosition,server)
      while rally :
           checkForEvent()
           time.sleep(0.05)
```

*continued*

Listing 5-4   **continued**

```
            drawScreen(ballPosition)
            ballPosition = moveBall(ballPosition)
        ballsLeft -= 1
    print "press space for",balls,"more balls"
    pause = True
    while pause :
        checkForEvent()


def waitForServe(p,player) :
    global batY, rally, delta, serve
    computerBatDelta = 2
    serve[player] = False
    serveTime = time.time() + 4.0 #automatically serve again
    while time.time() < serveTime and serve[player] == False:
            checkForEvent()
            drawScreen(p)
            batY[player] += computerBatDelta ⤵
# move bat up and down when waiting
            if batY[player] > limit[3] or batY[player] < ⤵
limit[2]:
                computerBatDelta = -computerBatDelta
        p[0] = batX[player]
        p[1] = batY[player]
        delta = deltaChoice[random.randint(0,maxDelta)]
        if player == 1 :
            delta[0] = -delta[0]
            p1hitSound.play()
        else:
            p0hitSound.play()
        rally = True
        return p

def moveBall(p):
    global delta, batY, rally, score, batThick, server
    p[0] += delta[0]
    p[1] += delta[1]
    # now test to any interaction
    if p[1] <= limit[2] : # test top
        bounceSound.play()
        delta[1] = - delta[1]
        p[1] = limit[2]
    elif p[1] >= limit[3] : # test bottom
```

```
        bounceSound.play()
        delta[1] = - delta[1]
        p[1] = limit[3]
    elif p[0] <= limit[0] : # test missed ball left player
        outSound.play()
        rally = False
        score[1] += 1
        server = 0
        p[0] = hw
        updateScore()
    elif p[0] >= limit[1] : # test missed ball right player
        outSound.play()
        rally = False
        score[0] += 1
        server = 1
        p[0] = hw
        updateScore()
    # Test left bat collision
    elif p[0] < limit[4] and p[1] >= batY[0] - ballRad ↵
and p[1] <= batY[0] + ballRad + batHeight:
        batBounce(p[1],batY[0],0)
        p[0] = limit[4]
    # Test right bat collision
    elif p[0] >= limit[5] and p[1] >= batY[1] - ballRad ↵
and p[1] <= batY[1] + ballRad + batHeight:
        batBounce(p[1],batY[1],1)
        p[0] = limit[5]
    return p

def batBounce(ball, bat, player) :
    global delta
    point = bat - ball
    delta[1] = int(-14.0 * ((point * 0.05) + 0.6))
    delta[0] = 16 - abs(delta[1])
    if player == 1 :
        delta[0] = -delta[0]
        p1hitSound.play()
    else:
        p0hitSound.play()

def updateScore():
    global scoreRect, scoreSurface
    scoreSurface = font.render(str(score[0])+" : "↵
```

*continued*

**Listing 5-4  continued**

```
+str(score[1]), True, cText, cBackground)
    scoreRect = scoreSurface.get_rect()
    scoreRect.centerx = hw
    scoreRect.centery = 24
    drawScreen(ballPosition)

def drawScreen(p) : # draw to the screen
    global rally
    screen.blit(background,[0,0]) # set background colour
    pygame.draw.rect(screen,(255,0,0), (hw - (box[0]/2),⤵
hh - (box[1]/2),box[0],box[1]), 4)
    pygame.draw.line(screen,(0,255,0), (batX[0], batY[0]),⤵
(batX[0], batY[0]+batHeight),batThick)
    pygame.draw.line(screen,(0,255,0), (batX[1], batY[1]),⤵
(batX[1], batY[1]+batHeight),batThick)
    screen.blit(scoreSurface, scoreRect)
    if rally :
        pygame.draw.circle(screen,cBall, (p[0], p[1]),⤵
ballRad, 2)
    pygame.display.update()

def updateBox(d,amount):
    global box, limit
    box[d] += amount
    limit[0] = hw - (box[0]/2) + ballRad #leftLimit
    limit[1] = hw + (box[0]/2) -ballRad #rightLimit
    limit[2] = hh - (box[1]/2) + ballRad #topLimit
    limit[3] = (hh + (box[1]/2))-ballRad #bottomLimit
    limit[4] = batX[0] + ballRad + batThick/2⤵
#x Limit ball approaching from the right
    limit[5] = batX[1] - ballRad - batThick/2⤵
#x Limit ball approaching from the left

def terminate(): # close down the program
    print ("Closing down please wait")
    pygame.quit() # close pygame
    sys.exit()

def checkForEvent(): # see if you need to quit
    global batY, rally, pause, serve
    event = pygame.event.poll()
```

```
        if event.type == pygame.QUIT :
            terminate()
        if event.type == pygame.KEYDOWN :
            if event.key == pygame.K_ESCAPE :
                terminate()
            if event.key == pygame.K_DOWN : ⤶
# expand / contract the box
                updateBox(1,-2)
            if event.key == pygame.K_UP :
                updateBox(1,2)
            if event.key == pygame.K_LEFT :
                updateBox(0,-2)
            if event.key == pygame.K_RIGHT :
                updateBox(0,2)
            if event.key == pygame.K_s :
                rally = True
            if event.key == pygame.K_SPACE :
                pause = False
            if event.key == pygame.K_q :
                serve[0] = True
            if event.key == pygame.K_HOME :
                serve[1] = True
            if event.key == pygame.K_PAGEDOWN :
                if batY[1] < screenHeight - batInc :
                batY[1] += batInc
            if event.key == pygame.K_PAGEUP :
                if batY[1] > batInc :
                batY[1] -= batInc
            if event.key == pygame.K_z :
                if batY[0] < screenHeight - batInc :
                batY[0] += batInc
            if event.key == pygame.K_a :
                if batY[0] > batInc :
                batY[0] -= batInc


if __name__ == '__main__':
    main()
```

Here more keyboard keys come into play. The Home key has been added for the right player's serve key, along with the bat movement keys of Page Up and Page Down. The A, Q and Z keys perform the same functions for the left player.

The `updateBox()` and `drawScreen()` functions are unchanged, but the `updateScore()` function has been altered to accommodate the score of both players. The `moveBall()` function has been enhanced to include top and bottom limits for the left player's bat, and for both players a new function `batBounce()` is called when a collision is detected. More on this shortly.

The `waitForServe()` function now includes code to allow either player to serve the ball, and there is a longer time before an automatic serve, along with a separate serve sound for each player. There are also a few changes to global variables, adding one to indicate who is serving.

So back to the `batBounce()` function. This performs two functions – the first to determine the ball's return velocity vector and the second to play a sound dependent on the player striking the ball. As the code is written this is the same as the serve sound, but it could be changed.

The major new feature in this function is in determining how far along the bat the collision occurred. This basically is a floating-point number between -1 and +1, with zero being returned if it is plumb center. After you have gotten this fraction it needs to be multiplied by the number that corresponds to the maximum Y velocity you want if the ball just grazes the top or bottom of the bat. In the code I have used a value of 14. Then to keep the overall speed of the ball constant, the X velocity is the maximum velocity you want it to be if there is a dead center hit minus any Y component of the speed. This is all done in the two lines

```
delta[1] = int(-14.0 * ((point * 0.05) + 0.6))
delta[0] = 16 - abs(delta[1])
```

Note how the floating-point calculation is converted to an integer before assigning it to the `delta` global variable. This keeps the delta values as integers, as operations on integers are much faster to perform for the computer.

The final bit of fun is the sound effects. What I did was scour the Internet looking for tennis sounds and found some interesting examples of famous tennis players' grunts as they hit the ball. Using Audacity, I clipped out the short hit/grunt noise and saved it as an `.ogg` format file. I found a line judge's "out" call, along with some real bounce sounds. These sounds enhance the playing of the game tremendously, especially because there is also some crowd noise. However, for that retro 70s sound, you can't beat simple tonal bleeps; the choice is yours.

## Over to You

Well, that is the end of my bit, but it is not the end of this project. There are many changes, enhancements and improvements you can make. This applies to both the single- and two-player version of the game. The simplest involves changing the colours: You might want green grass, for example, or filled coloured balls or bats. You could even draw a picture with a painting package or photo-editing package to act as the background, or you might want to include a net or white lines on the court. You could have different sounds for a serve and a return, which is easy because they are called up in different places in the code. You can upgrade the sounds in the single-player game to match what you did in the two-player game.

You might want to change things like the number of balls in a game or even the scoring to make it more like a real game of tennis, with a player winning a game only when he or she is two points ahead. You can even use the real tennis terms of *advantage* and *deuce* in the score box.

I have deliberately left in the code that alters the bounding box from the cursor keys. How about a variation of the game that allows the serving player to alter the size of the court as the serve takes place? Or how about a court that automatically shrinks as the rally gets longer? Basically, the whole game is one of anticipating where the ball will end up, and by changing the court size only slightly, you can make it more difficult to judge as you don't have any previous experience to go on.

It is only a small step from this game to making a "knock the bricks out of a wall" game with all the variants that can bring. It's within your grasp to do this now if you understand the basics of what was done here.

# Chapter **6**
## Pie Man

**by Mike Cook**

### In This Chapter

- ○ Learn to use animated sprites
- ○ Detect pixels previously drawn on the screen
- ○ Devise artificial intelligence algorithms
- ○ Use screen layers and transparent pixels
- ○ Discover how to detect colliding rectangles

ONE OF THE early great hits of computer gaming was Pac-Man, although I don't think many people had any idea about why it had this name. In the Japanese language there is a tradition of having words that sound like the spirit of what they convey. These are often two identical words said together. In the west the closest we have to that is the concept of onomatopoeia, but it is not quite what *giongo* and *gitaigo* is all about, although it is close. Two examples of this are *pyonpyon,* which is about hopping/skipping, and *niyaniya,* which is about a grin/smirk. As you can see there is not much sound associated with these, but if there was, those terms are what they would sound like. There is one such word, *pakupaku,* which is the sound of biting, chomping or eating – in other words, "the munchies" – and it is this phrase that gave the name to Pac-Man. How fitting, then, that my version of this game also has an eating connotation; only this time, the tables are turned, and it is the pie that does the eating.

There have been many variants of this basic game over the years, but some things are constant over different versions, such as the chomping "man" consuming pills distributed in a maze and being pursued by ghosts. Occasionally the tables can be turned on the ghosts by the consumption of a "power pill"; then it is the man that is lethal to the ghosts. (How you could actually kill a ghost, something already dead, is never quite explained.) This situation when the man can kill the ghost is known as a *power play.* The graphics in the game can range from simple to a stylistic complex 3D rendering, and the sound effects range from bleeps to a horror show. There are optional add-on bonus score items to eat often in the form of fruit, but mainly it is about eating the pills and avoiding the ghosts.

## The Pie Man Game

In the preceding chapter, "Ping", the Ping-Pong game was basically constructed with the technique of having a model of the action in the computer, and the graphics were generated from this model. So variables held the position of the bats, balls and walls, and you set the game going by changing some of these variables and making them interact, and then drawing the result. In this chapter I will show you the other way of making a game, which is in effect the exact opposite. The technique you will use for the Pie Man game involves not knowing in advance the location of anything; things are discovered from frame to frame by examining the pixels in the surrounding locality. This requires a whole bunch of new techniques that need to be learned. In many professional games a mixture of these two methods are used. So, to begin at the end, Figure 6-1 shows a screen dump of the final game, but there is a lot of work to do before you can get there.

Most chapters in this book show you how to build up software by getting increasingly complex and adding more features. However, if I were to take that approach in this chapter, it would probably double the size of the book. This is because each step involves a large piece of code, most of it very similar to the previous piece. So instead I will approach this program in chunks, with each chunk consisting of a number of functions. I will explain what is going on in these functions and talk about the techniques used and difficulties encountered. Each listing needs to be typed into the same file, and there is little that needs to be in any specific order, so let's get to it.

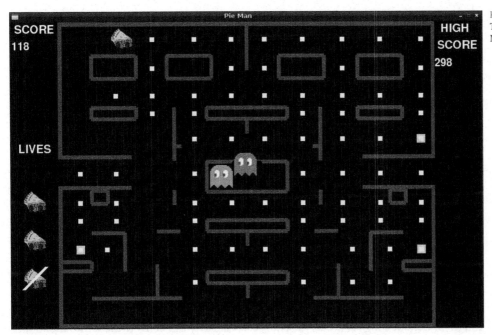

FIGURE 6-1:
The finished Pie
Man game.

## Gather Your Resources

Before you start writing any code there are a number of resources you need to construct or to gather. These are the sound effects and the graphic sprites, or small images, of the playing pieces. These are known as *sprites* because early in computing history they were separate entities with their own dedicated hardware memory that could be set to be displayed anywhere on the screen by simply setting an X and Y register. Nowadays they are always defined in software and the display position controlled by what address in memory you transfer them to, but the name has stuck. Getting these sprites "right" will greatly simplify the code that is needed. First and foremost is the Pie Man himself. It is vital that the sprite used for this be square and not rectangular. At first I made a rectangular Pie Man, but I ran into all sorts of problems with changing direction. The code that tested for the walls on a turn got very complex, and even then it would occasionally fail, causing the Pie Man to walk through a wall. The next thing to worry about is the actual size of the sprite; I settled on a size of 48 pixels square, which in turn governs the size between the walls. Finally, the maximum step size was chosen to be 8, which is a compromise between the speed of the game and the smoothness of the animation. There are a lot of things to calculate between each step, so having it too small will result in a slow game. The step size also governs the thickness of the walls that you need, but more on this when you look at the movement sections of the code.

## The Sounds

I found a good source of free sound effects at the Freesound website, www.freesound.org. You need to register in order to download sounds, but that is simple enough. Freesound has a good search engine to narrow down your choice of sounds, and you can hear them directly from your browser without having to download them first. Table 6-1 shows what sounds you need.

**Table 6-1    Sounds Required**

| Filename | Action |
| --- | --- |
| eatPill.ogg | Pie Man eats a pill. |
| powerPill.ogg | Pie Man eats a power pill. |
| ghostDie.ogg | Pie Man kills a ghost. |
| pieDie.ogg | A ghost kills Pie Man. |
| pieStart.ogg | Fanfare to indicate that you can start playing. |

Note here that the sound files are all in the .ogg format. I downloaded suitable files and used Audacity to trim them, so there was a minimum delay before the sound actually started, and there were no long silence at the end. Also, Audacity can convert them into mono files and save them in the .ogg format that Python on the Raspberry Pi handles with ease. Note that the Raspberry Pi can also handle WAV files, but I have found that it handles only some files, and I can't track down what the offending parameters or variations are. When you have these files put them in a folder called sounds inside your working folder.

## The Players

For the sprite I took the image of the racing pie slice used in Chapter 14, "Computer-Controlled Slot Car Racing", and made it square with a graphics package. I used Photoshop Elements for this, but most graphics programs will allow you to resize an image; however, to make it square, you have to remember to untick the Preserve Aspect Ratio box. Then with a copy of this image, using the Select tool, I carefully removed the pastry lid of the pie slice and pasted it back onto the pie at an angle. Make sure that the background is set to transparent, and save it as a .png file. This gives the two basic images for your Pie Man, shown in Figure 6-2. Make sure that both images are the same size (48 pixels square) and that they are aligned so that when you show one and then the other only the lid moves. Well, if you allow a pixel or two of misalignment in the Y direction, then Pie Man, when it is chomping stationary against a wall, does look like its motor is revving up and down, but don't overdo it.

FIGURE 6-2:
The two basic
Pie Man sprites.

Now with those two basic sprites, make copies of each pointing in the four directions. You can do this by using the Rotate function or the Flip Horizontally and Vertically function of your graphics package. When you have done this give them the names shown in Figure 6-3. Figure 6-3 also shows how you are going to use the sprites in the code. The numbers from zero to seven point at a different image, with the least significant bit of the number determining if the lid is open or closed, and the two most significant bits determining the direction Pie Man is pointing.

Next you need to consider the ghosts. I used six steps in the animation sprites for the ghosts. Basically the only change that happens from sprite to sprite is the position of the eyes and the ripple of the "skirt" at the bottom. In the game these are run in a shuffling loop – that is, they are used in the order 1 to 6 and then back from 6 to 1. In this way you don't have to worry about any discontinuities between sprites 1 and 6. You need three sets of ghost sprites, one set being blue and the others red and orange, or two other colours. This is easy in Photoshop. First I selected the eyes, and then inverted the selection so that the eyes were the only things *not* selected. Then I used the Change Hue function to change the ghost colour. Finally, you need a set of ghosts for the ghost dying sequence. I used a set of eight ghosts, all derived from the first blue ghost. I took the first ghost and shifted it down about three pixels, and carried on doing that in successive ghost sprites until the eyes reached the bottom of frame. Then I added more and more transparent pixels to the last few ghosts to give a fading-away effect. I went back to the first "sinking" ghosts and added a few transparent pixels to the body, putting more transparent pixels in subsequent frames. When played back this gave a nice dissolving effect. In order for the filenames to match up to the programs, the ghost's names are made from g for *ghost,* a number for the number in the sequence and finally a letter indicating the colour. These are shown in Figure 6-4. The dying ghost sequence is shown in Figure 6-5; these sprites are named similarly with a d for *die* as the last letter. Note that all the sprites should have a transparent background and they need to be put into a folder called pies, alongside the sounds folder.

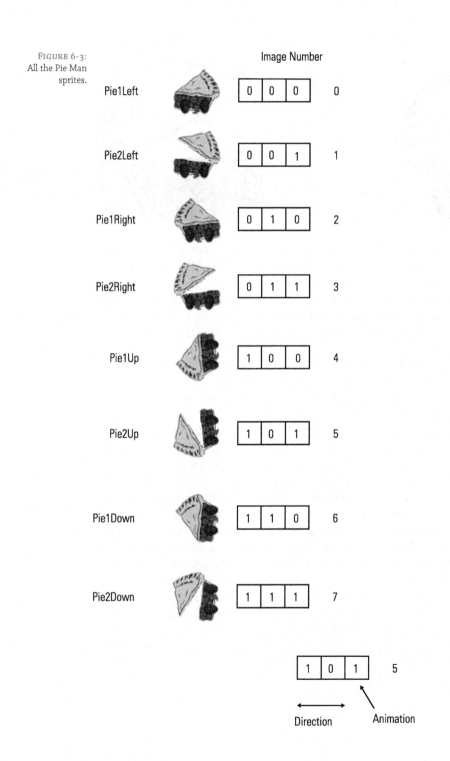

FIGURE 6-3:
All the Pie Man
sprites.

Image Number

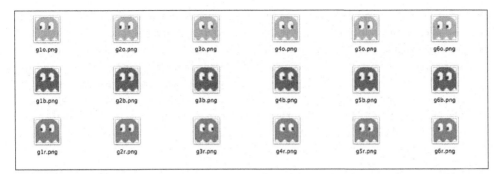

FIGURE 6-4:
All the ghosts.

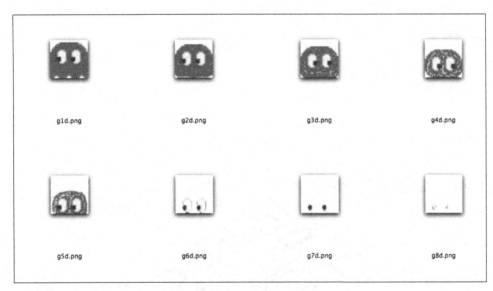

FIGURE 6-5:
The ghost dying sequence.

## Setting the Stage

Now with all the players in place, it is time to construct the stage for the action of your game. The trick in making the game play at a reasonable speed is to try and cut down on the number of drawing operations you have to make at each step. Basically the whole screen needs to be redrawn between steps; however, doing this with a set of draw commands would take too much time. To cut down on the amount of work needed, you can construct the game with three layers, or bitmaps. The lowest is the background layer, which contains all the walls of the maze and needs to be drawn only once. The next layer up contains the pills; after they are drawn you need to alter this layer only when a pill is eaten. Finally, the top layer is the screen, where Pie Man and the ghosts will be plotted. So redrawing the screen consists of copying or blitting the background layer into the screen layer, blitting the pill layer into the screen layer and finally blitting the sprites of Pie Man and the ghosts into the screen layer. Although blitting involves transferring a lot of data from one place to another, it is relatively quick and efficient because it is coded in a low-level machine code that can be executed quickly. One thing you must ensure, however, is that the pill layer's background is transparent so that it does not obscure the walls in the background layer. In Pygame this is done by telling the system that one colour should be treated as being transparent. This is known as the *color key*. Figure 6-6 shows the arrangement of the layers. Notice that the screen layer is wider than the background or the pills layer because first of all, you need to have room for the score and lives-left indicator and second, you need the extra space to cope with the tunnel from one side of the screen to the other.

FIGURE 6-6:
Screen drawing
planes.

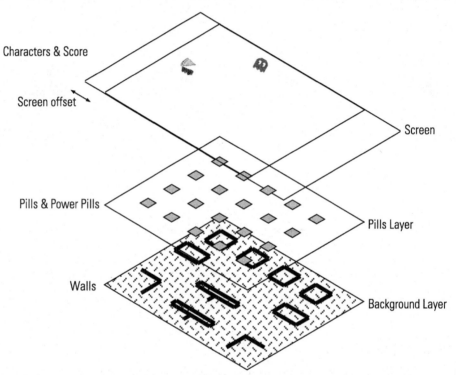

Now it is time for your first chunk of code – basically the functions that set up the background layer. As mentioned before, all these listings need to go into one file, so set up a file called `pieMan.py` in the same folder as the sound and graphics resources and type in the code in Listing 6-1.

Listing 6-1   **Setting Up the Background**

```
def setupBackground():
    walkIncrement = 8
```

```
    screen.fill(cBackground)
    background.fill(cBackground) # make background colour
    #screen bounding box
    pygame.draw.rect(background,(0,0,255), (0,0,↪
800,screenHeight),walkIncrement*2)

    block1(70,70, walkIncrement)
    block1(230,70, walkIncrement)
    block1(634,70, walkIncrement)
    block1(468,70, walkIncrement)
    block2(70,178, walkIncrement)
    block2(634,178, walkIncrement)
    block3(314,178, walkIncrement)
    block3(314,412, walkIncrement)
    block3(314,520, walkIncrement)

    pygame.draw.line(background, blue, (playWidth/2, 0),↪
(playWidth/2,100),walkIncrement) # centre bar
    pygame.draw.line(background, blue, (0, 280),↪
(155, 280),walkIncrement)#tunnel 1 left top
    pygame.draw.line(background, blue, (playWidth-155, 280),↪
(playWidth, 280),walkIncrement) # tunnel 1 right top

    pygame.draw.line(background, blue, (0, 344),(155,↪
344),walkIncrement)#tunnel 1 left bottom
    pygame.draw.line(background, blue, (playWidth-155, 344),↪
(playWidth, 344),walkIncrement) # tunnel 1 right bottom
    pygame.draw.rect(background, cBackground, (0,285, ↪
walkIncrement+1, 8 + pieMan),0) # clear tunnel sides
    pygame.draw.rect(background, cBackground, (playWidth-↪
walkIncrement,285, walkIncrement, 8 + pieMan),0)
    pygame.draw.line(background, blue, (245, 178),(245,↪
288),walkIncrement)
    pygame.draw.line(background, blue, (555, 178),(555,↪
288),walkIncrement)
    pygame.draw.line(background, blue, (245, 258),(260,↪
258),walkIncrement)
    pygame.draw.line(background, blue, (540, 258),(555,↪
258),walkIncrement)
    pygame.draw.line(background, blue, (245, 350),(245,↪
380),walkIncrement)
    pygame.draw.line(background, blue, (555, 350),(555,↪
```

*continued*

**Listing 6-1** **continued**

```
380),walkIncrement)

    pygame.draw.rect(background, blue, (314,290, 172,
64),walkIncrement) # ghost box
    pygame.draw.rect(background, cBackground, (370, 291,
60,walkIncrement-2),walkIncrement-2) #ghost door
    pygame.draw.line(background, blue, (70, 574),(260,
574),walkIncrement)
    pygame.draw.line(background, blue, (540, 574),(730,
574),walkIncrement)
    pygame.draw.rect(background,blue, (0,498, 70, 20),
walkIncrement) # left side block
    pygame.draw.line(background, blue, (140, 438),(140,
518),walkIncrement)
    pygame.draw.line(background, blue, (70, 438),(140,
438),walkIncrement)
    pygame.draw.line(background, blue, (208, 574),(208,
504),walkIncrement)
    pygame.draw.rect(background,blue, (730,498, 70,
20),walkIncrement) # right side block
    pygame.draw.line(background, blue, (660, 438),(660,
518),walkIncrement)
    pygame.draw.line(background, blue, (730, 438),(660,
438),walkIncrement)
    pygame.draw.line(background, blue, (592, 574),(592,
504),walkIncrement)
    pygame.draw.rect(background,blue, (70,350, 35,28),
walkIncrement) # under tunnel bump
    pygame.draw.rect(background,blue, (702,350, 35,
28),walkIncrement) # under tunnel bump

    pygame.draw.line(background, blue, (208, 435),(257,
435),walkIncrement)
    pygame.draw.line(background, blue, (592, 435),(543,
435),walkIncrement)
    drawWords(" SCORE",1,1)
    drawWords("  LIVES",1,250)
    drawWords("  HIGH",screenOffset+playWidth,1)
    drawWords(" SCORE",screenOffset+playWidth,textHeight)
    drawWords(str(hiScore),screenOffset+playWidth,textHeight*2)
    drawPills()

def block1(x,y, inc):
```

```
    global background
    pygame.draw.rect(background,blue, (x,y, 96, 48),inc)

def block2(x,y,inc):
    global background
    pygame.draw.rect(background,blue, (x,y, 96, 24),inc)

def block3(x,y, inc):
    global background
    pygame.draw.rect(background,blue, (x,y, 172, 24),inc)
    pygame.draw.line(background, blue, (x+86, y+24),(x+86, ⊃
y+54),inc)

def drawWords(words,x,y) :
        textSurface = pygame.Surface((screenOffset,textHeight))
        textRect = textSurface.get_rect()
        textRect.left = x
        textRect.top = y
        pygame.draw.rect(screen,cBackground, (x, y, ⊃
screenOffset, textHeight), 0)
        textSurface = font.render(words, True, cText, cBackground )
        screen.blit(textSurface, textRect)
```

Remember, you won't be able to run Listing 6-1 yet as the global variables haven't been set up, but it is worth examining the code to see what it does. Basically it sets up the background layer by drawing the walls. The thickness of the walls is set by the variable walkIncrement to make them thick enough to make their detection simple. This is basically a large number of draw commands that are, from a programming point of view, quite tedious. The only slightly interesting points are the use of black rectangles to create a hole in the walls for the tunnel from one side of the screen to the other, and to create a thinning of the wall in the ghost box to allow the ghosts to exit. It is not all background, however, and the drawWords function is used to set up the display on each side of the playing area. The screenOffset variable is used to adjust the X coordinates between the background layer and the wider screen layer. A bit more interesting is the next chunk of code shown in Listing 6-2.

---

Listing 6-2  **Drawing the Pills**
```
def drawPills():
    pillsLayer.fill((1,0,0)) # make transparent layer
    pillsLayer.set_colorkey((1,0,0),0)
    # basic grid of pills
    pillX = [142, 218, 295, 384, 463, 534, 614, 698, 777, 865 ]
    pillY = [32, 92, 149, 186, 239, 311, 372, 409, 469, ⊃
```

*continued*

**Listing 6-2**    **continued**

```
537, 600]
    powerPills = [(0,4), (9,4), (0,8), (9,8) ]
    # places in the grid where pills are not placed
    pillExclude = [(1,1), (3,1), (6,1), (8,1), (1,3), (4,3),⤵
(5,3), (8,3), (4,5), (5,5), (4,7), (5,7), (4,9), (5,9)]
    pillShift = [(1,8),(1,9),(2,8),(2,9),(7,8),(7,9),(8,8),⤵
(8,9) ]
    for X in range(0,10):
      if X > 5 :
        pillShiftOffset = -20
      else:
        pillShiftOffset = 20
      for Y in range(0,11):
       if not((X,Y) in pillExclude):
          if(X,Y) in pillShift:
             offset = screenOffset + pillShiftOffset
          else:
             offset = screenOffset
          pygame.draw.rect(pillsLayer,(255,255,0), ⤵
(pillX[X]- offset,pillY[Y], 10,10),0)
          if (X,Y) in powerPills:
              pygame.draw.rect(pillsLayer,(0,255,255), ⤵
(pillX[X]- offset-4,pillY[Y]-4,18,18),0)
              pygame.draw.rect(pillsLayer,(255,255,0), ⤵
(pillX[X]- offset,pillY[Y], 10,10),0)
```

This function sets up the pills layer and is called every time this layer needs to be refreshed, such as at the start of the game and when all the pills have been eaten. Whereas Listing 6-1 is a simple brute-force set of draw instructions, Listing 6-2 is a bit more subtle. The pills are mainly on a regular grid, so this lends itself to being programmed in an algorithmic way. However, not all the pills in the grid are drawn because some would be over walls or inside boxes. Similarly, some pills need to be dawn slightly off the grid to fit into the walls. This brings into play a new Python function – that of testing if any item in one list is contained in another list. The coordinates of the grid of pills is defined by the pillX and pillY lists, the coordinates pairs of the pills not to plot are in the pillExclude list and similarly the coordinates pairs of the offset pills are in the pillShift list. Two nested for loops generate the sequence of coordinates, and the line

```
if not((X,Y) in pillExclude)
```

checks whether those coordinates are contained in the exclusion list. That is quite a lot of functionality in a single statement and would be quite hard to code in another language. Finally, the
power pills are simply contained in another list, and they have a large square in a different colour
drawn around them. In fact, this did not look good when I drew a box around the existing pixel,
so the code draws the large solid square first and then the small yellow pill square on top of that.

## The Game Action

Now let's look at the action part of the program, which will move the sprite in a specific direction unless it is blocked by a wall. This is not quite as simple as it might sound. The position of
a sprite, Pie Man or ghost, is the point where you will plot it on the screen, which is in fact the
top-left corner of the sprite and, depending on what direction the sprite is moving, will depend
on where you have to check to see if it can move. Figure 6-7 shows this for Pie Man moving
both left and right. Note that the distance away from the plot position depends on the direction. When Pie Man is moving to the left the place to test is only the move increment away
from the plotted position, whereas when he is moving to the right the length of the image
needs to be added to the walk increment and then subtracted from the plot position. That is
only for the X coordinate; the Y coordinate needs to be scanned over the height of the image to
see if a part of a wall is blocking the progress. Note the pixels to test are not contiguous, but
every four pixels – that is, half the maximum walk increment. This reduces the number of pixels that need testing and thus speeds up the process. A similar process must be gone through
when checking up and down movement. The functions in Listing 6-3 do this.

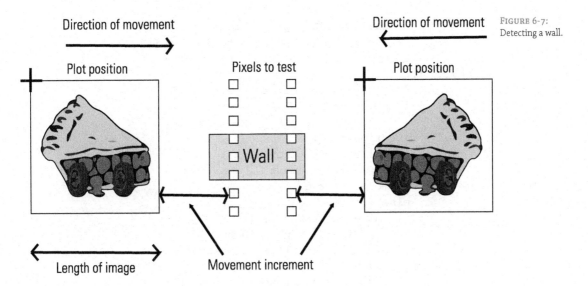

FIGURE 6-7:
Detecting a wall.

Direction of movement

Direction of movement

Plot position

Pixels to test

Plot position

Wall

Length of image

Movement increment

Listing 6-3   **Making a Move**

```python
def makeStep(p,direction, increment):
        global moved
        moved = False
        if direction == 6:
                if wallH(p,p[1]+pieMan+increment):
                    p[1] += increment
                    moved = True
                else:
                    while wallH(p,p[1]+pieMan+1):
                      p[1] +=1 # pull into bottom

        elif direction == 4:
                if wallH(p,p[1]-increment):
                    p[1] -= increment
                    moved = True
                else :
                    while wallH(p,p[1]-1):
                      p[1] -= 1 # pull into top

        elif direction == 2:
                if wallV(p,p[0]+pieMan+increment):
                    p[0] += increment
                    moved = True
                else :
                    while wallV(p,p[0]+pieMan+1):
                      p[0] += 1 # pull in to left side
                    if p[0] > screenOffset + playWidth:
# leaving the screen
                        p[0] = screenOffset - pieMan
                        moved = True

        elif direction == 0:
                if wallV(p,p[0]-increment):
                    p[0] -= increment
                    moved = True
                else :
                    while wallV(p,p[0]-1):
                      p[0] -= 1 # pull in to side
                    if p[0] < screenOffset - pieMan:
# leaving the screen
                        p[0] = screenOffset + playWidth
                        moved = True
```

```
    return p

def wallV(p,os):
    clear = True
    for pix in range(0,pieMan,4) :
        if screen.get_at((os,p[1]+pix)) == blue:
            clear = False
    return clear

def wallH(p,os):
    clear = True
    for pix in range(0,pieMan,4) :
        if screen.get_at((p[0]+pix, os)) == blue:
            clear = False
    return clear

def wallHt2(p,ox,oy,r): #test for turning
    clear = True
    for pix in range(0,r,4) :
        if screen.get_at((p[0]+pix+ox, p[1]+oy)) == blue:
            clear = False
    return clear
```

There are four functions here. The main one, makeStep, takes three parameters: The first, p, is a list containing the X and Y coordinates of the plot position, and the others are the direction and how far you need to go in that direction. This function has different code depending on the required direction, but the purpose of the code is the same. It is saying, "Is the space in front of the sprite enough to move the required distance?", and if so, it lets the sprite move. If not, it pulls in the sprite one pixel at a time until it is up against the obstacle. When that has been done the new position of the sprite is returned.

The three functions following this simply scan the pixels the required distance away to see if it is clear, where *clear* means not blue, the colour of the walls. Note that the exact colour is specified; you could draw something that was only one bit different from the full blue you are looking for, which would look identical, but you would be able to walk through it. Also, notice that it is the screen layer that is being tested; there is nothing to stop you from testing the background layer if you want to. In that way you could have an identical colour on the pills layer of the screen layer that would not act as an obstacle. Note there is also a global variable called move that is set if a step has been taken successfully, which is used later on for the ghost movements.

There is an additional test for directions 0 and 2 to cope with Pie Man exiting on one side of the screen and entering on the other. In early computers this was a pure consequence of the hardware; the way the memory was scanned meant that if you exceeded the coordinates, the sprite would wrap around and be displayed on the other side of the screen. These days, with a windowed environment, you have to do that effect in code.

## Eating the Pills

Next turn your attention to the consumption of the pills, which is a bit different from the detection of the walls. Basically you need to know if Pie Man is over a pill – put simply, you need to look at the pixel colour in the pill layer. As the pill is 10 pixels square, you need not look at any pixel within 10 of the boundary of the sprite. Then if you take a look over a horizontal line and vertical line at the center of the sprite and find any pixel that is yellow, you know the sprite is completely over a pill. Just as with checking for a wall, there is no need to look at every pixel on these lines – just every four. Note that there will be four small blind spots where the corner of a pill can be and still not be detected, but in practice this is not a problem because you will detect it on the next munch or step. Figure 6-8 shows the geometry of this situation.

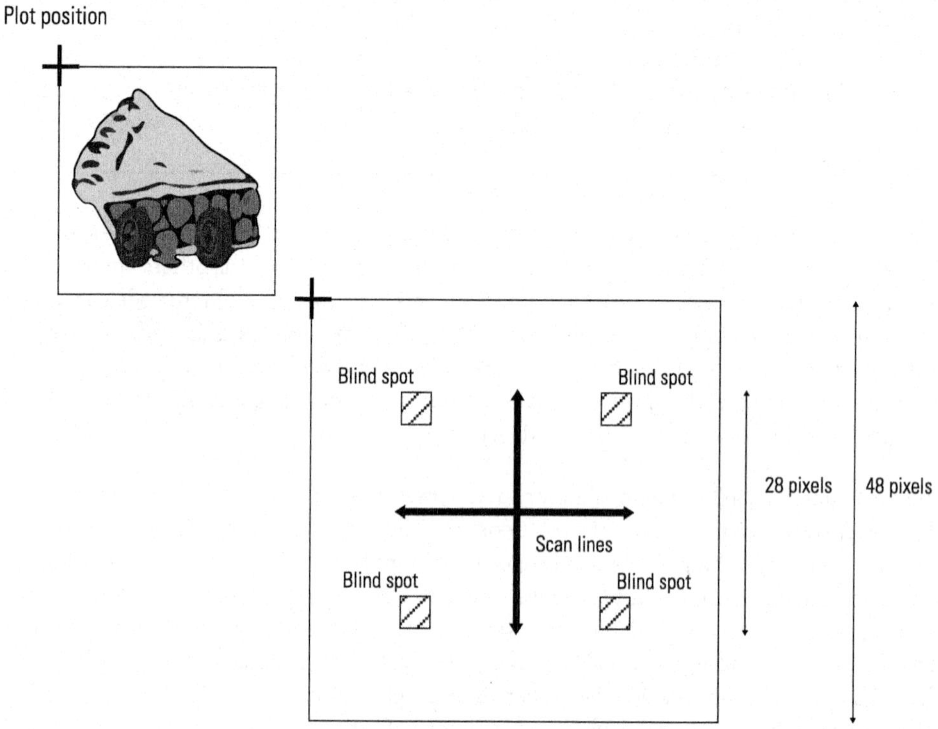

FIGURE 6-8:
Detecting a pill.

Detecting a power pill can in principle be done in the same way, but in practice I found that this was quite time-consuming and slowed the game down noticeably. Therefore, I had to come up with a more efficient way to do this. Basically if the scan for a pill has not detected one, there is no point in scanning for a power pill. If you make a note of where the last pill pixel was found, you can search close to that for the surrounding colour that indicates a power pill. The two functions involved with pill eating are shown in Listing 6-4.

**Listing 6-4   Eating the Pills**

```
def eat(p):
    global eaten, ghostPos, ghostRelease, gNumber
    if pillEat(p):
        eatSound.play()
        # wipe the pill area
        pygame.draw.rect(pillsLayer,(1,0,0), (p[0]- ↵
screenOffset, p[1], pieMan,pieMan),0)
        updateScore(3)
        eaten += 1
        if eaten >= 96:
            eaten = 0
            drawPills()
            ghostPos = copy.deepcopy(ghostInitalPos) ↵
# return ghosts to base
            gNumber = 0
            ghostRelease = time.time()+ 5.0 ↵
# time for first ghost
        pygame.display.update()

def pillEat(p): # test if you are over a pill
    global ppCount
    fpx = 0
    fpy = 0
    pill = False
    ppColour = (0,255,255,255)
    if p[0] > screenOffset and p[0] < rightLimit :
     piy = p[1]+24
     for pix in range(p[0]+10,p[0]+38,9):
            if pillsLayer.get_at((pix-screenOffset, piy))↵
  == pillColour:
                pill = True
                fpx = pix - screenOffset
     pix = p[0]+24
     for piy in range(p[1]+10,p[1]+38,9):
            if pillsLayer.get_at((pix-screenOffset, piy))↵
  == pillColour:
                pill = True
                fpy = piy
```

*continued*

**Listing 6-4    continued**

```
    if pill: #you have a pill is it a power pill?
        ppill = False
        if fpx != 0:
          for pix in range(fpx,fpx+12,2):
            if pillsLayer.get_at((pix, p[1]+24)) == ppColour:
              ppill = True
        if fpy !=0:
          for piy in range(fpy,fpy+12,2):
            if pillsLayer.get_at((pix-screenOffset, piy))↩
 == ppColour:
              ppill = True
        if ppill:
          #print" we have a power pill"
          ppSound.play()
          updateScore(40)
          ppCount = 0 # start off power play
      return pill
```

There are two functions here. The second, pillEat, deals with the pill detection in the manner already discussed. It returns a Boolean variable showing if it has detected a pill and also clears a global variable (ppCount) if a power pill has been found. The finding of the power pill also triggers the power pill sound as well as giving the score a bonus. The first function, eat, takes in a position list and calls the pillEat function as part of an if statement. When a pill is detected, the sound is played, and the score is updated as you might expect, but also the pill has to be removed from the display. This is done by simply drawing a rectangle covering the whole of the sprite in the pills layer of the colour that you have set to represent transparency. This wipes it from view. There is a count kept of how many pills have been consumed, and when this reaches the maximum number, 96, the ghosts are sent back to their box, and the pills are redrawn again on the pill layer. The line that resets the ghosts contains something you will have not seen before:

```
ghostPos = copy.deepcopy(ghostInitalPos) # return ghosts to base
```

This is what is known as a *deep copy*. When copying lists just putting

```
ghostPos = ghostInitalPos
```

will make the two lists the same object; that is, if you change one, the other will also be changed. When the deep copy is used every individual element in the list is transferred to each individual element in the other list. Also, when drawing a new lot of pills the global variable ghostRelease is set, which controls when the ghosts can come out of their box, but more on this later when you look at the main function.

## Death of a Pie Man – or a Ghost

Next, you look at the situation in which a ghost and Pie Man collide, which results in a death; however, whose death it is depends on the mode. If the power play is in force, the ghost dies. Otherwise, the ghost kills Pie Man. He is turned into a ghost because he is killed, and that ghost then dies. This conveniently allows you to use the same animated sequence for any sort of death. This is the only part of the game that relies on knowing where the objects are rather than looking at the screen pixels. This is done by creating a rectangle for Pie Man and the two ghosts, moving that rectangle to match the current playing position and then calling the collide-rectangle function in Pygame, which returns a logic value of true if the two rectangles overlap in any way. The functions that do this are shown in Listing 6-5.

Listing 6-5  **Detecting a Touch**

```
def kill(p,g1,g2): # see if man and ghosts are touching
    global ghostPos, lives, position, ghostRelease, gNumber
    playRect = pygame.Rect(0,0,pieMan,pieMan)
    g1Rect = pygame.Rect(0,0,pieMan,pieMan)
    g2Rect = pygame.Rect(0,0,pieMan,pieMan)
    playRect = playRect.move(p[0],p[1])
    g1Rect = g1Rect.move(g1[0],g1[1])
    g2Rect = g2Rect.move(g2[0],g2[1])
    if playRect.colliderect(g1Rect):
        if powerPlay:
            ghostDieSound.play()
            updateScore(150)
            ghostDisolve(g1)
            ghostPos[0]=[526,298]
    if playRect.colliderect(g2Rect):
        if powerPlay:
            ghostDieSound.play()
            updateScore(260)
            ghostDisolve(g2)
            ghostPos[1]=[422,298]
    if (playRect.colliderect(g1Rect) or playRect.colliderect⟳
(g2Rect) ) and not powerPlay:
            pieDieSound.play()
            ghostDisolve(p)
            time.sleep(0.4)
            lives -= 1
            updateLives()
            ghostPos = copy.deepcopy(ghostInitalPos) ⟳
# return ghosts to base
            position = [screenOffset +pieIncrement*2, ⟳
```

*continued*

Listing 6-5  **continued**

```
pieIncrement + 2] # position of the pieman
        ghostRelease = time.time()+ 5.0 ⟲
# time for subsequent ghosts
        gNumber = 0

def ghostDisolve(p):
    for i in range(0,8):
      pygame.draw.rect(screen, cBackground, (p[0],p[1], ⟲
pieMan, pieMan),0)
      screen.blit(ghostdPicture[i],[p[0],p[1]])
      pygame.display.update()
      time.sleep(0.1)
```

These two functions do the job of detection. After the rectangles have been created and moved to the correct position the two ghosts are checked to see if Pie Man has caught up with them. If this is true and the global variable powerPlay indicates that a power play is in force, the ghost is killed, the die sound is triggered, the score is updated, the death animation function ghostDisolve is called and the ghost is returned to its box. Note that the two ghosts are worth different amounts in the score. However, if a power play is not in force and one of the ghosts has struck a mortal blow to the brave Pie Man, then it is he who dies. One is subtracted from his total number of lives, the lives display is updated and the players are set back to their initial starting points. The ghostDisolve function simply draws successive ghost pictures on the screen. The sleep time controls the speed of this short animation, and makes it large for a slower, lingering death – or at least lasts as long as your dying sound effect.

## The Hunting Pack

Now it is time to look at the control of the ghosts. They must be set to chase Pie Man but run away when there is a power play in force. You need to write something that will determine the movement of the ghosts. Some of this work is done in the main function, but there is one function that hunts you down, getNewDir, which is shown in Listing 6-6.

Listing 6-6  **Finding a Way to You**

```
def getNewDir(g):
    deltax = ghostPos[g][0] - position[0]
    deltay = ghostPos[g][1] - position[1]
      #print deltax,deltay
    if abs(deltax) > abs(deltay) and abs(deltax)> pieMan:
      if deltax < 0:
        nd = 2
      else:
```

```
        nd = 0
    else:
      if deltay < 0:
          nd = 6
      else:
          nd = 4
    if powerPlay: # reverse direction
       nd ^= 0x2
    return nd
```

Here the function getNewDir takes in the ghost number and first works out the delta, or difference, between Pie Man and the selected ghost. This could be a positive or negative value depending on what side of the ghost Pie Man is on. Therefore, when you test these delta values, you need to discard the sign information and just look at the absolute magnitude, which is done with the abs function. The code then sets the direction number to be in the direction of the largest delta. The last few lines of this function check if there is a power play in force, and if there is, it reverses the direction. This is done in a rather clever way. If you refer back to Figure 6-3 and the numbers associated with direction and if you look at bit 1 of the number (remember you start numbering bits from zero, so bit 1 is the middle bit of the three), you will see that for any given direction number, if bit 1 is inverted, the direction is changed to the opposite direction. So by using the exclusive OR operation, ^, you can reverse the direction number no matter what it is. This clever code line saves you from writing many lines of if tests.

# Drawing the Screen

The functions for updating the screen are quite short because most of the heavy lifting has already been done, which is fortunate as this needs to be done every step. This is shown in Listing 6-7.

**Listing 6-7**   **Drawing the Screen**

```
def drawScreen(p,g1p,g2p) : # draw to the screen
    screen.blit(background,[screenOffset,0]) # draw background
    screen.blit(pillsLayer,[screenOffset,0]) # draw pills
    screen.blit(piPicture[pieDirection ^ step],[p[0],p[1]])
    if powerPlay:
       screen.blit(ghostbPicture[gStep],[g1p[0],g1p[1]])
       screen.blit(ghostbPicture[gStep],[g2p[0],g2p[1]])
    else :
       screen.blit(ghost1Picture[gStep],[g1p[0],g1p[1]])
       screen.blit(ghost2Picture[gStep],[g2p[0],g2p[1]])
    # blank out exit tunnels
    pygame.draw.rect(screen, cBackground, (0,285, ⊃
```

*continued*

**Listing 6-7  continued**

```
screenOffset, 12 + pieMan),0)
    pygame.draw.rect(screen, cBackground, (playWidth + ⤴
screenOffset,285, screenOffset, 12 + pieMan),0)
    pygame.display.update()


def updateLives():
    for pie in range(0,maxLives) :
        screen.blit(piPicture[2],[25,348+pie*80])
        if pie >=lives:
            y = 396 + (pie * 80)
            pygame.draw.line(screen,(255,255,0),(25,y),⤴
(25+pieMan, y-pieMan),8)

def updateScore(toAdd):
    global score
    score += toAdd
    drawWords(str(score),1,textHeight)
```

This is quite simple to follow. First the background is blited into the screen and then the pills layer, followed by the picture of Pie Man. Note here that all the sprites are held in an array, and the one chosen is given by the direction number along with the animation bit, which is toggled by the variable step. This simple method ensures that the sprite chosen is in the correct direction and alternates with the pie lid open and closed. This gives a nice chomping effect. Next the two ghosts are drawn. During a power play they are the blue versions; otherwise, they are the red and orange ones. The individual ghost sprite used is determined by the global variable gStep and is altered in the main function, along with Pie Man's step variable. Finally, the ends of the tunnels are blanked out in case Pie Man is making a trip through them, which makes it look like he is disappearing through the tunnel. The two other functions also update the screen but are called only occasionally. The updateLives function draws a number of Pie Man images on the left of the screen and draws a thick strikethrough line across one if that life has been spent. The updateScore function simply takes in a number, adds it to the total score and then draws that score on the screen.

Before you reach the main function that brings it all together and defines the game you must add the usual housekeeping functions. These are shown in Listing 6-8.

**Listing 6-8  Housekeeping Functions**

```
def terminate(): # close down the program
    print ("Closing down please wait")
    pygame.quit() # close pygame
```

```
        sys.exit()

def checkForEvent(): # see if you need to quit
    global pieDirection, position, start, ppCount
    event = pygame.event.poll()
    if event.type == pygame.KEYDOWN :
      start = True
      if event.key == pygame.K_ESCAPE :
          terminate()

      if event.key == pygame.K_DOWN :
          if pieDirection == 0 or pieDirection == 2: #check under
              if wallHt2(position,0,pieMan + 1,pieMan):
                  pieDirection = 6
          else :
              pieDirection = 6
      if event.key == pygame.K_UP :
          pieDirection = 4
      if event.key == pygame.K_RIGHT :
          pieDirection = 2
      if event.key == pygame.K_LEFT :
          pieDirection = 0
      if event.key == pygame.K_p : # cheat - power up at will
          ppCount = 0

    elif event.type == pygame.QUIT :
          terminate()

if __name__ == '__main__':
    main()
```

Unlike the other listings, which can be placed anywhere in the file you are building up, Listing 6-8 has to be at the end – or at least the last line in this listing must be the last line in your file. There is the terminate function that shuts things down when you press the Esc key or close the Pygame window, which is the same for many programs in this book. It is the checkForEvent function that actually provides the user with the controls to play the game – namely, the cursor keys. These mainly look at keyboard events and control the direction of Pie Man through the global variable pieDirection. Primarily, the key simply changes the direction number, but in the case of Pie Man going horizontally and wanting to turn down, an extra check of the wall underneath Pie Man must be made to avoid its walking through a wall. Putting the check here means you don't have to do it in the normal direction checks that have to be done on every step; you need to do this only on a turn in the downward direction from a left- or right-moving situation. Note as soon as any key is pressed a global variable start is set to be true. This is used at the start of the game on the first key press. Finally, there is a hidden cheat key, much in keeping with early computer games. Of course, because this is typed in a listing, it's not that "hidden", anyway: By pressing the P key, you can enter a power play at any time, so if the ghost is about to get you, you can quickly turn the tables. It is easy to remove these two lines for competition play.

# The Final Function

Now you are in a position to put it all together and define how the game actually plays. Basically, there are two nested loops: The outer one runs forever and plays game after game, whereas the inner one runs for only as long as there are lives left. The main function sets up all the parameters for a game, and then the inner loop generates the moves and evaluates the results by calling functions you have already typed in. So go ahead and enter the code in Listing 6-9 into your file. You need to place Listing 6-9 at the top of your file because it defines all the global variables and sets up the sounds, sprites and windows.

---

**Listing 6-9    The Global Variables and main Function**

```python
#!/usr/bin/env python
"""
Pie Man
A Raspberry Pi Game
"""

import time                       # for delays
import os, pygame, sys
import random, copy

pygame.init()                             # initialise graphics interface
pygame.mixer.quit()
pygame.mixer.init(frequency=22050, size=-16, channels=2, ⤶
buffer=512)
eatSound = pygame.mixer.Sound("sounds/eatPill.ogg")
ppSound = pygame.mixer.Sound("sounds/powerPill.ogg")
ghostDieSound = pygame.mixer.Sound("sounds/ghostDie.ogg")
pieDieSound = pygame.mixer.Sound("sounds/pieDie.ogg")
pieStartSound = pygame.mixer.Sound("sounds/pieStart.ogg")

os.environ['SDL_VIDEO_WINDOW_POS'] = 'center'
pygame.display.set_caption("Pie Man")
pygame.event.set_allowed(None)
pygame.event.set_allowed([pygame.KEYDOWN,pygame.QUIT])
textHeight = 36
font = pygame.font.Font(None, textHeight)

screenWidth = 1000
```

```
screenHeight =636
playWidth = 800
screenOffset = (screenWidth - playWidth) / 2
screen = pygame.display.set_mode([screenWidth,screenHeight],⤸
0,32)
background = pygame.Surface((playWidth,screenHeight))
pillsLayer = pygame.Surface((playWidth,screenHeight))

picName = [ "pie1left", "pie2left", "pie1right", ⤸
"pie2right", "pie1up", "pie2up", "pie1down", "pie2down" ]
piPicture = [ pygame.image.load("pies/"+picName[frame]⤸
+".png").convert_alpha() for frame in range(0,8)]

ghost2Picture = [ pygame.image.load("pies/g"+str(frame)⤸
+"o.png").convert_alpha() for frame in range(1,7)]
ghost1Picture = [ pygame.image.load("pies/g"+str(frame)⤸
+"r.png").convert_alpha() for frame in range(1,7)]
ghostbPicture = [ pygame.image.load("pies/g"+str(frame)⤸
+"b.png").convert_alpha() for frame in range(1,7)]
ghostdPicture = [ pygame.image.load("pies/g"+str(frame)⤸
+"d.png").convert_alpha() for frame in range(1,9)]

# define the colours to use for the user interface
cBackground =(0,0,0)
cText = (255,255,255)
cBlock = (0,0,0)
blue = (0,0,255,255)
pillColour =(255,255,0,255)
box = [screenWidth-100,screenHeight-40]
hw = screenWidth / 2
hh = screenHeight /2
pieIncrement = 8 # speed of pie man
pieDirection = 2
step = 0  # changing image of pie
gStep = 0 # changing image of ghost
gIncrement = 1
score = 0
hiScore = 0
eaten = 0 # number of pills eaten
ppill = False
maxLives = 3
lives = maxLives
pieMan = 48 # size in pixels each side of the pie man
```

*continued*

**Listing 6-9   continued**

```
rightLimit = playWidth+screenOffset-pieMan
position = [screenOffset +pieIncrement*2,pieIncrement+2] ⤵
# position of the pieman
ghostInitalPos = [ [526,298], [422,298] ]
ghostPos = copy.deepcopy(ghostInitalPos)
ghostRelease = time.time()
gNumber = 0
ghostDirection = [0, 2]
moved = True # see if something is blocked
start = False
powerPlay = False
ppCount = 90

def main():
    global position, step, gStep, gIncrement, ghostPos, ⤵
moved, ghostRelease, pieDirection
    global score, ghostDirection, cBackground, hiScore, ⤵
lives, eaten, gNumber, start, ppCount, powerPlay
    while True:
        score = 0
        eaten = 0
        lives = maxLives
        pieDirection = 2
        setupBackground()
        updateLives()
        ghostPos = copy.deepcopy(ghostInitalPos) ⤵
# return ghosts to base
        position = [screenOffset +pieIncrement*2, ⤵
pieIncrement+2] # position of the pieman
        drawScreen(position,ghostPos[0],ghostPos[1])
        gNumber = 0
        ppCount = 90
        start = False
        pieStartSound.play()
        while not start: # wait for a key
            checkForEvent()
        ghostRelease = time.time()+ 4.0 # time for first ghost
        while lives > 0:
                checkForEvent()
                if ppCount < 80: # sets length of ⤵
time for power play
                    if ppCount >70 and ppCount < 75: ⤵
# flash just before end
```

```
                    powerPlay=False
                else:
                    powerPlay=True
            else:
                powerPlay=False
            drawScreen(position,ghostPos[0],ghostPos[1])
            kill(position,ghostPos[0],ghostPos[1])
#collision check
            eat(position)
            position = makeStep(position,pieDirection, ⤶
pieIncrement)
            # move ghosts
            if powerPlay :
                ghostInc = 4
            else:
                ghostInc = 8
            if time.time() > ghostRelease:
                if gNumber < 2:
                    ghostRelease = time.time()+ 5.0 ⤶
# time for subsequent ghosts
                    gNumber += 1
            for i in range(0,gNumber):
                new = getNewDir(i)
                ghostPos[i] = makeStep(ghostPos[i],new, ghostInc)
                if not moved:
                    ghostPos[i] = makeStep(ghostPos[i], ⤶
ghostDirection[i], ghostInc)
                    while not moved:
                        ghostDirection[i] = random.randint(0,3)<<1
                        ghostPos[i] = makeStep(ghostPos[i], ⤶
ghostDirection[i], ghostInc)
                else:
                    ghostDirection[i] = new

        step ^= 1 # toggle pie animation
        ppCount +=1 # increment power play count
        gStep +=gIncrement
        if gStep == 5 or gStep == 0:
            gIncrement = -gIncrement
    # game over
    if score > hiScore : # new high score flash it
        hiScore = score
        for i in range (0,15):
```

*continued*

Listing 6-9   **continued**

```
        cBackground = (  (i & 1)*255, ((i>>1) & 1)*255,
((i>>2) & 1)*255)
        drawWords(str(hiScore),screenOffset+playWidth,
textHeight*2)
        pygame.display.update()
        time.sleep(0.2)
    cBackground = (0,0,0)
    drawWords(str(hiScore),screenOffset+playWidth,textHeight*2)
    pygame.display.update()
    time.sleep(2.0)
```

There is a lot going on here, so let's walk through it. Listing 6-9 starts off by initialising the sound, the window and the drawing planes – all stuff you have seen before. The lines

```
pygame.event.set_allowed(None)
pygame.event.set_allowed([pygame.KEYDOWN,pygame.QUIT])
```

restrict the number and type of events that can be generated. This is important because the event buffer can be filled up with mouse-movement events and other things you are not interested in. As these events are checked only once per step, it could make the game seem insensitive to the control keys. Next, the following lines associate each Pie Man sprite with the correct image number that is shown in Figure 6-3:

```
picName = [ "pie1left", "pie2left", "pie1right",
"pie2right", "pie1up", "pie2up", "pie1down", "pie2down" ]
piPicture = [ pygame.image.load("pies/"+picName[frame]
+".png").convert_alpha() for frame in range(0,8)]
```

This works by first generating a list of image names and then using that list to load in the image files into the piPicture list, with the index number matching the image number that you want. Then come a whole slew of variable definitions that control the game.

## The Game Begins

The main function is where it all happens. The part between the first two while statements sets up the game by initialising a lot of variables; you can't rely on the values they got in the global definitions because these will have changed by the time you play the second game. The second while statement pauses the program at this point until a key is pressed. You will remember that any key press event sets the variable start to true. So when it is the game proper starts. The first thing that happens is the variable ghostRelease is set to the current time plus 4 seconds, which means the player has four seconds of hassle-free pill munching.

The next section of code checks the value of the `ppCount` variable, which times the power play. The way it works is that the variable is incremented every step and, depending on the total, sets or clears the power play flag called `powerPlay`. This is set initially to be 90, so there is no power play at the start. However, this allows you to use a simple mechanism for starting a period of power play; you simply have to set the `ppCount` variable to zero, and it will start. The code also defines a period near the end of the power play when the ghosts will flash briefly. After that section of code the `drawScreen` function is called, and the positions of Pie Man and the ghosts are plotted. The following section of the code sees if there is a kill, or ghost/Pie Man collision, checks if Pie Man has eaten a pill and then updates Pie Man's position by calling the `makeStep` function.

## The Ghost Chase

Next comes the movement of the ghosts. First of all, the ghost speed is altered depending on if there is a power play in force. After all, there is little point in being able to kill a ghost if it can out-run you, or at least match your speed. In normal play the ghosts can move as fast as you can, which means errors you make in steering Pie Man will accumulate, so the ghosts will eventually catch you. If you want the ghosts to be able to move faster than Pie Man, don't increase the speed of the ghosts here; instead reduce the step size of Pie Man using the `pieIncrement` variable. After that, and providing the `ghostRelease` time has been exceeded, the moves for the ghosts are calculated by calling the `getNewDir` function and trying to move in that direction. If this move is blocked, an attempt is made to move in the previous direction. If this is blocked, a series of random directions are tried until one is found that is not blocked. It is this algorithm that gives the ghosts their movement, and it is interesting to see the emergent behaviour that this generates. Note that the `gNumber` variable is used to release the ghosts one at a time at set intervals.

The next section of code deals mainly with housekeeping. The `step` variable is toggled to display alternating lid-open and lid-closed images. The `ppCount` variable is incremented to time the power play period, and the `gStep` variable is changed up and down to define the ghost sprite to use. And that is it, until the game ends by reducing the number of lives left to zero.

## The Game Ends

The final part of the `main` function deals with what happens at the end of a game. First off, it checks to see if a new high score has been reached, and if it has, it flashes the new score with a number of changing colour backgrounds. The time between the flashes is controlled by the `time.sleep` statement. Then after another delay the whole thing starts again.

This is a long piece of code, so the odds are stacked against you for typing it in right the first time. However, if you have worked through the previous chapters, your debugging skills should be quite good by now. The main things to watch out for are getting the indentation correct and getting the case of the characters right; an uppercase *X*, for example, can look very close to a lowercase *x* in some fonts.

Using the four cursor keys for playing is quite good as you can concentrate on the screen action without needing to look at the keys. However, when you first play you may be a little frustrated as you might find that your Pie Man doesn't want to make a turn. This is because the whole of the sprite has to fit into the opening before you can move through it. Just a single pixel blocking the way is enough to prevent any movement. When this happens I have found it best to do a quick turn to one side, then do an about turn and then have another go at making the turn. You will get better the more you play.

## Over to You

What you have here is just the start; there are more things you can add to make the game even better. How about keeping a permanent record of the high score? You can write it out to a file in the terminate function and read it in at the start of the main function. Better still, how about a whole table of high scores with names alongside them? There is room on the right side of the screen to do that. See Chapter 8, "Colour Snap", for hints on how to add a high-score table. Additionally, you have the opportunity to add another sound effect for when a new high score is made. There are also several other places in the game where you can add sound effects, such as when restarting after losing a life and when the game ends altogether. You could add a continuous music soundtrack to play all the time, which is simple to do; you just need the normal command to play the sound but put a -1 in the brackets of the call – then the sound loops continuously.

You can add bonus fruit, like so many games of this type. There is room in the lower left of the screen to show the fruit in waiting. For the more adventurous, you could add some extra code that makes Pie Man wriggle into gaps that he is not initially exactly lined up to fit in. Perhaps the biggest challenge would be to change the behaviour of the ghosts. You might want to have an initial phase in which a ghost can escape from the top of the ghost box no matter where the Pie Man is. Or you can put an exit in the lower part of the ghost box. You could even have each ghost performing a different strategy to hunt. What about using more ghosts? You can also make the ghosts flash more than once toward the end of the power play period.

One other thing you could do is make a level editor. As you have seen, the background consists of many drawing commands; well, you could do this in a separate program and produce an image file of the background. Then, in the game-playing program in place of the drawing, you could simply have an instruction that loads the image file into the background layer. You can also have another file for the pills layer; then when all the pills are eaten you can load in another, different layout.

There is really a lot more you can do, but whatever you do, keep on munching.

# Chapter 7
# Minecraft Maze Maker

**by Sean McManus**

**In This Chapter**

- ○ Installing Minecraft
- ○ Exploring the Minecraft world
- ○ Manipulating the Minecraft world in Python
- ○ Generating a random Minecraft maze in Python

**MINECRAFT APPEALS TO** the Lego fan in everyone. It enables you to build immersive 3D worlds from blocks of materials, and it's fired up imaginations to the extent that an estimated 20 million copies have been sold across platforms including the PC and Xbox.

An early development version of Minecraft is available for the Raspberry Pi. It features only the creative mode, where you can build things peacefully without the threat of monster attacks or starvation, but it has one neat twist: You can program it using multiple languages, including Python. This means that you can build a grand palace without having to manually place every block, and can write programs that can invent original new structures for you to roam around and explore, as you'll see in this chapter.

This project uses a Python program to build a maze in Minecraft. Each time you run the program, it will build a new maze for you, and you can control how big you want it to be and which materials you want it to be made of. During the course of this project, you'll learn how to place and remove blocks in Minecraft using Python, so you'll have the skills to write your own programs that supercharge your construction work.

At the time of writing, Minecraft: Pi Edition is alpha software, which means that it's a very early test version (less well developed than a beta version). I had only a couple of minor issues with it: The window and its content were strangely aligned using a screen resolution of 1024 x 768 (so I switched to 1280 x 1024), and the cursor misbehaved when I maximised the window. Nevertheless, I recommend that you always back up any important data on your Raspberry Pi when you use any alpha software, just in case something goes wrong.

| **TIP** | The easiest way to back up files on your Raspberry Pi is to connect a USB storage device and use the File Manager in the desktop environment to copy them across. |
|---|---|

You can download the code for this chapter from my website at www.sean.co.uk.

## Installing Minecraft

Although Minecraft is distributed commercially on other platforms, the Raspberry Pi alpha version is free to download. To use it, you'll need to have the Raspbian Wheezy version of Linux on your Raspberry Pi. It's the operating system version recommended by the Raspberry Pi Foundation, and you can install it using the New Out of Box Software (NOOBS) image available through the Downloads section at www.raspberrypi.org. For help with installing the operating system, see Chapter 1, "Getting Your Raspberry Pi Up and Running".

To install Minecraft, follow these steps:

1. Make sure that your Raspberry Pi is connected to the Internet. You'll be downloading Minecraft over your web connection.

2. Start your Raspberry Pi, type `startx` and press Enter to go into the desktop environment.

3. Double-click the Midori icon on the desktop or use the Programs menu in the bottom left to start your browser.

4. Visit `http://pi.minecraft.net` and click the link to download Minecraft. When prompted, click Save As to check that you're saving into your `pi` folder. In the file browser, it should be highlighted in your Places on the left. Click the Save button. Close Midori. (You don't need it any more.)

5. Double-click the LXTerminal icon on the desktop to open a terminal session.

6. Enter the command `tar -zxvf minecraft-pi-0.1.1.tar.gz` to uncompress the file you downloaded. Linux is case sensitive, so make sure that you type everything in lowercase. The last bit of that command is the name of the file you just downloaded, so it is likely to change as new versions of Minecraft are released, especially the numbers near the end of it. You need to type only the first few letters of the filename and then press the Tab key to have it automatically completed for you, though. As the files are uncompressed, you'll see a list of them on-screen. You can see the files in your `pi` directory by typing in `ls`.

7. Enter the command `cd mcpi` to go into the folder containing the uncompressed Minecraft files.

8. Type in `./minecraft-pi` and press Enter to start Minecraft.

If all has gone according to plan, you should see the Minecraft title screen appear.

## Starting Minecraft

After you've installed Minecraft, the next time you want to play you can start it by going into the desktop environment (step 2 in the installation instructions in the section "Installing Minecraft"), opening a terminal session (step 5), and typing in the commands `cd mcpi` and `./minecraft-pi`. It won't work if you try to run Minecraft from the command line without first going into the desktop environment.

---

If you close your LXTerminal window, you'll close your Minecraft session immediately too, so try to ignore that window that doesn't look as if it's doing anything. It is!    **TIP**

## Playing Minecraft

When you start Minecraft on the Raspberry Pi, the title screen gives you two options:

○ Start Game: This is the option you'll be using in this chapter to generate your own game world to explore. You can also use this option to choose a previously generated world to revisit, when you replay Minecraft later. To choose between the different worlds, click and drag them left and right to position your chosen one in the middle, and then click it to open it.

○ Join Game: This option is used if you want to join other players in a game on a local network. It's outside the scope of this chapter, but can enable collaborative or competitive play in a Minecraft world.

Click Start Game, and then click Create New, and Minecraft will generate a new world for you, with its own distinctive terrain of mountains, forests and oceans. When it's finished, you'll see a first-person view of it (see Figure 7-1).

FIGURE 7-1:
Minecraft on
the Pi.

 **TIP**     You can change your perspective to show the player's character in the game. Press the Esc key to open the game menu, and then click the icon beside the speaker icon in the top left to change the perspective.

When you've finished playing, you can quit the game by pressing the Esc key to open the game menu.

## Moving Around

Minecraft is easiest to play using two hands, one on the mouse and one on the keyboard. Use the mouse to look around you and change your direction, sliding it left and right to turn sideways, and forwards and backwards on the desk to look up and down. To move, you use the keys W and S for forwards and backwards, and A and D to take a sidestep left and right. Those keys form a cluster on the keyboard, which makes it easy to switch between them.

You character will automatically jump onto low blocks if you walk into them, but you can deliberately jump by pressing the spacebar.

For the best view of your world, take to the skies by double-tapping the spacebar. When you're flying, hold the spacebar to go higher, and the left Shift key to go lower. Double-tap the spacebar to stop flying and drop to the ground. There's no health or danger in this edition of Minecraft, so you can freefall as far as you like.

## Making and Breaking Things

To break blocks in your world, use your mouse to aim your crosshair at the block you want to destroy and click and hold the left mouse button. Some blocks are easier to break than others. There's a limit as to how far away you can be, so move closer if you can't see chips flying off the blocks as you attempt to smash them.

The panel at the bottom of the window shows the blocks you can place in the world (refer to Figure 7-1). You choose between them using the scroll wheel on your mouse, or by pressing a number between 1 and 8 to pick one (from left to right). Press E to open your full inventory, and you can use the movement keys (W, A, S, D) to navigate around it and Enter to choose a block, or simply click your chosen block with the mouse.

To position a block, right-click where you would like to place it. You can put a block on top of another one only if you can see the top of it, so you might need to fly to make tall structures.

---

You can build towers and rise into the air on them by looking down and repeatedly jumping and placing a block under you.          **TIP**

---

Although Python makes it much easier to build things, I recommend that you spend some time familiarising yourself with how players experience the world. In particular, it's worth experimenting with how blocks interact with each other. Stone blocks will float in the air unsupported, but sand blocks will fall to the ground. Cacti can't be planted in grass, but can be placed on top of sand. If you chip away at the banks of a lake, the water will flow to fill the space you made. You can't place water and lava source blocks within the game, although you can program them using Python and they can cascade down and cover a wide area. When they come into contact with each other, water sometimes cools lava into stone.

## Preparing for Python

One of the peculiarities of Minecraft is that it takes control of your mouse, so you have to press Tab to stop it from doing that if you want to use any other programs on your desktop. To start using the mouse in Minecraft again, click the Minecraft window. You'll soon become used to pressing Tab before you try to do any programming. Press Tab now to leave Minecraft running, but bring the mouse cursor back into the desktop.

To make your Minecraft programs, you're going to use IDLE, so double-click its icon on the desktop to start it. You might have to click the top of the Minecraft window and drag it out of the way first.

One of the first things you'll notice is that Minecraft sits on top of other windows, and your IDLE window might well be underneath it, so a certain amount of reorganisation is necessary. To move a window, you click and drag the title bar at the top of it, and you click and drag the edges or corners of a window to resize it. I recommend that you arrange your windows so that you can see them all at once. On my reasonably standard size monitor, I have room for Minecraft in the top left, a small box for the Python shell in the top right, and the window I'm writing my program in the bottom half of the screen. I don't recommend resizing the Minecraft window: In the version I'm running, the mouse controls became unresponsive when I did that. You can ignore (but not close) the LXTerminal window.

## Using the Minecraft Module

You're now ready to write your first Python program for Minecraft, which will send a message to the chat feature in the game.

From the Python shell, click the File menu and choose New to open your programming window. Enter the following in the window, use the File menu to save it in your pi directory and press F5 to run it. You must have a Minecraft game session running for this to work.

```
import sys, random
sys.path.append("./mcpi/api/python/mcpi")
import minecraft
mc = minecraft.Minecraft.create()
mc.postToChat("Welcome to Minecraft Maze!")
```

The first line imports the sys and random modules. The random module you'll need later to build a random maze as you develop this program. Use the sys module straight away to tell IDLE where it can find the Minecraft Python module, which enables you to pass commands to Minecraft to carry out. After telling IDLE where it is, you import the module.

To issue Python commands to Minecraft, you use minecraft.Minecraft.create() and then add the command at the end. For example, to put a greeting in the chat window, you might use the following:

```
minecraft.Minecraft.create().postToChat("Welcome to ⤸
Minecraft Maze!")
```

That soon gets hard to read, so in the previous program, you set up mc so that you can use it as an abbreviation for minecraft.Minecraft.create(). As a result, you can use the shorter line that you see in the program to post a message.

---

If your code isn't working, pay particular attention to the case. Python is case sensitive, so you have to use upper- and lowercase exactly as shown here. Look out for the camel case in postToChat, and the capital M in minecraft.Minecraft.create(). **TIP**

---

## Understanding Coordinates in Minecraft

As you might expect, everything in the Minecraft world has a map coordinate. Three axes are required to describe a position in the game world:

- x: This axis runs parallel to the ground. The values run from -127.7 to 127.7.

- y: This axis runs vertically and could be described as the height. You can fly at least as high as 500, but you can't see the ground from higher than about 70, so there's not much point. Sea level is 0. You can break blocks to tunnel under the sea too. I made it down to about -70 before I fell out of the world and died. This is the only way I've seen that you can die in Minecraft on the Pi.

- z: This is the other axis parallel to the ground. The values run from -127.7 to 127.7.

I put them in that order deliberately because that's the order that Minecraft uses. If, like me, you often use x and y to refer to positions in 2D, such as points on the screen, it takes a short while to get your head around the fact that y represents height. Most of the time in this chapter, you'll be using the x and z coordinates to describe a wall's position (which differs depending on the wall), and the y coordinate to describe its height (which doesn't).

As you move in the game, you can see the player's coordinates in the top left of the Minecraft window change. If you try to move outside the game world, you hit a wall of sky that you can't penetrate, like in the *Truman Show* (except that he had a door).

## Repositioning the Player

You can move your character to any position in the Minecraft world, using this command:

```
mc.player.setTilePos(x, y, z)
```

For example, to parachute into the middle of the world, use

```
mc.player.setTilePos(0, 100, 0)
```

---

**TIP**    You don't have to put this command into a program and run it. If you've already run the program to set up the Minecraft module, you can type commands to move the player and add blocks in the Python shell.

---

Assuming that you are not in flying mode, you'll drop from the sky into the middle of the world. If you are in flying mode, click the Minecraft window and double-tap the spacebar to turn it off and start your descent.

You can put the player anywhere in the game world, and sometimes that means they'll appear in the middle of a mountain or another structure, where they can't move. If that happens, reposition the player using code. Putting them somewhere high is usually a reasonably safe bet because they can fall to the highest ground from there.

## Adding Blocks

To add a block to the world, you use this command:

```
mc.setBlock(x, y, z, blockTypeId)
```

blockTypeId is a number that represents the material of the block you're adding. You can find a full list of materials at www.minecraftwiki.net/wiki/Data_values_(Pocket_Edition). (Take the number from the Dec column in the table on that page. You want the decimal number, rather than the hexadecimal one.) Any number from 0 to 108 is valid, and a few higher numbers are as well. Table 7-1 shows some of the materials you might find most useful for this project and for experimentation.

## Table 7-1   Materials in Minecraft: Pi Edition

| blockTypeId | Block Type |
|---|---|
| 0 | Air |
| 1 | Stone |
| 2 | Grass |
| 3 | Dirt |
| 5 | Wooden plank |
| 8 | Water |
| 10 | Lava |
| 12 | Sand |
| 20 | Glass brick |
| 24 | Sandstone |
| 41 | Gold brick |
| 45 | Brick |
| 47 | Bookshelf |
| 53 | Wooden stairs |
| 57 | Diamond block |
| 64 | Wooden door |
| 81 | Cactus |

If you use the water and lava blocks, you could flood your world, so create a new world to experiment with.    **TIP**

There is another command you can use to create a large cuboid shape built of blocks of the same material. To use it, you provide the coordinates of two opposite corners, and the material you'd like to fill the space with, like this:

```
mc.setBlocks(x1, y1, z1, x2, y2, z2, blockTypeId)
```

You can quickly build a brick shelter by making a large cuboid of brick, and then putting a cuboid of air inside it. Air replaces any other block, effectively deleting it from the world. Here's an example:

```
mc.setBlocks(0, 0, 0, 10, 5, 7, 45) #brick
mc.setBlocks(1, 0, 1, 9, 5, 6, 0) #air
```

These lines build a shelter that is 10 × 7 blocks in floor space, and 5 blocks high, starting at coordinate 0, 0, 0. The walls have a thickness of 1 block because you fill the space from 1 to 9 on the x axis, 1 to 6 on the z axis, and 0 to 5 on the vertical axis with air, leaving 1 block of brick from the original cuboid intact on four sides, and the roof open.

> **TIP** Remember that the # symbol represents a comment that's just there as a reminder for you. The computer ignores anything on the same line after the #.

Although players can have coordinate positions with decimal portions (such as 1.7), when you place a block, its position is rounded down to the nearest whole number.

## Stopping the Player from Changing the World

I know you wouldn't cheat, but there's no fun in a maze that you might *accidentally* just hack your way through, is there? To stop players from being able to destroy or place blocks in the world, use the following:

```
mc.setting("world.immutable",True)
```

The word *immutable* is often used in programming, and just means "unchangeable".

## Setting the Maze Parameters

Now that you know how to place blocks in the world and use the air block to remove them again, you're ready to start making the maze program. In this program, you'll use a number of constants to keep track of important information about the maze. Constants are just variables which you *decide* not to change the values of as the program is running, so their values are always the same. It's conventional to use uppercase for the names of constants to signal your intent to others reading the program, and to remind yourself that you're not supposed to be letting the program change these values. Replacing numbers in your program with constants makes it easier to customise your program later, but also makes it much easier to read your program and understand what different numbers represent.

> **TIP** Variable names are case sensitive, so Python would think SIZE and size were two different variables. You'd be mad to use both in the same program, though!

The program starts by setting up these constants:

```
SIZE = 10
HEIGHT = 2
```

```
MAZE_X = 0
GROUND = 0
MAZE_Z = 0
MAZE_MATERIAL = 1 #stone
GROUND_MATERIAL = 2 #grass
CEILING = False
```

To build the maze, you will start with a grid of walls with one-block spaces (or cells) between them, which looks a bit like a potato waffle (see Figure 7-2). Each cell starts with four walls, and the program knocks walls down to create paths between them and build the maze. The maze is square, and its SIZE is measured in cells. A maze with a SIZE of 10 will have 10 cells in the x and z dimensions, but will occupy double that space in the Minecraft world (that is, 20 blocks by 20 blocks) because there is a one-block wall between each cell. This will become clearer as you start to build the maze. I've tried mazes as big as 40, but they take some time to build and ages to explore. 10 is big enough for now. The program will stop with an error if there isn't enough room for all of the maze in your world.

The HEIGHT is how many blocks tall the maze walls are. I chose 2 because a value of 1 means that the player can just walk over the maze. (The player automatically steps up onto blocks 1 unit high.) Higher values obscure any mountains in the distance that can otherwise give a nice visual hint to the player.

The constants MAZE_X, GROUND and MAZE_Z are used for the starting coordinates of the maze. The MAZE_MATERIAL is stone (1), and the GROUND_MATERIAL is grass (2). I've added an option for a ceiling, to stop players from just flying out of the top of the maze, but I've turned it off for now so that you can freely explore the maze as you're building it.

---

A maze of bookshelves (MAZE_MATERIAL=47) looks great! **TIP**

---

## Laying the Foundations

One of the first things you need to do is make sure that you're building on solid land. Because Minecraft worlds are dynamically generated, you might find that you're building a maze inside a mountain or in the sea, otherwise.

As well as the area the maze will occupy, you'll clear an area of 10 blocks all the way around it, so the players can approach it easily and walk around the outside of it. First you clear the area by filling it with air blocks, which will wipe out anything else in that space.

FIGURE 7-2:
The starter grid.

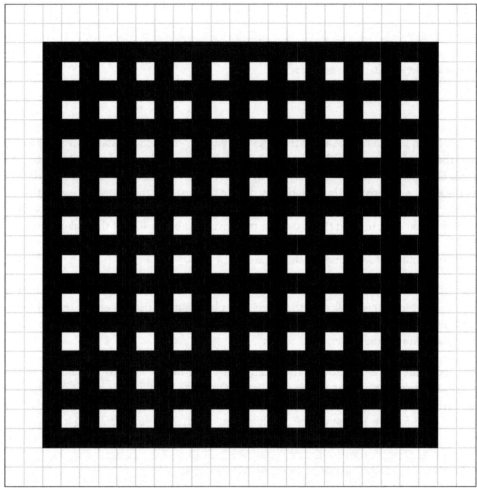

The maze occupies a ground space measured in blocks from `MAZE_X` to `MAZE_X+(SIZE*2)`, and from `MAZE_Z` to `MAZE_Z+(SIZE*2)`. The number of blocks is twice the number of cells (`SIZE`) because each cell has a wall on its right and below it. The middle of the maze in the Minecraft world is `MAZE_X+SIZE`, `MAZE_Z+SIZE`.

You need to clear 10 blocks further in each direction. The following code clears everything as high as 150 above the ground level of the maze to stop the risk of any remaining mountain blocks falling from the sky into the maze and lays the floor:

```
mc.setBlocks(MAZE_X-10, GROUND, MAZE_Z-10, ⤵
MAZE_X+(SIZE*2)+10, GROUND+150, MAZE_Z+(SIZE*2)+10, 0)
```

```
mc.setBlocks(MAZE_X-10, GROUND, MAZE_Z-10, MAZE_X+↲
(SIZE*2)+10, GROUND, MAZE_Z+(SIZE*2)+10, GROUND_MATERIAL)
```

I recommend adding a block to indicate the starting corner of the maze (where MAZE_X and MAZE_Z are). You will find it useful when writing and debugging the program because it will enable you to tell which way around the maze is as you fly around it. To do so, use the following:

```
mc.setBlock(MAZE_X, GROUND+HEIGHT+1, MAZE_Z, MAZE_MATERIAL)
```

Put your player character above the middle of the maze, too, so you can watch it being built by looking down, as follows. If you're not flying, you'll fall onto the maze wall, but you can just fly up again.

```
mc.player.setTilePos(MAZE_X+SIZE, GROUND+25, MAZE_Z+SIZE)
```

## Placing the Maze Walls

To make the potato waffle-like grid, use the following code:

```
for line in range(0, (SIZE+1)*2, 2):
    mc.setBlocks(MAZE_X+line, GROUND+1, MAZE_Z, ↲
MAZE_X+line, GROUND+HEIGHT, MAZE_Z+(SIZE*2), MAZE_MATERIAL)
    mc.setBlocks(MAZE_X, GROUND+1, MAZE_Z+line, ↲
MAZE_X+(SIZE*2), GROUND+HEIGHT, MAZE_Z+line, MAZE_MATERIAL)
```

The for loop gives the variable line the values of even numbers starting at 0 and finishing at SIZE*2, in turn. You have to add 1 to SIZE before doubling it because the range function doesn't include the last number in the sequence. If you use range(1, 10), for example, you get the numbers 1 to 9. The number 2 at the end of the range function is the step size, so it adds 2 each time it goes around the loop, and only gives you the even numbers. That means you leave a gap for the cell between each wall. Each time around the loop, it uses cuboids to draw two walls that stretch across the maze from edge to edge in the x and z dimensions. It doesn't matter that the same block is set twice where those lines intersect. You build the wall starting at GROUND+1, so the grass is still underneath when you knock down the walls to make paths.

---

Don't forget the colon at the end of the for statement, and that the next two lines should each be indented to tell Python that they belong to the loop. **TIP**

---

You should now have a grid that looks like Figure 7-3.

FIGURE 7-3:
Your grid in
Minecraft.

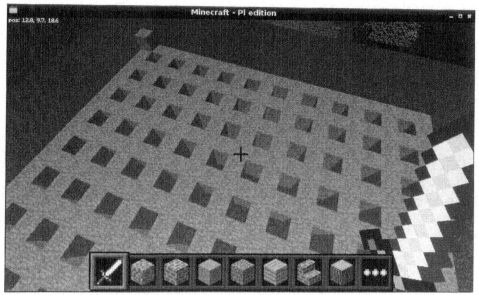

## Understanding the Maze Algorithm

Before you dig into the code that turns your waffle into a maze, let me tell you how it works. You're going to make what's known as a "perfect maze" (that's a technical term, not me bragging). That means there are no loops in it, and no parts of the maze you can't get into. There is only one path between any two points in the maze.

Here's how the program works:

1. You start with the "waffle" you've built, with every cell having all four walls.

2. You pick a random cell in the maze to start at.

3. You look at your current cell's neighbours, and make a list of all those that have all four walls intact. These are the cells that have not yet been visited.

4. If you found some unvisited neighbours, you pick one at random, knock down the wall between it and your current cell, and then move into that cell, making it your current cell.

5. If your current cell has no unvisited neighbours, you go back one cell in the path you've taken, and make that your current cell.

6. You repeat steps 3 to 5 until you've visited every cell.

## Setting Up the Variables and Lists

To implement this algorithm, you'll use the following variables:

- numberOfCells: This is the total number of cells in the maze, which will be SIZE*SIZE. (* is the symbol for multiplication.)

- numberOfVisitedCells: This keeps track of how many cells you've visited so far. When this is the same as the numberOfCells, every cell has been visited and had a wall demolished, and is therefore reachable. The maze is finished.

- xposition: This remembers your x position as you move through the maze generating it. It's measured in cells, and starts as a random number between 1 and the maze SIZE.

- zposition: This remembers your z position as you move through the maze generating it, also measured in cells, and also starting as a random number.

- cellsVisitedList[]: This is a list that stores the path you've taken, so the program can retrace its steps. When you set it up, you put your starting position into it using the append() list method.

- playerx and playerz: These are used to remember the starting position, so you can put the player there when the maze has been built.

When an algorithm like this is implemented (it's called a *depth-first maze generation algorithm*), it often requires a list or similar data structure to be used to store the locations of walls. You don't need that because you have actual walls in Minecraft you can look at. The game world stores your maze, if you like.

The following code lines set up your starting variables:

```
numberOfCells = SIZE*SIZE
numberOfVisitedCells = 1
cellsVisitedList = []
xposition = random.randint(1, SIZE)
zposition = random.randint(1, SIZE)
playerx = xposition
playerz = zposition
cellsVisitedList.append((xposition, zposition))
```

## Creating the Functions

There are a number of basic functions you will need for your program:

- realx(x) and realz(z): These convert coordinates in the maze (measured in cells) into coordinates in the Minecraft world (measured in blocks, and offset from the maze's starting position).

○ showMaker(x,z) and hideMaker(x,z): These functions use a gold block to show which cell the program has reached as it builds the maze. It's fun to watch from above, and is useful while building and debugging the program.

○ demolish(realx,realz): This knocks down a wall in the maze, and takes a real coordinate in the Minecraft world as its parameters.

○ testAllWalls(cellx, cellz): This checks whether the four walls on a cell are intact. If all of them are, it returns True. Otherwise, it returns False. It uses the command mc.getBlock(x, y, z), which tells you the blockTypeId at a particular location. You use two equals signs, as usual, to test whether a block in a wall position is the same as the MAZE_MATERIAL, which means that there's a wall there.

Add these function definitions at the start of your program, after where you set up the Minecraft module:

```
def realx(x):
    return MAZE_X+(x*2)-1

def realz(z):
    return MAZE_Z+(z*2)-1

def showMaker(x, z):
    mc.setBlock(realx(x), GROUND+1, realz(z), 41) # 41=gold

def hideMaker(x, z):
    mc.setBlock(realx(x), GROUND+1, realz(z), 0)

def demolish(realx, realz):
    mc.setBlocks(realx, GROUND+1, realz, realx, ⤸
HEIGHT+GROUND, realz, 0)

def testAllWalls(cellx, cellz):
    if mc.getBlock(realx(cellx)+1, GROUND+1, ⤸
realz(cellz))==MAZE_MATERIAL and mc.getBlock⤸
(realx(cellx)-1, GROUND+1, realz(cellz))==MAZE_MATERIAL ⤸
and mc.getBlock(realx(cellx), GROUND+1, realz(cellz)+1)== ⤸
MAZE_MATERIAL and mc.getBlock(realx(cellx), GROUND+1, ⤸
realz(cellz)-1)==MAZE_MATERIAL:
        return True
    else:
        return False
```

If you have an error, check for missing colons at the end of your def and if statements.

**TIP**

# Creating the Main Loop

Your maze algorithm runs until you've visited every cell, so it starts with the following statement:

```
while numberOfVisitedCells < numberOfCells:
```

You need to test whether your current cell's neighbour cells have all their walls intact. To do that, you check each direction in turn, using the testAllWalls(x, z) function. When you find a cell with all the walls intact, you add its direction to the list possibleDirections[] using the append() list method. This implements step 3 in the algorithm (remember it's all indented underneath the while statement):

```
possibleDirections = []

if testAllWalls(xposition-1, zposition):
    possibleDirections.append("left")

if testAllWalls(xposition+1, zposition):
    possibleDirections.append("right")

if testAllWalls(xposition, zposition-1):
    possibleDirections.append("up")

if testAllWalls(xposition, zposition+1):
    possibleDirections.append("down")
```

The values of up, down, left and right are somewhat arbitrary in 3D space, but I've used them because they're easy to understand. If you fly into the air and look down on the maze as it's being generated and you have the block identifying the starting corner of the maze (MAZE_X, MAZE_Z) in the top left, these directions will look correct to you.

Incidentally, you might have noticed that there's no check for whether these cell positions are inside the maze borders. What happens if you look for a cell off the left edge of the maze, or off the bottom edge? No problem. The program implementation automatically respects the borders of the maze because when it looks at "cells" outside the borders, they don't have all four walls (their only wall is the maze's border), so they are never visited.

Step 4 in the algorithm is to pick a random direction if you found any unvisited neighbours, knock down the wall in that direction and move into that cell. To decide whether you found any possible directions, you check the length of the `possibleDirections` list and act if it is not equal to 0 (`!=0`). All of this should be indented under the `while` loop. If you get lost in the indenting, consult the full code in Listing 7-1 near the end of this chapter.

Before you start moving your position, you hide the gold brick that shows where you are in the maze:

```
hideMaker(xposition, zposition)
if len(possibleDirections)!=0:
    directionChosen=random.choice(possibleDirections)

    if directionChosen=="left":
        demolish(realx(xposition)-1, realz(zposition))
        xposition -= 1

    if directionChosen=="right":
        demolish(realx(xposition)+1, realz(zposition))
        xposition += 1

    if directionChosen=="up":
        demolish(realx(xposition), realz(zposition)-1)
        zposition -= 1

    if directionChosen=="down":
        demolish(realx(xposition), realz(zposition)+1)
        zposition += 1
```

After you've moved into a new cell, you need to increase your tally of cells visited by one, and add the new cell to the list that stores the path taken. This is also a good time to show the gold block in the cell to highlight how the maze is being built:

```
numberOfVisitedCells += 1
cellsVisitedList.append((xposition, zposition))
showMaker(xposition, zposition)
```

The way you've stored the list of cells visited deserves some explanation. You've put the xposition and zposition in parentheses, which are used to indicate a tuple. A *tuple* is a data sequence, a bit like a list, with a key difference being that you can't change its values.

(It's immutable.) So `cellsVisitedList` is a list that contains tuples, which in turn contain pairs of x and z coordinates. You can use the Python shell to take a look inside this list. Here's an example from one run of the program, showing a path taken through the maze:

```
>>> print cellsVisitedList
[(6, 6,), (6, 7), (6, 8), (5, 8), (4, 8), (3, 8), (3, 7)]
```

For step 5 in the algorithm, you go back to the previous position in the path if your cell has no unvisited neighbours. This involves taking the last position out of the list. There's a list method called `pop()` you can use to do that. It takes the last item from a list and deletes it from that list. In your program, you put it into a variable called `retrace`, which then stores a tuple for the x and z positions in the maze. As with a list, you can use index numbers to access the individual elements in a tuple. The index numbers start at 0, so `retrace[0]` will hold your previous x position, and `retrace[1]` will hold your previous z position. Here's the code, including a line to show the gold block in its new position:

```
else: # do this when there are no unvisited neighbours
    retrace = cellsVisitedList.pop()
    xposition = retrace[0]
    zposition = retrace[1]
    showMaker(xposition, zposition)
```

Note that your `else` statement should be in line with the `if` statement it's paired with, in this case the one that tests whether you found any possible directions to move in.

Step 6 in the algorithm has already been implemented because the `while` loop will keep repeating the indented code underneath it until every cell has been visited.

## Adding a Ceiling

Personally, I think it's more fun to leave the ceiling open and be free to fly up and marvel at your maze, and drop into it at any point. If you wanted to build a game around your maze, though, and stop people from cheating, you can add a ceiling using the following code. Just change the variable `CEILING` to `True` at the start of the program. I've made the ceiling out of glass bricks, so it doesn't get too dark in there:

```
if CEILING == True:
    mc.setBlocks(MAZE_X, GROUND+HEIGHT+1, MAZE_Z, ⤵
MAZE_X+(SIZE*2), GROUND+HEIGHT+1, MAZE_Z+(SIZE*2), 20)
```

## Positioning the Player

Finally, let's place the player at the random position where you started generating the maze. You could put the player anywhere, but this seems as good a place as any, and it uses random numbers you have already generated:

```
mc.player.setTilePos(realx(playerx), GROUND+1, realz(playerz))
```

Now you're ready to play! Figure 7-4 shows the maze from the inside.

FIGURE 7-4: Finding your way around the maze.

## The Final Code

Listing 7-1 shows the final and complete code.

---

Listing 7-1    **The Minecraft Maze Maker**

```
#!/usr/bin/env python

"""
Minecraft Maze Maker
By Sean McManus
From Raspberry Pi Projects
```

```
"""

import sys, random
sys.path.append("./mcpi/api/python/mcpi")
import minecraft
mc = minecraft.Minecraft.create()

mc.postToChat("Welcome to Minecraft Maze!")

def realx(x):
    return MAZE_X+(x*2)-1

def realz(z):
    return MAZE_Z+(z*2)-1

def showMaker(x, z):
    mc.setBlock(realx(x), GROUND+1, realz(z), 41) # 41=gold

def hideMaker(x, z):
    mc.setBlock(realx(x), GROUND+1, realz(z), 0)

def demolish(realx, realz):
    mc.setBlocks(realx, GROUND+1, realz, realx,⤴
HEIGHT+GROUND, realz, 0)

def testAllWalls(cellx, cellz):
    if mc.getBlock(realx(cellx)+1, GROUND+1, ⤴
realz(cellz))==MAZE_MATERIAL and mc.getBlock⤴
(realx(cellx)-1, GROUND+1, realz(cellz))==MAZE_MATERIAL ⤴
and mc.getBlock(realx(cellx), GROUND+1, realz(cellz)+1)==⤴
MAZE_MATERIAL and mc.getBlock(realx(cellx), GROUND+1, ⤴
realz(cellz)-1)==MAZE_MATERIAL:
        return True
    else:
        return False

mc.setting("world_immutable", True)

# Configure your maze here
SIZE = 10
HEIGHT = 2
MAZE_X = 0
```

*continued*

**Listing 7-1   continued**

```
GROUND = 0
MAZE_Z = 0
MAZE_MATERIAL = 1 # 1=stone
GROUND_MATERIAL = 2 # 2=grass
CEILING = False

mc.setBlocks(MAZE_X-10, GROUND, MAZE_Z-10, MAZE_X+⤶
(SIZE*2)+10, GROUND+150, MAZE_Z+(SIZE*2)+10, 0) # air
mc.setBlocks(MAZE_X-10, GROUND, MAZE_Z-10, MAZE_X+⤶
(SIZE*2)+10, GROUND, MAZE_Z+(SIZE*2)+10, GROUND_MATERIAL)
# lay the ground

mc.setBlock(MAZE_X, GROUND+HEIGHT+1, MAZE_Z, MAZE_MATERIAL)
# origin marker

mc.player.setTilePos(MAZE_X+SIZE, GROUND+25, MAZE_Z+SIZE)
# move player above middle of maze

mc.postToChat("Now building your maze...")

# build grid of walls
for line in range(0, (SIZE+1)*2, 2):
    mc.setBlocks(MAZE_X+line, GROUND+1, MAZE_Z, ⤶
MAZE_X+line, GROUND+HEIGHT, MAZE_Z+(SIZE*2), MAZE_MATERIAL)
    mc.setBlocks(MAZE_X, GROUND+1, MAZE_Z+line, MAZE_X+⤶
(SIZE*2), GROUND+HEIGHT, MAZE_Z+line, MAZE_MATERIAL)

# setup of variables for creating maze
numberOfCells = SIZE*SIZE
numberOfVisitedCells = 1 # 1 for the one you start in
cellsVisitedList = []

xposition = random.randint(1, SIZE)
zposition = random.randint(1, SIZE)
playerx = xposition
playerz = zposition
showMaker(xposition, zposition)
cellsVisitedList.append((xposition, zposition))
```

```
while numberOfVisitedCells < numberOfCells:
possibleDirections = []

if testAllWalls(xposition-1, zposition):
    possibleDirections.append("left")

if testAllWalls(xposition+1, zposition):
    possibleDirections.append("right")

if testAllWalls(xposition, zposition-1):
    possibleDirections.append("up")

if testAllWalls(xposition, zposition+1):
    possibleDirections.append("down")

hideMaker(xposition, zposition)

if len(possibleDirections)!=0:
    directionChosen=random.choice(possibleDirections)

    #knock down wall between cell in direction chosen
    if directionChosen=="left":
        demolish(realx(xposition)-1, realz(zposition))
        xposition -= 1

    if directionChosen=="right":
        demolish(realx(xposition)+1, realz(zposition))
        xposition += 1

    if directionChosen=="up":
        demolish(realx(xposition), realz(zposition)-1)
        zposition -= 1

    if directionChosen=="down":
        demolish(realx(xposition), realz(zposition)+1)
        zposition += 1

    numberOfVisitedCells += 1
    cellsVisitedList.append((xposition, zposition))
showMaker(xposition, zposition)
```

*continued*

Listing 7-1   **continued**

```
    else: # do this when there are no unvisited neighbours
        retrace = cellsVisitedList.pop()
        xposition = retrace[0]
        zposition = retrace[1]
        showMaker(xposition, zposition)

if CEILING == True:
    mc.setBlocks(MAZE_X, GROUND+HEIGHT+1, MAZE_Z, ⤵
MAZE_X+(SIZE*2), GROUND+HEIGHT+1, MAZE_Z+(SIZE*2), 20)

mc.postToChat("Your maze is ready!")
mc.postToChat("Happy exploring!")
mc.player.setTilePos(realx(playerx), GROUND+1, realz(playerz))
```

## Over to You

When the maze is built, the gold brick is left showing, so you could try to solve the maze to find the brick. You could also plant other objectives in the maze, and time how long it takes the player to find them. The mc.player.getTilePos() command checks where the player is in the Minecraft world, and gives you a result in the form x, y, z. Code to create a timer can be found in Chapter 9, "Test Your Reactions".

You could add an entrance and exit in a random position in the border of the maze, so the goal is to travel from one side to the other. You could make huge mazes more playable by adding landmarks. (Try using different wall materials, or putting blocks on top of some walls.) After the maze has been generated, you could knock out random walls, so there are some shortcuts through the maze. Or maybe just replace them with glass blocks, to provide a tantalising glimpse into another corridor. What about a multistorey maze, with stairs between the levels? The possibilities are . . . ahem! . . . amazing.

# Part III
# Hardware Projects

# Chapter **8**
## Colour Snap

**by Mike Cook**

### In This Chapter

- ○ Make your first interactive game hardware
- ○ Power an LED safely
- ○ Use surface mount components
- ○ Make boxes simply
- ○ Implement a high-score table

THE GAME IN this chapter is just the thing to get going on your first hardware project. There does not seem to be an end to the sorts of things you can do with LEDs and switches. All the projects I have ever worked on, even highly complex transmodulation systems consisting of 8000+ components, have started with an engineer making an LED flash. By adding a bit of imagination you can make something unique with LEDs, and this project is, as far as I know, totally unique. It is a colour snap game.

I am sure that most children have played the card game snap in one form or other either with special cards or a regular pack. The procedure is simple: The pack is divided into two, and the cards are laid face up on the table by alternate players. When two of the same cards are turned up the first player to shout "SNAP!" wins all the cards, but if you shout "SNAP!" and the cards do not match, your opponent gets them. The player to lose all his cards is the loser.

You can implement this as a hardware game in many ways, but the one I have chosen here is to use a coloured light. The light flashes on and off, and each time it comes on, it is normally a different colour from the last time. However, occasionally it will be the same colour as the previous one, and that is the cue for the players to claim a snap by pushing a button. There are no arguments over who pressed first; the computer has split second timing. Also, at the same time the computer shouts out, "SNAP!" in one of two voices, depending on which player was fastest to press the button.

## Implementing the Game

So how are you going to implement this game? You need two switches and a source of controllable coloured light. You could use the push switches that are already on the PiFace board, but to make a decent job of the project you will take them off the board into a separate box. (For more information on setting up PiFace, see Chapter 9, "Test Your Reactions".) For the source of changing colour, you are going to use three LEDs. An LED, or *light emitting diode*, is a cheap and easy-to-drive source of light, so most hardware projects have at least a few. Moreover, LEDs come in a rich variety of colours. There is however a rather special form of LED which is known as an RGB LED. Basically this is three LEDs in one package: red, green and blue. Using these you can mix up an almost infinite number of colours. So to start off, let's see how to drive an LED from the PiFace board.

### The Theory

Unlike with a flashlight bulb, you can't connect an LED directly to a source of power. Well, you can, but it will end up burning out. This is because LEDs have a special form of electrical characteristic: They are a *nonlinear device*. What this means is that unlike other components, such as resistors, the current through LEDs is not directly proportional to the voltage across them. They have an effective resistance that switches sharply depending on the voltage across them. Figure 8-1 shows the graph of voltage against current for a typical LED. You will see that at low voltages there is little or no current through them. As the voltage rises there is little change in current until a sort of threshold is reached, and then a small increase in voltage gives a large increase in current. This threshold, or *breakpoint*, is known as the *forward voltage drop*, and you need to run an LED at this voltage. This is not done by supplying a voltage of "just the right value" for various reasons – the two main ones being that producing this right voltage takes some complex electronics and the value that is "right" changes with the temperature and the age of the device.

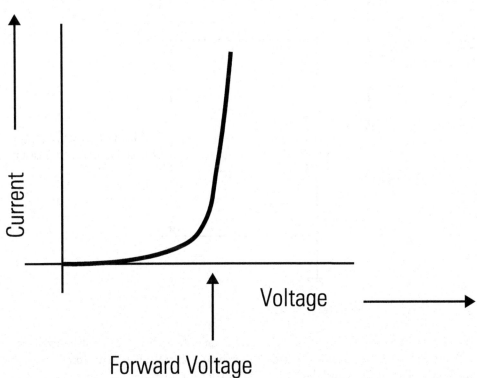

## Current vs. voltage for an ideal LED

FIGURE 8-1:
The voltage against current relationship for an LED.

What you have to do is to arrange for a constant current through the device. For low-current LEDs, which is what you will be using here, it is simplest to use a resistor to simply limit the current. Most LEDs work with currents of up to a maximum of 20mA, so that is normally the target to aim for, although the more current you have, the brighter the LED will shine. Figure 8-2 shows a resistor and LED connected to a 5V power source.

FIGURE 8-2:
How to use
an LED.

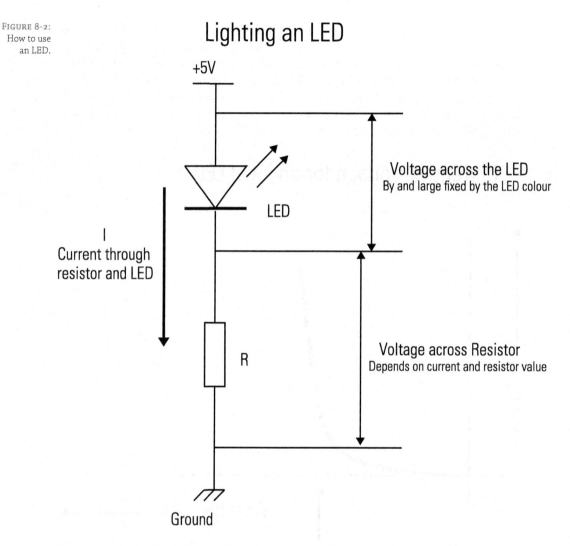

# Lighting an LED

+5V

LED

I
Current through
resistor and LED

R

Voltage across the LED
By and large fixed by the LED colour

Voltage across Resistor
Depends on current and resistor value

Ground

You want to have 20mA flowing through the LED, and when you do there will be a voltage of 3.2V across the LED. This voltage is said to be *dropped across* the LED. So first off, how do you know the voltage dropped will be 3.2V? Well, you look it up in the LED's data sheet. If you haven't got a data sheet, you guess because the voltage drop of an LED is determined mainly by the material it is made of and the material determines the colour. So most LEDs with the same colour have the same sort of voltage drop; 3.2V is typical for a green one and the newer type of blue LEDs. Red LEDs have a much lower drop of typically 1.8V. So look at Figure 8-2: If there is 3.2V across the LED, there has to be 5 - 3.2 = 1.8V across the resistor. If you know the voltage across a resistor and you know what current you want to have flowing through it, you can calculate the resistance it has to have in Ohms by using Ohm's law in the form of Resistance equals Voltage over Current, or

$R = E / I$

E is the voltage in volts, and I is the current in amps. So if you want to have 20mA flowing through the LED, which means 20mA flowing through the resistor as well because these two components are in *series,* which means the same current flows through both of them, you plug those figures into the formula to get the following:

$R = 1.8 / 0.02 = 90$ Ohms (also stated as *90R*)

Unfortunately, you can't get a 90R resistor because you can get only certain standard values, but the value closest to 90R is 91R, so you can use that. If you plug that value back into Ohm's law, you will see that your actual current is

$I = E / R = 1.8 / 91 = 19.78$mA (which is almost spot on)

So let's see what happens if the forward voltage drop changes slightly. How will that affect the current? You can plug some different values into the equation, as shown in the graph in Figure 8-3. You can see that the current through the LED doesn't vary dramatically with small changes in forward voltage like it does when you drive the LED with a fixed voltage. The resistor has acted to minimise variations and stabilise the operating current.

To allow the PiFace board to control an LED, all you need to do is to connect the resistor not to ground but to the PiFace's output. These outputs are what is known *current sinks;* that is, they allow current to flow through them to ground, or not, depending on the logic level set by the Raspberry Pi. This means that you can turn the LED on or off by setting the output high or low. When you set the PiFace output high, that makes the current sink through the output buffers and thus allows current to flow through the LED, thus allowing the LED to emit light. What you are going to do for this project is not to have one resistor to sink the current through but to have two. If you arrange the currents the resistors provide carefully, you can get three different brightness levels from one LED. This means having one resistor supply twice the current of the other to give a current of one unit, or two units or three units of current, where three units of current is less than or equal to the maximum working current.

In practice, the eye has a nonlinear response to brightness, so although you might increase the current in equal steps and the light output from the LED changes in equal steps, we do not perceive it as being in equal steps. In fact, the brighter something gets, the less a fixed step in brightness appears to make it change; this is a logarithmic law.

FIGURE 8-3:
Voltage drop
against current
for an LED and
resistor circuit.

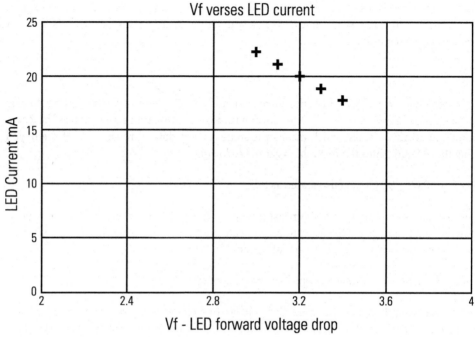

FIGURE 8-3: Voltage drop against current for an LED and resistor circuit.

To make your game, you are going to apply that design to an RGB LED – that is the three colours built into one package. This means that the sources of light are close together and it is easy to get them to mix or blend together. Red, green and blue are the three primary colours, although don't tell the art department. To be more precise, they are the additive primary colours; that is, when light is added in various amounts in these colours you can make any other colour. When dealing with paint you are restricting the colours it will reflect, which is known as *subtractive colour mixing*. The subtractive primary colours are yellow, magenta and cyan, although they are often inaccurately referred to as yellow, red and blue.

The final design for the game, as far as the electronics is concerned, is shown in Figure 8-4. It consists of an RGB LED with two resistors on the cathode of each colour. The anodes of all three LEDs are connected to +5V. Many RGB LEDs have these connected together inside the chip and bring out only one anode connection; these are known, not unsurprisingly, as *common anode LEDs*. The other type you can get is where the cathodes are common. As you might guess, these are called *common cathode LEDs* and are not the type you want for this project.

The other part of the game is the player switches, which are simply wired between the PiFace's input connections and ground. When they are pressed the input bit reads as a logic zero. This goes to a logic one when they are released.

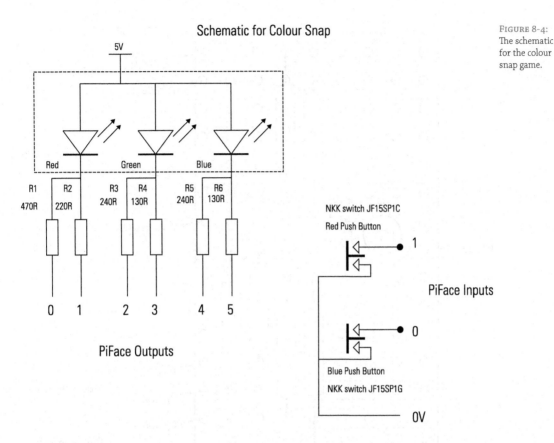

FIGURE 8-4:
The schematic
for the colour
snap game.

The construction of the game has two aspects – electrical and mechanical. The electrical is the wiring, resistors, switches and LEDs, and the mechanical is the box and light diffuser. There are many ways of making each aspect; here I will discuss two ways to make the electrical part.

It all hinges on the sort of LED and resistor you use. Traditionally, components have been what is known as *through-hole components*. That is, they have wires, leads or legs that push though holes in a board and are soldered to a copper laminate on the other side of the board. These components are big and bulky and thus are easy to handle. The newer sort of components are known as *surface mount* because they are simply soldered onto the surface of a copper laminate. They are small – some say too small – so they reduce the size of the circuit. Also, surface mount LEDs offer flatter and more even illumination than a through-hole part.

Let's look at the through-hole method of construction first (although I recommend the surface mount instead). Figure 8-5 shows the LED layout using through-hole components. This is built on a small piece of strip board, sometimes known as *veroboard*. You might come across this being called *BusBoard Prototype System*, *Vectorbord*, *Circbord*, or *breadboard* but not solderless breadboard.

FIGURE 8-5:
Circuit layout
using
through-hole
components.

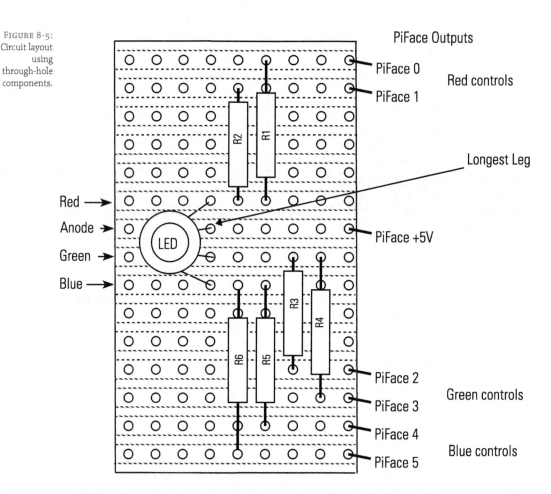

A piece of strip board 0.8″ long and 1.6″ high will suffice, although you can use a bigger size. The dotted lines represent the copper strip on the other side of the board. You will not see them; this is what engineers call *hidden detail*. There are no tracks to cut, so it is nice and simple. Make sure that the LED is the right way around; note that all the legs are of different length and that the longest one is the anode, as marked in Figure 8-5. Just to make sure, you can test the LED with a multimeter set to resistance. Put the red lead of your meter on the anode, and then by putting the black lead on each of the other legs in turn, you should see a faint glow in the LED for each colour. Make sure that the leads of the LED are bent close to the body so that they align with the hole spacing. Then push the LED down as close as you can to the board, so the LED sits as low as possible. If you have a water-clear package, you can improve the diffusion by lightly sanding the LED with as fine a sandpaper as you can get. This makes the resulting colours blend a lot better.

However, for a much better result, you can use surface mount components. Not only will this be smaller, but the light output also will be flatter and more even, producing a much better distributed level of colour. Surface mount can be a bit scary, but it is not as difficult as you might think. Despite the fact that the RGB LED I used is not the right pitch for the strip board, you can easily make it fit using a scalpel or sharp knife.

Start off with a piece of 0.7″ by 0.5″ strip board with the strips running vertically, as shown in Figure 8-6. There are some shaded parts in Figure 8-6 that show the area where you are going to remove the copper. There are two types of cuts you need to make – from the hole to the edge of the strip and between holes. The first is the easiest; simply put the point of the knife in the hole and put the blade at an angle touching the side of the track. With a rotary wrist movement, cut the copper. This will leave a flake of copper standing up. Remove this by repeating the action from the other direction, and remove the copper. You need to do this on both sides of the hole to break the connection.

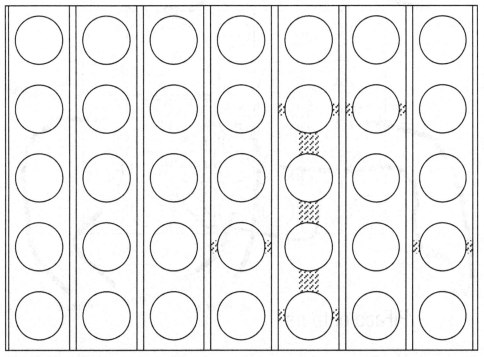

FIGURE 8-6: Cutting out some of the copper on a strip board to make the LED fit.

There are five holes to cut like this. The next cut is to remove a strip of copper between the holes. Start with your blade in the hole and score down to the next hole. Repeat this for the other side of the hole. Then use the blade and lift out the copper between the two score marks. This sounds complex when written down, but it is actually quite easy to do. In the end you will have split one of the 0.1″ copper strips into two 0.05″ spaced strips.

Next you need add the components. Figure 8-7 shows how they are arranged. You need a fine pair of tweezers and a magnifying glass. Take the 5050 LED and make sure that the polarity mark is at the top. It marks the three anodes; if you are not sure, use the multimeter test technique described earlier. The critical point is to line things up so that the left-most two anode connections connect to different strips of the half strip you have cut out. Now remove the LED and just put the smallest dab of solder on the strip board where the left cathode connection is going to be. Now with your iron in one hand and the tweezers with the LED in the other, align the LED again and touch the iron on the solder. Position the LED flat on the board and then remove the iron. Keep the LED still while the solder sets. Now check that it is aligned correctly. If not, reapply the iron and straighten it with the tweezers. Only when you are sure that it is positioned correctly apply solder to the other connections. The anodes should be joined together by applying sufficient solder so that the two tracks are bridged.

FIGURE 8-7:
Circuit layout
using surface
mount
components.

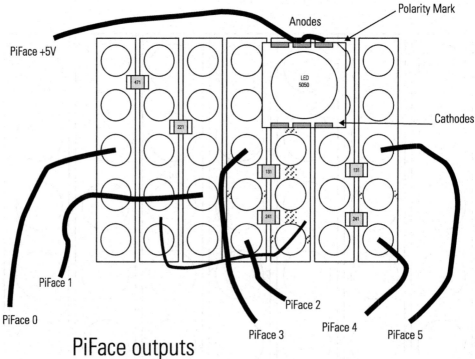

Now you need to add the resistors. You could use through hole at this point, but you might as well go for surface mount. A surface mount resistor should sit nicely between the tracks of 0.1″ pitch strips. Note how surface mount resistors are labeled. They use three numbers: The first two are actual numbers, and the third one says how many zeros there are. So a resistor marked "471" is 470 ohms. There are two sizes that will do this: The larger is known as *0806*, and the smaller as *0604*; either size will do. (I used the smaller resistor size.) A photograph of the final layout is shown in Figure 8-8. For a prediffuser you can either sand the surface of the LED or glue a small piece of translucent plastic over the top of it.

FIGURE 8-8: A photograph of the surface mount circuit layout.

This LED board, however you make it, will require fixing to a base. You can either use hot melt glue or a larger piece of strip board and drill some holes for fixing. Finally there is the matter of the player switches. I have found that the tactile switches made by NKK are rather good-looking and not too expensive. They come in a round or rectangular style with a variety of coloured tops. For this project I used the JF15SP1C with a red top and the JF15SP1G with the blue top. Of course, you can use any other type of switch you like, as long as it is a momentary push-to-make type. Many switches like this have four connections, and the ones on each side are electrically joined; when the button is pressed one side electrically connects to the other. To prevent confusion about which side is which, I have developed a neat trick: Always connect the wires to two opposite corners and leave the other two unconnected, so you will always have the correct connections.

## Creating the Box

The mechanical construction of the box is vital to the final look and feel of the project. Don't be tempted to skimp here if you want a top-notch result. You can make or buy a box, but by far the most satisfactory choice is to make one. There are many construction techniques you can use as well. With the advent of fab labs and hackspaces, many ordinary people have access to laser cutters, and they can make a very neat job. However, I want to show you a simple but effective method of box construction using only small hand tools and low-cost materials.

You can make the box from 6 mm (1/4″) plywood. Start by simply cutting out two rectangles 92 mm (3 5/8″) by 180 mm (7″). Then clamp them together, and making sure that they are square, drill a 3 mm (1/8″) hole 10 mm in from each corner. After you drill the first hole remove the clamp and put a nut and bolt to temporary hold the two pieces together while you drill the next hole. Use a nut and bolt for the second hole as well to keep the pieces together while you drill the last two holes. This ensures that your holes line up. You can then use hexagonal tapped spacers to hold the two sheets apart. Make the sides from four lengths of strip pine. The exact height of the strip pine depends on the construction method you used to make the LED board. If you used the surface mount technique, you can make your box nice and thin, using 5 mm strip pine. However, if you used a through-hole LED, you need to use 12 mm strip pine. This is because you want the LED at the same level or slightly below the lid of the box to get good coverage of light on the diffuser. Glue the four pieces of strip pine to the base, and make sure that they are level with the edge of the base. This sandwich arrangement is shown in Figure 8-9.

FIGURE 8-9:
How to put your
box together.

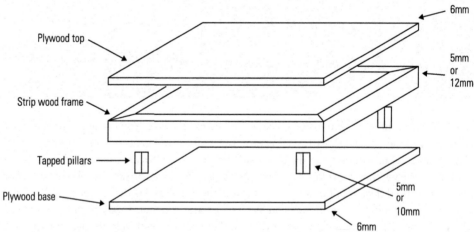

Construction of the Colour Snap box

Mark out four holes for each switch and drill them at 0.8 mm. When fitting the switches, solder some thin wires to the connections in the opposite corners, thread the wires through the holes and push them into place. It should hold simply by the fit, but you can add a blob of glue at the switch center first. Don't do it yet, though, until the box is finished and painted.

To act as the diffuser and place to see the colour, I used a half table tennis ball. You can cut one in half using various methods, but I found the best way is by using a hot wire cutter of the type sold in hobby shops for cutting expanded polystyrene. Clamp the cutter so that the wire is horizontal to the table, and put the ball in the hole of a stick tape reel to stop it from moving. Then adjust the height of the wire so that it comes as close as possible to the center of the ball, and slide the ball through the wire. Keep your fingers out of the way – that wire is hot! (The clue is in the name – *hot wire cutter*.) You now have enough half balls to make two games.

Table tennis balls are a standard size of 40 mm, so you need to cut a 40 mm hole in the middle of the top of the box. You can do this easily with a saw drill. Then you have to fix the half ball into this hole. What I did was to take a small square of 1 mm thick styrene sheet, trace a pencil line around the ball and cut out the hole with a scalpel (see Figure 8-10). Then using model airplane glue, I attached the ball to the sheet, as shown in Figure 8-11.

FIGURE 8-10: The half ball ready to be glued into the supporting base.

It is time to paint the box. I decided to make mine a two-tone finish to emphasise the two player's sides. First give the top and sides of the box a coat of wood primer. Then lightly sand it down and apply the top coat. I used a water-based enamel paint sold in hobby shops. I bought two pots, black and white, and used black for the sides and then mixed a portion of black and white together to make a light grey. I masked off half the top along the middle with painter's tape and painted the other half grey. I removed the tape while the paint was still wet. When the paint dried, I mixed a little more black with the grey I had made for the first half, masked the join and painted the other side – and again removed the tape while the paint was still wet. This produced a very pleasing effect, and the colours show up well against a grey background.

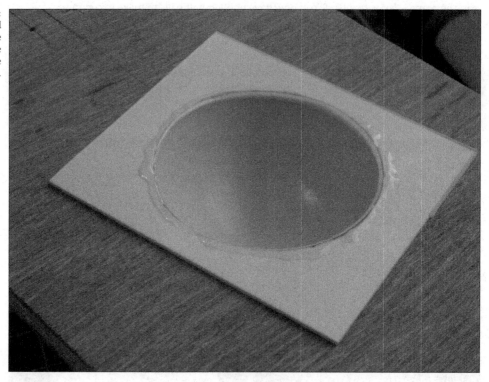

It's time to put it all together! Figure 8-12 shows the view with the lid off.

Mount the LED board in the center of the base with either two screws as shown here or a spot of glue. You can glue the diffuser table tennis board and its sheet through the hole in the lid. The wires from the switches can go to the LED board as well. (They are kept tidy by small spots of hot melt glue.) Finally, make the connections out to the PiFace board using a length of 10-way flat ribbon cable. Just cut a slot in the top of a side piece to allow the cable to sit just under the lid when it is screwed on. The ribbon cable has a red stripe on one wire that is useful as a marker. It doesn't matter what order the wires are in as long as you know what wire to connect to what terminal on the PiFace module. I used the sequence shown in Figure 8-13. As the two switches are around the other side of the board, I extended those two wires by soldering an extra length on and putting some heat shrink sleeving over the joint to insulate it. You can make the sleeving shrink by applying a hot hair dryer to it. The finished unit is shown in Figure 8-14.

FIGURE 8-12:
The box with its
lid off.

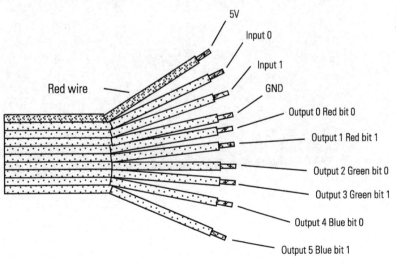

## Connections from a ribbon cable to the PiFace board

5V

Input 0

Input 1

GND

Red wire

Output 0 Red bit 0

Output 1 Red bit 1

Output 2 Green bit 0

Output 3 Green bit 1

Output 4 Blue bit 0

Output 5 Blue bit 1

FIGURE 8-13:
The wire
connections to
the PiFace
board.

FIGURE 8-14:
The finished box
for the game.

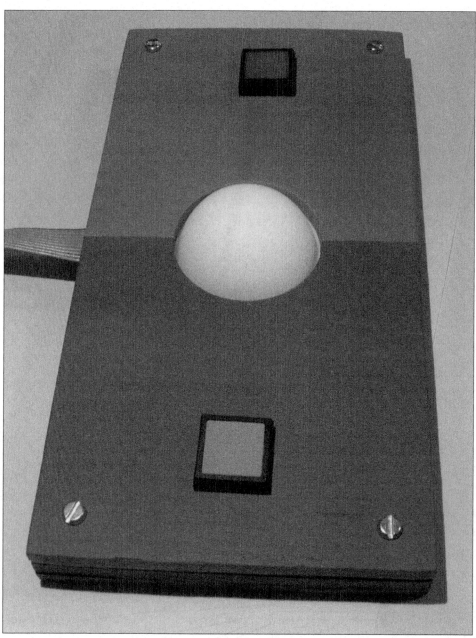

## The Software for Testing the Game

All that you need now is the software to bring your game to life, but before you write that let's write some software to test the hardware. It is vital that before you delve into the complexities of making anything work you have confidence that the hardware is working properly. Therefore, it is common when working on a project to write some simple software to exercise the hardware. Then you have the confidence that if the project doesn't do what you expect it to in the end, it is the software that is wrong, not the hardware. Although Figure 8-4, earlier, showed the schematic of the hardware, how that hardware looks to a programmer is totally different. Figure 8-15 shows that. You can see here that there is a byte that represents the output to the PiFace module. The top two bits are shown as X, which means that you don't care what state they are in. The other bytes are shown in groups of two, each group controlling the intensity of one of the LED colours.

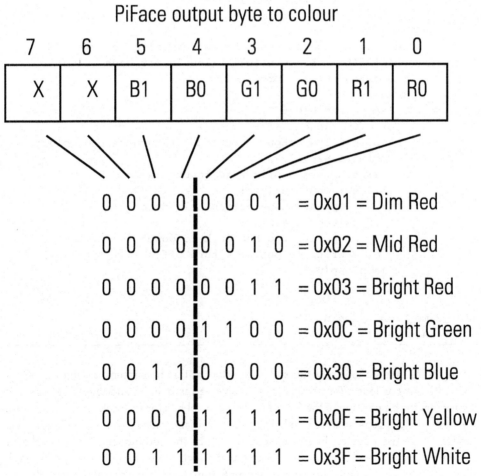

FIGURE 8-15: This top byte shows the output to PiFace.

Although it might be tempting to write a program that cycles through all the colours, what you actually want to see is if each colour works at each of its intensities. It is also helpful to know that the switches are working as well. The test program is shown in Listing 8-1.

---

**Listing 8-1    Colour Snap Hardware Test**

```python
#!/usr/bin/env python
"""

Colour Snap test
"""
import time                 # for delays
import piface.pfio as pfio  # piface library

pfio.init()             # initialise piface

def main():
    print"Testing the colour snap hardware Ctrl C to quit"
    print"showing the three intensity levels for each colour"
    print"& showing buttons pressed"
    while True:
        for led in range(0,6,2) :
            for c in range(1,4) :
                pfio.write_output(c << led)  # turn on the colour
                time.sleep(.5)
                switchState = pfio.read_input() & 3
                if switchState & 1 :
                    print "blue button held down"
                if switchState & 2 :
                    print "red button held down"
                pfio.write_output(0) # turn off the light
            time.sleep(0.8)


if __name__ == '__main__':
    main()
```

---

Listing 8-1 is simply a loop that turns on each colour at the three intensities in turn. This is done with two for loops. The first uses the variable led as an index and counts up in two, so it gives you the bit position of the first of the two control bits for each colour of LED in turn. The next for loop generates the numbers 1 to 3 in a variable called c (for "colour"). Then you combine these two numbers by shifting c to the left by the led number. That gives you the bit pattern you need to write out to the PiFace board to light only one LED at a specific level. When you run this you should see the red colour first in three intensities, the green colour in three intensities and finally the blue colour in three intensities. If you don't see this, check the wiring, soldering and PiFace connections.

The colour changing the state of the input switches is checked, and a message is printed out if a button is held down. You will notice there is some bit manipulation code in this part that you might not have come across before – the use of the bitwise AND operation; in Python and many other languages the symbol to do this is the ampersand (&). Basically, an AND operation is used to selectively zero bits so that you are left with just the bits you are interested in. The AND operation is performed between two numbers or bit patterns; one is called the *subject* and the other the *mask,* although these names are arbitrary. The AND rules are simple: There will be a logic one in the result if there is a logic one in that bit position in both the subject AND the mask. So if you have a zero in the mask, you have a zero in the result; if you have a one in the mask, you will have that position in the result, depending on what the bit was in the subject. In effect you use it for selectively clearing bits. So the line

```
switchState = pfio.read_input() & 3
```

sets the variable switchState to whatever is on the two least significant bits of the PiFace input connectors. The 3 is the mask that is zeroing out all the other bits except bits zero and one. If you write the number 3 in binary, you will see that it looks like 0000011, with ones in the positions you are interested in. To test a bit, you can use another AND operation; the line

```
if switchState & 1 :
```

takes the switchState variable and ANDs it with 1 (or in binary, 00000001). If the result of doing this is a zero, the if operator sees a false; with any other result, it sees a true. So there is no need, for example, to say in this line

```
if (switchState & 1) == True :
```

although the result would be the same. The same augment applies to looking at the switch on bit 1: You simply AND the switchState variable with the number 2 (or in binary, 00000010).

Now go on and succumb to the temptation of showing all the colours just for fun. The simplified program in Listing 8-2 does this.

---

**Listing 8-2  Colour Snap Hardware Test 2**

```
#!/usr/bin/env python
"""

Colour Snap test 2
```

*continued*

Listing 8-2    **continued**

```
"""
import time                    # for delays
import piface.pfio as pfio  # piface library

pfio.init()           # initialise piface

def main():
    print"Testing the colour snap hardware Ctrl C to quit"
    print"showing all the colours"
    while True :
        for c in range(1,63) :
            pfio.write_output(c)  # turn on the colour
            time.sleep(.5)
            pfio.write_output(0) # turn off the light
        time.sleep(0.8)
        print "repeating sequence"


if __name__ == '__main__':
    main()
```

If you find that colours such as yellow look a little mottled, try a bit more prediffusion of the LED – either sand it some more or find a bit of more textured translucent plastic to put over it. The colours seen on the table tennis ball should be smooth and even.

## The Software for the Game

Now on to the full game! There are many ways this game could be programmed to play, so what I give here is just one implementation. It is important, when writing any piece of software, to have the numbers that define it stored in a variable name at the start of the code so that it can be easily changed with an edit in only one line. The way this is set up is that there are two players and the program asks for their names first. It looks up their score in the high-score table and makes an entry for them if they are not in it already. There are three rounds, and the player that wins a round by correctly pressing the Snap button is awarded points based on the difficulty level of the game. At the end of the game, a winner is announced, and the points acquired in the game are transferred to the high-score table. After the names have been inputted, you are asked to enter a difficulty level, which is a number from one to three and refers to how much a colour can change from one presentation to the next. In the easiest level, the colours displayed are only the primary and secondary colours, so it is simple to distinguish one from the other. In the middle level, any colour can be chosen from the 63 possible colours; however, because these are picked at random, most of the time they are very different colours. In the advanced level, only one bit in the colour is changed from one presentation to the next, so this means that there is a good chance of getting a slightly different colour, fooling you into thinking it is the same as the previous one. If you press the Snap button and it is *not* snap, points are deducted.

All the sounds the game produces are stored in a folder called `sounds`. They are all `.ogg` format sounds and are mainly self-explanatory. There are two "snap" sounds (one for each player), a success and fail sound called *applause* and *doh* and finally a "tick" sound. This sound should be very short and is played just before a new colour is displayed.

The inner workings of the game might surprise you as you might think that this way of doing things is counterintuitive. However, it is actually simpler to program the game this way. First of all, a random number function makes a number from 3 to 10 to control how many colour presentations there will be before a match. There is a new colour function whose job is to generate a colour that is different from the last one according to an algorithm chosen by the difficulty level. The program goes on presenting these colours until the number of presentations has been reached; then the last colour is simply repeated. If no player sees the matching colour, the process repeats. You could have the program penalise both players if this happens, but that is not how I have written this code. The full listing is shown in Listing 8-3.

Listing 8-3 **The Colour Snap Game**

```python
#!/usr/bin/env python
"""
Colour Snap
"""
import time               # for delays
import piface.pfio as pfio  # piface library
import sys
import os
import random
import pygame
from pygame.locals import *
import shelve
pygame.init()
pygame.mixer.quit()
pygame.mixer.init()
pfio.init()            # initialise piface

snapSound1 = pygame.mixer.Sound("sounds/snap1.ogg")
snapSound2 = pygame.mixer.Sound("sounds/snap2.ogg")
```

*continued*

**Listing 8-3    continued**

```python
tickSound = pygame.mixer.Sound("sounds/tick.ogg")
applauseSound = pygame.mixer.Sound("sounds/applause.ogg")
dohSound = pygame.mixer.Sound("sounds/doh.ogg")

easyCols = [ 0x3, 0xC, 0xF, 0x30, 0x33, 0x3C, 0x3F ]
intCols = [ 0x3, 0xC, 0xF, 0x30, 0x33, 0x3C, 0x3F,
              0x1, 0x4, 0x5, 0x10, 0x11, 0x14, 0x15]
colours = [ easyCols, intCols ]
level = 2 # 0 = easest level 2 = hardset
playerName = ["no player", "Blue player","Red Player"]
countToMatch = 0
roundToPlay = 1 # current round number
maxRound = 5 # number of rounds to play
redScore = 0
blueScore = 0

def main():
        global level
        print"Colour Snap, ctrl C to quit"
        show_table()
        playerName[1] = raw_input("Enter the name ⊃
of the player using the blue button ")
        p1Score = set_table(playerName[1], 0); ⊃
#make sure player is in database
        print "The score for",playerName[1],"so far is ",p1Score
        playerName[2] = raw_input("Enter the name of the ⊃
player using the red button ")
        p2Score = set_table(playerName[2], 0); ⊃
#make sure player is in database
        print "The score for",playerName[2],"so far is ",p2Score
        il = raw_input ("Enter a difficulty level 1 Easy ⊃
to 3 Hard ")
        level = int(il)-1
        #make sure the level is within range
        if level>2:
                level=2
        if level < 0:
                level = 0
        lc = random.randint(0,63) # the last colour shown
        while roundToPlay <= maxRound :
            print "Round ",roundToPlay, " of ",maxRound
            countToMatch = random.randint(3, 10)
```

```
            while countToMatch !=0 : ⤾
# do this until you get a match
                countToMatch -= 1
                if countToMatch != 0 : ⤾
#don't generate a new colour on last turn
                    c = newColour(lc);
                tickSound.play()
                time.sleep(0.5)
                pfio.write_output(c)  # turn on the colour
                checkInput(0.8, c, lc)
                pfio.write_output(0) # turn off the light
                checkInput(0.9, c, lc)
                lc = c # record the last colour
        print "End of the game"
        if blueScore == redScore:
                print"It is a DRAW!!! "
        else:
                win = 2
                if blueScore > redScore:
                    win = 1
                print"The winner is ",playerName[win]
        p1Score += blueScore
        set_table(playerName[1], p1Score);
        p2Score += redScore
        set_table(playerName[2], p2Score);
        print"Updating high score table"
        show_table()
        # end of main function


def newColour(lastColour):
        nc = lastColour
        if level == 2 : # hardest
                nc ^= 1 << random.randint(0,5) ⤾
# change by only a single bit
        else:
                while nc == lastColour : ⤾
# repeat until you find a new colour
                    nc = colours[level][random.randint⤾
(0,len(colours[level])-1)]
        return nc


def checkInput(delay, c, lc) : # has someone pressed a button
```

*continued*

**Listing 8-3**    **continued**

```
        nextTime = time.time() + delay
        buttonPress = 0
        while nextTime > time.time() and buttonPress == 0 :
            buttonPress = pfio.read_input() & 3
        if buttonPress != 0 :
                if buttonPress & 1 :
                    snapSound1.play()
                else :
                    snapSound2.play()
                checkResult(buttonPress, c, lc)
                while buttonPress !=0 : ⟳
# hold until button is released
                        buttonPress = pfio.read_input() & 3


def checkResult(player, newColour, lastColour) :
        global countToMatch, roundToPlay, blueScore, ⟳
redScore, level
        pfio.write_output(0) # turn off the light
        time.sleep(0.8)
        count = 0 # minimum number of flashes
        print playerName[player],
        if lastColour == newColour :
                print"yes"
                applauseSound.play()
                roundToPlay += 1
                # add successful player score
                if player == 1 :
                        blueScore += level +1
                else:
                        redScore += level +1
        else :
                print "sorry not snap"
                dohSound.play()
                # penalise wrong press
                if player == 1 :
                        blueScore -= 1 * (level +1)
                else:
                        redScore -= 1 * (level +1)


        while player !=0 or count < 6: ⟳
#until button is released or 6 flashes
```

```
                    pfio.write_output(lastColour)
                    time.sleep(0.3)
                    pfio.write_output(newColour)
                    time.sleep(0.3)
                    player = pfio.read_input() & 3
                    count +=1
            pfio.write_output(0) # turn off the light
            time.sleep(2)
            countToMatch = random.randint(3, 10)


def set_table(name, score):
        scoreTable = shelve.open('score_table.snap')
        if not name in scoreTable:
                scoreTable[name] = score
        elif score > scoreTable[name]:
                scoreTable[name] = score
        else :
                score = scoreTable[name]
        scoreTable.close()
        return score


def show_table():
        print
        print "The current high scores are"
        scoreTable = shelve.open('score_table.snap')
        highscores = scoreTable.items()
        highscores.sort(key=lambda elem: elem[1], reverse=True)
        for entry in highscores:
                print entry[0], "has a score of",entry[1]
        scoreTable.close()
        print


if __name__ == '__main__':
    main()
```

First off, you will see that you use the pygame module, but you are using that only for the generation of sound. The main function starts off by asking for all the user input and then enters an outer while loop that plays all the rounds. This is followed by another while loop that does the actual playing of the round; this calls up the generation of the colours and the checking of the user input in addition to playing the appropriate sound. At the end of all the rounds, one player is declared the winner, and the updated high-score table is displayed.

In order to implement the high-score table, I have used the `shelve` module, which is a useful module that handles most of the work in making a persistent database. Basically, it maintains a dictionary and stores its entries in an unsorted manner. It is a simple enough matter to transfer this to a list, and sort the list before displaying it. When you run this code for the first time a file containing the high-score table will be generated; subsequently, the file will be used. If you want to start afresh, simply delete this file.

Generating the next colour is done in the `newColour` function. For the two simplest levels, it simply picks a colour from a list defined at the start of the code as `easyCols` and `intCols`. However, if the game is running at the most complex level, a random bit is toggled or changed. This function generates a number with only a single bit set in it by shifting a one a random number of places to the left; it then uses the exclusive or function, or `XOR`, to change that bit in the colour number.

The `checkInput` function does two jobs: First it acts as a delay, and while it is delaying it constantly checks to see if a button has been pressed. If a button has been pressed, it triggers the snap sound and calls the `checkResult` function to see if the call is correct. If the snap is correct, an applause sound is played, along with a printout of the successful player's name; otherwise, a fail sound is played, and the incorrect player's score is decremented. Then the last two colours are alternated; you will see them flash if they are different.

## Over to You

The first thing you can customise are the sounds, especially the snap sounds. It is great to have those said by a person you actually recognise. You could change colours in the colour list. You could even add an extra resistor to two of the LEDs to get an even wider range of subtle colour variations.

You could make the scoring more sophisticated so that instead of simply storing the score of a player, you also stored the number of rounds he or she has played and sorted the list on the ratio of score-to-rounds played.

# Chapter **9**
# Test Your Reactions

**by Dr. Andrew Robinson**

## In This Chapter

○ Getting started interfacing hardware with the Raspberry Pi

○ Working with basic electronic circuits

○ Getting started with electronic components, including transistors and resistors

○ Wiring up a switch and an LED

THINK YOU'VE GOT fast fingers? Find out in this chapter as take your first steps in hardware interfacing to build a reaction timer. You'll program the Raspberry Pi to wait a random time before turning on a light and starting a timer. The timer will stop when you press a button.

# Welcome to the Embedded World!

For some people the idea that computers aren't always big black or beige boxes on desks is a surprise, but in reality the majority of computers in the world are embedded in devices. Think about your washing machine – to wash your clothes it needs to coordinate turning the water on, keeping it heated to the right temperature, agitating your clothes by periodically spinning the drum, and emptying the water. It might repeat some of these steps multiple times during a wash, and has different cycles for different types of fabric. You might not have realised it's a computer program. It takes inputs from switches to select the wash and sensors that measure water temperature, and has outputs that heat the water and lock the door shut, and motors to turn the drum and open and close valves to let water in and out.

---

**YOUR TURN!**    Take a moment to consider the number of appliances and gadgets that need to measure inputs, do some processing to reach a decision and then control an output in response.

---

A modern kitchen is crammed with computers that watch over and automate our appliances to save us effort. Computers aren't just embedded in practical products either; they're in electronic toys and entertainment devices. After working through this chapter and the other examples in this book you'll be on your way to designing your own embedded systems to make your life easier, or entertain you.

Before you get too carried away connecting things up it's worth considering a couple of warnings that will protect you and your electronic components.

## Good Practice

Electricity can be dangerous, so it is important to use it safely. The muscles in your body are controlled by tiny electrical signals, and these can be affected if electricity flows through your body. Your heart is a muscle that can be stopped by an electric shock.

The flow of electricity can cause heating, which will either cause burns to your body (sometimes deep within tissue) or can cause a fire.

---

**WARNING**    Electricity can kill! Only experiment with low voltages and currents, and never work with mains. If you are ever in doubt, then you should check with someone suitably qualified.

---

Hardware is less forgiving than software; if you make a mistake with code, you might get an error, the program might crash, or in rare cases you might cause your Raspberry Pi to reset. If you make a mistake in hardware, then you can cause permanent damage. As such, hardware engineers tend to check and double-check their work before applying the power!

When experimenting you should beware of short-circuiting your projects. Make sure that nothing conductive touches your circuit. Tools, metal watchstraps and jewellery, unused wires, spare components and tin foil have all been known to damage circuits – keep your working area clear of anything you don't need and make sure that nothing metallic can accidentally touch your Raspberry Pi or circuit.

### Static Discharge

You may have felt a small electric shock due to static sometimes. This occurs when a charge builds up and then discharges to a conductor, which you feel as a small shock. If you are holding a component when this happens, that large voltage will flow through the component and may damage it. Other objects such as plastic can become charged too and then discharge through a component. As such, you should take care to avoid this static discharge through components or circuits. In industry, conductive work surfaces and wrist straps are earthed to prevent static buildup. This may be an extreme solution for a hobby; you can discharge yourself by touching something earthed like a water tap, and avoid working on surfaces that are prone to picking up static charge like plastics – for example, avoid working on nylon carpets or plastic bags.

---

You may have noticed components are supplied in antistatic bags, or static-dissipative bags or static-barrier bags. These bags are made from special plastic designed to protect the contents from being zapped by static discharges and conduct any charge away. Beware that some of these bags can be slightly conductive and so may interact with your powered-up circuit.          **TIP**

---

# Obtaining Components

Another difference with hardware is that you can't download everything you need from the Internet! However, you can do the next best thing and order parts online. There are a number of online electronics retailers that supply parts, including the two worldwide distributors of the Raspberry Pi, element14/Premier Farnell/Newark and RS Components. Pimoroni, SparkFun, SK Pang, Cool Components, Adafruit and other web stores have a smaller range but cater well to electronic hobbyists.

Maplin Electronics and Radio Shack have shops on the high street with a smaller selection of parts.

## An Interface Board

Although the Raspberry Pi has a general purpose input/output (GPIO) connector that you can connect to directly, as a beginner, it is easier to use an add-on board. An interface board can offer some protection to your Pi against burning out if you get your wires crossed!

## PiFace Digital

This chapter uses the PiFace Digital interface because it is very easy to use. PiFace Digital has eight LEDs on it so that you can start controlling hardware without any electronics knowledge. Later in this chapter you'll connect your own LEDs and switches to PiFace Digital with the screw terminals. Hopefully you'll go on to use more advanced boards, and eventually you may want to design an interface board of your own!

---

**TIP**    In computing, *digital* refers to things that can either be on or off – there's no in between. In contrast, *analogue* devices have many points between their maximum and minimum values. A button is digital in that it is either on or off. A temperature is an example of something that is analogue.

---

## Setting up PiFace Digital

PiFace Digital communicates using *Serial Peripheral Interface* (SPI) bus. It's a standard means of connecting peripheral devices to microprocessors. Before you use PiFace Digital with the Raspberry Pi you need to install some software.

## SPI

SPI consists of four wires to communicate data from a master (the microprocessor) to a slave device (the peripheral). Data is sent *serially* (that is, the voltage on a wire is switched on and off to communicate a binary number) over time using four wires as shown in Figure 9-1.

FIGURE 9-1:
Example SPI transaction: The microprocessor sends data 11011101, and the device sends 11110011.

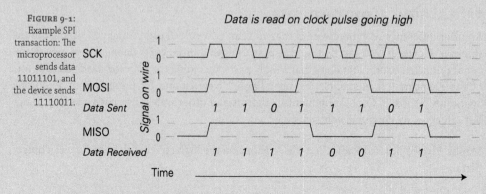

○ One wire is used for data from the master to the slave (named *master output slave input* [MOSI]).

○ Data going to the master from the slave is sent on another wire (named *master input slave output* [MISO]).

○ The *serial clock* (SCK) wire is used to synchronise the master and slave so they know when a valid value is being sent (that is, that MISO and MOSI have momentarily stopped changing).

○ The *slave select* wire, or sometimes called *chip select* (SS or CS), selects between multiple slave devices connected to the same MOSI, MISO and SCK wires.

## Installing PiFace Digital Software

Chapter 1, "Getting Your Raspberry Pi Up and Running", mentions drivers that the operating system loads. These make it easy for programmers to write code to interact with hardware devices. Rather than bloat the operating system with drivers for every possible type of hardware, Linux has driver modules. These are loaded separately when needed. As PiFace Digital talks over SPI you need to ensure that the SPI driver is loaded so the Raspberry Pi hardware sends the correct electrical signals on the expansion pins. You will also need to install a Python library that makes the SPI driver easy to use from your Python code.

It is possible to install PiFace Digital software on Raspbian as a Debian package with one command. However, in the future you might need to install software that isn't packaged, or perhaps want to use PiFace Digital on a different distribution that doesn't use Debian packages. As such the following steps show how to manually install software from the source.

### Loading the SPI Driver Module

Check to see if the SPI driver is loaded. Type `lsmod` to list all modules. If it is loaded, you will see the following line. Don't worry about the numbers on the right; it is the module name `spi_bcm2708` which is important.

```
spi_bcm2708             4401  0
```

If it is not listed, you need to enable the module. Although the driver module is included, Linux "blacklists" some modules so they are not loaded. To un-blacklist the module, edit the file /etc/modprobe.d/raspi-blacklist.conf. You can insert a # in front of the line `blacklist spi-bcm2708` to comment it out, or delete the line completely. Use your favourite editor to edit the file, such as leafpad, nano or vi. For example, you use nano by typing the following:

```
sudo nano /etc/modprobe.d/raspi-blacklist.conf
```

Enter # at the start of the line `blacklist spi-bcm2708` like so:

```
#blacklist spi-bcm2708
```

Save the file. If using the nano editor, press Ctrl + X and then confirm that you want to save the file before exiting.

---

**TIP**

Commenting out is a way of making the computer ignore what is on that line. It works by turning the line into a comment. *Comments* are text intended for the user and not interpreted by the computer.

It is better to comment a line out rather than delete it as it makes it easier to restore later by uncommenting (that is, removing the comment marker). Python also uses # for comments, so you can temporarily remove a line of code by putting a # at the start of the line.

---

Restart the Raspberry Pi by typing `sudo reboot`.

After reboot log in and type `lsmod` again, and you should see `spi_bcm2708` listed. Programs send a message over the SPI bus by writing characters to a special file. Type `ls -la /dev/spi*` to check whether the special file exists. If you're successful, Linux will show at least one file. If you receive a message such as `No such file or directory`, you need to check that the SPI driver module is functioning correctly.

### Installing Python Modules

With the `spi_bcm2708` module loaded, Linux can talk SPI to peripherals. The next step is to install programs that will make the driver easier to use and send the correct messages over the SPI bus to control the hardware:

1. Make sure that the Raspberry Pi is up to date. Because the Raspberry Pi will check the Internet for updates, you need to make sure that your Raspberry Pi is online. Then type `sudo apt-get update`.

   Wait until Linux downloads and updates files, which can typically take a couple of minutes.

2. Install the necessary packages by typing `sudo apt-get install python-dev python-gtk2-dev git`.

   Linux will list any other programs necessary and tell you how much additional disk space is required. Confirm that you want to continue by typing Y and pressing enter. After a few minutes the programs will be installed.

3. Type cd to return to your home directory and then get the latest software to control PiFace by typing the following:

```
git clone https://github.com/thomasmacpherson/piface.git
```

This will copy the latest PiFace code and examples into your home directory. Type ls piface to list the contents of the directory that have just been downloaded.

## Git and Source Code Management

Git is a *source code management* (SCM) system that keeps track of different versions of files. SCMs are necessary when multiple people work on the same project. Imagine if two people were working on a project and changed the same file at the same time. Without SCM the first person's changes might get overwritten by the second. SCMs instead help manage the process and can merge both contributions. They also keep previous versions (like wikis do) so it's possible to go back.

Git was initially developed by Linus Torvalds for collaborative development of the Linux operating system but then used by many other projects. There are other SCMs such as SVN, CVS and Mercurial, which provide similar functions.

GitHub (http://github.com) is a website that hosts projects using Git. It's designed for social coding, so everyone can suggest changes and contribute to improving a project. As the Raspberry Pi has such a strong community, there are many projects on GitHub (including the code for Linux itself) for the Raspberry Pi that everyone can contribute to.

GitHub offers free accounts and tutorials so as you become a more proficient coder, you might as well try using source code management for your project. It can be really useful if you start working with a friend or want to go back to a previous version of your code.

4. So that all users of the Raspberry Pi can use the SPI bus, you need to change the permissions on the /dev/spi* files. PiFace Digital provides a handy script to set SPI permissions. Run the script by typing

```
sudo piface/scripts/spidev-setup
```

5. Restart by typing

```
sudo reboot
```

Lastly, you need to install the Python modules that will make it easy to send the correct messages on the SPI bus.

6. Log in again and type cd to get back to the home directory.

7. Change the directory to the piface directory and then the python directory by typing `cd piface/python`.

8. Install the Python module that talks to PiFace Digital by typing `sudo python setup.py install`. After a few minutes the necessary files will be installed, and you will be ready to start testing with real hardware.

9. Finally, shut down the Pi and remove the power before connecting the PiFace interface by typing `sudo halt`.

---

**TIP**     It is useful to know how to install software manually, but if in the future you want to install PiFace Digital with one command, instructions are provided at `www.piface.org.uk`.

---

## Connecting PiFace Digital

Disconnect the power before connecting or disconnecting anything to or from the Raspberry Pi. This ensures that you don't accidentally short anything and is generally safer. Position PiFace Digital so it lines up with the edges of the Raspberry Pi and check that all 26 pins of the expansion port line up with the holes in the connector. Gently push the PiFace interface down, making sure that you don't push sideways to bend the pins. If it is correctly lined up, it should slide smoothly. Connect the power, log in and start X, as described in Chapter 1.

## Using the Emulator

This book mentions the importance of regular testing and checking that subsystems work before moving on. This is a great excuse for turning some lights on and off. There's something satisfying about seeing a computer responding to you, lighting a light, obeying your command! Next you will use the PiFace emulator to check that your Raspberry Pi can talk to your PiFace Digital.

Start the emulator by typing `piface/scripts/piface-emulator` in a Terminal window. The emulator window will appear as shown in Figure 9-2.

As you want to manually control the outputs, in the PiFace Emulator window click Override Enable.

Toggle Output Pin 1 on by clicking it. The PiFace interface will click as the relay turns on, and the corresponding LED will illuminate. Notice the graphic on-screen updates to show the LED being on, the contacts have changed over on the relay and the first output pin is on.

Try turning multiple output pins on, and notice how the on-screen display updates. Try the All On, All Off and Flip buttons to discover what they do.

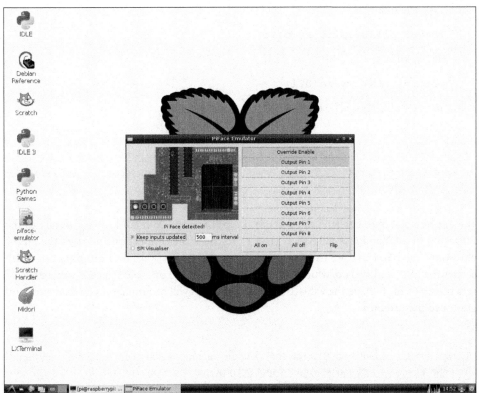

FIGURE 9-2:
The PiFace
Emulator.

When you are finished flashing lights and trying the various options close the emulator. You're now ready to program your Raspberry Pi to take control!

## Interfacing with Python

You first meet the Hello World program in Chapter 2, "Introductory Software Project: The Insult Generator". The hardware equivalent of Hello World is flashing a light, which similarly, although not exciting in itself, is the first step in getting a computer to start controlling the world. After you've mastered this, there's no limit to what you can start controlling!

## Turning a Light On

First, write the code to turn an LED on:

1. Double-click IDLE to begin entering code interactively.

2. Type the following:

```
import piface.pfio as pfio

pfio.init()

pfio.digital_write(0,1)
```

3. The first LED should be lit.

**TIP**    Chapter 2 mentions that there are two versions of Python – Python 2 and Python 3. Similarly there are two versions of IDLE; IDLE (used in this book) that corresponds to the Python 2 command python and IDLE3 that corresponds to Python 3.

The `import` statement tells Python to use the `piface.pfio` module so it can talk to the PiFace interface. You must call `pfio.init()` to check the connection and reset the PiFace hardware. The `digital_write(outputpin, value)` function takes *outputpin*, which selects the LED, and *value*, which determines if it is turned on. So `digital_write(0,1)` sets the first LED to have the value 1 (on). This function will be familiar if you have ever programmed the Arduino.

**TIP**    Computers start counting at 0 as this makes some operations and calculations more efficient. You should see why as you learn more about computers and programming.

## Flashing a Light On and Off

Next, you're going to write a program that flashes the LED with a timer:

1. Create a new window in IDLE by going to the File menu and clicking New Window.

2. Type the following:

```
from time import sleep

import piface.pfio as pfio

pfio.init()

while(True):

  pfio.digital_write(0,1)

  sleep(1)

  pfio.digital_write(0,1)

  sleep(1)
```

3. Go to the Run menu and choose Run Module (or press F5).

4. Click OK when Python displays the message Source Must Be Saved.

5. Enter a filename and then click Save.

6. You will see a message saying RESTART, and then Python should run your code. If an error message appears, go back and correct your code and try running it again.

You've now written the hardware equivalent of Hello World – an LED that flashes. The next examples will show how to make the Raspberry Pi respond to the world, as you will learn how to read inputs.

---

As an extension, you could try flashing a more complex pattern – change the rate the LED flashes at or try flashing multiple LEDs. **YOUR TURN!**

---

## Reading a Switch

For a computer to respond to its environment, it needs to be able to read inputs. First you will use the graphical emulator to display the status of the inputs.

### Showing Input Status Graphically

In the emulator, click the Keep Inputs Updated check box as shown in Figure 9-3. The interval sets how often the inputs are read; for most cases, it is fine to leave it on 500ms.

FIGURE 9-3:
Enable the Keep
Inputs Updated
check box to
show the status
of inputs.

Test the input by pressing one of the buttons on the bottom left of PiFace. As shown in Figure 9-4, the on-screen representation changes to indicate the switch that has been pressed.

FIGURE 9-4:
The status of
inputs are
shown in the
emulator.

You can close the emulator for now by clicking the cross in the top-right corner of the window.

### Reading Inputs with Code

As you saw earlier, you can control outputs using the function `digital_write`. Logically, as you might expect, to get the value of inputs, you use the `digital_read` function. Let's write a simple example:

1. Type the following Python code interactively:

   ```
   import piface.pfio as pfio

   pfio.init()

   pfio.digital_read(0)
   ```

   Python prints 0.

2. Hold down button number S1 and type `pfio.digital_read(0)` again.

   Python prints 1.

3. Now read the next button along (S2). Type `pfio.digital_read(1)`. Notice how the argument of the function specifies which input to read.

You have seen how easy it is to read an input. Next, you are going to combine turning a light on and reading an input to build a reaction timer.

## The Reaction Timer

Now is the time to find out if you've got fast fingers by building a reaction timer game.

Type the following code in a new window and then save it as reactionTimer.py:

```python
from time import sleep, time
from random import uniform
import piface.pfio as pfio
#Initialise the interface
pfio.init()
print "press button one when the light comes on"
#Sleep for a random period between 3 and 10 seconds
sleep(uniform(3,10))
#Turn LED on
pfio.digital_write(0,1)
#Record the current time
startTime = time()
#Wait while button is not pressed
while(pfio.digital_read(0)==0):
    continue #continue round the loop
#Button must have been pressed as we've left loop
#Read time now
stopTime = time()
```

```
#Time taken is difference between times
elapsedTime = stopTime-startTime
#Display the time taken. str is required to convert
#elapsedTime into a string for printing
print "Your reaction time was: " + str(elapsedTime)
#Turn LED off when finished
pfio.digital_write(1,0)
```

Run the code by pressing F5 from IDLE.

All the lights will go out. Wait until the LED comes on and then press button 0 as fast as you can. The program will print your reaction time.

Next, you'll see if your reactions are any faster with a big red button as you wire up a simple circuit.

## Meet PiFace Digital's Connections

The PiFace Digital interface makes it very easy to wire up simple digital circuits so that you can connect your Raspberry Pi to switches and actuators like lights or motors in the real world. Figure 9-5 labels the connectors on PiFace Digital.

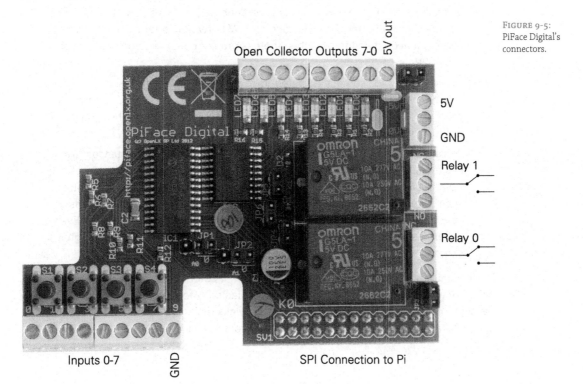

FIGURE 9-5:
PiFace Digital's
connectors.

# Electrical Circuits

Modern computers work with electricity, so to interface with them, you need to understand the basics of how it behaves.

*Electricity* is the flow of tiny particles, called *electrons,* that carry a charge. Think of electrons as always wanting to get home; for example, with a battery, the electrons want to get back into the other terminal. As the electrons move through components in a circuit on their way home they do work. This work might be to emit light in an LED or move a motor around. If the electrons do not flow, no work is done (and the LED does not shine). Figure 9-6 shows three circuits, but only one has a path for electrons to leave the power source, pass through a component to do work and return home again!

Electronics is all about controlling electrons' journeys! In many cases it is about making or breaking a complete path for electrons to flow.

In describing circuits, there are a few terms that you may come across:

○ Voltage – this is, in electrical terms, how "strongly" the electrons are pulled home – that is, how much work they can do while they flow through the circuit. Think of it a bit like a water wheel and a reservoir. The greater the distance the water falls, the more work it can do turning the water wheel as it flows past. *Voltage* describes the work that can be done and is measured in volts – for example, an AA battery has a voltage of 1.5V between its terminals. If another one is connected end to end, then there is greater potential to do work, a voltage of 3V.

○ Ground, or 0V (or sometimes referred to as *negative*) – a reference point to measure voltage from. If a point in a circuit is at ground, then it is at 0V, and no work can be done. With the water example, if the water is on the ground, it can't fall any further so can't be harnessed to do any work.

○ Resistance – how easily the electrons can flow. Different substances allow electrons to flow with different degrees of ease. Conductors, such as metals, have a low resistance and make it easy for the electrons to flow. Insulators, such as plastics, have high resistances, which make it hard for electrons to flow. Different materials resist the flow of electrons by different amounts. Even water has a fairly low resistance, so it will allow electricity to flow through it, which is why you shouldn't use your Raspberry Pi in the bath!

You can think of these like this: *Voltage* describes the potential to do work (analogous to the height of water), and *current* describes the rate electricity follows (the rate of flow of water passing a point). *Resistance* describes how easily electricity flows through a material – voltage, resistance and current are interrelated – without a voltage existing between two points, no current will flow. The resistance between the two points affects how much current will flow. If you want to know more, look up Ohm's law online.

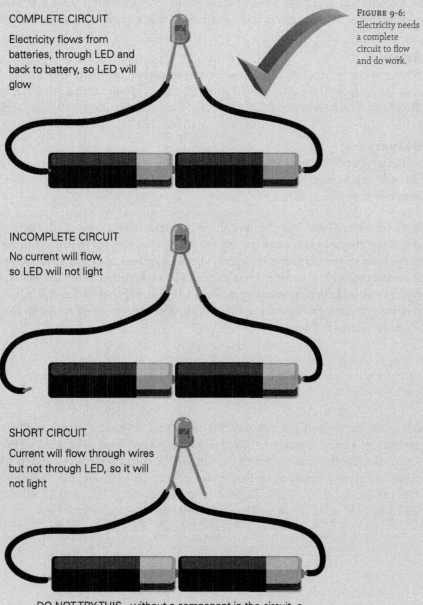

**COMPLETE CIRCUIT**

Electricity flows from batteries, through LED and back to battery, so LED will glow

FIGURE 9-6: Electricity needs a complete circuit to flow and do work.

**INCOMPLETE CIRCUIT**

No current will flow, so LED will not light

**SHORT CIRCUIT**

Current will flow through wires but not through LED, so it will not light

DO NOT TRY THIS - without a component in the circuit, a large current will flow, which will result in heating

### Inputs

The screw terminals next to the on-board switches are used to connect external switches. There are eight inputs, numbered 0-7 from the outside of the board to the middle, followed by a connection to ground. PiFace Digital will register an input if there is an electrical connection between the input terminal and ground – that is, there is a path for electrons to flow.

### Relays

When you turn either of the first two outputs on you should notice that PiFace clicks. This sound is as the contacts in the relay (the large rectangular components) change over. A *relay* can by thought of as a computer-controlled switch. You'll use relays in Chapter 10, "The Twittering Toy".

### Outputs

As well as controlling the on-board LEDs and relays, PiFace Digital has "open-collector" outputs that can be used to control circuits. You can connect to these outputs with the screw terminals next to the LEDs.

The term *open collector* describes how the output transistor is connected. *Transistors* are the switches at the heart of computers – there are tens of millions of transistors in the processor at the heart of the Raspberry Pi. Luckily they're only tens of nanometres (a *nanometre* is a thousand millionth of a metre – you could fit 2000 transistors across the width of a human hair) in size. Although transistors behave in a similar way to switches and relays, the direction current flows through them affects how they behave, which needs to be considered when connecting to them.

---

**TIP**     There are different types of transistors, which allow current to flow in different ways. For simplicity this chapter just uses examples of the type NPN.

---

Open-collector outputs can just sink current. That is, they allow current to flow to ground; they are not a source for current. This means that circuits have to be wired up from a power source, through the component being controlled, through the transistor and then to ground. Figure 9-7 shows a typical setup. Remember, current has to flow for electricity to do work, so until the transistor turns on and allows current to flow to ground the LED will not come on. The transistors on PiFace already have the connection to ground wired up.

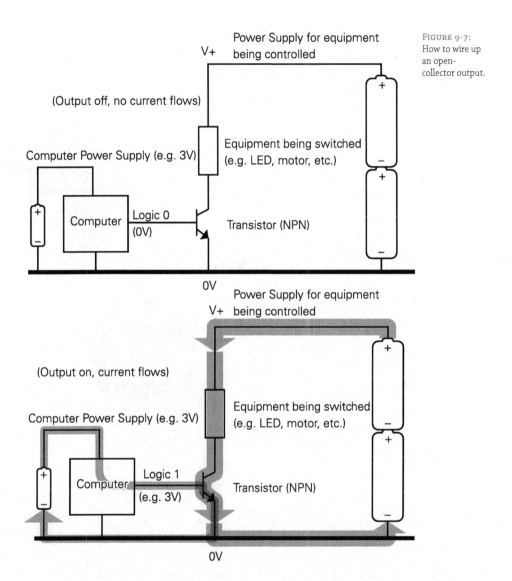

FIGURE 9-7:
How to wire up
an open-
collector output.

## Connecting a Switch and an LED

Enough theory! It's time to wire up the components. For the example, you're using a switch that incorporates an LED, but you could use a separate LED and switch. You will wire them up as shown in Figure 9-8.

FIGURE 9-8:
Wiring up
the LED and
switch to the
Raspberry Pi.

FIGURE 9-8: Wiring up the LED and switch to the Raspberry Pi.

## Making Connections

There are a variety of ways to join wires and components together. Figures 9-9 through 9-12 show different ways of making connections. Important considerations are that the joint is secure and that you have a good connection; otherwise, the joint will create a high resistance or come apart.

○ Wires can be twisted together (as shown in Figure 9-9) – this is a quick and easy method, but not very secure. Wrapping insulation tape helps to hold things more securely and prevents other connections from shorting.

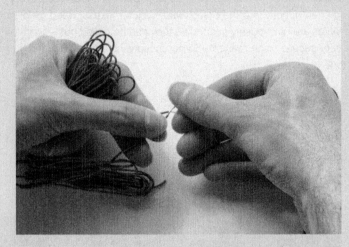

**FIGURE 9-9:**
Twisting wires.

○ Screw connectors (in some forms, sometimes called *choc-bloc*) (see Figure 9-10) – these hold wires together under a screw. They're quick, easy and fairly secure, but are quite bulky.

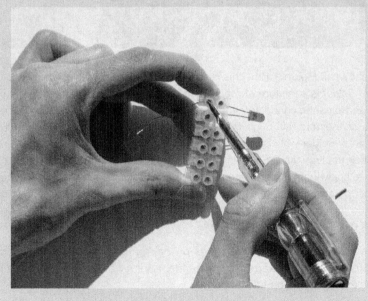

**FIGURE 9-10:**
Screwing terminals.

*continued*

*continued*

○ Breadboard, sometimes called *binboard* (see Figure 9-11) – is great for experimenting. Breadboard has rows of strips of metal that grip and connect wires. Components can be inserted directly into the breadboard, which makes it good for prototyping circuits. Wires are only loosely gripped so they can be pulled out – good for reuse, but not very secure or permanent. Some cheaper breadboards suffer from poor connectors.

**FIGURE 9-11:**
Using a
breadboard.

○ Solder (shown in Figure 9-12) – this is the most permanent way of making connections. *Solder* is a mixture of metals and is heated with a soldering iron until it melts and joins the connectors together. It's also possible to re-melt solder to separate connectors, although this is not always easy without damaging the components. Solder will also only join certain types of metals – for example, it won't stick to aluminium. Soldering can be a bit tricky at first; it takes a bit of practise to apply just the right amount of heat in the right place to avoid melting insulation, damaging sensitive components or burning your fingers! It's best to practise to join some scrap components and wire as your first few attempts might be unsuccessful.

It's best to become familiar with all methods of making connections; then you can use whichever method is most appropriate at the time. And, if nothing else, learning how to solder with molten metal can be fun!

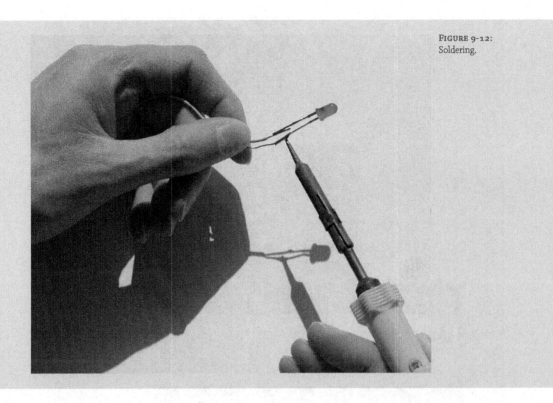

FIGURE 9-12:
Soldering.

Cut four lengths of wire 20cm long and strip about 7mm of the insulation off each end. If you are using stranded wire (that is, there isn't a single core, inside the insulation, but lots of fine strands), twist the strands together with your fingertips.

---

You can "tin" the wires with a soldering iron. This prevents metal whiskers sticking out that can accidentally short, causing undesired connections. To tin wires, twist them together, then run along the metal from the insulation to the tip with a soldering iron on the top and solder on the bottom. Try and get the speed right so just enough solder flows to bind all the strands together.

**TIP**

---

## Connect a Switch

Connect one switch to an input terminal (such as input 0) and the other to the ground (0V) terminal as shown in Figure 9-13. Start the emulator up to show the state of the inputs. Press the button and check that the input is registered. If nothing happens, check your wiring. Note that as pins 0-3 are wired in parallel to the switches, the terminal and corresponding switch indicate together.

FIGURE 9-13:
Wiring up a
switch.

### Connect an LED

You will connect the LED to the open-collector outputs. Remember open-collector outputs cannot supply current; they are essentially a switch that connects the terminal to ground. You'll create a circuit where the current will flow from the 5V terminal, through a resistor (to limit the current so the LED is not damaged) and through an LED and into the output terminal. When the output terminal is turned on it allows current to flow to ground, completing the circuit and illuminating the LED. Remember LEDs only work if current flows through them one way, so it matters which lead you connect to positive. For most LEDs the longer leg indicates the *anode*, which should be connected to the resistor and then the 5V terminal. A complete circuit diagram is available on the book's website (www.wiley.com/go/raspberrypiprojects).

Some switches with built-in LEDs can safely work at 5V so you do not need a resistor. However, most normal LEDs would be damaged by a voltage of over 2V. If you are using a normal LED, you need to put about a 330Ω resistor in series with the LED. Chapter 8 has more information about using resistors with LEDs. Connect the longer leg of the LED and resistor together and then connect the other leg of the resistor to the 5V terminal. Now is a good time to check if the LED will work. Briefly touch the other lead of the LED, called the *cathode*, to GND. You should see the LED glow. If not, check your wiring and make sure that you have identified the anode and cathode correctly. (You shouldn't have damaged the LED if you got the polarity wrong.)

When you know the circuit works, disconnect from the ground and then connect to the transistor via one of the output terminals – such as output 0. When the transistor is turned on, it will allow the current to flow to ground and complete the circuit, so the LED will illuminate. Turn the output on from the emulator and check that it lights.

## Playing with the Reaction Timer

Now that you have connected an LED and switch, rerun the reaction timer program. Again the LED should light after a random time, and the switch should stop the timer. Now that you know your wiring and circuit works, you can really start to have fun – try different output devices, wire up a buzzer instead of the LED and see if your reactions to sound are quicker. You could perhaps mount a feather on a motor and test your reaction to touch. You might find this reaction to be quicker. This is because the inputs (nerves in the skin) can send a message to the outputs (muscles) without going through a complicated processing system (your brain) – the principles of computing apply to lots of other systems too! Experiment with different input switches too – you could attach a switch to different parts of your body and see if they respond as fast as your hand.

Have a go at making your own switch! Instead of a pre-made switch, you could wire up pieces of aluminium foil as the contacts and detect when they are connected. Maybe you could make a pressure pad for your foot, or have pieces of foil taped to your knees and complete the circuit by bringing them together.

---

**YOUR TURN!** Connect up multiple switches and LEDs and modify the code to make a game. You could have a different score for each button, or deduct points if you press the wrong button at the wrong time. You could build your own game like whack-a-mole.

When you become more experienced at coding, if you are really adventurous, you could create a network version and play against a friend over the Internet.

---

## What Will You Interface?

Computing becomes more interesting when it is connected to the world. Interfacing allows computers to sense and manipulate the world through inputs and outputs. Most computers sense the world by detecting a voltage on an input pin, and affect the world by allowing a current to flow through an actuator such as an LED or motor. Relays can be considered as an equivalent to switches, whereas open-collector outputs have to be wired up in a particular way.

With a basic understanding of electricity and the right sensors and actuators you can make the world a smarter place. As computers become more sophisticated we can build even smarter solutions. In the future, you might build a robot that would listen for your commands. Although that may seem complicated to program, as you have seen, computing is about breaking a challenge down into lots of simple parts, and then each little part becomes solvable.

# Chapter **10**
## The Twittering Toy

**by Dr. Andrew Robinson**

### In This Chapter

- ❍ Make a soft toy read out tweets and move
- ❍ Learn about text-to-speech
- ❍ Discover object-orientated programming
- ❍ Gain experience building Python modules
- ❍ Access Twitter from your program

**IN THIS CHAPTER** you'll make use of the Twitter library to bring a soft toy to life. At the end of this chapter, you can have your very own animatronic chicken that waddles and moves its beak as it reads aloud tweets from a particular user or containing a certain hash tag.

This project illustrates that one of the joys of the Raspberry Pi is the ease of reusing existing code. Programmers strive for efficiency (some people call it laziness) and aim to never type the same thing twice. What's even better is never having to write the code in the first place and using someone else's!

This chapter will cover how to hack a toy to connect it to the Raspberry Pi and how to install a Python module to talk to Twitter and interact with an external program (in this case a text-to-speech engine) from Python.

## Hacking the Toy

You are going to take an animated toy and "hack" it so the Raspberry Pi can control its movement. You'll do this by wiring one of the relays on the PiFace interface to replace the toy's on-off switch.

| NOTE | The word *hack* in regard to computing has become associated with illegal activity. In this sense, hacking is bad and not something to engage in. However, to programmers, a *hack* is a way to make something work, particularly when reusing something or repurposing it in a clever way. |
|------|----|

There are many animatronic and robotic toys available online and in novelty shops. It's easy to modify the simple toys that have just a basic on-off switch. Before hacking your toy, it's worth considering what happens if something goes wrong – it's best not to hack an expensive toy or one you're particularly fond of, just in case you struggle to put it back together again. You may wish to build your own toy from components instead.

## Building the Chicken

I chose to build a twittering chicken around the Head and Mouth Mechanism shown in Figure 10-1 from Rapid Electronics (www.rapidonline.com/Education/Head-and-mouth-mechanism-60675). The mechanism contains a battery case, a motor, gears and a switch. On this web page, you'll find a free data sheet with a fabric pattern for making the chicken cover (as well as for a bird and a whale with other mechanisms).

Yellow fur for the body and red felt for the wattle and comb can be purchased from a local fabric shop, and a local craft shop or market is an ideal hunting ground for suitable materials like stick-on eyes. What's great about building your own toy is the opportunity for customisation – feel free to experiment. It shouldn't be too hard to modify the chicken pattern into the Linux mascot "tux the penguin". You could share your pattern online for other people too.

FIGURE 10-1:
A naked
chicken – the
mechanism that
makes the toy
move.

## Wiring

You will connect the relay in parallel with the switch. This allows the relay to override the switch to turn the toy on.

Open the case by removing the four screws as shown in Figure 10-2, taking care not to lose any bits or move parts too far out of alignment.

An important skill of hacking is remembering how you take something apart so you can put it all back together. You could try filming it with a camera phone or similar, so you can play it back to see which part goes where.

**TIP**

# Series and Parallel Circuits

*Series* and *parallel* are two names to classify how components in a circuit are connected. In series, as the name suggests, the electric current flows through all the components in a series, one after another. As such, if you have switches wired in series, then all of them have to be closed for the current to flow. Breaking one of them will break the circuit.

In parallel, the flow of electricity splits and so closing any switch wired in parallel will allow the current to flow. This is because electricity tends to take the path of least resistance, which in parallel circuits will be through any closed switch. For the toy, the closed PiFace Digital relay contacts will bypass the toy's open switch.

FIGURE 10-2:
Removing the
case of the
movement
mechanism.

Try and identify how the wires are connected to form the circuit. Find the terminals on the power switch. These may be covered with glue, but this can be carefully peeled or scraped away. In many cases, there will be only two wires going to the switch; if there are more, then the wiring is more complex, and it may be better to hack a different model if you cannot easily identify how the circuit works.

Attach another wire to each of the wires already connected to the terminals as shown in Figure 10-3. A soldering iron is the most secure way to do this, but you could also twist the wire onto the terminal and secure with tape. Briefly, touch the free ends of the wires you just joined together to check that your model moves. Find an appropriate hole to pass them through to the outside of the model, taking care that they don't catch on any moving parts. Adding a blob of glue or tying a loose knot on the inside will relieve some of the strain on the connections.

FIGURE 10-3: Add wires (shown as white in the figure) in parallel to the switch and add a knot to stop it from pulling through.

It is now time to reassemble your toy and the time when you discover how much attention you were paying when you took it apart! All things being well, your toy should go back together looking no worse after its surgery, as shown in Figure 10-4, and you shouldn't have any parts left over. Briefly touch the wires together again to make sure that your toy still comes to life.

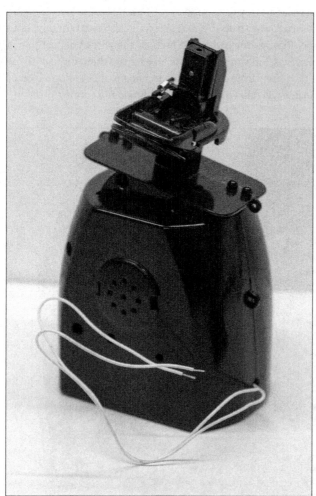

FIGURE 10-4:
Toy post-surgery showing no ill effects. Touch the wires together to make the toy move.

## Making It Talk

You'll use the espeak text-to-speech (TTS) program to read aloud the tweets.

## How TTS Works

A TTS engine typically works by splitting the words into syllables and then synthesising the word by concatenating (combining) corresponding sounds. In most TTS engines, the computer has no understanding of the words, so the output is monotone. However, TTS is an exciting area of research in computer science, attempting to make it sound more human. Latest research efforts include modelling the human voice box to generate more realistic sounds on virtual vocal chords, and another project to try and understand what is being said to vary pitch, delivery speed and rhythm.

After you've followed the instructions below to install espeak, you can see more about what espeak is doing if you run it with -X. For example, from a terminal run espeak -X "hello world".

## Uses of TTS

TTS is used when a visual display isn't appropriate. This includes assistive technology for people with visual impairments or when it is not possible to look at a screen, a satnav or automatic telephone exchanges.

If the computer is required to say just a few hundred different words, then for better quality, an actor will record the separate words, with the computer forming sentences and playing back a sequence of clips separated by short pauses. In some applications, there are too many different words to have a recording of each one, so the computer will generate them from syllables. In the case of a satnav, it's a lot of work recording the name of every road and every place. Some words will be frequently used so they may be recorded, and a mixture of synthesized TTS and recorded may be used. You might like to try putting your own voice in the soft toy by recording a set of words and writing a program that plays them back. See the "More Ideas" section at the end of this chapter.

Install espeak by typing the following in a terminal:

```
sudo apt-get install espeak
```

Plug in some speakers and then test that TTS works by typing this in a terminal:

```
espeak "hello world from espeak"
```

**TIP** If you cannot hear sound, you may need to change how audio is routed. The Raspberry Pi can output sound via the HDMI cable or the audio jack socket. It will try to automatically select the correct one, but that doesn't always work with some displays. To switch it by hand, type `sudo amixer cset numid=3` $n$, where $n$ is 0 for automatic, 1 for audio jack and 2 for HDMI.

## Using Espeak in Python

The next step is to call the espeak program from Python. Because you might want other programs that you write in the future to use espeak, you'll create a module for it. It's worth studying how the module works because it shows how you can run another program from Python, which can be very useful. Enter the following code into `espeak.py`:

```
import subprocess

def say(words):
    #Speaks words via espeak text to speech engine
    devnull = open("/dev/null", "w")
    subprocess.call([
            "espeak",
            "-v", "en-rp", # english received pronunciation
            words],
            stderr=devnull)
```

Let's take a brief tour of the code. The first line imports the subprocess module that allows other programs to be called. Put simply, a program running on a computer is called a *process*, so if it wants to run another program, then (similar to calling a function) it creates another subprocess with a call.

`def` defines the `say` function that is passed a string of words to say. Next, the file `/dev/null` is opened for writing. On Linux, `/dev/null` is a special file that throws away anything written to it. It's a really good way of ignoring any output produced. In this case, it's used to hide any error messages produced by espeak. If you replaced `/dev/null` with a real filename, then any error message would be saved there instead.

Finally, the `subprocess.call` function calls the program `"espeak"` with an array of arguments to pass to it. In this case, if the `words` argument contained `hello`, it would be the same as typing the following:

```
espeak -v en-rp hello
```

This shows that multiple arguments can be passed to a command. The `-v en-rp` is used to specify how espeak sounds. It can be fun to play around with different pronunciations, or even languages.

## Testing the Espeak module

Now is a good time to check the Python module you've just created. Enter the following into the file `try_espeak.py`:

```python
#!/usr/bin/env python
# try_espeak.py
# Show use of espeak.py
import espeak as talker
def main():
    talker.say("Hello World")
if __name__ == '__main__':
    main()
```

Run `try_espeak.py` and check that you hear "Hello World" from the speakers.

---

Try espeak with different pronunciation options, such as American or caricatures of British accents such as Northern, West Midlands or Scottish. The codes needed are described in the espeak documentation at `http://espeak.sourceforge.net/languages.html`. You could add another argument to the `say` function in Python and pass information to set the accent. If you are really adventurous, you could try passing pitch, speed and voice arguments, and you'll get some very silly sounding voices.

**YOUR TURN!**

---

## Making It Move

The next step is to turn on the motors of the toy to make the mouth move while it is speaking. To control the motors, you'll use PiFace Digital. You should have set up PiFace Digital as specified in Chapter 9, "Test Your Reactions". Because there are LEDs on the board, these will indicate that the outputs are active so you can test the code before connecting the chicken. Create a new file named `chicken.py` and enter the following:

```python
import piface.pfio as pfio
import espeak as talker

VERBOSE_MODE = True


class Chicken():
```

```
#The wobbling/talking chicken
def __init__(self, pfio, pin):
    pfio.init()
    self.pfio = pfio
    self.relay_pin = pin

def start_wobble(self):
    #Starts wobbling the chicken
    self.pfio.digital_write(self.relay_pin,1)
    if VERBOSE_MODE:
        print "Chicken has started wobbling."

def stop_wobble(self):
    #Stops wobbling the chicken
    self.pfio.digital_write(self.relay_pin,0)
    if VERBOSE_MODE:
        print "Chicken has stopped wobbling."

def say(self, text_to_say):
    #Makes the chicken say something
    if VERBOSE_MODE:
        print "Chicken says: %s" % text_to_say
    talker.say(text_to_say)


def test_chicken():
    #create a sample Chicken object called tweetyPi
    tweetyPi = Chicken(pfio,1)
    tweetyPi.start_wobble()
    tweetyPi.say("hello world")
    tweetyPi.stop_wobble()

if __name__ == '__main__':
    test_chicken()
```

With a speaker connected, run the preceding script and check that it works. You should hear the relay click (and see the corresponding LED illuminate) on the PiFace interface, the sound "hello world" come from the speaker and then the relay click off again.

Looking back at the code, you should notice a couple of points. The line VERBOSE_MODE = True is an example of a constant. It is set by the programmer and then never changes – in other words, it remains constant. In this case, it provides an easy way to turn on and off debugging information in one place. With it turned on, you'll receive messages saying when the chicken should start moving and stop. Without these messages, if the chicken wasn't moving, you wouldn't know if the problem was with this module, or whether the problem was elsewhere.

Being able to see what is going on in a program is very important when debugging. Computer scientists describe it has having *good visibility*. One way to achieve this is to have print statements at key points in a program so as it executes you can follow its progress and the state of data. It's very common for a program to not work perfectly the first time, so designing it to make it easy to debug can save time in the long run, particularly when you might add a new feature later.

**TIP**

## Creating Classes

The file chicken.py makes uses a particular style of programming called *object-orientated programming (OOP)*. You don't need to worry too much if you don't understand the code at the moment; there are more examples of OOP in other chapters in the book.

OOP is a handy way to group code and data together. Think about any object in the real world: It has characteristics, also called *attributes,* and it has things that can be done to it. For example, a balloon's attributes include its colour and if it is inflated. Actions that can be done to it include blowing it up or popping it. You may have a room full of different balloons, but they can all be considered to share the same set of attributes and actions (even though the value of the attribute, like the colour, might be different). As such, they are all the same class of object.

In OOP, the programmer designs his or her own classes of objects, which have a set of attributes and functions. In chicken.py, the Chicken class of the object is defined by class Chicken():. The next indented block defines the methods (another name for functions) of the class. There are methods to start and stop the chicken from moving and one to make it speak. The __init__ method is a special method that is called when an object is created. In this case, it calls the pfio initialisation method (to initialise the PiFace interface) and sets up the object's attributes. This can be handy, as you can use your object without worrying about what you need to do to initialise things first. So far, the program has only created a class for the chicken. It hasn't created an actual object, merely a description of what a Chicken object will be like. It's a bit like creating a cookie cutter – you've defined what shape the cookies will be, but you've not actually created any cookies yet.

## Creating Objects

A Chicken object is created in the test_chicken function. It is outside the class definition (and therefore not part of the Chicken class) because it's not within the indented block. The statement tweetyPi = Chicken(pfio,0) creates a new Chicken object called tweetyPi. The arguments are used to pass in the PiFace Digital interface and identify which pin the motor is connected to.

Imagine if you had multiple chickens, one connected to each of the relays on PiFace. You could create two chickens by typing the following:

```
tweetyPi1 = Chicken(pfio,0)
tweetyPi2 = Chicken(pfio,1)
```

Now, if you wanted to start them both wobbling you could type this:

```
tweetyPi1.start_wobble()
tweetyPi2.start_wobble()
```

By using objects, you can use the same function for each chicken. You don't have to worry about which pin they are connected to after you've created the object because the object stores it for you. This is an example of why using OOP can be advantageous.

OOP can be tricky to understand at first, but it should become clearer as you see more examples. For now, you can ignore the details, accept that it works and hide it in the chicken module, in the same way you use other modules without knowing what is inside them. Believe it or not, professional programmers do this too – as long as the interface to a module is clear (that is, the functions it provides are clearly documented), it doesn't matter if they don't fully understand how it works!

## Breaking Up Your Code

Chapter 2, "Introductory Software Project: The Insult Generator", talks about splitting programs up into functions and how important it is to structure your code in computing.

In this example, separate files are used for modules to help structure the program. Classes also help by grouping related data and functions together.

As you will see, what may have sounded like a daunting task of making a Twitter-enabled soft toy move and talk becomes manageable when tackled in smaller chunks. You also tested each chunk so it's easier to see where a problem is. Similarly, as you become more experienced, you'll be able to take almost any big and seemingly hard problem, and split it up into little steps. Why not try it? Think of a project you want to do, and then think how you can split it up into smaller parts. Hopefully, as you complete the projects in this book, you'll learn the skills necessary to implement each of these little parts, and you'll be able to build almost anything!

## Testing As You Go

If you wrote a huge program and tried to run it, chances are it wouldn't work the first time. You'd then have to go through all of it trying to find where the problem was. Instead, it is better to test as you go, checking each component before moving on to the next. Python provides a good means to do this. Toward the end of the file are the following lines:

```
if __name__ == '__main__':
    test_chicken()
```

This code calls the `test_chicken()` function if the file is being run by itself, but doesn't call the function if it is imported as a module. As such, it's a good way of writing code that will test the behaviour of a module. As you learn more about programming, you will understand the importance of testing and which tools and techniques can help.

---

Surrounding or starting a word with __ in Python (and some other languages) indicates a special meaning. As such, it's better not to start and end your own variables and functions this way unless you really know what you're doing!

**TIP**

---

# Connecting to Twitter

The `python-twitter` module makes it very easy to read from Twitter. Unfortunately the module isn't prepackaged for Debian Linux. Luckily it's not too difficult to build it from source and doing so will give you good experience that will come in handy if you need to install another module in the future. You'll also see what it's like to use someone else's module, which will be an advantage if you write modules that you want other people to reuse. You'll discover that it is just as important to write good documentation as it is to write good code.

## Building and Installing Python Modules

The module's home page `http://code.google.com/p/python-twitter` contains a summary of how to build the module. If you've never built a module before, you're better off following the more detailed steps in this chapter.

The website lists and links to dependencies; these are other modules that must be built first. `python-twitter` requires `simplejson`, `httplib2` and `python-oauth2` to be installed. Step-by-step installation instructions are provided in this chapter.

**TIP** It's possible to download files from the command line in Linux without using a web browser. There are two main programs to choose from: either `curl` or `wget`. Both provide similar functionality, so deciding which one to use comes down to personal preference and/or availability. `wget` is used for the examples in this chapter.

### simplejson

Clicking the `http://cheeseshop.python.org/pypi/simplejson` link redirects you to `http://pypi.python.org/pypi/simplejson`.

**TIP** Note that the version numbers may be different as the library is updated, in which case, you should replace `simplejson-3.3.0.tar.gz` with whatever filename you have downloaded.

From a terminal, type the following (all on one line) to download the code:

```
wget http://pypi.python.org/packages/source/s/simplejson/
simplejson-3.3.0.tar.gz
```

The `tar.gz` file extension tells you that the file is zipped to save space and is a *tar archive*. A tar archive is often used in Linux as it provides a convenient way to package multiple files and preserve file permissions and other attributes. It is possible to unzip the file and then untar a file as separate operations, but because so many tar archives are compressed, it is possible to do it in a single action. To unzip and untar the compressed archive, type the following on the command line:

```
tar xvf simplejson-3.0.7.tar.gz
```

As the command executes, it lists the files as they are expanded (unpacked) from the archive.

## Using tar

You can create your own zipped archives by typing the following:

```
tar czvf <archivename.tar.gz> <list of files and directories>
```

Tar has many different options, but in most cases `czvf`, `xvf` or `tvf` will be sufficient. `t`,`c` and `x` mean test (list the contents of an archive), compress and expand an archive, respectively. `v` indicates that tar should be verbose and list the files as it expands them. `f` is used to specify the filename of the archive.

Change into the newly expanded directory by typing the following in a terminal:

```
cd simplejson-3.3.7
```

On Linux, most software that is supplied as source code shares a similar installation process of extract, build and install. Many Python modules follow this same pattern. Because a malicious user could insert a module that would cause harm, you need to use sudo to provide enough access privileges to install the module. Type the following to install the package:

```
python setup.py build
sudo python setup.py install
```

After the module has installed, return to the parent directory by typing the following:

```
cd ..
```

### httplib2

Follow the same procedure to install the httplib2 package from http://code.google.com/p/httplib2. In a terminal, type the following:

```
wget http://httplib2.googlecode.com/files/httplib2-0.8.tar.gz
tar xvf httplib2-0.8.tar.gz
cd httplib2-0.8
python setup.py build
sudo python setup.py install
cd ..
```

### python-oauth2

python-oauth2 is hosted on GitHub at http://github.com/simplegeo/python-oauth2, so you obtain it through git rather than wget. In a terminal, type the following:

```
git clone "http://github.com/simplegeo/python-oauth2"
cd python-oauth2
python setup.py build
sudo python setup.py install
cd ..
```

The final step is to install the `python-twitter` module:

```
wget "http://python-twitter.googlecode.com/files/⤴
python-twitter-0.8.2.tar.gz"
tar xvf python-twitter-0.8.2.tar.gz
cd python-twitter-0.8.2
python setup.py build
sudo python setup.py install
cd ..
```

If you have IDLE open, close all the windows and restart it so it can access the newly installed modules.

# Talking to Twitter

Twitter requires programs that access it automatically to send authentication information with requests. This allows Twitter to prevent abuse by blocking programs that put too much load on its servers. Your program will authenticate itself to Twitter by sending secret tokens.

### Getting Access Tokens for Twitter

You will need to get four pieces of information by signing into the developers' part of Twitter. This section explains how to get a `consumer_key`, `consumer_secret`, `access_token_key` and `access_token_secret`. The names sound confusing, but all they are is a secret code that will identify you and your program to Twitter.

Visit `https://dev.twitter.com/apps/new` and log in. (You will need to sign up to Twitter if you don't have an account.) If you're not old enough to have your own Twitter account you could ask a parent, guardian or teacher to do this for you.

Enter the name of your application, a brief description and a website. If you don't have a website you could enter `www.example.com` as a placeholder. Read the terms and click to indicate your acceptance of the terms. Fill in the CAPTCHA and then click Create Your Twitter Application. You may need to enter a different name for your application if it is already in use; you could try prefixing it with your Twitter username.

Upon success, scroll down and click Create My Access Token. Wait up to a minute and reload the page.

Make a note of the Consumer Key and Consumer Secret entries from the OAuth section, and Access Token and Access Token Secret from the Your Access Token section because you will need to include these in your program.

**Writing Code to Talk to Twitter**

With the Python modules installed, it is time to write the code that will talk to Twitter. Create a new file named twitter_tag_listen.py, containing the following code:

```python
#!/usr/bin/env python

#twitter_tag_listen.py
#listens for new tweets containing a search term

import time
import sys
import twitter

DEFAULT_SEARCH_TERM = "chicken" #what we search twitter for
TIME_DELAY = 30 # seconds between each status check

def main():
#replace values for consumer_key, consumer_secret,
#access_token_key and access_token_secret with the values
#you made a note of from the Twitter website.
        api = twitter.Api(consumer_key='xxxxxxcxK9I3g',⤸
consumer_secret='xxxxxfLBmh0gqHohRdkEH891B2XCv00',⤸
access_token_key='xxxxx25-Dw8foMCfNec2Gff72qxxxxxwMwomXYo',⤸
access_token_secret='xxxxxxjIuFb88dI')

        previous_status = twitter.Status()

        # has user passed command line argument?
        if len(sys.argv) > 1:
                search_term = sys.argv[1]
        else:
                search_term = DEFAULT_SEARCH_TERM

        #alternative form of print statement to display contents ⤸
                of a variable
        print "Listening to tweets containing the word '%s'."⤸
                % search_term

        while True:
                # grab the first tweet containing the ⤸
                search_term
                current_status = api.GetSearch(term=search_term,⤸
                count=1)[0]
```

```
    if current_status.id != previous_status.id:
                        #if the result we get from twitter is
                        #different from what we got last time,
                        # we know there's a new tweet
                        print current_status
                        previous_status = current_status

            # wait for a short while before checking again
            time.sleep(TIME_DELAY)

if __name__ == "__main__":
        main()
```

Run the code to test it. Obviously, you need to be connected to the Internet for it to work. The program should print the latest tweets that contain the word *chicken*. Press Ctrl + C to stop the program.

You are nearly ready to add in the code that controls the toy, but before you do, it is worth looking at how the code works.

By now you should be recognising statements in the program. First you import three modules that you need. The `Time` module provides the `sleep()` function that creates the delay between each time you check Twitter. The `Sys` module provides a way to get command-line arguments. Next constants are defined before the main function begins.

The Twitter module is written in OOP style, so you create a Twitter `api` object with the following statement:

```
api = twitter.Api(consumer_key='xxxxxxcxK9I3g',⮐
consumer_secret='xxxxxfLBmh0gqHohRdkEH891B2XCv00',⮐
access_token_key='xxxxx25-Dw8foMCfNec2Gff72qxxxxxxwMwomXYo',⮐
access_token_secret='xxxxxxjIuFb88dI')
```

You check if any command-line arguments were used by checking the length (that is, the number of items) in `sys.argv`. If there's at least one, then you set the `search_term` to be the first argument:

```
# has user passed command line argument?
if len(sys.argv) > 1:
```

```
        search_term = sys.argv[1]
else:
        search_term = DEFAULT_SEARCH_TERM
```

## Command-Line Options and Arguments

When you run a Python program from the command line, you can follow it with a list of arguments. This provides an easy way to pass data into a program at startup and is typically used to pass names of files or configuration options. For many programs, if you run it with just the –h option, it will display simple help and summarise the options and arguments available. To try this with espeak, type the following from a terminal to display a summary of command-line options:

```
espeak -h
```

In the `twitter_tag_listen.py` example, because your program only takes one argument, you read it from the list held by `sys.argv`. However, as you begin to master Python and your programs get more complicated, you may wish to use the `argparse` module that splits up the arguments and can automate generating usage information.

Finally, you enter the main loop – a block of code that will keep going around in a loop, running again and again. This is a `while` loop, which is discussed in Chapter 2.

In this program you use the condition `True`, to make it loop indefinitely. To stop the program, press Ctrl + C. In Linux, this keyboard combination sends a message from the operating system to interrupt the program, which in most cases will *terminate* it (cause it to stop running).

With all the components written and tested, it's the moment of truth: Will they work together?

## Putting It All Together

Connect the wires from your toy to the common and normally open relay contact terminals on PiFace Digital as shown in Figure 10-5. The code example in this chapter uses relay 0, which is the bottom two terminals nearest to JP3 and the Raspberry Pi expansion pins. You can use the manual override button in the emulator as described in Chapter 9 to check that the toy moves when the relay is turned on.

FIGURE 10-5:
Wiring the toy
up to the
normally open
relay contacts.

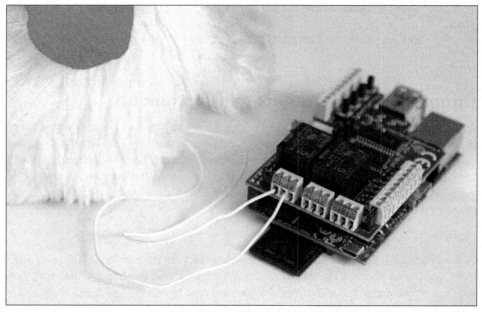

Update the `twitter_tag_listen.py` code to control the hardware and speak as follows:

1. Import your `chicken` and `piface.pfio` modules.

2. Create a Chicken object called `chick` and pass in the number of the output pins wired up to the toy.

3. Instead of printing a tweet, add three statements to start the chick wobbling, say the tweet and then stop the chick from wobbling.

The code for `twitter_tag_listen.py` is shown in full in Listing 10-1, with the necessary updates in bold.

**Listing 10-1**    twitter_tag_listen.py

```
#!/usr/bin/env python

#twitter_tag_listen.py
#listens for new tweets containing a search term
#and then wobbles a chicken

import time
import sys
import twitter

import chicken
```

```python
import piface.pfio as pfio

DEFAULT_SEARCH_TERM = "chicken" #what we search twitter for
TIME_DELAY = 30 # seconds between each status check

def main():
        api = twitter.Api(consumer_key='xxxxxxcxK9I3g',↲
consumer_secret='xxxxxfLBmh0gqHohRdkEH891B2XCv00',↲
access_token_key='xxxxx25-Dw8foMCfNec2Gff72qxxxxxwMwomXYo',↲
access_token_secret='xxxxxxjIuFb88dI')
        previous_status = twitter.Status()
        chick = chicken.Chicken(pfio,0)

        # has user passed command line argument?
        if len(sys.argv) > 1:
                search_term = sys.argv[1]
        else:
                search_term = DEFAULT_SEARCH_TERM

        #alternative form of print statement to display contents↲
                of a variable
        print "Listening to tweets containing the word↲
'%s'." % search_term

        while True:
                # grab the first tweet containing the
                # search_term
                current_status = api.GetSearch(term=↲
search_term, count=1)[0]

                # if the status is different
                # then pass it to the chick.say function
                if current_status.id != previous_status.id:
                        chick.start_wobble()
                        chick.say(current_status.text)
                        chick.stop_wobble()
                        previous_status = current_status

                # wait for a short while before checking again
                time.sleep(TIME_DELAY)

if __name__ == "__main__":
        main()
```

Try it! Run the code and you should have an animated, talking toy that responds to Twitter. Don't forget you can make the file executable by running the following in a terminal:

```
chmod a+x twitter_tag_listen.py
```

Try out different search terms by passing in arguments. For example, type the following in a terminal to search for the hash tag `RaspberryPi`:

```
./twitter_tag_listen.py "#raspberrypi"
```

**TIP**   Note that you have to enclose the tag in quotes. This tells the command line to ignore the special meaning that # has, and to pass it through to your program as part of the argument. It's the same principle as putting strings in quotes in Python.

# Wrapping Up

By now you should have your own animatronic, twittering soft toy. You've also seen the advantages of breaking a program up into manageable parts and reusing other people's code. Becoming a programmer is sometimes like being a plumber – it's about connecting up functions, with data flowing between them. If you're struggling with your own program design, try splitting it up into a set of smaller problems, and keep splitting until all the problems are really simple to code. Not only is it less daunting at the design stage, but by testing stage-by-stage, it's harder for bugs to hide and easier for you to find them. When writing functions, you've seen the need for good *observability for testing and debugging* – that is, you can see what is going on inside them so you can check that they work and fix them when they don't!

You've also seen the need for good documentation. If other people are going to reuse your code, then they need clear instructions about how to install the program, what other modules it depends on and what arguments each function takes and does.

Practically, you've also learned about using tar and untar for packaging up sets of files and how to build and install Python modules.

**YOUR TURN!**   There are lots of ways you can customise the twittering soft toy; why not try some of the following suggestions? Don't forget to film what you make, upload it to YouTube and tag it with `Raspberry Pi Projects Book`.

## More Ideas

There are many things you can do with your own toy. Here are some suggestions:

○ Try changing the arguments passed to espeak. (Don't forget that –h will give you a list of options.) For example, you could try

- Different languages

- Different voices, both male and female

- Changing pitch

- Changing speed

Here's an example of how you could change espeak.py:

```
import subprocess

DEFAULT_PITCH = 50  # 0-99
DEFAULT_SPEED = 160 # words per min


def say(words, pitch=None, speed=None):
    if not pitch:
        pitch = DEFAULT_PITCH

    if not speed:
        speed = DEFAULT_SPEED

    devnull = open("/dev/null", "w")
    try:
        subprocess.call([
            "espeak",
            "-v", "en-rp", # english received pronunciation
            "-p", str(pitch),
            "-s", str(speed),
            words],
            stderr=devnull)
```

○ You could change the speech parameters depending on who is talking or the content of the tweet.

○ You could connect multiple soft toys, each with different voices, and have a conversation. (Hint: Create `chick0 = chicken.Chicken(pfio,0)` and `chick1 = chicken.Chicken(pfio,1)` and then wire a different chicken up to each relay.)

○ You could control more motors in your soft toy and make it dance if it detects certain hash tags.

○ If you're really adventurous, you could replace the `espeak.py` module completely with a module that splits simple phrases up into words and plays a sound recording of yourself saying each of the words for a more natural sound. Chapter 17, "The Techno-Bird Box, a Wildlife Monitor", uses the `split` function, and Chapter 5, "Ping", shows how to play sounds.

# Chapter **11**
## Disco Lights

**by Mike Cook**

## In This Chapter

○ Using individual bits in variables to define individual LEDs

○ Connecting external LEDs to your PiFace board

○ Writing a Python program user interface that looks like any windowed application

○ Customising the user interface to use your own choice of colours

○ Getting input from music

IN MY YOUTH, during the late 60s, I answered an advertisement in the *Manchester Evening News* for someone to turn lights on and off in time to the music in an Ashton-under-Lyne night club. I went to the interview that Friday evening, which consisted of their showing me the lighting control rig and saying I had to be there by 7:30 p.m. on Saturday and Sunday. To be honest, I didn't fancy five hours of switching lights on and off for just £1.00, so I arrived the following evening on my Lambretta with a rucksack full of electronics. I had a large multiway switch used in telephone exchanges called a uniselector (you can still get these on eBay), which was wired up to make an on/off control of five circuits. I started hacking the lighting panel, and before long, I had five coloured spotlights flashing away while I put my feet up.

These days, you cannot go hacking about with mains like that – health and safety would have a fit. And with the Raspberry Pi, you have the opportunity to do something a lot more sophisticated. So in this chapter, you are going to see how to control those disco lights, and change the pattern with a click of a mouse. Not only that, but you will see how to drive the light sequence from the beat of the music.

In this chapter, you'll learn how to write a Python program to define a sequence of lights. You'll also learn about various aspects of electronics and control.

## Defining Your Sequence

So far in this book, you have written programs that interact through the Python console. Now you are going to produce a proper desktop application. This would be quite a daunting prospect if it were not for the help that you can get from a Python package that does a lot of the under-the-hood hard work for you. This just leaves you to specify exactly what things should look like. This package also integrates the windows style selected for your whole desktop, so the result looks consistent with other applications.

This package is called `pygame` and comes preloaded in most Raspberry Pi distributions. It consists of a number of functions to create and update windows, draw in the windows, register a mouse click and read the keyboard. It will also handle sound and music, but you will not be looking at that function this time.

Start IDLE, and select a new window. For a start let's look at Listing 11-1, a very basic piece of code to open a window and close it down.

---

Listing 11-1  **Windows1 Test Program**

```
#!/usr/bin/env python
"""
Window1 to open up a window on the desktop
"""
```

```python
import os, pygame, sys

pygame.init()                      # initialise graphics interface
os.environ['SDL_VIDEO_WINDOW_POS'] = 'center'
pygame.display.set_caption("Test Window 1")
screen = pygame.display.set_mode([788,250],0,32)

def main():
        while True :
            checkForEvent()

def terminate(): # close down the program
    print ("Closing down please wait")
    pygame.quit()
    sys.exit()

def checkForEvent(): # see if we need to quit or
                     # look at the mouse
    #print "checking for quit"
    event = pygame.event.poll()
    if event.type == pygame.QUIT :
            terminate()
    elif event.type == pygame.KEYDOWN and event.key == ⏎
pygame.K_ESCAPE :
            terminate()

if __name__ == '__main__':
    main()
```

When you run this, you should get just a black window in the middle of the screen. It won't do much, but it is a real window. You can drag it around the screen, and clicking the minimise icon at the top-right corner will fold up the window and put it on the task bar at the bottom of the screen. Clicking the close cross will quit the program as will pressing the Esc key. When the program quits, you will get a message printed out in blue in the console window along with several lines of red debug information telling you where the program quit.

If you look at the anatomy of the program, you will see things are quite simple. The first few lines tell pygame to create a window, of a certain size, with a certain title and put it in the middle of the screen. The main part of the program is an infinite loop that constantly checks to see if an event has occurred.

In programming terms, an *event* is something happening, which is normally how user interaction gets input to the program. You are looking for a close event or a key up event on the

Esc key. A *close event* is either the user clicking the close cross on the window or the operating system telling the program to quit because it is going to shut down. If your program sees any of those events, it calls a `terminate` function that prints out a message. Then it quits pygame to release any memory it grabbed, and it exits to the operating system.

## Getting the Code to Do More

Well, that was not very exciting, was it? Let's get the code to do a little more. Take a look at Listing 11-2.

Listing 11-2　**Windows2 Test Program**

```python
#!/usr/bin/env python
"""
Window2 to open up a window on the desktop, draw something in it
    and read the mouse position upon a click
"""

import piface.pfio as pfio        # piface library
import os, pygame, sys

pygame.init()                      # initialise graphics interface
pfio.init()                        # initialise pfio
os.environ['SDL_VIDEO_WINDOW_POS'] = 'center'
pygame.display.set_caption("LED controll")
screen = pygame.display.set_mode([190,160],0,32)
box = False

def main():
        drawBox(box)
        while True :
            checkForEvent()

def drawBox(state):
        boxNum = 0
        # first draw the box
        # - fill colour depends on sequence bit state
        if state :
                pygame.draw.rect(screen,(255,0,0), ⤶
(50, 70, 40,40), 0)
        else :
                pygame.draw.rect(screen,(180,180,180),
                    (50, 70, 40,40), 0)
```

```
        #now draw the outline of the box
        pygame.draw.rect(screen,(0,0,180),(50, 70, 40,40), 3)
        pygame.display.update() # refresh the screen
        pfio.write_output(state)

def mouseGet() : # see where we have clicked
        global box
        x,y = pygame.mouse.get_pos()
        print "The mouse has been clicked at ",x,y
        if x in range(50,90) and y in range(50,110) :
                box = not box # toggle the state of the box
                drawBox(box)

def terminate(): # close down the program
    print ("Closing down please wait")
    pygame.quit()
    sys.exit()

def checkForEvent(): # see if we need to quit
                     # or look at the mouse
    #print "checking for quit"
    event = pygame.event.poll()
    if event.type == pygame.QUIT :
            terminate()
    elif event.type == pygame.MOUSEBUTTONDOWN :
            mouseGet()
    elif event.type == pygame.KEYDOWN and event.key == ⤶
pygame.K_ESCAPE :
            terminate()

if __name__ == '__main__':
    main()
```

When you run this, you will get a much smaller window on the desktop with a single square in it. Click in the square, and four things will happen. First the square will turn from grey to red, and then you will hear the relay on the PiFace board come on and see one of the LEDs come on. Finally you will see the position of the mouse when it was clicked printed out in window coordinates. That means that the coordinate value will be the same when clicking the same spot within the window, irrespective of where that window is positioned on the screen. Let's see what's been done here.

This time you add in the call to import the piface library, which is going to control the relay and lights. You set a variable called box to be false, which is called a *logic* or *Boolean value* and can only take on one of two values. You can call these values one and zero or true and false. The main function calls a drawBox function and then enters an endless loop that simply checks the events.

Take a closer look at the drawBox function. It takes in a variable, called state, that defines what colour the box is going to be. It is tested and you use the draw rectangle command from pygame. At first this looks complex, with lots of parameters or numbers in it, but it is quite simple. The first parameter in the command tells where you are going to draw the rectangle, in this case in an area called screen you defined at the start of the program. The next three numbers define the colour you will use in red, green and blue values – these are in brackets because they are one entity that could be replaced by a suitable variable later on called a *tuple*. Next you have four values bracketed as a tuple that define the X and Y coordinates of the rectangle, followed by how wide and how high to draw it. The final value tells the computer how wide a pen to draw this with. A zero is a special case and fills in the whole rectangle. Finally after drawing the rectangle, you have to tell the computer to update what is being shown on the screen.

This way of working means that no matter how complicated or time consuming it is to draw, the user always sees the screen change in a flash. The technical name for this is *double buffering* because one buffer, or area of memory, is being used to display the picture, and the other is being used to construct the next picture. The display update call copies the construction buffer into the display buffer. Note that at this point the display and construction buffers both contain the same thing. Finally in this function the variable state is written out to the PiFace board. As this Boolean variable can only be a zero or a one, then the least significant LED is turned on or off, and all the other LEDs are turned off.

The last thing to look at in this program is the mouseGet function, which is called by the checkForEvent function when it detects a mouse button down event. The mouseGet function first recovers the coordinates of the mouse pointer when it was clicked. Then the compound if statement checks if both the x and y fall within the coordinates of the box. If it does, then you toggle or invert the state of the variable box and then call the function that draws it and writes to the outputs.

So with a mouse click, you can control a light.

## A Small Detour into Theory

Now you've got a program that doesn't just act like a real window application; you can click in the window and control an output. However, before you can go on to looking at a complete sequencer you need to look a little bit about how the LEDs on the PiFace board are related to the value you write to the interface.

The basic unit of storage in a computer is the byte. A *byte* consists of eight bits, each bit being a separate logic level. Rather than think in bit terms, it is easier if you group these bits and consider storage in terms of bytes. However, as you will see you sometimes want to manipulate individual bits in that byte. In the last program you saw that a Boolean variable could only have one of two possible values; however it takes a byte to store that one variable, so all the other bits in it are wasted. If you take a byte, you can store the state of eight LEDs in it. The relationship between the byte, the bits and the LEDs is shown in Figure 11-1.

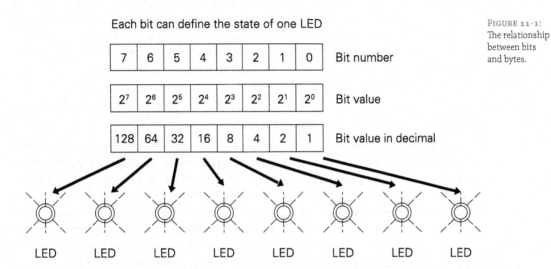

FIGURE 11-1: The relationship between bits and bytes.

So by using a byte variable to store the state of all eight LEDs you can then use a list of these variable to store a sequence of LED patterns. To output each pattern all you have to do is to write out the next variable in the list to the PiFace board.

## Designing the Sequencer

Now that you have all the elements in place you can begin to think about how you want this to look and operate. This is called *top-down design* because you start with a top-level view of what you want the software to look like.

I envisaged a grid of squares, each one representing an LED and its position in the sequence. A column of eight squares would represent the states of the LEDs at any instance in the sequence. A marker under the column will indicate what LEDs are being lit at any time. A mouse click in one of these squares will toggle the LED.

In order to help set up the sequence there should be some control buttons, one to clear or turn off all the LEDs in all sequence positions, and another to toggle or invert all the LEDs. There should be control buttons to determine the speed of the sequence and finally one to select where to take the trigger to advance the sequence from. This last point is important if you want to synchronise the changing of the lights to the beat of the music. The sequence can either be stepped at a regular rate determined by the speed controls, or locked into the beat of the music. This last feature will require a little bit of extra hardware and is optional – you can skip it for now and add it later if you like.

Finally it would be good if all the colours used in the sequence software were customisable; that is, it should be easy to change by changing a single value at one point of the code only. This means that whenever you use a colour you do not hard code it in by putting the colour numbers into a function call, but rather use a variable to define that colour. Those variables for all the colours should be grouped in one place in the code for easy access.

# Implementing the Sequencer

After designing the sequencer from the top down, when it comes to implementing the design it is better to write the code in what is known as a *bottom-up* implementation. That means starting at the lowest possible function and working your way up. Of course, if you just look at the finished code, you don't see that. I started by taking the window test program and writing the functions that showed the columns representing the LEDs in the sequence. Then I expanded it so that I could click on each LED to turn the box on or off. Next came the controls to clear and invert, followed by step indicator. This was followed by the speed controls, and at this point I added the code to actually output something to the LEDs. Finally the auto/external step control was added and the code tidied up. This might not be the sequence of building up a program that first springs to the mind of a beginner, but the idea is to do a little coding and then test. So you are always looking to do something that can be instantly tested, even if it means writing the odd line of code that is not going to make it in the final mix. It also means that if something goes wrong with the test you know you have just written the code with the error in it.

Listing 11-3 shows the sequencer application.

---

**Listing 11-3   The Sequencer Application**

```python
#!/usr/bin/env python
"""
Disco LED sequence display on the PiFace board
"""
import time                      # for delays
import piface.pfio as pfio       # piface library
import os, pygame, sys

pfio.init()                      # initialise pfio
pygame.init()                    # initialise graphics interface
```

```python
os.environ['SDL_VIDEO_WINDOW_POS'] = 'center'
pygame.display.set_caption("LED sequence controller")
screen = pygame.display.set_mode([788,250],0,32)
background = pygame.Surface((788,250))

# define the colours to use for the user interface
cBackground =(255,255,255)
cLEDon = (255,0,0)
cLEDoff = (128,128,128)
cOutline = (255,128,0)
cText = (0,0,0)
cTextBack = (220,220,220)
cStepBlock = (0,255,255)

background.fill(cBackground) # make background colour
font = pygame.font.Font(None, 28)
seq = [ 1 << (temp & 0x7) for temp in range (0,32)]
   # initial sequence
timeInc = 0.3
stepInt = True # getting the step signal from inside the Pi
step = 0 # start point in sequence
nextTime = time.time()
lastSwitch = 0

def main():
        setupScreen()
        while True :
            checkForEvent()
            checkStep()

def checkStep() :
        global step, nextTime, lastSwitch
        if stepInt :
  # if we are getting the step command from the internal timer
            if time.time() > nextTime :
  # is it time to do a next step
                    updateSeq(step)
                    step += 1
                    if step >31 :
                            step = 0
                    nextTime = time.time() + timeInc
        else: # if not look at lowest switch
```

*continued*

**Listing 11-3    continued**

```
                  switchState = pfio.read_input() & 1
                  if switchState != lastSwitch and ⤵
lastSwitch == 0:
                        updateSeq(step)
                        step += 1
                        if step >31 :
                              step = 0
                  lastSwitch = switchState

def updateSeq(n) :
      pygame.draw.rect(screen,cBackground, ⤵
(10, 202,768 ,10), 0) # blank out track
      pygame.draw.rect(screen,cStepBlock, ⤵
(14 + n * 24, 202,10 ,10), 0) # draw new position
      pygame.display.update()
      pfio.write_output(seq[n])

def setupScreen() : # initialise the screen
      screen.blit(background,[0,0]) # set background colour
      drawControl(10,58,"Clear")
      drawControl(86,62,"Invert")
      drawControl(168,68,"Faster")
      drawControl(250,74,"Slower")
      drawControl(350,132,"Auto Step")

      for x in range(0,32) :
            drawCol(x,seq[x])
      pygame.display.update()

def drawControl(xPos,xLen,name) :
      pygame.draw.rect(screen,cTextBack, ⤵
(xPos, 216, xLen,32), 0)
      pygame.draw.rect(screen,cOutline, ⤵
(xPos, 216, xLen,32), 2)
      text = font.render(name, True, cText, cTextBack )
      textRect = text.get_rect()
      textRect.topleft = xPos+4, 220
      screen.blit(text, textRect)

def drawCol(x,value):
      boxNum = 0
      x = 10 + x*24
```

```
        y = 10
        for bit in range(0,8):
                # first draw the box -
                # fill colour depends on sequence bit state
                if ((value >> boxNum) & 1) != 1 :
                        pygame.draw.rect(screen,cLEDoff, ⤸
(x, y + 24*boxNum, 20,20), 0)
                else :
                        pygame.draw.rect(screen,cLEDon, ⤸
(x, y + 24*boxNum, 20,20), 0)
                #now draw the outline of the box
                pygame.draw.rect(screen,cOutline, ⤸
(x, y + 24*boxNum, 20,20), 2)
                boxNum +=1

def mouseGet() : # see where we have
                # clicked and take the appropriate action
        global timeInc, stepInt
        x,y = pygame.mouse.get_pos()
        if y in range(10, 202) and x in range(10, 778 ) :
                bit = (y -10) / 24
                byte = (x- 10) / 24
                seq[byte] ^= 1 << bit
                drawCol(byte,seq[byte])
                pygame.display.update()
        elif y in range(216,248) :
                if x in range(10,58) : # the clear control
                        for a in range(0,32):
                                seq[a] = 0
                                drawCol(a,seq[a])
                        pygame.display.update()
                if x in range(86,148) : # the invert control
                        for a in range(0,32):
                                seq[a] ^= 0xff
                                drawCol(a,seq[a])
                        pygame.display.update()
                if x in range(168,236) : # the faster control
                        timeInc -= 0.05
                        if timeInc <= 0 :
                                timeInc = 0.05
                if x in range(250,324) : # the slower control
                        timeInc += 0.05
                if x in range(350,482) :
```

*continued*

**Listing 11-3   continued**

```
                                # the step source control
                                    stepInt = not stepInt
                                    if stepInt :
                                        drawControl(350,132,⤸
"Auto Step")
                                    else:
                                        drawControl(350,132,⤸
"External Step")
                                    pygame.display.update()
            else:
                    #print "mouse ",x,y

def terminate(): # close down the program
    print ("Closing down please wait")
    pfio.deinit()                                    # close the pfio
    pygame.quit()
    sys.exit()

def checkForEvent():
   # see if we need to quit or look at the mouse
    #print "checking for quit"
    event = pygame.event.poll()
    if event.type == pygame.QUIT :
            terminate()
    elif event.type == pygame.MOUSEBUTTONDOWN :
            mouseGet()
    elif event.type == pygame.KEYDOWN and ⤸
event.key == pygame.K_ESCAPE :
            terminate()

if __name__ == '__main__':
    main()
```

So let's walk through the major sections of the code. It starts off by importing the required libraries and then initialising them and the program's window. Next comes the section where you can customise the colours for the program. I found a black background looks best when you are using the program but a white background looks a lot better when viewed in a book. The next section defines the few global variables needed by the program.

The main function is simple, just four lines: Set up the screen, and then loop forever checking for events to quit or mouse clicks to change what is happening. Finally check if you need to advance the sequence. This sequence advance function follows next, although as you know, the order of the function definitions is not important.

The checkStep function first looks at the variable that defines where the trigger to the next step is coming from. If this is from the internal timer, the time now is compared to when the next step should occur, and if it is time, the updateSeq function is called, and the step variable is incremented and tested to see if it has not gone over the maximum number of steps. If it has then the step variable is reset to zero. This is known as *wrapping around the counter*. Finally the time for the next change is set up by adding the time now to the time increment variable. If the system is set up so that the sequence is advanced on a hardware input then that input is looked at to see if it is different from last time. This indicates a level change or an edge has been detected, and if the input level is now high, it is time to advance the sequence in the same way as before. One line that might puzzle beginners is this:

```
switchState = pfio.read_input() & 1
```

What the & operator does is to perform a bitwise AND operation between what is read and the number 1. The result of this is that the variable switchState just contains the least significant bit of the byte that is read from the PiFace board's input lines. This means you can advance the sequence from the lowest switch or the music by attaching the special beat following circuit to it. I will describe that circuit later in this chapter.

The updateSeq function basically does two jobs; first it updates the position of the sequence indicator square by drawing a long thin rectangle in the background colour to erase the old square, and then drawing a new one. Finally it outputs the next pattern in the sequence with the following line:

```
pfio.write_output(seq[n])
```

This takes the list called seq and extracts the value that is next in the list given by the variable in the square braces and then writes it out to the PiFace board. This single line is what actually does the turning on and off of the lights; everything else just supports this one line.

The setUpScreen function simply calls other functions that draw the basic framework of the screen. So after wiping out everything in the screen buffer and setting it to the background colour there are five calls to draw control boxes. This call takes the parameters of the words in the box, its location in the x axis and the width of the box. Finally the drawCol, or draw column, function is called in a loop 32 times, one for each step in the sequencer. The two parameters it takes is what step in the sequence it is and what bit pattern it is to set it at.

Drawing text under the pygame module is a bit complex. First you have to define your font, which was done at the start of the code; the None parameter is the name of the default font file, and the number used is the font size. You then have to render the font into a bitmap, which is a little bit of a screen buffer that contains only the font characters you want. You then define a rectangle that encompasses the whole of this small bitmap. Then you have to position this rectangle to the correct part of the screen. Finally you transfer that small screen buffer to the main one with the `screen_blit` call giving it the parameters of the screen buffer and where you want it put. See if you can follow those steps in the `drawControl` function.

The `drawCol` function draws a column of boxes, with one colour if that corresponds to a lit LED in the sequence or another colour if it is unlit. In order to do this you have to separate out all the bits from the sequence value. This is done by this line:

```
if ((value >> boxNum) & 1) != 1 :
```

What is happening here is that the variable called `value` is shifted to the left a number of times, defined by what box you are drawing. The AND operation then separates out just the least significant bit of this, as you saw before, and then makes the decision of what to draw based on this bit.

Finally the `mouseGet` function does all the work of dealing with clicks. First it gets the location of the mouse and checks to see if it is in the range of out array of LEDs in the sequence. If it is, it works out what byte or value this location represents in the sequence and what bit within that byte it is. Then this line toggles the bit:

```
seq[byte] ^= 1 << bit
```

It will look a bit odd and so calls for some explanation. The right side of the equals sign makes a number with a one in the bit position that you want to change. This is done by taking the value 1 and shifting it to the left the number of times you calculated when you worked out what bit was clicked. The equals sign is preceded by a caret symbol ^ and means the exclusive OR operation. So this number you have created by shifting is exclusive ORed with the value of the sequence at this point, and it is then put back into the sequence list. It is a shorthand way of saying this:

```
seq[byte] = seg[byte] ^ (1 << bit)
```

When you exclusive OR, or XOR as it is sometimes called, two numbers, the result is that you set bits that are only set to a logic one in one of the numbers and you invert the bits that are a set to a logic one in both numbers. So doing this operation simply inverts the bit corresponding to the bit you have clicked. You can then go and draw the whole column; again you update the screen image when you have finished all the drawing.

Next, the `mouseGet` function looks to see if the mouse has been clicked in any of the control boxes. If it has, it does the appropriate action. Clearing the sequence writes zero in every value in the sequence, while inverting applies an exclusive OR operation to all the bits in every value.

The number 0xff is simply a byte with all bits set to one. This notation is called *hexadecimal* and believe it or not is simpler to think about than decimal when it comes to creating bit patterns. The faster and slower control boxes change the value to add to the nextTime variable. There are also some checks which stop the value from going below zero. Finally the last control changes the variable that determines where the sequence advance is coming from. In order to inform you where the advance trigger is coming from the text in this control box is changed when you click it. Figure 11-2 shows the sequencer as it appears on the screen.

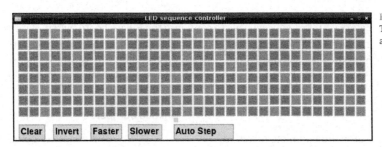

FIGURE 11-2: The sequencer application.

Notice the structure of the code. There is a data structure in a list called seq; it is the values in this list that control what is displayed on the screen, and what is output to the lights. Any changes are made to this list, and then the list is used to change the display as well as providing the output. Note that the screen display is not used to hold data – only reflect it. This is an important principle and is used whenever you try and write a nontrivial piece of code.

## The Lights

The next step is to control some lights rather than the LEDs that are on the PiFace board. While these LEDs are good for testing they are not going to be very impressive in a disco.

The buffer on the PiFace board is capable of switching voltages up to 40V with currents up to half an amp. Now although it can do this on any output, it cannot do this on all the outputs at the same time. That is, there is a collective sum total of current the buffer can switch without getting too hot; this is about 650mA. This works out at about 80mA per output if you are to allow for all outputs to be on at once. What you are going to do is drive an LED strip off each output by using a 12V external power supply. There are two types of LED strips, those that have electronics embedded along the strip so that you can control individual lights in the strip, and those where the whole strip lights up at the same time when you apply voltage to it. You are going to use the latter type, which fortunately is cheaper as well.

These LED strips can be cut up at a point every third light, and every three lights consumes 20mA. Therefore you can tailor the amount of current drawn by simply cutting the appropriate length of strip. Some places sell these by the meter and others by the group of three. The absolutely cheapest place to get them is from the Far East through eBay, although the quality you get can be a bit hit and miss. There will be plenty of stockists that carry them in your home country.

In this project you have two options when it comes to powering these strips. The first is where the length of strip is restricted to 12 LEDs – that is about 130mm. The second is where you can power a strip length up to 0.7 of a meter, but more on that later. First you will look at the 130mm option.

Before you start you will have to configure the PiFace board by removing some of the links. This involves removing jumpers JP4, JP5, JP6 and JP7; this disconnects the internal 5V supply from the PiFace board's output devices and disables the relays. See Figure 11-3 for the position of these on the PiFace board. It is important you do this before connecting anything else up.

FIGURE 11-3:
PiFace jumpers.

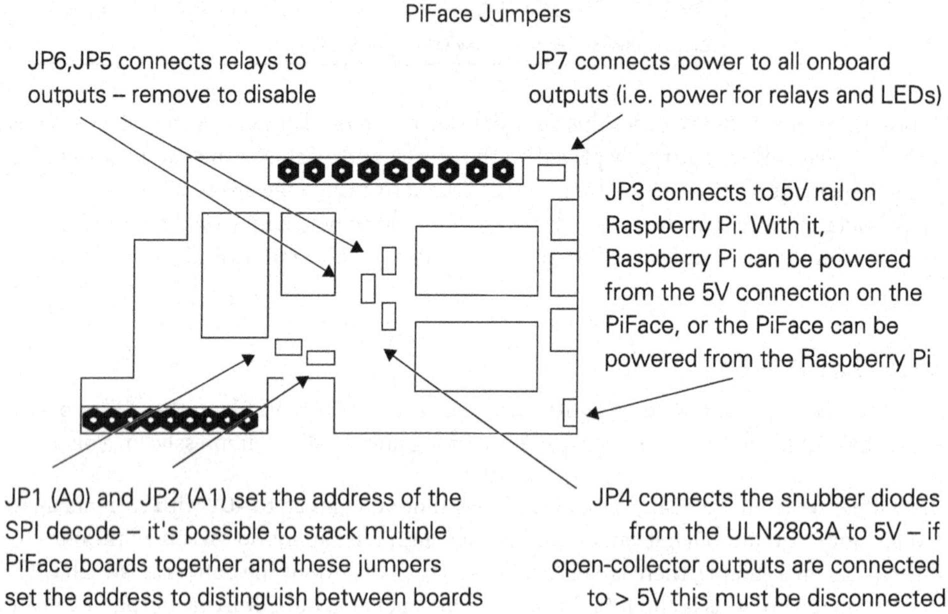

PiFace Jumpers

JP6,JP5 connects relays to outputs – remove to disable

JP7 connects power to all onboard outputs (i.e. power for relays and LEDs)

JP3 connects to 5V rail on Raspberry Pi. With it, Raspberry Pi can be powered from the 5V connection on the PiFace, or the PiFace can be powered from the Raspberry Pi

JP1 (A0) and JP2 (A1) set the address of the SPI decode – it's possible to stack multiple PiFace boards together and these jumpers set the address to distinguish between boards

JP4 connects the snubber diodes from the ULN2803A to 5V – if open-collector outputs are connected to > 5V this must be disconnected

Now the LED strips come in different colours. Normally these are white, red, green, blue and amber, so no doubt you will be wanting some of each. You need to cut up each strip you want to light into smaller strips of 12 LEDs. Figure 11-4 shows you where to cut; you will need a sharp hobby knife or better still a scalpel. Every nine LEDs there is a copper soldering area; however this will not appear on the end of every strip of twelve lights. Not to worry – it is very easy to scrape the green solder mask off the board with a scalpel. If you don't fancy that, you can always use the solder areas in the middle of the strips. You will end up with eight strips all the same length, but you might want a good mix of colours; the white ones do produce the most light however.

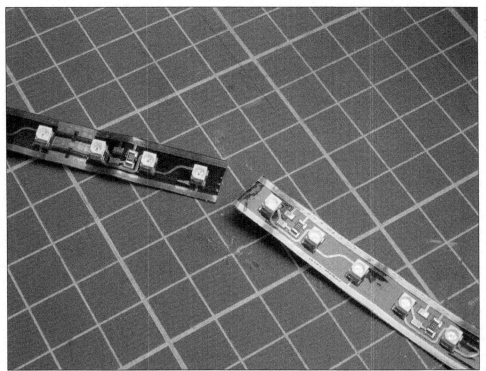

FIGURE 11-4:
Where to cut the
LED strip.

Then, you wire them up so that the positive for each strip is wired to the positive of your 12V power supply. The LED strips are marked with a + and - on the strips at every soldering area. The negative for each strip goes into a separate input of the PiFace board, and finally the right-most connector on the input strip is connected to the negative wire of your power supply. This is shown in Figure 11-5, and it is vital that you get the positive and negative wires from your power supply the right way around. Check this before wiring the strips to the PiFace board. When you have wired up the strip's positive leads to the positive of the power supply, just take the negative lead from the strip and touch it against the negative lead of the power supply; if all is well the strip should light.

Now remove the power and touch the two negative wires again just to discharge the power supply before wiring it up to the PiFace board. Then attach the PiFace board to the Raspberry Pi and boot it up, plug in the 12V power supply and run the software. A note of caution: Never connect anything to the Raspberry Pi when it is powered up; it is easy to have an accident, and you can damage things with incomplete or partial wiring.

FIGURE 11-5:
Wiring the LED
strip to the
PiFace board.

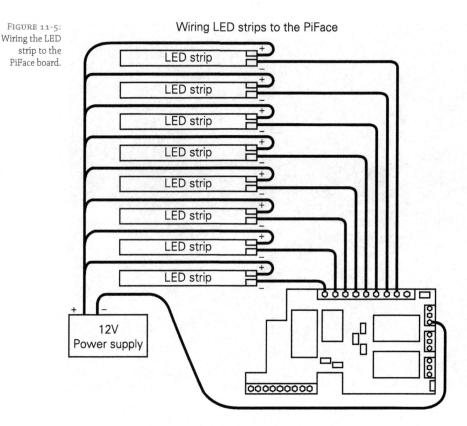

## Using Longer Strip Lights

Now what about the longer strip light I mentioned at the start of the last section? You can draw up to 450mA from each of the outputs from the PiFace board so you can have longer strips of LEDs. This amount of current will drive 66 LEDs or 22 groups of three – this is a strip of 0.7 meters long. However, the down side is that you can't have more than one LED strip lit at any one time. With the existing software it is too easy to make a mistake and set two or more LEDs to come on in each column, but with the changing of just one line in the code you can make the software act as a safety watch dog and only allow one strip light to be on at any one time. The line is in the mouseGet function six lines in, and it is one that has been discussed already:

```
seq[byte] ^= 1 << bit
```

Now take that line and change it to

```
seq[byte] = (seq[byte]  &  (1 << bit) ) ^ (1 << bit)
```

You might also want to change the title of the window and the colour scheme at the start so you can distinguish between the two programs. Also, save it under a different name. What this line now does is clear out the sequence value for all bits except the bit you have clicked, and then it toggles that bit. So if any other bit has been set in that step, it is cleared, and the bit you have clicked is toggled. This prevents you from setting more than one strip to be lit at any one time. However, there is still a slight danger because if you click the invert control, all the outputs but one will be on. To be on the safe side you should remove the following line (10 lines down from the one you just changed):

```
seq[a]  ^= 0xff
```

To tidy up the screen display you should remove the call to `drawControl` that sets up the invert control in the `setupScreen` function. You don't have to buy a strip 0.7 meter long; if you want, you can join strips together if you cannot buy them in the length you want.

Now all you need to do is mount your light strips in some way – maybe a display board above the decks, or hanging down from the ceiling. I mounted the eight strips on an 8 × 10-inch piece of MDF painted black. I arranged them in a fan shape over half a circle. This would stand up nicely under my monitor. The display is startlingly different depending on what you put in front of the LEDs. If you use nothing, they are very raw but do shed a lot of light. A thin styrene sheet of 0.5mm or less thickness acts as a good diffuser if placed close to the LEDs. However, if you set it just a few inches in front of them, the diffusion is much greater, and you no longer see the individual lights but bars of colour. Finally another good diffuser is a few layers of clear bubble wrap, the round bubbles in it nicely complementing the individual round LEDs. Your imagination, design skill and venue will allow you to put these strips, be they short or long, into many a pleasing configuration. However, if you want to cover the dance floor with them, you will have to install them behind acrylic sheets to prevent their being stamped on.

## Making the Lights Move

Now so far you have looked at stepping the sequence along using the internal timers or an external push button, and if that is as far as you want to take this project, then fine. However, the next step is to have the music drive the change in sequence. Unfortunately this may not work as well as you might be expecting, but you can make a good stab at things relatively easily.

An audio signal, the sort that comes out of an MP3 player or from record decks, is a very complex waveform, consisting of lots of very rapid changes. The speed of the rapid changes carry the frequency content information of sound. The size of the waveform – that is, over what range of voltage values they cover – is the amplitude or loudness information. However, the amplitude is varying rapidly to convey the frequencies. What you need to do is to isolate the loudness factor – that is, to measure just the size of the peak of the waveform, but it is not quite as simple as that. With a loud sound you get a large positive value and a symmetrically large negative one, so in order to get a measure of loudness you have to ignore the negative value and hold the positive value at its peak. Such a circuit is possible and is called, rather unsurprisingly, a *peak detector*.

Now the beat of music is normally carried in the low frequencies. There are electronic circuits that will separate or filter a mishmash of frequencies so that only a specific range of frequencies get through. The two simplest type are known as *high pass* and *low pass*. In a low-pass filter only the low frequencies can pass through it. Exactly how low is low depends on what is known as the filter's *break frequency*. This is defined as the frequency where the output is cut down by half compared with the input. By correct choice of components you can make this break frequency any value that you want. Most of the low frequencies in music are between 200Hz and 30Hz – any lower and you tend to feel it more than hear it. So to get at the beat of the music you must filter it with a low-pass filter at a break frequency of 200Hz. The key to filters is the capacitor component, which acts a bit like a frequency dependent resistor. The higher the frequency, the lower its resistance is to AC signals or its capacitive reactance.

The final piece in the jigsaw is called a *comparator*, which compares two voltages and gives a logic one output if one output is higher than the other or a logic zero if it is lower. By varying one voltage with a control knob or potentiometer and feeding a varying signal into the other, you can trigger a digital input when the varying voltage exceeds that set by the knob. If you feed the output of a peak detector into this you can, by turning the knob, set the level that will trigger the sequencer to advance to the next step.

## Designing the Circuit

So to implement all that you need a couple of components called *operational amplifiers*, or *op amps* for short. These are very simple on the outside but quite complex on the inside. Basically there are two inputs marked + and – with a single output. The way it works is that the output is equal to the difference in voltage between the two inputs multiplied by a big number called the *open loop gain*, which is typically 100,000. So you might think that if you put one volt into the amplifier, you will get 100,000 volts out. Well, you would if you powered it with a 100,000 volt power supply and you could find an op amp that would work at that level. What happens in practice is that the output will only go as high as the power supply. Also the open loop gain is too high to be useful most of the time, and so when you design a circuit that you want to use as an amplifier some negative feedback is applied, as shown in Figure 11-6. Don't confuse this with positive feedback, sometimes known just as *feedback* or *howl around,* when an amplifier's output is fed into an input, like a microphone picking up the amplified sound.

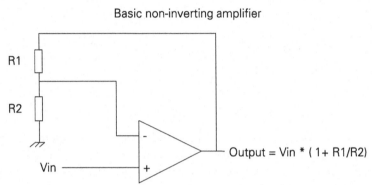

Basic non-inverting amplifier

Output = Vin * ( 1+ R1/R2)

FIGURE 11-6:
A non-inverting
amplifier.

Negative feedback means feeding a proportion of the output back into the – (negative) input so that the input in effect gets turned down. Consider the circuit in Figure 11-6 and assume that there is zero volts on Vin, and also zero volts on the output. Also imagine that the two resistors have the same value. Now suddenly Vin is changed to 1V so the difference between the two inputs is also 1V. So the output sets off to amplify this difference into 100,000V. However, as the output rises to one volt then the voltage on the negative input will have risen to half a volt, because the two resistors act as a potential divider and feed half the voltage of the output back into the negative input. At this stage the difference between the two voltages is only half a volt, so the output tries to amplify this by 100,000 to give an output of 50,000V. But the higher the voltage gets on the output the more of it is fed back to the negative input. Eventually a balance point is reached when the voltage on the two inputs is exactly the same, and so the amplifier's output will not get any higher. This balance point, in this case, happens when the output is exactly twice the input, so in effect the whole circuit has a gain of 2. You can make the gain anything you want, within reason, by simply altering the ratio of the two resistors. So if you feed a tenth of the output back into the negative input, you will have a gain of 10. The actual formula for calculating the gain is shown in Figure 11-6.

So armed with that information you can set about to design the beat extracting circuit whose schematic is shown in Figure 11-7.

FIGURE 11-7:
The schematic of
the beat driver.

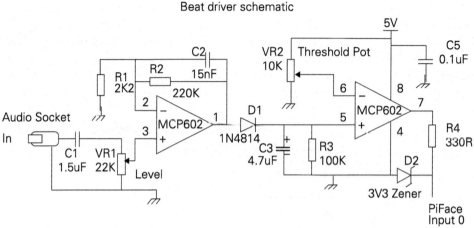

Beat driver schematic

This uses two op amps which conveniently come in one package. The signal passes through C1 to remove any DC component and then into a pot so that you can set the level into the amplifier. This first op amp is configured just like the previous example as a non-inverting amplifier, only this time there is a capacitor across the feedback resistor. This means that for low frequencies the gain is determined by the value of resistor R2. But as the frequency increases, the capacitive reactance of the capacitor shorts out the feedback resistor to lower the gain. So in this section you have combined a low-pass filter with an amplifier.

The output of this amplifier is passed through a diode. This is a component that will only let electricity flow in one direction, in this case from the amplifier into capacitor C3. So as the waveform goes up and down rapidly it will start to charge up C3; it only gets more charge when the output of the first amplifier exceeds the voltage on C3 so this capacitor remembers the peak voltage of the audio signal. That is all well and good but you need some way of forgetting a peak signal that happened some time ago, and so R3 discharges the capacitor at a slower rate. The result is that the voltage on C3 represents the peaks of the signal or, as we say, it is an envelope follower. The value of R3 determines how quickly the envelope decays.

This envelope voltage is fed into the second op amp. Here you have no feedback, and you just use the open loop gain. The negative input is fed by a voltage set by a knob or pot VR2; this is a threshold voltage. If the envelope voltage is above this, then the output goes crashing up to the supply rail of 5V. If, however, the envelope voltage is below this threshold, then the output gets put firmly at zero volts or ground. This digital signal is too big to be fed into the PiFace board so it needs cutting down with R4 and D2 to make it a 3.3V signal suitable to dive the sequencer. D2 is a special sort of diode known as a *zener diode;* it starts to conduct at a set voltage. You can get these diodes that conduct at all sorts of voltages; you want one here to conduct at 3.3V or, as it is often written, *3V3.* The ground is shown by the hatched symbol at the end of R1. All the points with this symbol must be connected together.

# Building the Circuit

So what you need to do as the final step is construct this circuit. I much prefer making circuits on strip board and not solderless breadboard. The problem with breadboard is that it can make poor or intermittent contact which means that you could appear to have wired it up correctly but it is not. Therefore you can waste a lot of time just jiggling the components around hoping this will make it work. A small piece of veroboard or prototyping strip board is all you need. You can also use sockets for the integrated circuits, which means you can reuse them or replace them if they are damaged. The physical layout of the circuit is shown in Figure 11-8.

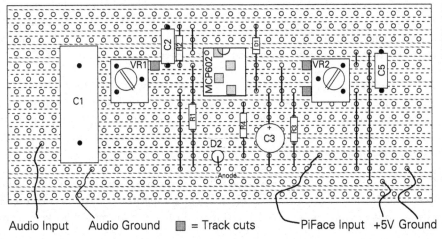

FIGURE 11-8:
The physical
layout of the
beat driver
circuit.

This shows the view of the board looking from the top or component side. The dotted lines indicate the copper strips on the underside of the board.

# Running the Circuit

After you have built the circuit you need to attach it to your audio input and wire the output, 5V and ground into the PiFace board. Adjust the threshold knob until it is at the mid-point, and boot up your Raspberry Pi. Then run the sequence program and switch to the external step. Start off the music and adjust the volume until you start to see the sequence advance. If it won't turn up far enough, you might have to increase the value of R2; try changing it to 470K. Then adjust the threshold until you see the sequence pick up the beat of the music. You might have to go back and adjust the volume. It works better on some types of music than others.

# Over to You

Well, that comes to the end of my bit but not of your bit. You can extend and improve this in many ways. You can use transistors or FETs to drive longer LED strips and have many of them on all the time. You can extend the software to save your sequence in a file. Then make it so you can save different patterns in different files. You can implement a shift function where you can concatenate several sequences to make a much longer one and even display an extended sequence by drawing the new pattern when the old one is done. Better yet you could have the display scrolling. Or make the window bigger and the boxes smaller to fit more steps in.

You can add some software that keeps the sequence kicking over if you have switched to an external input and have not had a trigger for a certain amount of time. You could add a small delay after an external trigger to stop them from happening too rapidly. You can add an extra control button to set the sequence to a random pattern.

On the hardware side, you might have noticed that the dynamic range of some music makes it drop out of the trigger zone. There are special amplifiers called *gated compressors;* they are made so that things like walkie-talkies have a constant audio signal into the transmitter. The gain of the amplifier is adjusted automatically to keep the output constant. The SSM2165 is one example of such an amplifier.

You might want to replace the envelope follower's discharge resistor with a pot, something like 220K. Finally you might want to adjust the filter capacitor, or even have a more sophisticated second or fourth order filter on the input. However, whatever you do, keep on dancing.

# Chapter **12**
## Door Lock

**by Dr. Andrew Robinson**

### In This Chapter

- ○ Learn about computer security
- ○ Create a door lock controlled by RFID tags
- ○ Extend your knowledge of OOP
- ○ Discover more about computer authentication
- ○ Use Python's dictionary object to store key/value pairs

**I'M FOREVER FORGETTING** things – usually important documents. Luckily with computers and the cloud, I can go online and access my documents whenever and wherever I need to. Unfortunately, I can't download physical objects, such as a door key, particularly when the door has swung shut behind me. Luckily, the Raspberry Pi can come to the rescue.

In this chapter you'll build a computer-controlled door lock that will unlock the door when you prove to it who you are. You'll take advantage of the general-purpose nature of the Raspberry Pi, so you can extend it to have a range of different ways of unlocking your door. This chapter shows you how use an RFID reader, but you could go on to modify it to unlock using your mobile phone; lucky for me, as I'm just as bad at remembering passwords as keys.

If you don't have a door lock, you can instead use the Raspberry Pi to activate and deactivate an alarm – it won't physically prevent entry, but it can warn you that someone has been in your room without permission.

There's a bit of an art to designing computer programs, and hopefully, after this chapter you'll also appreciate the need to design things modularly – that is, in a way that allows chunks to be easily switched out for another one. You'll also see that it can be easier to design with a simple block, get the system working and then go back later to make it more complicated. In this chapter you'll see how to break the task down into separate aspects, and then switch out one block and switch in another.

## The System Overview

When starting work on a new system, computer scientists will often sketch out a system diagram showing how the main components will work together – it would be far too complicated to try and design everything all at once.

Figure 12-1 shows the system diagram for the door lock. It shows how the system needs to get input (this could be from a code pad) and check whether the input is valid, and if it is, then it unlocks the door. You should recognise that Figure 12-1 maps well to the familiar "input, process, output" of computers.

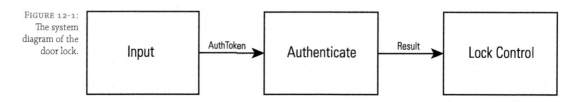

FIGURE 12-1:
The system
diagram of the
door lock.

## Safety-Critical Systems

This project also introduces an important aspect in computing, that of *safety-critical systems*. If your desktop computer crashes, you might lose hours of work, which probably at worst is just frustrating. If a computer flying a plane malfunctions, it may lead to death or serious damage. This is a *safety-critical system*, in which computers can cause harm if they do not function correctly. There are particular tools, techniques and standards that apply to try to safeguard the public. This is relevant to the project at hand because you should make sure that you have a manual override for the door lock – because you don't want to be locked in a room by your Raspberry Pi. Typically, most electric door lock systems can also be opened with a mechanical key.

Furthermore, just as a mechanical lock can be picked, computers can be hacked, so it's important to be aware of how secure your system and code are. You don't want someone opening your door because you didn't design your program properly.

---

Don't rely on your Raspberry Pi keeping your house secure unless you know what you're doing. Also, have a manual override, so you don't get locked in, or out! **WARNING**

---

## How Are Computers Hacked?

Most hacking incidents work by sending the computer data it is not expecting – too much or the wrong format perhaps. In the C language, if the programmer is not careful, the program will continue to accept input, which will overflow from the area of memory that had been put aside for it. Think of this like filling in a form and going off the end of one line and continuing onto the next. Sometimes the extra input data can overwrite something else in the program. Programs are just a series of instructions the computer obeys that are held in memory, and these instructions can be overwritten. If the attacker sends the right data, it's possible to change the instructions to make the program do something else.

This particular type of attack is called a *buffer overflow* – the *buffer* being the area reserved for input data. Luckily, Python manages the size of its buffers for you, so this shouldn't happen. You should still be careful, and whenever you take input from a user expect the unexpected!

## The Door Lock Hardware

You need a door lock that the Raspberry Pi can control through an electric signal. There are two main types:

○ Electromagnetic locks – Use an electric current to create a magnetic field to hold the door shut. When the current is switched off the field collapses, and there is nothing to hold the door shut. Typically, a flat metal plate is attached to the door that is held by the electromagnet attached to the frame.

○ Electromechanical keepers (as shown in Figure 12-2) – Tend to work in conjunction with traditional locks. They are typically fitted to the doorframe and accept the bolt from the door. A small spring holds a plate in place that stops the bolt from escaping. If a voltage is applied to a small coil, the keeper allows the bolt to pull out and the door to open. When the current stops flowing, the bolt will be captured again when the door is closed.

FIGURE 12-2:
An
electromechanical
keeper door
lock.

Clearly, the Raspberry Pi needs to produce a different signal for each type of lock – the electromagnetic lock needs a voltage continually applied to keep the door shut, whereas the electromechanical keeper needs voltage supplied only to open the door. You will use a relay on PiFace Digital to control the door lock, and because it has a changeover contact, you can use the same software to control both types of locks – you just need different wiring.

At this stage it's also worth thinking about the default state of the outputs. What happens if the Raspberry Pi crashes; would the door stay locked, or would it open? This too will be considered when wiring up the lock.

## The Initial High-Level Software Simulation

If you tried to write your entire door-lock controller all at once, chances are it wouldn't work the first time. Furthermore, with lots of code, there would be many places for bugs to hide.

Instead you should limit the number of places to look by writing something very simple, and testing it. Only then should you add more complexity, step by step. Also, before working with pesky real-world hardware that makes it harder to see what's going on (and so harder to find bugs) you'll first simulate the hardware in software.

Figure 12-1, earlier, identified the major blocks needed for your door controller system. The first step is to implement it in Python. Enter Listing 12-1 in a new file called door_controller.py.

**Listing 12-1  The Initial Code for the Door Controller**

```python
#!/usr/bin/env python
"""Door Lock: System to control an electric door lock
class AuthToken:
    def __init__(self, id, secret):
        self.id=id
        self.secret=secret


class TestDoorController:
    def send_open_pulse(self):
        print "unlock the door"


class BasicAuthenticator:
    id = "Andrew"
    secretPassword = "1234"
    def check(self,token):
        print "checking input of '" + token.id + "', ⤶
password: " + token.secret + ", against secret password ⤶
'" + self.secretPassword +"'"
        result = (token.secret == self.secretPassword) & ⤶
(token.id == self.id)
    print "authentication is: " + str(result)
    return result


class TestInput:
    def getInput(self):
        print "checking for input"
        authToken = AuthToken("Andrew","1234")
        return authToken

def main():
    authInput = TestInput()
```

*continued*

Listing 12-1    continued
```
  authenticator = BasicAuthenticator()
    doorController = TestDoorController()

if(authenticator.check(authInput.getInput())):
    doorController.send_open_pulse()
if __name__ == '__main__':

    main()
```

Run the program in Listing 12-1, and you'll see it print the following messages that describe what is happening in that part of the program. Note that at the moment the test data is hard coded into the program so it is not interactive, but it shows how the blocks work together.

```
checking for input
checking input for 'Andrew', password: 1234 against ⏎
secret password '1234'
authentication is: True
unlock, wait and relock
```

Change the value returned by the getInput() function to something other than 1234 and rerun the program. Check that you don't see the message about unlocking the door.

By now, much of the code should be familiar as functions, if statements, variables, print statements and delays are covered in earlier chapters. Not covered so far are the keywords class and self, which are concerned with object-oriented programming, or OOP for short. In this example OOP is used as a means to break the task into manageable objects that represent the blocks in your system diagram. Later in the chapter you'll swap out one object for another, which makes it very easy to modify your programs, and reuse objects in other projects. You'll learn more about OOP later in the section "Testing the Program and Fitting the Lock".

Your simulated system may not appear very exciting at the moment, but building up a system with firm foundations can save hours of debugging later. The next steps are to start expanding the blocks that actually take input and control the door.

# The Output Block

Having a simple system complete means that you don't always have to start coding "at the beginning" of a system – that is, you don't have to complete the getting-input stage first. Instead, you can write the code that controls the door (which is much more fun!).

---

If you don't have a door lock, you can still follow along by wiring up an LED instead of the lock to show when the door would be locked.    **TIP**

---

# Connecting the Door Control Circuit

You want the door to stay locked even if the Raspberry Pi crashes, yet in the case of the electromagnetic lock, a current needs to flow to hold the door shut. This functionality is provided by a changeover relay on the PiFace Digital interface.

Wire the door lock up as shown in Figure 12-3 or Figure 12-4. You will need an appropriate power supply for your lock. You can buy plug-in power adapters for a range of voltages. Check the voltage and current required by your lock. Connect your lock to either the normally open or normally closed contacts, depending on whether it needs current to unlock the door, or hold the door locked.

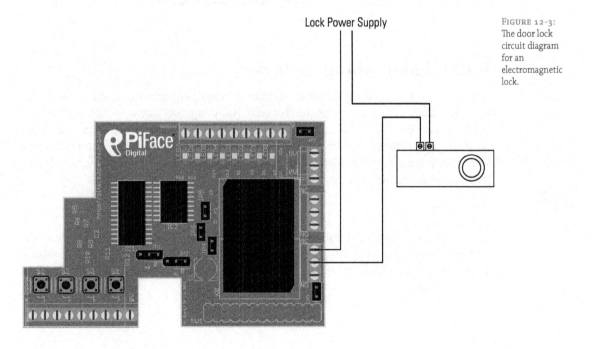

Lock Power Supply

FIGURE 12-3: The door lock circuit diagram for an electromagnetic lock.

FIGURE 12-4:
The door lock
circuit diagram
for an electro-
mechanical
keeper.

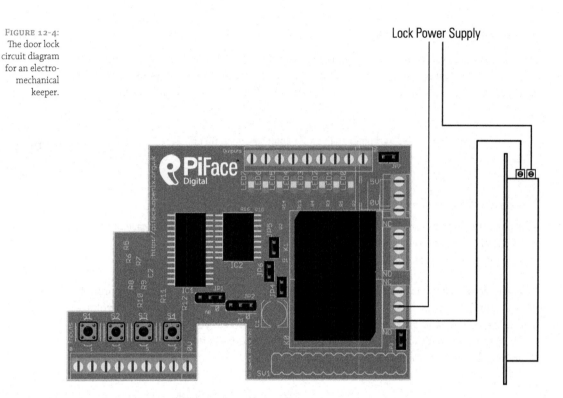

FIGURE 12-4:
The door lock circuit diagram for an electro-mechanical keeper.

## A Reminder About Relays

Relays are switches that are operated electrically. They have contacts that are moved by passing an electric current through a coil of wire. Relays are available with different configurations of contacts. The relays you will use here are changeover, or sometimes called *double throw*. This means that with no current flowing through the coil, the centre contact is connected to one pin on the relay. When current flows the centre contact changes-over and becomes connected to the other pin.

In line with a test-as-you-go strategy, now is a good time to check whether you have control of the door lock. Connect up the power supply for the door lock and use the PiFace emulator (as described in Chapter 9, "Test Your Reactions") to check the lock holds and releases when you change output 0.

## Programming the Door Control Block

With the door lock connected to the interface, it is time to write the software. The function of the door controller is to send a short signal to unlock the door. You will edit the `TestDoorController` class.

Open the file `door_controller.py` and edit the code to add the following lines.

Add these statements to the beginning of the program:

```
import piface.pfio as piface
from time import sleep
```

Add this before the `main` function:

```
class DoorControllerPiFace:
    def send_open_pulse(self):
        piface.digital_write(0,1)
        sleep(5)
        piface.digital_write(0,0)
```

Update the `main` function to make use of this class. Change

```
doorController = TestDoorController()
```

to

```
doorController = DoorControllerPiFace()
```

Run the entire program, and check that instead of printing `unlock the door`, the door lock is released for five seconds and then locks again.

Now that you've successfully built and tested the output stage, it's time to get the input from the user when he or she wants to open the door.

## The Input Block

Continuing with the theme of keeping things simple at first, you will start with the input block asking the user to type a password on a standard USB keyboard.

## Getting Input

Edit the door_controller.py code by adding the following class:

```
class KeyboardInput:
    def getInput(self):
    print "checking for input"
    id = raw_input("please enter your name: ")
    password = raw_input("please enter your password: ")
    authToken = AuthToken(id,password)
    return authToken
```

You need to tell the program to use this class to get input rather than the TestInput class. Change the line

```
authInput = TestInput()
```

to

```
authInput = KeyboardInput()
```

Check that the code works; the door should open only if you type the name Andrew and the password 1234.

The next step is to implement the authentication block.

## The Authentication Block

*Authentication* is about checking that someone is who he or she claims to be. You will probably use authentication systems many times a day. For example, you need to authenticate yourself to use websites such as Facebook and Twitter.

The class you have written so far to do authentication is very simple; it checks to see if the string passed to it matches a hard-coded value. This has a number of drawbacks, including the following:

○ If anyone looks at the source code, it is possible for him or her to read your password.

○ Changing the password requires you to edit the source code.

A better solution is to store the password information separately, which is what you will do next.

## Storing Secrets in a File

One of the simplest ways to store data is in a *flat file*. This is nothing more than a list of entries in a basic text file. To read a username and password pair of values from a file, change the `door_controller.py` code by adding the following `FileAuthenticator` class before the `main` function:

```
class FileAuthenticator:
    filename = "secrets.txt"
    def readFile(self):
        secrets = open(self.filename, 'r')
        print "reading from file"
        for line in secrets:
            line = line.rstrip('\n')
            self.id, self.secretPassword = line.split(',')
    def check(self,token):
        self.readFile()
        print "checking input of '" + token.id + "', ⊃
password: " + token.secret + ", against secret password ⊃
'" + self.secretPassword +"'"
        result = (token.secret == self.secretPassword) & ⊃
(token.id == self.id)
        print "authentication is: " + str(result)
        return result
```

Now tell the main part of the program to use the new `FileAuthenticator` class instead of `BasicAuthenticator`. Change the line

```
Authenticator = BasicAuthenticator()
```

to

```
Authenticator = FileAuthenticator()
```

The file `secrets.txt` will hold the your secret authentication information. Use a text editor to create the file `secrets.txt` in the same folder as your program file and add the following sample line:

```
Andrew, 9876
```

Run your program and enter your name as Andrew and the password as 1234. You will see the following output:

```
checking for input
please enter your name: Andrew
please enter your password: 1234
reading from file
checking input of 'Andrew', password: 1234, against ⊃
secret password '9876'
authentication is: False
```

Notice how the password 9876 is read from the file. Add more usernames and passwords (commas separated) to the file secrets.txt, one per line. Test the program with different usernames and passwords to check that the door opens when it should, and more importantly, that it doesn't when it shouldn't! For the full code listing, go to the book's website at www.wiley.com/go/raspberrypiprojects.

---

TIP    It is tempting to think that your program works when it gives the behaviour you want – such as in the case of the door lock, if the door is unlocked when the correct password is entered. However, it is just as important to test programs for other cases; for the door lock example, you need to test that the door isn't opened if the incorrect password is entered. In industry, testing is very important, and programmers aim for high levels of *code coverage* – that is, that much of the code has been tested. This may mean running the program with a wide range of sample inputs.

---

## Unlocking Doors Without Touching

You may have seen door locks for which you can wave a card or plastic fob against a reader. These work using *radio frequency identification* (RFID) technology. The Raspberry Pi makes it easy to incorporate an RFID reader into your door lock.

You will need to buy a USB RFID reader and matching tags, similar to those shown in Figure 12-5. Although these are available from the major component distributors, you may find online auction sites to be cheaper. USB RFID readers can appear in different ways to the computer – for example, as an HID USB device (which sends input as if it were a keyboard typing in characters from the tag) or as a serial port. The USB RFID reader used in this chapter is an HID USB device as it is simplest to program. You could use a USB serial RFID reader, but you would have to modify the code yourself.

FIGURE 12-5:
An RFID reader
and tags.

There are two main frequencies used by RFID systems, 13.56MHz and 125kHz. These frequencies are incompatible with each other, so whichever reader you get make sure that you buy matching tags. 13.56MHz is more commonly found in industrial systems, so with a 13.56MHz reader you may find that you can use a staff/student ID badge, or even a biometric passport or prepaid travel card. *Near field communications* (NFC) on some smartphones also use 13.56MHz tags.

**TIP**

There are different levels of security offered by RFID with the cost of increased complexity, and more expensive hardware. As this is your first RFID system, it is best to start with the simple version of RFID, which offers a basic level of security (comparable with the cheaper commercial systems). As you become a more accomplished programmer, you could upgrade to a more sophisticated system.

## Connecting the RFID Reader

In this subsection you will check if your RFID reader works with your Raspberry Pi and read your first RFID tag. As the Raspberry Pi has only two USB ports, you will need to use a USB hub or unplug the mouse before plugging in additional USB devices. Linux is designed so that it can be used without a mouse from the command line. Follow these steps to test the reader from a command line:

1. If you are running a graphical X environment, choose Logout from the program menu. You will be returned to the command line.

2. Unplug your mouse and plug in the RFID reader into the USB port.

3. Start the text-based editor nano (or your preferred text-based text editor) by typing nano on the command line.

4. Bring an RFID tag near to the reader. It should bleep, and you will see a string of characters are typed to the screen. Bring a different tag near to the reader and check that a different string of characters is displayed on the next line.

---

**TIP** Remember that whenever you present a tag to your reader it will type its serial number wherever the cursor is, followed by a new line. So don't present a tag when you're in the middle of typing something else!

---

5. Now is a good time to create the data file that will contain the tags that you want to grant access to open the door. Still in nano, add the name of the person who will be given the tag followed by the ID from the tag separated by a comma. There should be a separate line for each tag. Save the file by typing Ctrl + X, followed by Y to confirm that you want to save the buffer, followed by the filename tag.txt and then Enter. Your tags and reader may produce codes that look slightly different, but the file should look similar to this:

```
Andrew,1c477cd5
Mike,54bfc314b
```

---

**TIP** If your RFID reader does not send any data, check that it works with your tags with a desktop computer. To check that the Raspberry Pi has recognised your USB reader, type dmesg into a terminal shortly after plugging it in and look for a reference to RFID and USB HID.

---

**YOUR TURN!** Experiment with reading other items containing RFID tags, such as ID cards, payment cards, travel passes and biometric passports. If successful, you should notice that a string of characters is printed.

---

# How RFID works

RFID works by exchanging messages between a reader and tag by radio waves. RFID tags consist of an aerial (a loop of wire), a capacitor to store electricity and a small silicon chip. The silicon chip is actually a small computer processor! This demonstrates just how small computers have become and how they are everywhere!

An ingenious feature of the system is that the tags do not need their own power source to transmit. They can receive their energy by radio waves from the reader when they are first placed nearby. The radio waves also contain a message from the reader that it wants to read the tag. The tag stores the energy and uses it to compute a response and then transmit it back to the reader. In the simple case this message is a fixed number, but more sophisticated tags contain read/writable *nonvolatile memory* (memory that stores state even without power) to store data. In the most sophisticated tags, their computer processor performs a calculation in the tag. This allows the tag to perform challenge-response authentication.

# Challenge-Response Authentication

One problem with authentication is the threat of *replay attacks* – that is, that an attacker may copy the secret reply given to a system. An example of this might be watching a user type in a password, and then typing it in to impersonate that user. A solution is never to reveal the secret information. This may seem impossible at first, but can be implemented if a challenge is set that can be achieved only if the subject possesses the secret information. In everyday life you might want to know if someone knows the same secret you do but don't want to reveal the secret to him or her. In this situation you find a question that a person can only answer if he or she knows the secret, yet the two of you don't actually share the secret itself. In computing this is known as *challenge-response authentication*.

The more sophisticated RFID tags have a processor to answer questions posed by the reader. In this case the question is usually numbers that the tag has to do a sum with together with the secret number it is storing. If the tag transmits the correct number back, the reader is sure that the tag knows the secret. The next time the tag is presented to the reader a different challenge will be issued, which makes it very difficult to copy the tag.

# Using the RFID Reader in Python

You will need to write a new input block and an authentication block for the RFID tag reader.

### The RFID Input Block

As the RFID reader inputs data from tags as if it had been typed on a keyboard, you will use the `raw_input` function in Python. Add the following code (before the `main` function) to get input from the RFID reader to your `door_controller.py` program:

```
class RfidInput:
    def getInput(self):
        print "waiting for tag"
        tag = raw_input()
        return AuthToken(None,tag)
```

### The RFID Authentication Block

The RFID authentication block looks up the value from the tag to see if it is valid. It does this by checking if it is in the `tags.txt` file you created earlier. Add the following code to the `door_controller.py` program so that you can check if the value read from the tag is valid:

```
class RfidFileAuthenticator:
    filename = "tags.txt"
    tags = dict()
    def __init__(self):
        self.readFile()
    def readFile(self):
        secrets = open(self.filename, 'r')
    print "reading from " + self.filename + " file"
        for line in secrets:
            line = line.rstrip('\n')
            id, tag = line.split(',')
            self.tags[tag] = id
    def check(self,token):
        print "checking if " + token.secret + " is valid"
        if token.secret in self.tags:
            print "tag found belonging to: " + ↩
self.tags[token.secret]
            return True
        else: "tag not found"
            print
            return False
```

You will notice that the `RfidFileAuthenticator` class uses a `dict` – a dictionary. A *dictionary* in Python is a way of storing a set of values that have a unique identifier. The unique identifier is called the *key*. A value is stored with its associated key. For example, the following example creates a dictionary stored in the variable `ages` and then associates the value 21 with the key `jim` and 43 with the key `tony`:

```
ages = dict()
ages["jim"] = 21
ages["tony"] = 43
```

The following code looks up the value for the key `jim` in the `ages` dictionary:

```
print ages["jim"]
```

This prints the value 21.

---

Open up an interactive Python session and try it yourself. Create a dictionary, add some key-value pairs and then retrieve them. **YOUR TURN!**

---

In the `RfidFileAuthenticator` class a dictionary is used to store who has which RFID tag. The RFID tag is used as the key (which is unique), and the name of the tag owner is stored as the associated value. The dictionary is populated by reading each line in the file in a `for` loop when the object is initialised.

```
self.tags[tag] = id
```

The `check` function checks if the tag that has been read is present in the dictionary with the following line:

```
if token.secret in self.tags:
```

If the key is present, the associated value is looked up so that the name of the owner can be printed.

---

Other languages may call a dictionary an *associative array*, a *hash*, a *hash table* or *key/value pairings*, but they all have similar functionality. They are very useful in computing. **TIP**

## Putting It All Together

With the new input and authentication blocks written, the next step is to use them in the main function.

Update the main function to use the new classes by changing the authInput and authenticator variable initialisations to

```
authInput = RfidInput()
authenticator = RfidFileAuthenticator()
```

Run the program and bring a tag that is listed in tags.txt near the reader. The program will print

```
reading from tags.txt file
waiting for tag
1c477cd5
checking if 1c477cd5 is valid
tag found belonging to: Andrew
unlock, wait and relock
```

Rerun the program and check that a tag that is not listed in tags.txt doesn't open the door. If your program works successfully, you need to add a while loop to the main function so that you do not have to keep running it each time a tag is presented. Do this by wrapping the if statement with an unconditional while loop, as shown here:

```
while(True):
    if(authenticator.check(authInput.getInput())):
        doorController.send_open_pulse()
```

## Testing the Program and Fitting the Lock

Now is the time to test the complete program. Run the program and check that the electric door lock is locked. Wave a valid tag at the reader and check that the door lock unlocks for a few seconds and then relocks. Wave the valid tag again to check whether the sequence is repeated. Finally, use an invalid tag and make sure that the door doesn't open.

If the system appears to work, it's time to fit the electric lock to the door and the tag reader. You should secure the wiring running to the door lock; otherwise, an attacker could tamper with it to unlock it. As mentioned earlier, it's a good idea to be able to manually unlock the door if you have an error in your program that means it fails to unlock the door! If your Raspberry Pi is on the inside of your door, it can be useful to have remote access to it so that you can stop or edit your program. Look up how to SSH into your Raspberry Pi online for more information.

# Object-Orientated Programming

You have seen how easy it is to swap blocks out with OOP. OOP allows programmers to structure their code by creating and using objects as they may do with real-world objects.

Think of a real-world object – it has a set of properties (characteristics, such as its colour) and a set of things that you can ask it to do. As an example, think of a balloon – there is data about the balloon, properties that it has – for example, it may have the colour red and be inflated. There are actions you can cause the balloon to do, such as inflate or pop. These actions may affect the balloon's properties; causing a balloon to pop will cause its is `Inflated` property to change from true to false.

The key thing to notice about OOP is that it organises functions and variables together. In the door lock example the variable `tags` is only useful to the RFID authentication part of the program, so it is part of the `RfidFileAuthenticator` class. The alternative would be to have all the variables together, which would be more confusing as you would not know which part of the program needed them. If you were working as a part of a team on a program, OOP would provide a way to split the code into fairly independent parts that can be worked on separately and eventually assembled.

OOP is there to help you write programs by providing a framework for structure. Objects can be swapped out as you have seen. You can also build more complex objects from component objects, just as you can in the real world. As you become more advanced, you can learn about another feature of OOP, *inheritance,* which enables you to create child objects that inherit the behaviour and variables of their parents, but with additions.

You don't have to write in an OOP style, but using it can be a great help. In the code lock example it allows you to change behaviour by swapping an object in one line. This is only easy because the OOP helps manage abstraction, breaking a problem into manageable parts.

# Networking Multiple Doors

Now that you have one door lock working it's time to think about expansion. Imagine in the future that you have lots of door locks, and want to allow access to some of the doors to other users. With the current system you would have to visit each door controller and set the same password. It might also be hard to keep track of who has access to each door.

TIP Do not confuse a *user directory* with a *filesystem directory* – although they use the same word, they are separate unrelated concepts.

A better solution would be to keep all the information stored in one place, on a central server. With this approach, when a user requests access to a resource (that is, he or she wants to open the door) his or her credentials are sent to the directory server over the network, which grants access or not. A similar process is used online to allow users to log in to other websites using their Twitter or Facebook accounts.

## Authentication and Directories in Industry

The standard way to share and store authentication information is the *lightweight directory access protocol* (LDAP). Its history can be traced back to the 1980s around the time of the birth of the Internet. Nowadays it is the basis for Active Directory, the system used for network user management on Microsoft Windows. Linux supports running LDAP servers and user logon through open-source implementations of LDAP. The main version for Raspbian is OpenLDAP.

If you own multiple Raspberry Pis, you could network them and manage who can log in to them centrally. You could perhaps manage a classroom of Raspberry Pis for a school this way. There would be no difference between this setup and the way large institutions such as banks, universities or offices manage all their machines and users. There are tutorials online that show how to set up an OpenLDAP server and client specifically on Raspberry Pis.

In your door lock program, because the authentication is separated into a class, you can easily replace it with a network version that would look the user's input up in a directory or other authentication service. You could even replace it with code that sends the user's input to validate against Facebook. Clearly putting a Raspberry Pi next to every door in your house starts becoming expensive, but there are a number of other fun ways you can expand the project which do not require additional hardware.

## Over to You

This project, like all the others in this book, has many opportunities for extensions. Why not try swapping out one or more input, authentication and output blocks to implement some of the following:

○ You could have the lock greet the user and announce that access has been granted. Make use of the code for text-to-speech in Chapter 10, "The Twittering Toy".

○ Write a log of who is granted access so that you know who enters your room. You could reuse the code from Chapter 17, "The Techno–Bird Box, a Wildlife Monitor". A variation on this would be to send an e-mail or tweet when access was granted or attempted. You could trigger the Raspberry Pi camera too to record a photograph of a person trying to gain access. Using the other outputs on PiFace Digital, you could trigger an electric water pistol to deter unauthenticated access.

○ The authentication block could be extended so that access was granted only at certain times of day.

○ If you're familiar with web programming, you could set up a web server on the Raspberry Pi and unlock your door by sending a password via a web page on your smartphone.

○ You could experiment with different input devices, such as a biometric scanner if you can afford one. Barcode and magstripe readers are more affordable alternatives.

○ If you are feeling really ambitious, you could find code online to do image recognition and use the Raspberry Pi camera. OpenCV is a useful library.

○ Another ambitious extension would be to use Asterisk or Twilio to unlock the door when you dial a telephone number or send a text.

○ You could be really creative and come up with your own authentication method.

## The Art of Programming

This chapter should have shown you an important feature about computer programs – that they change. Requirements change during the life of a program, which means parts need to be swapped out or rewritten. Part of the art of programming is structuring code so that it is easy to maintain later, particularly when you start working with other programmers.

Managing software development is difficult; for more information about how large, complicated programs are written in industry, search online for "extreme programming" or "agile methodologies" such as "scrum".

---

Programmers may talk about refactoring. *Refactoring* is basically the matter of tidying up code to improve its structure without changing its behaviour. It requires discipline, but makes maintaining code easier in the long term.   **TIP**

---

You should have seen that a good approach is to build a simple system with limited features that works, and then add more features later. The goal is to write code in such a way that you're always fairly close to having a program that runs, even if parts of it are massively simplified, rather than have an unmanageable mass of uncompleted features, which show no sign of working!

Most importantly, to master writing code takes practise. So, if you haven't already, get your Raspberry Pi working for you. As you've seen in this chapter, if you're forever forgetting your keys, the Raspberry Pi can provide a solution. Why not create a new gadget to solve a problem for you or your friends?

# Chapter **13**
# Home Automation

**by Jonathan Evans**

## In This Chapter

- ○ Interface the following sensors to the Raspberry Pi: door switch, motion sensor and temperature gauge
- ○ Create e-mail alerts that can be used with each project in this chapter
- ○ Convert a webcam into a surveillance camera that records footage and takes pictures when motion is detected
- ○ Control the Raspberry Pi using a radio frequency remote key fob

**IN THIS CHAPTER** you will be creating some home-automation projects to make your home environment more intelligent and provide you with the foundational knowledge to further the automation of your home. A key part of home automation is being able to interface with sensors. This is something that the Raspberry Pi is very good at. There has been a recent explosion of cheap and reliable sensors available to the DIY enthusiast, and combined with the small form factor of the Pi, its high processing power, network connectivity and low cost, it makes the Raspberry Pi an ideal platform for the DIY home-automation enthusiast.

Home automation can be distilled into three categories: control, alert and monitor. During the course of this chapter, you will create five projects covering each of these categories.

In this chapter you will not be making use of PiFace, which is used in other chapters in this book. You will interface directly with the GPIO ports of the Raspberry Pi using male-to-female jumper wires (described later). If you have to remove your PiFace, remember to always power down the Raspberry Pi before disconnecting (or connecting) anything to the GPIO headers.

## The Internet Of Things

The Internet Of Things (IOT) describes the rapidly expanding phenomenon of connecting things to the Internet. Network connectivity and IP addresses are no longer just used to connect computers. Increasingly we are seeing everyday appliances and sensors connecting to a network, providing us with real-time information from, and control over, those devices. The IOT is an emerging technology, so as it matures and interoperability standards are developed it will become easier and cheaper to connect devices to the IOT which will have a positive impact on home owners wanting to automate their environment. Again the Raspberry Pi has a role to play in connecting devices cheaply to a network. As you work through this chapter you will be contributing to the rapidly expanding network of things connected to the IOT.

## Project 1: How to Create a Motion Sensor and Door Switch

In your first home-automation project you will create a motion sensor and door switch. Motion sensors and door switches allow you not only to create alarms or alerts, but also to monitor flow and movement throughout your home. Using the information created by these sensors, you can apply rules and actions using Python. For example, you could turn off a light in a room if motion is not detected for a period of time, or send an e-mail alert to yourself if your garage door is open for a period of time. So by combining sensors, rules and actions, you can create a more intelligent home environment.

A door switch contains a reed switch (see Figure 13-1) that is triggered when the two pieces come apart. One piece is attached to the door and the other to the door frame. One of the two halves contains a magnet and the other a reed switch that is held closed when the magnet is near. When the two come apart the magnetic field loses its strength, and the switch is broken. This type of switch is closed when the pieces are together and open when they come apart. So when the door is closed current flows through the switch, and when the door is open the current is broken. This type of switch is called *normally open*. The motion sensor, sometimes known as a *passive infrared* (PIR) sensor (see Figure 13-2), is packaged with an integrated circuit and a lens that will focus the moving objects for the sensor. A motion sensor is also normally open, so both of the sensors interact with the Raspberry Pi through the GPIO port in the same manner, which makes the software for both identical. You will be writing some Python script to monitor the sensors and produce an action when either sensor is triggered. In this tutorial you will trigger a message to the screen, but you could take any number of other actions as explained before.

FIGURE 13-1:
A door switch.

FIGURE 13-2:
A motion
sensor.

Table 13-1 shows what you need.

## Table 13-1   What You Will Need

| QTY | Item | Description |
| --- | --- | --- |
| 1 | Door switch | Can be obtained from a home security outlet or online. |
| 1 | Motion sensor | Usually 5V-12V with three terminals, +VE, GND and 3.3V Pi-friendly output. |
| 2 | 10kΩ resistors | Brown, black, red, gold. |
| 2 | 1kΩ resistors | Brown, black, orange, gold. |

| QTY | Item | Description |
|-----|------|-------------|
| 1 | Solderless breadboard | A prototyping board for which parts and wires can be connected by clipping them into the board. It is used for prototyping electronics without having to solder parts together. |
| 3, 5 | Jumper wires | Male to male for breadboard connections, male to female for connecting the breadboard to the GPIO pins. Jumper wires usually come in packs of various quantities, colours and sizes. Although you need only 8 for this project, having 20 to 30 of each should see you through most projects. Any size will do for this project, but shorter male to male (10 cm) and longer male to female (20 cm) are best. |

## Construction

You are going to be using the Raspberry Pi GPIO ports to interface with the sensors. GPIO ports can be configured for input or output. In this case you are going to use them for input as you are collecting data from an external sensor. A GPIO port can have three different states: high (positive), low (ground) or floating (either). For you to be able to accurately determine the state of the GPIO pin, you need to tie it either to positive or negative (ground). You do this using what is known as a *pull-up* or *pull-down resistor*. When the GPIO is connected to a positive current the GPIO pin's value is high. When it is connect to ground it is low. Figure 13-3 shows a pull-up resistor (10kΩ) that connects the GPIO to positive when the switch is open. However, when the switch closes there is a lower resistance path to ground, and the GPIO state will go low. Figure 13-4 shows a pull-down resistor (10kΩ) connecting the GPIO pin to ground, making it low. When the switch is pressed there is a lower resistance to positive, which changes the GPIO state to high. The 1kΩ resistor is there to protect the GPIO pin from a short circuit when the switch is pressed.

---

Always double-check your circuits before powering on the Raspberry Pi. You can very easily damage the Raspberry Pi by not protecting the GPIO pins with resistors. Be especially careful of the 5V pins, which if connected to a GPIO pin will cause permanent damage.   **TIP**

---

In your project you want a closed circuit (low state) when the door is closed or when there is no motion and a high state when the door is opened or motion is detected, so you want a pull-up resistor to set the GPIO high in an alarm state. You will therefore base your circuitry on the diagram in Figure 13-3.

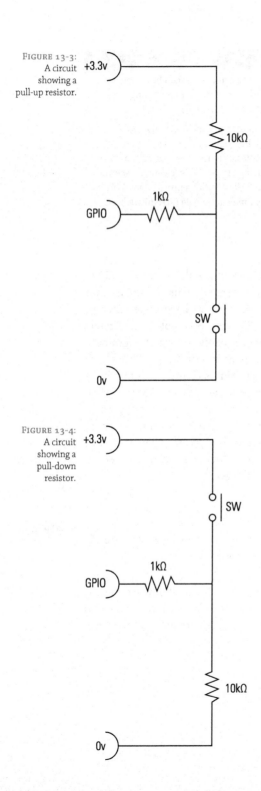

FIGURE 13-3:
A circuit
showing a
pull-up resistor.

FIGURE 13-4:
A circuit
showing a
pull-down
resistor.

The PIR sensor has three coloured wires: ground, positive and alarm. The colours and pin positions may differ, depending on which one you buy, so be sure to check the data sheet of your PIR. The alarm pin is an *open collector*, meaning you will need to connect a pull-up resistor on the alarm pin (see Chapter 9, "Test Your Reactions", for details on open collectors).

In Figure 13-5 you can see the circuit diagram with all the components, and in Figure 13-6 there is the breadboard prototype diagram.

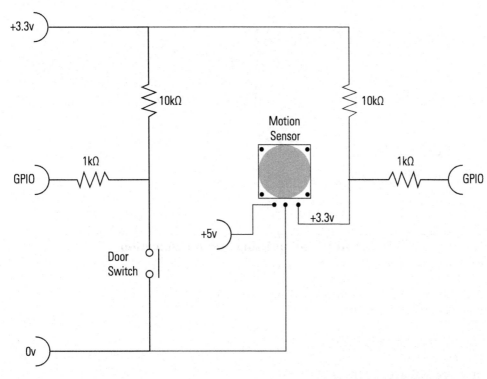

FIGURE 13-5: A circuit diagram for the door switch and motion sensor connected to two GPIO pins on the Raspberry Pi.

## Software

The software will print to the screen whenever motion is detected or the door sensor is triggered. You want to print to the screen only once per event, so you will use variables (motion and door) to keep track of when you are in an alarm state and prevent the trigger reoccurring for the same event. If you were logging these events to a database, or taking another action such as switching on a light or sending an e-mail alert, you would use this method to prevent multiple actions being created for the same event. The code is provided in Listing 13-1.

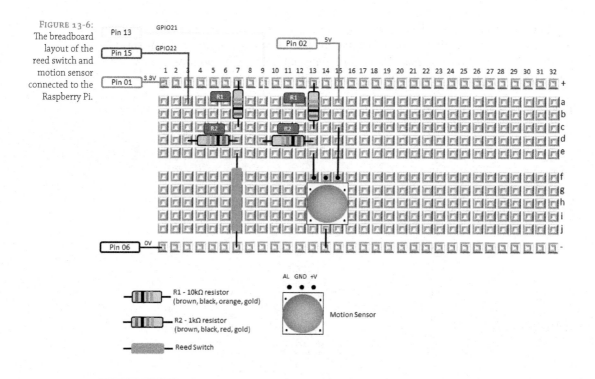

FIGURE 13-6:
The breadboard
layout of the
reed switch and
motion sensor
connected to the
Raspberry Pi.

R1 - 10kΩ resistor
(brown, black, orange, gold)

R2 - 1kΩ resistor
(brown, black, red, gold)

Reed Switch

Motion Sensor

---

## Listing 13-1    Home Automation Using Motion Detection

```python
#!/usr/bin/env python
"""
Home Automation using motion detection
For the Raspberry Pi
"""
import RPi.GPIO as GPIO
import time
GPIO.setmode(GPIO.BOARD)
GPIO.setup(13, GPIO.IN)
GPIO.setup(15, GPIO.IN)

def main():

        motion = False
        door = False

        while True:
```

```
        if GPIO.input(13):
                if motion == False: print "Motion Detected"
                motion = True
        else:
                motion = False

        if GPIO.input(15):
                if door == False: print "Door Opened"
                door = True
        else:
                door = False

        time.sleep(.3)

if __name__ == "__main__":
        main()
```

# Project 2: How to Monitor Your Home with a Webcam

Webcams have been around for quite some time, but when you combine one with the small form factor of the Raspberry Pi you can put surveillance easily anywhere in the home without having to run cables back to a recorder or PC. In this project you will construct a webcam surveillance monitor that will

○ Stream real-time video to a browser

○ Create e-mail alerts when motion is detected

○ Create stills and video files when motion is detected

You can use this to increase the security of your home but also for other purposes, such as keeping an eye on the kids around the house, knowing whether you left the garage door open or receiving alerts and be able to see when someone walks through the front door. Table 13-2 shows what you need.

**Table 13-2   What You Will Need**

| QTY | Item | Description |
|-----|------|-------------|
| 1 | Webcam | Most webcams will work, but a good frame rate (30 fps), autofocus and screen resolution (640 x 480) are webcam features that will all add to the quality of the picture. |
| | Network connection to the Raspberry Pi | A network connection is needed for the video streaming. You will most likely want a Wi-Fi connection so that you can place your webcam where you need it. Configuring a USB Wi-Fi device for your Raspberry Pi is beyond the scope of this tutorial; however, there are a number of online resources available on how to do this. If you have an Ethernet network point, that will work fine too. |
| | An Internet connection for your Raspberry Pi | You will need this to install the webcam software. |

**TIP**    Visit this website to check for compatibility of your webcam, or any other hardware, with the Raspberry Pi: `http://elinux.org/RPi_USB_Webcams`.

## Construction

The USB webcam plugs into the USB port of the Raspberry Pi, and the Raspberry Pi is connected to your home network either via Wi-Fi or network cable. You need to be connected to the Internet at the time you install the webcam software, but you do not need an Internet connection for the webcam to store video footage or to stream on your home network. The video footage is stored directly on the Raspberry Pi and is streamed to a predefined port. If you don't know what a port is, don't worry; it's like a television channel that the Raspberry Pi will broadcast to. You will use a browser to tune into that channel (port) to view the live video stream. You will be able to view the video using any browser-enabled device (PC, tablet, smartphone) connected to your home network. You will not be able to view the video footage from the Internet without opening up the port on your router. Your router will typically only allow traffic from the Internet to pass through port 80, which is used for Internet browsing and e-mail. However, you can configure your router to open up the port you choose for video surveillance. I'll explain that in more detail later in the "How to View the Webcam over the Internet" subsection of this project.

You will most likely want to run your Raspberry Pi headless (without a TV, keyboard and mouse attached). If you are not familiar with how to do this, I advise you to do some research and become comfortable with accessing your Raspberry Pi remotely. It is not difficult; you just need to know the IP address of your Raspberry Pi and then unplug the TV, keyboard and mouse and access it using a remote access SSH application such as Putty.

---

**TIP**

You can find the IP address of your Raspberry Pi by typing

`/sbin/ifconfig | less`

The output will look something like this:

`wlan0 Link encap:Ethernet HWaddr d8:eb:97:18:16:ef`

`inet addr: 192.168.0.2 Bcast:192.168.0.255 Mask:255.255.255.0`

Your IP address is the number provided after `inet addr:`, which in this case is `192.168.0.2`.

---

## Software

You will be using a great piece of open-source software to do all of this called *Motion*. Motion was founded by Jeroen Vreeken and has since had over 100 people contribute to the code. At the time of this writing, Motion is being maintained by Kenneth Lavrsen and Angel Carpintero at `www.lavrsen.dk/foswiki/bin/view/Motion/WebHome`. Installing Motion requires that you run a command from the command prompt on your Raspberry Pi. Unless you are familiar with assigning permissions in Linux, I recommend that you use the root user and not the standard user for this project.

---

**TIP**

You can create the root user by typing

`sudo passwd root`

The system will prompt you for a password twice. After that is complete log in to your Raspberry Pi using `root` as the username and the new password you just set.

---

After you are logged in as the root user, your command prompt should look like this:

`root@raspberrypi:~#`

If you have not done so recently, you should make sure that your Raspberry Pi is up to date by typing

```
sudo apt-get update
sudo apt-get upgrade
```

These updates will take some time to complete. You are now ready to install Motion. At the command prompt type

`sudo apt-get install motion`

The install process is automatic and should complete in a few minutes (depending on your Internet connection speed). After this is complete you are ready do to some configuration. In order to configure Motion, you will need to be able to edit a file in Linux. If you are familiar with editing in Linux, you can use your favorite editor; otherwise, you will be using a very simple text editor called *nano*. Table 13-3 shows the commands you will use for editing. You can refer to this table as needed.

**Table 13-3   Nano Editing Commands**

| Action | Command |
| --- | --- |
| Start editing a file called `filename` | `nano filename` |
| Navigate | Use the up, down, left and right keys. |
| Exit and save | Ctrl + X, followed by Y, followed by pressing the Enter key. |
| Exit without saving | Ctrl + X, followed by N. |
| Search for text | Ctrl + W, followed by entering the text that you want to search for, followed by pressing the Enter key. To search again for the same text, press Ctrl + W, followed by the Enter key. |

The installation process will have placed a configuration file in the /etc/motion directory. Edit the configuration file by typing the following at the command prompt:

```
nano /etc/motion/motion.conf
```

A screen similar to Figure 13-7 will appear.

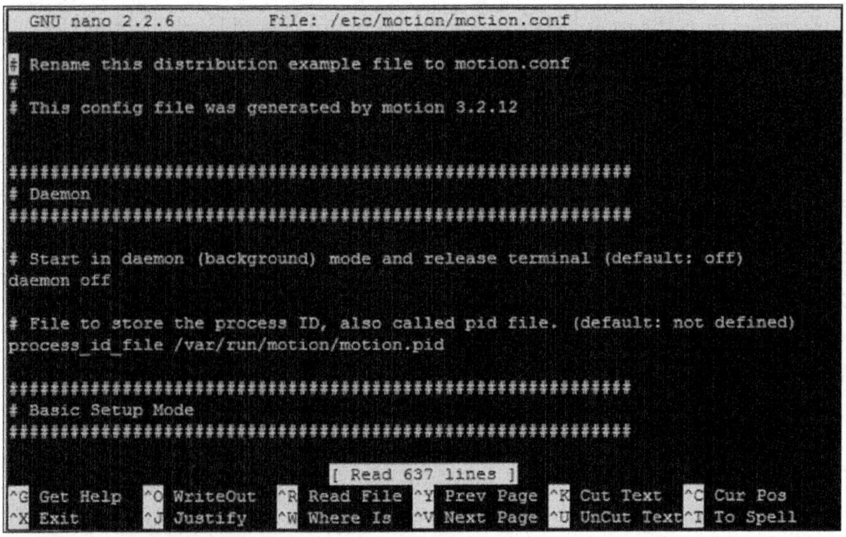

FIGURE 13-7:
The configuration file for Motion.

```
GNU nano 2.2.6          File: /etc/motion/motion.conf

# Rename this distribution example file to motion.conf
#
# This config file was generated by motion 3.2.12


################################################################
# Daemon
################################################################

# Start in daemon (background) mode and release terminal (default: off)
daemon off

# File to store the process ID, also called pid file. (default: not defined)
process_id_file /var/run/motion/motion.pid

################################################################
# Basic Setup Mode
################################################################
                        [ Read 637 lines ]
^G Get Help  ^O WriteOut  ^R Read File ^Y Prev Page ^K Cut Text  ^C Cur Pos
^X Exit      ^J Justify   ^W Where Is  ^V Next Page ^U UnCut Text^T To Spell
```

The first configuration you want to change will make Motion run in daemon mode, which will make sure that it is always running in the background. This means if you log off from your Raspberry Pi, the webcam will still run as long as it is plugged into power. You will see a setting called *daemon* close to the top of the configuration file. Change the setting from off to on. Then continue to make the configuration changes in Table 13-4.

**Table 13-4  Motion Configuration Changes**

| Configuration | New Value | Comment |
|---|---|---|
| framerate | 30 | |
| threshold | 500 | |
| gap | 10 | |
| max_mpeg_time | 30 | |
| output_normal | center | |
| ffmpeg_video_codec | msmpeg4 | For viewing video footage in Windows; otherwise choose your preferred codec. |
| target_dir | /home | You can choose any other directory where you want your video footage to be stored. |
| webcam_motion | on | |
| webcam_maxrate | 30 | |
| webcam_port | 8085 | Or any other port. |
| webcam_localhost | off | |

Save the file and exit (Ctrl + X, Y, Enter) to complete editing the configuration. After you're back at the command prompt you need to restart Motion so that the new configuration can take effect. You do this by typing the following:

```
service motion stop
motion
```

If your webcam has an activity light on it, you should have noticed it come on. Check that it is working by doing a directory listing of the /home directory (type dir /home) and see if there are .avi and .jpg files being written. It is configured so that it will store video footage only when motion is detected, and it will store a maximum of 30 seconds of footage per file. You probably noticed when you were editing the configuration that this application is highly configurable and can be changed to suit your needs. Next you will test that the real-time video streaming is working.

Open a browser other than Internet Explorer on a PC, tablet or smartphone connected to your home network. (Internet Explorer does not support MJPEG streaming, so you need to use another browser such as Chrome, Firefox or Safari.) Now type the IP address and port of your Raspberry Pi. For example, type something like this:

```
http://192.168.0.2:8085
```

The real-time webcam video will now appear in the browser.

In order to view the video and picture files that have been saved in the /home directory, you have a number of options. I recommend connecting remotely to the Raspberry Pi using an FTP client (such as FileZilla) and then either copying the footage to a PC or executing the file directly through FileZilla (which actually copies the file across to the PC, runs it and then destroys the local copy).

### How to Send an E-Mail When Motion Is Detected

One of the great features of Motion is the ability to run a Python script when movement is detected. Later in this chapter, there is a project describing how to send an e-mail. (See the section "Project 4: How to Send an E-mail Alert".) You can use the code from that project to have an e-mail sent to you when movement is detected on your webcam. You can do this by editing the configuration file and looking for a configuration called on_event_start, which can be configured as follows:

```
on_event_start sudo python /home/sendemail.py 'Webcam ⊃
motion detected'
```

This configuration tells Motion to execute the sendemail.py script when movement is detected. The content of sendemail.py is located in the section "Project 4: How to Send an E-mail Alert" later in this chapter. You can also learn how to attach a file to an e-mail in that project, which allows you to e-mail a picture from the webcam when movement is detected. For this there is another configuration called on_picture_save. Set this configuration as follows:

```
on_picture_save sudo python /home/emailphoto.py 'Webcam ⊃
picture attached' %f
```

This configuration tells Motion to execute the emailphoto.py script, which is located in the /home directory, when movement is detected. Additionally, it passes a parameter (%f) to the script of the filename of the picture that the webcam took at the time the movement was detected. Motion will replace %f with the filename of the picture it took.

Both of these scripts are listed in project 4 of this chapter.

Remember, of course, to restart Motion after any configuration change by typing the following:

```
service motion stop
motion
```

### How to View the Webcam over the Internet

This subsection comes with a big security warning. If you open up your Raspberry Pi to the Internet, anyone on the Internet can see your webcam. They will of course need to know your IP address and port, so you do have some measure of safety, albeit fairly weak. Internet hackers look for open ports, so it won't be long before they figure out that there is a video stream on that port.

So if you are still reading this, this is how to make your webcam visible from the Internet. In a typical home installation there is a router that connects all the PCs and Wi-Fi devices in the house to the Internet. You need to configure your router to allow the video stream through the port you configured earlier in this project. Getting access to your router requires that you know how to do this, and may require that you contact your Internet service provider (ISP) or cable company. You will need to know the IP address of your router. Many routers use the `192.168.0.1` or `192.168.1.1` address as a default. Type your router IP address into a browser. This will take you to a login page where you need to log in to the router with the username and password for the router. It is beyond the scope of this chapter to provide you with detailed instructions for this part as there are many different routers, each with their own configuration applications. Look for "port range forwarding" or "port forwarding" settings, often under a "Gaming" menu. (Gamers need to open a port to be able to participate in peer-to-peer games over the Internet.) Add a new entry called `rpi-web`. `FromPort=8085`, `ToPort=8085`, `IpAddress=`*(Raspberry Pi IP address)*. Take note of the Internet IP address of the router under the Gateway settings of the router. This is the address that has been assigned to you by your ISP, and you will use this address to access from the Internet. Now type `http://InternetIPAddress:8085` into a browser connected to the Internet. This should take you to your webcam video stream. From time to time your ISP may recycle IP addresses, so you will need to repeat the earlier steps to determine your new IP address. Alternatively, most ISPs will sell you a static IP address.

---

> **WARNING**
>
> Your webcam is now accessible to anyone accessing the Internet who knows your Internet address and port number. It's a good idea to install a firewall on your Raspberry Pi to protect your computer from port scanners and other malicious programs. A *firewall* is basically a set of rules that limits or blocks incoming or outgoing web requests. One more thing you may want to protect against is Internet users attempting to access your SSH account by trying a dictionary attack against your password. There is a handy utility called *Fail2Ban* that monitors your log files for failed login attempts and temporarily blocks offending users. Detailed instructions on these precautions are beyond the scope of this book.

---

# Project 3: How to Make a Temperature Gauge

In this project you are going to be using a DS18B20 sensor to detect the temperature and display it on the screen. You will also write some Python code to monitor temperature and send an e-mail alert if the temperature exceeds a predefined threshold. The sensor returns a Celsius value, so you will also have some optional Python code to do a Fahrenheit conversion if that is your preference. Table 13-5 shows what you will need.

### Table 13-5 What You Will Need

| QTY | Item | Description |
|-----|------|-------------|
| 1 | DS18B20 | This sensor looks like a transistor but is actually a highly accurate 1 wire temperature sensor. |
| 1 | 4.7kΩ resistor | A pull-up resistor. |
| 1 | Solderless breadboard | A prototyping board for which parts and wires can be connected by clipping them into the board. It is used for prototyping electronics without having to solder parts together. |
| 3, 3 | Jumper wires | Male to male for breadboard connections, male to female for connecting the breadboard to the GPIO pins. Jumper wires usually come in packs of various quantities, colours and sizes. Although you need only 6 for this project, having 20 to 30 of each should see you through most projects. Any size will do for this project, but shorter male to male (10 cm) and longer male to female (20 cm) are best. |

## Construction

The circuitry for this sensor is very easy to build. Besides the power and ground connections all you need to do is connect the 4.7Ωk pull-up resistor between the signal and power as shown in Figures 13-8 and 13-9. It is important to use pin 7 for the sensor connection. The software you will use to interface with the DS18B20 is hard-coded for pin 7, so you cannot use another pin for this sensor.

## Software

Luckily the software required to interface with the DS18B20 has already been written and is built into your Raspberry Pi kernel. You will be using an application called *Modprobe* to retrieve the temperature value.

At the Raspberry Pi command prompt type the following two commands:

```
sudo modprobe w1-gpio
sudo modprobe w1-therm
```

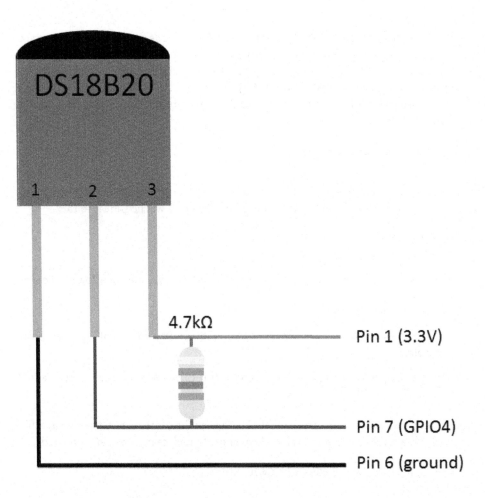

FIGURE 13-8:
A wiring
diagram for a
DS18B20
temperature
sensor
connected to a
Raspberry Pi.

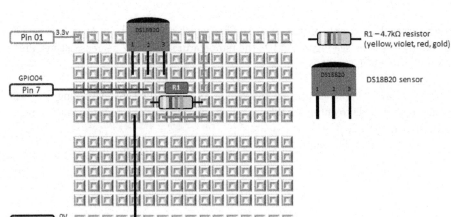

FIGURE 13-9:
A breadboard
diagram for a
DS18B20
temperature
sensor
connected to a
Raspberry Pi.

One of the nice features of the DS18B20 sensor is it has a unique number that allows you to use multiple sensors and uniquely identify the temperature of each sensor. The preceding command interfaces with the sensor and retrieves the temperature, which it then writes to a new directory on the Raspberry Pi. This directory can be found in `/sys/bus/w1/devices/`. In order to check if this file was created, you can do a directory listing by typing the following command:

```
ls /sys/bus/w1/devices/
```

You should see a directory that correlates to the unique number of your sensor. Every sensor has a unique number, so it won't be the same as my file, but it will be similar to this:

```
28-0000040be5b6
```

If you don't see a directory with lots of numbers and letters like this one, then do the following:

- Check your circuit wiring.
- Make sure that you have the correct resistor. (This is very important – yellow, violet, red, gold.)
- Feel the temperature gauge with your finger. If it feels hot, you have it wired back to front.

If you do see the new directory, navigate into it and view the contents of the `w1_slave` file, which will contain the temperature value. (Remember to replace my number with yours.)

```
cd /sys/bus/w1/devices/28-0000040be5b6
nano w1_slave
```

You will now see the contents of the `w1_slave` file, which contains the temperature data in Celsius. In my example (see Figure 13-10), the temperature is 20.812 degrees Celsius. Press Ctrl + X, followed by N, to exit.

Now that you have completed testing your circuit and have the sensor working, you will write some Python code to automate the preceding and print the temperature to the screen, as shown in Listing 13-2.

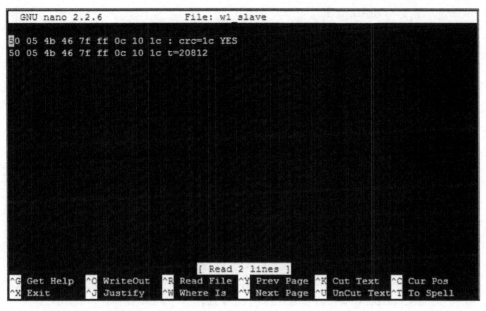

FIGURE 13-10: The temperature shown in the `w1_slave` file that was created by Modprobe.

---

## Listing 13-2  Temperature Check

```
#!/usr/bin/env python
"""
Home Automation: temperature check
For the Raspberry Pi
"""
import subprocess
import time

def fileexists(filename):
        try:
                with open(filename): pass
        except IOError:
                return False
        return True

def GetTemperature():
        #set this variable to true if you want a Fahrenheit
        #temperature
        Fahrenheit = False

        #These two lines call the modprobe application to get the
        #temperature from the sensor
```

*continued*

Listing 13-2   **continued**

```
        subprocess.call(['modprobe', 'w1-gpio'])
        subprocess.call(['modprobe', 'w1-therm'])

        #Open the file that you viewed earlier so that Python can
        #see what is in it. Replace the serial number with
        #your own number
        filename = "/sys/bus/w1/devices/28-0000040be5b6/w1_slave"
        if (fileexists(filename)):
                tfile = open(filename)
        else:
                return 0
        # Read the w1_slave file into memory
        text = tfile.read()
        # Close the file
        tfile.close()
        # You are interested in the second line so this code will
        # put the second line into the secondline variable
        secondline = text.split("\n")[1]
        # You are interested in the 10th word on the second line
        temperaturedata = secondline.split(" ")[9]
        # You are interested in the number of the 10 word so
        # you discard the first two letters "t=" and convert
        # the remaining number $
        temperature = float(temperaturedata[2:])
        # Divide the value by 1000 to get the decimal in the
        # right place
        temperature = temperature / 1000
        temp = float(temperature)
        # Do the Farenheit conversion if required
        if Fahrenheit:
                temp=temp*1.8+32
        temp = round(temp,2)
        return(temp)

def main():
        # This is the main routine of the program
        print "The temperature is " + str(GetTemperature())

if __name__ == "__main__":
        main()
```

Lastly, let's create some code that will monitor the temperature and send an e-mail when the temperature exceeds a particular value. You will use the `SendEmail` function from the e-mail project (project 4 in this chapter). Using the program you created to print the temperature to the screen, replace the `main` routine with the code in Listing 13-3.

**Listing 13-3  Temperature Alert**

```
# This is the main routine of the program
        tempind=False
        while True:
            temperature=GetTemperature()
            if temperature > 25 and tempind==False:
                    #Use the SendEmail routine from the
                    #e-mail project
                    SendEmail("The temperature is "+ ↩
str(temperature))
                    tempind=True;
            else:
                    #This will ensure you only receive one e-mail
                    #once the temperature is above 25
                    #This variable is set back to false when the
                    #temperature is less than or equal to 25
                    tempind=False;
            #Fetch the temperature every 10 seconds
            time.sleep(10)
```

# Project 4: How to Send an E-mail Alert

The sensors play an important role in monitoring your home but are not much use without having an action associated with them. An e-mail alert is a useful type of action as you can pack as much information as want into the body of the e-mail and send it to a smartphone. Other useful alerts (not detailed in this chapter) are a flashing LED, an LCD display and a buzzer or siren, which are all easily achievable tasks with a Raspberry Pi. Another useful tool for home automation, but also beyond the scope of this chapter, is a web page and a database. You can log sensor data to a database and design web pages to represent that data to you so that you can monitor your home.

## What You Will Need

This project is all software based and can be used in conjunction with all the other projects in the chapter. All you will need is your Raspberry Pi, an editor and some Python code that I will provide.

## Software

In order to send an e-mail from your Raspberry Pi, you need to send it from an e-mail server. You need to know your e-mail account details. There are three pieces of information you will need:

○ The URL or IP address of the e-mail SMTP server

○ Your username

○ Your password

If you do not have these, you can use a Gmail or Yahoo! account. You will be creating a Python program called `sendemail.py` that will send a plain-text e-mail. The program accepts two command-line parameters. A *command-line parameter* is a value that you pass to the program. In this case you are passing the e-mail content as a parameter, as follows:

```
sudo python sendemail.py "Web cam motion detected"
```

sudo is a command telling the operating system to use super user rights when executing the command. Python tells the operating system to run some Python script. `sendemail.py` is the Python script you want to execute, and `"Web cam motion detected"` is the parameter you are passing into the `sendemail.py` program.

Create a file called `sendemail.py` that contains the code in Listing 13-4. Go through each line of code and ensure that you have filled in the details specified in the code comments.

---

**Listing 13-4    Send E-mail**

```python
#!/usr/bin/env python
"""
Home Automation: send e-mail
For the Raspberry Pi
"""

import sys
import smtplib
from email.mime.text import MIMEText
import time

def SendEmail(MessageText):
        #enter the e-mail account username between the quotes
        smtp_user = ""

        #enter the e-mail account password between the quotes
        smtp_pass = ""

        #sys.argv[1] is the 1st parameter that is passed to
        #this program and it contains the text for the body
```

```
        #of the e-mail
        msg = MIMEText(MessageText)

        #enter the target e-mail address between the quotes
        msg['To']   = ""

        #enter the e-mail account username between the quotes
        msg['From'] = ""

        #enter the message subject between the quotes
        msg['Subject'] = ""

        #enter the SMTP server URL or IP Address between the quotes
        s = smtplib.SMTP("")

        s.login(smtp_user,smtp_pass)
        s.sendmail(msg['From'], msg['To'], msg.as_string())
        s.quit()

def main():
    SendEmail(sys.argv[1])

if __name__ == "__main__":
        main()
```

Most e-mail servers use e-mail encryption, so there are two variations of the code in Listing 13-4, depending on which type of encryption is being used – transport layer security (TLS) or SMTP SSL encryption. You can find out what encryption is being used from your ISP, or through trial and error. If you have a Gmail or Yahoo! account, I have included details on how to send e-mails from their e-mail servers (providing you have an e-mail address with them).

**Transport Layer Security**

The code in Listing 13-5 will send an e-mail using TLS encryption.

Listing 13-5   **Send E-mail Using TLS Encryption**

```
#!/usr/bin/env python
"""

Home Automation: send e-mail using TLS encryption
For the Raspberry Pi
```

*continued*

Listing 13-5    **continued**

```python
"""

import sys
import smtplib
from email.mime.text import MIMEText

def SendEmail(MessageText):
        #enter the e-mail account username between the quotes
        smtp_user = ""

        #enter the e-mail account password between the quotes
        smtp_pass = ""

        #sys.argv[1] is the 1st parameter that is passed to
        #this program and it contains the text for the body
        #of the e-mail
        msg = MIMEText(MessageText)

        #enter the target e-mail address between the quotes
        msg['To']   = ""

        #enter the e-mail account username between the quotes
        msg['From'] = ""

        #enter the message subject between the quotes
        msg['Subject'] = ""

        #enter the SMTP server URL or IP Address between the quotes
        s = smtplib.SMTP("",587)
        s.ehlo()
        s.starttls()
        s.ehlo()

        s.login(smtp_user,smtp_pass)
        s.sendmail(msg['From'], msg['To'], msg.as_string())
        s.quit()

def main():
    SendEmail(sys.argv[1])

if __name__ == "__main__":
        main()
```

## SMTP SSL Encryption

The code in Listing 13-6 will send an e-mail using SMTP SSL encryption.

---

**Listing 13-6   Send E-mail Using SSL**

```python
#!/usr/bin/env python
"""
Home Automation: send e-mail using SSL encryption
For the Raspberry Pi
"""

import sys
import smtplib
from email.mime.text import MIMEText

def SendEmail(MessageText):

        #enter the e-mail account username between the quotes
        smtp_user = ""

        #enter the e-mail account password between the quotes
        smtp_pass = ""

        #sys.argv[1] is the 1st parameter that is passed to
        #this program and it contains the text for the body
        #of the e-mail
        msg = MIMEText(MessageText)

        #enter the target e-mail address between the quotes
        msg['To']   = ""

        #enter the e-mail account username between the quotes
        msg['From'] = ""

        #enter the message subject between the quotes
        msg['Subject'] = ""

        #enter the SMTP server URL or IP Address between the quotes
```

*continued*

**Listing 13-6**   **continued**

```
        s = smtplib.SMTP_SSL("", 465)

        s.login(smtp_user,smtp_pass)
        s.sendmail(msg['From'], msg['To'], msg.as_string())
        s.quit()

def main():
        SendEmail (sys.argv[1])

if __name__ == "__main__":
        main()
```

## Sending E-mail Using a Gmail or Yahoo! Account

If you have a Gmail or Yahoo! account, you use your e-mail address as the e-mail account and the e-mail password as the e-mail account password. Gmail uses SSL, so edit the SSL encryption code (in Listing 13-6) with the following SMTP server details:

```
smtp.gmail.com
```

Yahoo! uses TLS, so edit the TLS encryption code (in Listing 13-5) with the following as the SMTP server details:

```
smtp.mail.yahoo.com
```

## How to Attach a File to an E-mail

In the section "Project 2: How to Monitor Your Home with a Webcam", a command was introduced that enabled you to send a photograph attachment when the webcam detected motion. The code in Listing 13-7 will allow you to do it. You will build on the `sendemail.py` program you created earlier (in Listing 13-4) by adding a new parameter to pass the filename of the photo you want to attach to the e-mail. Remember to update this program with the code depending on the type of encryption you require as explained earlier. In this example I've assumed SSL encryption. The `emailphoto.py` program accepts two parameters: the first for the message text and the second for the filename of the photo you want to send. For example, you will run this program using the following command:

```
sudo python sendemail.py 'Webcam motion detected', ↵
'/home/photo.jpg'
```

Listing 13-7 is the code for `emailphoto.py` that will attach a photograph to the e-mail. I have created a function called `emailphoto` because it is used in other programs within this chapter.

**Listing 13-7    Send E-mail with a Photo Attachment**

```python
#!/usr/bin/env python
"""
Home Automation: sends an e-mail with a photograph attachment
For the Raspberry Pi
"""

import sys
import smtplib
from email.mime.text import MIMEText
from email.mime.application import MIMEApplication
from email.mime.multipart import MIMEMultipart

def emailphoto(msgtext, afilename):
        #enter the e-mail account username between the quotes
        smtp_user = ""

        #enter the e-mail account password between the quotes
        smtp_pass = ""
        msg = MIMEMultipart()

        #enter the target e-mail address between the quotes
        msg['To']   = ""

        #enter the e-mail account username between the quotes
        msg['From'] = ""

        #enter the message subject between the quotes
        msg['Subject'] = ""

        #That is what you see if don't have an e-mail reader:
        msg.preamble = 'Multipart message.\n'

        #sys.argv[1] is the 1st parameter that is passed to this
        #and it contains the text for the body of the e-mail
        part = MIMEText(msgtext)
        msg.attach(part)
```

*continued*

Listing 13-7   **continued**

```
       #The next 3 lines attach the photo using the filename
       #passed in as the second parameter to this program
       part = MIMEApplication(open(afilename,"rb").read())
       part.add_header('Content-Disposition', 'attachment', ⟳
filename=afilename)
       msg.attach(part)

       #enter the SMTP server URL or IP Address between the quotes
       s = smtplib.SMTP_SSL("", 465)
       s.login(smtp_user,smtp_pass)
       s.sendmail(msg['From'], msg['To'], msg.as_string())
       s.quit()

def main():
    emailphoto(sys.argv[1], sys.argv[2])

if __name__ == "__main__":
        main()
```

# Project 5: How to Send an E-mail Using a Wireless Remote

In this project you will use a wireless remote to send a signal to the Raspberry Pi to check the status of the sensors that you have built in the other projects in this chapter and then send yourself an e-mail report of all the sensors in the house. This is an example of the control category of home automation. The e-mail will contain the temperature, status of door switches and motion sensors and a picture of the last motion detected by the webcam. Other typical uses of a wireless remote in home automation are switching lights on and off (particularly external lights), switching or sounding an alarm system, opening and closing a garage door and automating blinds and curtains. As you get access to more home-automation sensors and controllers within your home you can use what you learn in this chapter to add remote control to those devices. Table 13-6 shows what you need.

## Table 13-6 What You Will Need

| QTY | Item | Description |
|-----|------|-------------|
| 1 | Wireless remote kit | This is shown later in Figure 13-11. There are a number of kits available on the market that consist of a key-fob remote and a receiver. The receivers are usually 5V-10V and have four digital outputs. The key fobs vary from one button to four buttons. There are different kinds of receivers (momentary, toggle and latch). You are using a momentary receiver here (explained further later). |
| 1 | 5V power supply | Although this is not mandatory because the Raspberry Pi does have a 5V power supply, I recommend a separate power supply for the receiver. It is best to not overload the Raspberry Pi, and I have found that the current required by this RF receiver exceeds that of the Raspberry Pi, which affects the distance you can get between the key fob and the receiver. An old cell phone power supply should work (5V 700mA). Be sure to check the voltage and current of both input and output in the data sheet of the receiver you purchase. The output signal voltage should be 5V. |
| 1 | PN2222A transistor | Switching NPN bipolar transistor 40V/.6A. |
| 1 | 10kΩ resistor | Brown, black, red, gold. |
| 2 | 1kΩ resistors | Brown, black, orange, gold. |
| 1 | Solderless breadboard | A prototyping board for which parts and wires can be connected by clipping them into the board. It is used for prototyping electronics without having to solder parts together. |
| 3, 4 | Jumper wires | Male to male for breadboard connections, male to female for connecting the breadboard to the GPIO pins. Jumper wires usually come in packs of various quantities, colours and sizes. Although you need only 7 for this project, having 20 to 30 of each should see you through most projects. Any size will do for this project, but shorter male to male (10 cm) and longer male to female (20 cm) are best. |

## Construction

Radio frequency circuits are complex and not worth building yourself when they are readily available prebuilt for a minimal cost (as shown in Figure 13-11). As discussed earlier, there are different types of radio frequency circuits available on the market (momentary, latch and toggle) that all work slightly differently. A momentary receiver's digital output will remain on as long as the key-fob button is pressed. The latch receiver will ensure that only one output pin is on at any one time. For example, if you press button A, digital output A will go on. If you press B, A will go off, and B will go on – and so on. A latching receiver digital output goes on when a button is pressed in and out, and off when the same button is pressed in and out. In this project you will use a momentary receiver, but you can use any type and adjust the Python code to suit the type of the receiver.

FIGURE 13-11:
A wireless
remote kit.

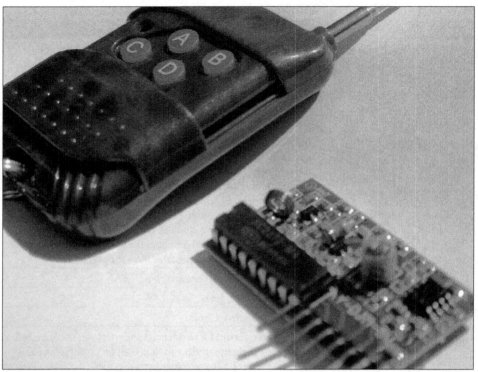

This is the first time in this chapter you have used a transistor. Although transistors have many uses, one of the lesser-known uses is the capability of a bipolar transistor to switch things off and on. With the flat surface facing you, the PN2222 transistor has three pins from left to right: the emitter, the base and the collector. When voltage is applied to the base the transistor allows the current to flow through the emitter (source) to the collector (drain). You will construct a switch similar to what you did in the section "Project 1: How to Create a Motion Sensor and Door Switch", but instead of a door switch you will use the transistor to switch the Raspberry Pi GPIO when the wireless receiver receives a signal. The reason you do not connect the receiver directly to the GPIO pin is that it has an external 5V supply and will damage the GPIO pin, which has a 3V maximum.

---

**WARNING**     Be extremely careful when working with circuits (especially 5V) that connect to the GPIO pins as they are not protected and you can very easily cause permanent damage to your Raspberry Pi. Double-check the wiring before powering on the Raspberry Pi and the external power supply.

---

Figure 13-12 is the circuit diagram, and Figure 13-13 is the breadboard layout diagram. Depending on which key-fob receiver you have, you may need to alter the receiver pin connections. In this example pin 1 is ground, pin 2 is 5V and pin 3 is data. The other pins are usually allocated to additional key-fob buttons or a receiver aerial. Before you buy a kit refer to the data sheet of the receiver to check the pin configuration and check the output voltage.

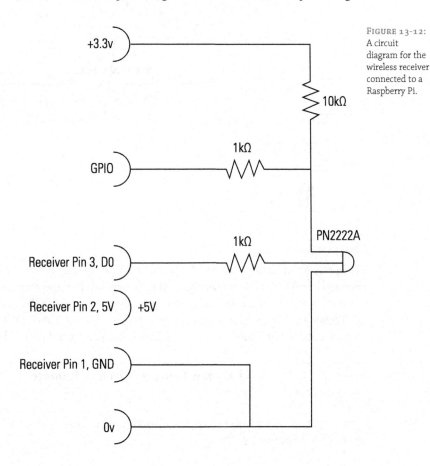

FIGURE 13-12: A circuit diagram for the wireless receiver connected to a Raspberry Pi.

FIGURE 13-13:
A breadboard
layout for the
wireless receiver
connected to a
Raspberry Pi.

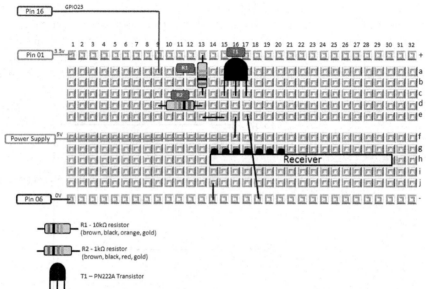

## Software

The program in Listing 13-8 will loop and wait until the key-fob button is pressed. When it is pressed it will poll the door switch, motion detector and temperature sensor and get the latest picture created by the webcam. You then send an e-mail using the `sendemail.py` program you created in Listing 13-4. The status of all the sensors is in the body of the text, and the latest webcam photo is attached to the e-mail. Every time you press the key fob, an e-mail will be sent.

**Listing 13-8   Send E-mail Using a Wireless Remote**

```python
#!/usr/bin/env python
"""

Home Automation: send e-mail using wireless remote
For the Raspberry Pi
"""

import os, glob, time, operator
import RPi.GPIO as GPIO
import time
import sys
import smtplib
from email.mime.text import MIMEText
from email.mime.application import MIMEApplication
from email.mime.multipart import MIMEMultipart
```

```python
from time import gmtime, strftime

def get_latest_photo(files):
    lt = operator.lt
    if not files:
            return None
    now = time.time()
    latest = files[0], now - os.path.getctime(files[0])
    for f in files[1:]:
            age = now - os.path.getctime(f)
            if lt(age, latest[1]):
                    latest = f, age
    return latest[0]

def emailphoto(msgtext, afilename):
        #enter the e-mail account username between the quotes
        smtp_user = ""

        #enter the e-mail account password between the quotes
        smtp_pass = ""
        msg = MIMEMultipart()

        #enter the target e-mail address between the quotes
        msg['To']   = ""

        #enter the e-mail account username between the quotes
        msg['From'] = ""

        #enter the message subject between the quotes
        msg['Subject'] = ""

        # That is what u see if don't have an e-mail reader:
        msg.preamble = 'Multipart message.\n'

        #sys.argv[1] is the 1st parameter that is passed to this
        #and it contains the text for the body of the e-mail
        part = MIMEText(msgtext)
        msg.attach(part)

        #The next 3 lines attach the photo using the filename
        #passed in as the second parameter to this program
        part = MIMEApplication(open(afilename,"rb").read())
        part.add_header('Content-Disposition', 'attachment', ⤶
    filename=afilename)
```

*continued*

Listing 13-8 **continued**

```
        msg.attach(part)

        #enter the SMTP server URL or IP Address between the quotes
        s = smtplib.SMTP_SSL("", 465)
        s.login(smtp_user,smtp_pass)
        s.sendmail(msg['From'], msg['To'], msg.as_string())
        s.quit()

def sendreport():
        msgtext = "This is a sensor status report for " +⤸
  strftime("%Y-%m-%d %H:%M:%S", gmtime()) + "\n"

        if GPIO.input(13) == True:
                msgtext = msgtext + "Status of door switch is :⤸
  Door open\n"
        else:
                msgtext = msgtext + "Status of door switch is :⤸
  Door closed\n"


        if GPIO.input(15) == True:
                msgtext = msgtext + "Status of motion detector ⤸
  is : No motion\n"
        else:
                msgtext = msgtext + "Status of motion detector ⤸
  is : Motion detected\n"

        # Use the GetTemperature routine we
        # created in the temperature project
        Temperature = GetTemperature()
        msgtext = msgtext + "The temperature is :⤸
  "+str(Temperature)+"\n"

        # Change this to your path where the
        # web cam pictures are stored.
        # *.jpg means all JPEG files
        photopath = "/home/*.jpg"
        files = glob.glob(photopath)
        latestphoto = get_latest_photo(files)
        msgtext = msgtext + 'Latest photo:' + latestphoto + "⤸ is
  attached to this e-mail\n";

        # Send e-mail using the emailphoto()
        # function we created in the e-mail
```

```python
    # project
    emailphoto(msgtext, latestphoto)
    print "Report has been sent."


#main program
def main():
        GPIO.setmode(GPIO.BOARD)
        GPIO.setup(16, GPIO.IN) #RF Remote Receiver
        GPIO.setup(13, GPIO.IN) #Door switch
        GPIO.setup(15, GPIO.IN) #Motion sensor

        rfkey = False

        while True:
                if GPIO.input(16) == False: #RF key-fob key pressed
                        if rfkey == False:
                                rfkey = True
                                sendreport()
                else:
                        rfkey = False

                time.sleep(.3)

if __name__ == "__main__":
        main()
```

## Over to You

Over the course of this chapter, you learned how to interface with sensors that give you information about your home (movement, temperature, video and pictures). You acted on this information by creating e-mail alerts, and in the last project I introduced an element of remote control. You now have the building blocks for your next home automation project. Here are some ideas:

○ Place a door switch on a dog flap and send an e-mail every time your dog enters or leaves the house.

○ Detect when your garage door has been open for more than 10 minutes.

○ Switch off a light when no motion is detected for a period of time.

These projects, plus many more, are now well within your reach.

# Chapter 14

# Computer-Controlled Slot Car Racing

by Mike Cook

## In This Chapter

○ Learn how to use your Raspberry Pi to enable and disable a slot car set

○ See how to make your own illuminated joystick pad

○ Discover how to use an external text file as a question bank

○ Understand the interactions between the software and hardware

**THIS PROJECT IS** a rather different twist on the multiple-choice quiz theme. Not only does it have a novel way of inputting answers, but it also has a rather novel way of keeping the score.

The idea is that you are going to hack into a slot car game and allow the Raspberry Pi to control when the game can be played. Then players can drive their cars for three seconds at a time, if they are the first to answer a question correctly. If they get the question wrong, their opponent gets the time. The game continues until one player crosses the finishing line after completing a set number of laps. The questions come from a plain text file and can be added to, or the subject of them changed. They are multiple-choice questions with four possible answers, and players indicate their answer by moving a special joystick button. The successful player's joystick button will light up green, whereas the other player's button will light up red.

## Obtaining a Slot Car Racer

So how are you going to implement this game? First you need a slot car racing game. These come in all sorts of shapes and sizes, from sleek Formula One racing cars to heavy trucks and even grannies on Zimmer frames. In essence they are very similar: It's a race between two players. Mostly they are set up so that if you go too fast at the corners, the vehicle will come off the track, so it is not just a matter of running the cars at top speed all the time. Normally the track is some form of figure eight, so the track length can be made the same for both players. Sometimes the two vehicles cross at the same level, giving opportunities for crashes, and other times the tracks go over and under each other. Although there are very expensive racing games, some can be had cheaply in thrift shops or second-hand stores.

## Hacking Your Slot Car Racer

You need to hack into your slot car racer, and, as there are lots of different types of them, I can't be too prescriptive about what you need to do. However, from the electrical point of view, it is basically all the same. What you are going to do is to wire a PiFace relay in series with each hand controller. This will involve cutting one of the two wires coming from the controller, and connecting each end of your cut wire into the NO and common relay connections. NO stands for *normally open* – this connection is only connected to the common line when the relay is energised; when the relay is not energised, that is the normal state – no electrical connection is made. Figure 14-1 shows how you can do this using a screw connection block. These are the type you use for electrical wiring around the house. They come in various sizes, and the size you want is the smallest, which is often marked something like *3 Amps*. A sharp hobby knife can slice the two wires apart, and then you can cut one of them; it doesn't matter which one. You should cut back the insulation and then, following the diagram, attach each end to two of the connector blocks. Take the other end and run wires off to the PiFace board. Do the same for the other controller. When you want to play with your slot car game normally you simply replace the long wires trailing back to the PiFace board with a simple link. Do this close to the track connections so that you have the maximum length of wire on the hand controllers.

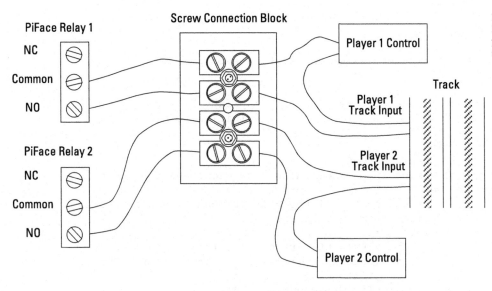

FIGURE 14-1: Hacking into your slot car racing game.

Sometimes the wires coming from the hand controller are all bundled into one cable, so it is impossible to cut just one wire. If this is the case, you will have to cut both of them and join the other wire back up again. This sort of thing is shown in Figure 14-2. In this case the wire consists of an inner conductor and an outer braided wire sheath. Strip back the outer sheath and make sure that no thin strands of wire are shorting out to the other wire. Use insulation tape or heat shrink sleeving to insulate the sheath. Then wire it up as shown in Figure 14-2. Note that this diagram is for one controller; you will have to duplicate this for the other player's controller.

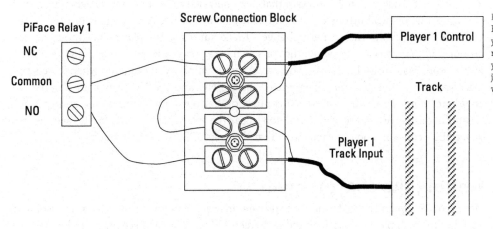

FIGURE 14-2: Hacking into your slot car racing game if you can't cut just a single wire.

## Testing Your Slot Car Racer Hack

Now you need to test the slot car hack. Power up your slot car racing game as normal and run the program in Listing 14-1.

Listing 14-1    **Slot Car Racer Hack Test**

```python
#!/usr/bin/env python
"""
Slot Racer Hack tester on the PiFace board
"""

import piface.pfio as pfio      # piface library
pfio.init()                     # initialise pfio

def main():
        lastInput =0
        print "Slot Racer Hack test press the two input ⟲
switches"
        print "on the PiFace board to change who is racing"
        print "Ctrl - C to quit"
        while True :
            buttons = pfio.read_input()
            if (buttons & 1) ==1 and buttons != lastInput:
                print "player 1 racing"
                pfio.write_output(0x01)
            if (buttons & 2) ==2 and buttons != lastInput:
                print "player 2 racing"
                pfio.write_output(0x02)
            lastInput = buttons

if __name__ == '__main__':
    main()
```

You will see it is a very simple program that just energised each of the relays depending on if you press one of two buttons on the end of the PiFace board. A message is printed to say which player is racing each time it changes. Make sure that the players are the right way around and that you can play when the console message says you can. If you find the control is the wrong way around – that is, when it says you can play you can't and when it says you can't you can – then you may have mixed up the NO and the NC relay connections. NC stands for *normally closed* – there is a connection between the common line and this one when the relay is not energised. If you don't hear the relay clicking at all but do see the two lower LEDs come on and off, then check that the links JP5 and JP6 are made.

## Getting the Player Input

Next you need to find a way to input the players' answers. You could just arrange a row of four switches for each player along with red and green LEDs. In fact the schematic in Figure 14-3 can be implemented in exactly that way. However, at this stage in the game you can be a lot more adventurous than that, so I am going to show you how to make an illuminated switch joystick using that same schematic. Not only is this useful for this project, but you also can use the joystick on other projects in this book, replacing a keyboard input. In Chapter 8, "Colour

Snap", the colour snap project shows you how useful half table tennis balls are at acting as a light diffuser. Well, now they are back, and this time they are even more useful. You are going to mount four tactile button switches on a board, and, in each of the corners, have foam pads that are slightly taller than the switches. Then, if you put the board switch side down, you can click each switch in turn by simply pushing the board in that direction. The feel of the switch is down to the rigidity of the foam pads you use. On the track side of the board, you mount a red/green LED and cover the board in a half table tennis ball. Let's see how to do that in detail.

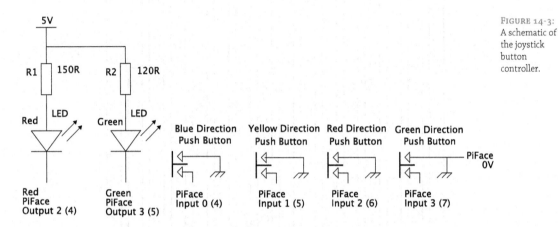

FIGURE 14-3:
A schematic of the joystick button controller.

> The LED needs to be a bright one: Look for one with at least 60 mcd on the red, and 40 mcd on the green at 20mA – brighter if you can get it; otherwise the switch could look a bit washed out. I found 90 mcd red and 45 mcd green, which looked good.
>
> **TIP**

## Making the Joystick Buttons

Take a small piece of strip board 17 holes long, and 16 strips wide. I like to take the corners off the board to give it an octagonal shape, just to make it look neater and ensure that the corners don't snag on the base. Cut the tracks on the back of the board where the dark marks are on Figure 14-4. Make sure that you count the tracks and holes carefully. Then solder a surface mount red/green LED at the centre of the board, as shown between the two tracks and two track cuts. Make sure that the orientation mark on the LED is correctly aligned. There are two types of surface mount LEDs that you can get. One has the LEDs pinned out to the package in parallel; that is, the two anodes are on one side and the two cathodes on the other. This is sometimes known as a *parallel LED pinout*. The other way is known as *antiparallel*, where one anode and one cathode are together at each end; these normally have a bar or some other marker, often green, denoting the cathode. Make sure that you know which you are using. I have designed the board so that the tracks you need to cut are the same for both versions. However, the links on the component side are different for each LED type. When the LED is in place solder the two surface mount resistors as shown between the cut marks. If you haven't got surface mount resistors, then one-eighth watt, or one-tenth watt, resistors should be small enough to mount on the tracks.

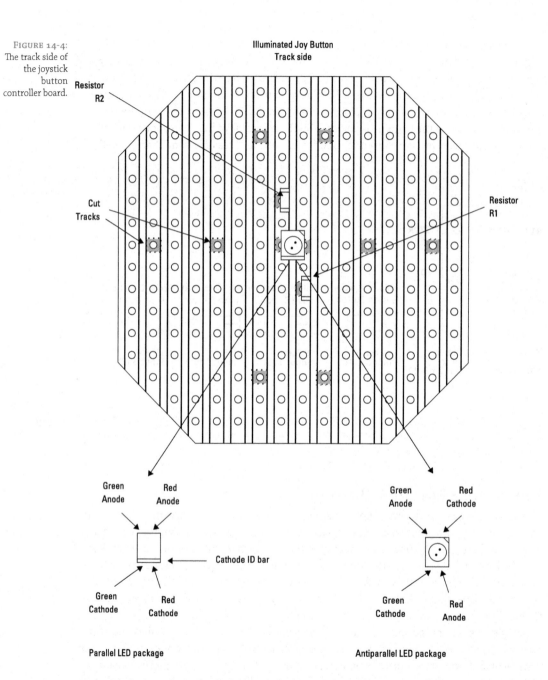

FIGURE 14-4:
The track side of
the joystick
button
controller board.

Now turn the board over and mount and solder the four tack buttons. This is shown in Figure 14-5 for an antiparallel LED package and Figure 14-6 for a parallel LED package. The differences are minor but important. The switches' contacts should be either side of the cut tracks as you insert them through the board. Note that in these figures, the copper strips are shown as hidden detail dotted lines, and the cut tracks are also shown as shaded. This is for ease of orientation, although you won't actually see this when you look at the board for real. The solid lines are tinned copper links; these can be the scrap from cutting the legs of components or simply stripped-back solid core wire. The foam pads can be glued on using impact adhesive; you can cut them out from some packing material. Finally, a strip of 8-way ribbon cable is soldered to the board to make the connections, and spots of hot melt glue make sure that the wires do not foul the switches or pads. A photograph of this is shown in Figure 14-7; note that it is a photograph of the antiparallel LED version of the joystick so it corresponds to Figure 14-5. At this point you should test the board as described later in the subsection "Joystick Testing". In that way you can correct any mistakes before too much gluing is done. However, I will first continue the building narrative as the finished article needs testing as well.

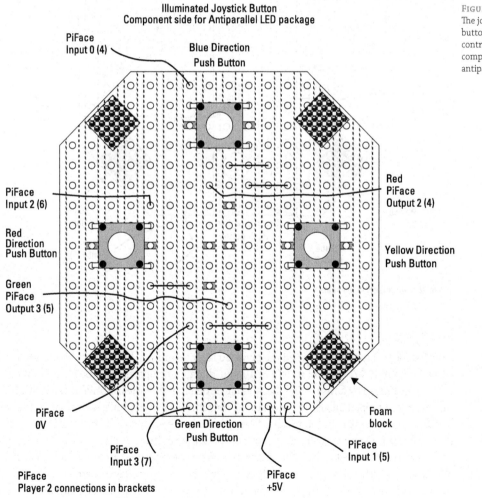

FIGURE 14-5: The joystick button controller components for antiparallel LED.

FIGURE 14-6:
The joystick
button
controller
components for
parallel LED.

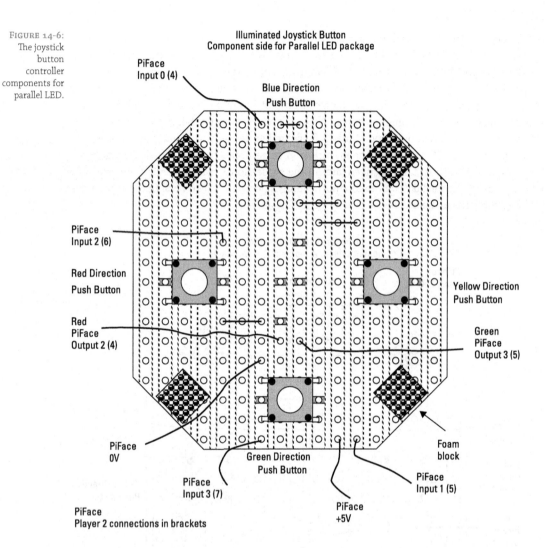

**Illuminated Joystick Button**
**Component side for Parallel LED package**

PiFace
Input 0 (4)

Blue Direction
Push Button

PiFace
Input 2 (6)

Red Direction
Push Button

Red
PiFace
Output 2 (4)

Yellow Direction
Push Button

Green
PiFace
Output 3 (5)

PiFace
0V

Foam
block

Green Direction
Push Button

PiFace
Input 3 (7)

PiFace
Input 1 (5)

PiFace
+5V

PiFace
Player 2 connections in brackets

## Boxing It Up

Now for the box to put it in. I used the plywood layer technique described in Chapter 8 to make
a box 116 mm (4 5/8") by 92 mm (3 3/4"), but the dimensions are not too critical. I made the
sides from 12 mm by 5 mm strip pine, and I fastened together the top and bottom with 10 mm
M3 spacers or tapped pillars. The holes in the bottom sheet were countersunk, and in the centre
of the top I used a saw drill to make a 40 mm hole. I gave it a coat of primer and then painted.
Each radial direction was painted a colour to match the software in the game – blue up, green
down, red right and yellow left. The spaces in between were painted grey. Figure 14-8 shows the
box taped up with painter's tape, ready to receive the grey paint layer. Remove the tape while
the paint is still wet, and then when it has dried mask off the grey areas and paint in the colours.

FIGURE 14-7: A photograph of the joystick button controller components for antiparallel LED.

FIGURE 14-8: The joystick button box masked up before painting.

To make sure that the top of the board is flush with the top of the hole, I mounted the board on a piece of 4 mm acrylic by gluing the foam pads with impact adhesive. Figure 14-9 shows a side view of this arrangement; note how the buttons are not in direct contact with the acrylic. I filed a slot in the side of the box to allow the ribbon cable to come through, as shown in Figure 14-10.

FIGURE 14-9:
A side view of the joystick button controller button switches.

FIGURE 14-10:
The joystick button controller slot for connecting ribbon cable.

Next is the most important part: You have to glue the acrylic in the correct place in the board. Make sure that the copper strips are parallel with the box edge and that the LED is in the centre of the hole when the lid is on. Then hold the board through the hole and remove the lid of the box. Add some hot melt glue to the corners of the acrylic sheet without moving it. What makes this difficult is the wire that is wanting to twist the orientation of the board. Bend the wire to your will. Figure 14-11 shows the board with the hole correctly aligned.

FIGURE 14-11: The joystick button controller aligned under the central hole.

Finally, fix the ribbon cable to the slot in the top side with a bit more hot melt glue. When it has finally tested correctly you can glue the half table tennis ball by dropping it through the hole as shown in Figure 14-12. When this has dried remove the lid and add a fillet of glue neatly round the whole of the ball. Just remember you need two of these joysticks; the connections to the PiFace board for the second player's joystick button are shown in Figures 14-5 and 14-6 in brackets.

## Joystick Testing

Just as with the slot car hack, you need to test your joystick buttons using a simple program before you try anything fancy with it. The test program is shown in Listing 14-2.

FIGURE 14-12:
The complete
joystick button
controller.

## Listing 14-2   Testing the Joystick Buttons

```python
#!/usr/bin/env python
"""
Joystick button tester on the PiFace board
"""

import piface.pfio as pfio      # piface library
pfio.init()                     # initialise pfio

positions = ["nothing", "north (blue)", "west (yellow)", ⤵
"north west", "east (red)","north east","east & west??", ⤵
"big north", "south (green)", "north & south??", "south ⤵
west", "big west", "south east", "big east", "big south", ⤵
"all on"]
def main():
        lastInput =0
```

```
        print "Joystick test press the joystick button"
        print "Ctrl - C to quit"
        while True :
            buttons = pfio.read_input()
            if buttons != lastInput and buttons != 0:
                print "bits are",hex(buttons)
                print "player 1",positions[buttons & 0xf]
                print "player 2",positions[buttons >> 4]
                print " "
                leds = (buttons & 0xC) | ((buttons >> 2) & 0x30)
                pfio.write_output(leds)
            lastInput = buttons

if __name__ == '__main__':
    main()
```

When you first run this you will get the introductory message. Then any press on the joystick will print out the bit pattern, in hex, read from the PiFace inputs, and followed by a message telling you the state of each player's buttons. These are displayed as the points of the compass with the colours used in the slot car racing game in brackets. If you press in the east or south direction, the red or green LED comes on and stays on until there is a change in either button.

The program is quite simple. First the inputs are polled as fast as possible, and then an if statement is used to see if the input has changed since the last time it was looked at and also that the input has a nonzero value. This ensures that you get only one message per key press and you don't get a message when the key is released. The bit pattern is then printed in hex, and the joystick button positions for each player are printed out. These position messages are held in a list called positions, and there is an entry for each of the possible 16 different combinations. Player 1 has the four least significant bits of the input, and a simple bitwise AND operation just leaves player 1's input bits to use to look up what to print. For player 2 the top four bits in the input are shifted down to the bottom four bits so that the same lookup table list can be used. Finally a bit pattern is calculated to see what LEDs to light. This takes bits 6 and 7 and shifts them into the position of bits 4 and 5. Then this is merged with bits 2 and 3 to give the output you need.

Notice that there are some positions with question marks; it is quite hard for example to press both east and west without pressing either north or south – it is easier without the table tennis ball attached, but that is not something you want to require when using the joystick button in an application. These intermediate positions have to be included in the positions list because you have to cater for all combinations, physically possible or not. There are also positions such as a "big south", which is one where east, west and south are all being pressed at one time. One thing you might notice when testing some positions is that you get two messages such as one saying south followed by another saying south west. This is because it is almost impossible to press two buttons simultaneously; one goes down first followed by the other and so there is a message for each. This is something to consider when using the joysticks in your own game.

# The Software

After you have all the hardware prepared you are ready to put together the software support for this project. This consists of two files, a question bank and a screen background logo. You need at least one file containing the questions and answers; later on you might extend this to more question banks, but for a start let's look at just one file. You need a simple text file, just like those you can create with Leafpad. Place one question per line, with the question first, followed by the correct answer, and followed by three incorrect answers. Separate all the sections with commas including the last answer. You will see that there is a space between the end of the last word and the comma, which allows the spacing in the box to look right. Listing 14-3 is a sample of the file format with just a few questions on the subject of IT. You should save it under the name questions.txt.

---

**Listing 14-3    Sample Questions**

```
How many bits in a byte? , 8 , 10 , 4 , 16 ,
Which company did Bill Gates start? , Microsoft , Apple , Google ,
  Facebook ,
What is the largest? , Terabyte , Gigabyte , Megabyte , Kilobyte ,
Which country owns the WWW suffix .de? , Germany , France , Denmark
  , Dominica ,
What is the command to list files in Windows? , dir , ls , cat ,
  files ,
What does UNIX stand for? , Nothing , UNIt eXchange , The creators
  name , UNidentified Integrated eXchange ,
Which of the following is an operating system? , Linux , Bantex ,
  Hopex , Bandx ,
What computer language uses the tags <body> and <meta/>? , HTML ,
  Java , Python , Scratch ,
What does DBMS stand for? , Database management system , Database
  migration statistics , Database management statistics , Database
  migration statistics ,
Who invented the web? , Tim Berners-Lee , Alan Turing , Clive
  Sinclair , Stephen Hawking ,
What was the forerunner to the Internet called? , ARPANET , SKYNET
  , OUTERNET , FASTNET ,
What does LAN stand for? , Local Area Network , Legitimate Access
  Network , Local Access Network , Legitimate Area Network ,
What was the first stored-program computer called? , The Baby , The
  Infant , The Newborn , The Tiny ,
```

```
What is another name for a CPU? , Processor , Disk drive , Memory ,
  Thinker ,
What is Magnetic Ink Character Recognition often used on? , Cheques
  , Bar codes , QRC , Laundry ,
Which of these is a mobile operating system? , Android , Windows
  Vista , OS X , RISCOS ,
What are the tiny points of colour on your monitor called? , Pixels
  , Pacsels , Points , Pica ,
What does WYSIWYG stand for? , What you see is what you get , What
  you see is where you go , What you see is what you give , What
  you seek is where you go ,
```

Where the question overruns a single line in this listing, you should type it in all on one line when you create the file.

The other thing you need to prepare is the background screen logo. I made mine in Gimp, but you can use any graphics drawing program. The image size needs to be 555 pixels by 540 pixels and should mirror the joystick buttons in some way. Figure 14-13 shows the program running, and you can see the background logo underneath the multiple-choice boxes. The file should be called racingLogo.png and be in the same directory as the game code and the questions file. However, the program will cope without its being present, but it's not so colourful.

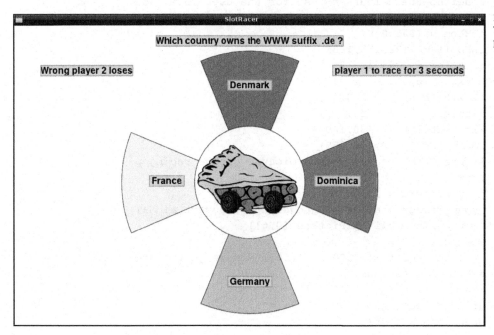

FIGURE 14-13: The game in progress.

# The Game

Now you can get down to the game itself, which is shown in Listing 14-4.

**Listing 14-4    The Slot Car Racing Game**

```python
#!/usr/bin/env python
"""
Slot Racer on the PiFace board
"""
import time                    # for delays
import piface.pfio as pfio     # piface library
import random
import os, pygame, sys

pfio.init()                        # initialise pfio
pygame.init()                      # initialise graphics interface
os.environ['SDL_VIDEO_WINDOW_POS'] = 'center'
pygame.display.set_caption("SlotRacer")
screen = pygame.display.set_mode([980,610],0,32)
background = pygame.Surface((980,610))
piSurface = pygame.Surface((555,540))

# define the colours to use for the user interface
cBackground =(255,255,255)
cLEDon = (255,0,0)
cLEDoff = (128,128,128)
cOutline = (255,128,0)
cText = (0,0,0)
cTextBack = (220,220,220)
altcText = (255,255,255)
altcTextBack = (180,180,180)
cStepBlock = (0,255,255)
# cope with not having the picture of the racing pi
try:
    piPicture = ⏎
pygame.image.load("racingLogo.png").convert_alpha()
    piSurface.blit(piPicture,[0,0])
except:
    piSurface.fill((220,220,220)) # make just a grey area
# Set up questions

qfile = open("questions.txt","r")
questions = list()
```

```
numberOfQuestions = 0
for line in qfile.readlines():
        questions.append(line)
        numberOfQuestions +=1
qfile.close()
random.shuffle(questions)
placeX = [490,490,355,625,490, 150, 800]
placeY = [ 20, 110, 305, 305, 510, 80 ,80]
aPos = [-1,-1,-1,-1]
single = [0, 1, 2, 0, 3, 0, 0, 0, 4, 0, 0, 0, 0, 0, 0, 0]

background.fill(cBackground) # make background colour
font = pygame.font.Font(None, 28)
seq = [ 1 << (temp & 0x7) for temp in range (0,32)]
# initial sequence
timeInc = 0.3
stepInt = True # getting the step signal from inside the Pi
step = 0 # start point in sequence
nextTime = time.time()
answer = "answer"
answerPos = -1

def main():
        ask =0
        while True :
            while pfio.read_input() != 0:
                checkForEvent()  # wait until switch is released
            setupScreen(ask)
            checkInput()
            ask += 1
            if ask >= numberOfQuestions :
                ask = 0
                random.shuffle(questions)

def checkInput():
    buttonsInput = 0
    while buttonsInput == 0:
        buttonsInput = pfio.read_input()
        checkForEvent()
    if buttonsInput >= 0x10 :
        first = " player 2 "
        second = " player 1 "
```

*continued*

**Listing 14-4   continued**

```
      buttonsInput = buttonsInput >> 4
      bits = 0x26
   else:
      first = " player 1 "
      second = " player 2 "
      bits = 0x19
   #print hex(buttonsInput), single[buttonsInput] , answerPos
   if single[buttonsInput] == answerPos:
      drawWords("Correct"+first+"wins", 5, False)
      drawWords(first+"to race for 3 seconds", 6, False)
      pfio.write_output(bits)
   else:
      drawWords("Wrong"+first+"loses", 5, False)
      drawWords(second+"to race for 3 seconds", 6, False)
      pfio.write_output(bits ^ 0x3f)
   correct()
   pfio.write_output(0)
   correct() # keep on flashing for a bit


def scramble():
   global aPos
   aPos = [-1,-1,-1,-1]
   for p in range(0,4):
      match = True
      while match:
         match = False
         candidate = random.randint(1,4)
         for i in range(0,4):
            if aPos[i] == candidate:
               match = True
         aPos[p] = candidate

def setupScreen(question) : # initialise the screen
   global answer, answerPos
   screen.blit(background,[0,0]) # set background colour
   screen.blit(piSurface,[210,50])
   pygame.display.update()
   time.sleep(2.0) # delay while the players settle down
   q = questions[question].split(",")
   scramble()
   drawWords(q[0],0, False)
```

```
        drawWords(q[1],aPos[0], False)
        drawWords(q[2],aPos[1], False)
        drawWords(q[3],aPos[2], False)
        drawWords(q[4],aPos[3], False)
        pygame.display.update()
        answer = q[1]
        answerPos = aPos[0]

def drawWords(words,pos,inv) :
        if inv :
            text = font.render(words, True, altcText, ⤵
altcTextBack )
        else :
            text = font.render(words, True, cText, cTextBack )
        textRect = text.get_rect()
        if pos == 2 :
           textRect.right = placeX[2]
        elif pos == 3:
           textRect.left = placeX[3]
        else:
           textRect.centerx = placeX[pos]
        textRect.top = placeY[pos]
        pygame.draw.rect(screen,cTextBack, textRect, 0)
        screen.blit(text, textRect)
        pygame.draw.rect(screen,cOutline, textRect, 2)

def correct() :
    nextTime = 0
    for flash in range(0,10) :
      while time.time() < nextTime :
         pass
      if flash & 1:
         drawWords(answer,answerPos, False)
      else :
         drawWords(answer,answerPos, True)
      pygame.display.update()
      nextTime = time.time() + 0.3

def terminate(): # close down the program
    print ("Closing down please wait")
    pfio.deinit() # close the pfio
    pygame.quit() # close pygame
```

*continued*

**Listing 14-4    continued**

```
    sys.exit()

# see if we need to quit or look at the mouse

def checkForEvent():
    event = pygame.event.poll()
    if event.type == pygame.QUIT :
            terminate()
    elif event.type == pygame.MOUSEBUTTONDOWN :
            pass
            #print pygame.mouse.get_pos()
    elif event.type == pygame.KEYDOWN and event.key == ⤵
pygame.K_ESCAPE :
            terminate()


if __name__ == '__main__':
    main()
```

The program starts with a lot of initialisation for screens, colours and variables. Then the question file is opened, and all the lines are read into a list, called, appropriately enough, `questions`. The lines are counted, and then the order of the questions is shuffled so it is different every time. After that are some variables that define where things are going to appear on the screen: the question, the four answers, the player who is correct message and the player who gets to race message. It is convenient having them all in one place for when you want to tinker with the screen layout. What's left is a useful development tool in this code, one that prints out the position of the pointer when you click the mouse. This is useful for knowing where to place things. If you want to use it, just remove the # in front of the `print   .mouse.get_pos` instruction. Finally, the list called `single` has the conversion lookup table required to translate between the button press, and the answer number it signifies.

The main function is, as always, the heart of the program and controls the top-level flow. You can see that it is mainly one endless loop asking the questions one at a time in the list. The first thing it does is hold the program in a loop until all buttons are released. Then the screen is set up with the question on it, and the `checkInput` function holds until an answer is entered and the winning player rewarded. When all the questions have been asked, the question number is set back to the beginning, and the list of questions is shuffled again. This is because the end of the game is defined by a player's racing car completing the required number of laps; the Raspberry Pi knows nothing of this. That is why it is important to have a decent number of questions in the question file so that the game does not get too repetitive.

The setUpScreen function does just that – it puts everything onto the screen. First off it clears the screen and then puts up the background picture. Then there is a small delay for the players to prepare themselves, and the components of the question are separated out into distinct variables in a list as delimited by the commas. Next you need to put the answers in random positions. Although in the question file the correct answer is always the first one, it would be a bit of a dead giveaway if the correct answer always appeared in the same place on the screen, so the game has to scramble the positions. This is done by creating a list called aPos, short for *answer position*, that holds numbers 1 to 4 to show where each one is to be displayed. This is done in a function called, surprisingly enough, scramble. The way this is done is by generating a random number between 1 and 4 and then checking through the list to see if that number appears already. The first time around it doesn't appear, so it is stored in the first position. Next a candidate for the second position is generated, and the list searched to see if it has used it before. If it has, it generates more random numbers, and continues doing so until it finds one that hasn't been used before. This is done for all four positions. Although it might sound a bit silly to do this for the last position, you can simply use the same code as you did before. This is sort of like the instruction to throw a six before continuing, which is found in some simple board games. However, as the computer is very fast it will eventually come up with the missing number before a noticeable time has passed.

So having got the list of where to put each answer, the setUpScreen function continues by drawing the question and answer on the screen. It does this by calling up the drawWords function, which takes in three variables – the text to draw, the position number to draw it in and a logic input that determines if the text is to be rendered in the alternate text colour or not. You will see at the end of this section how that feature is used when the program flashes the correct answer in response to an incorrect one. The position number is used to access the global lists placeX and placeY defined at the start of the code. Normally this position defines the centre of the text rectangle but in the case of positions 2 and 3, the X position defines an end of the text rectangle. This is so that those answers can be placed close to the central graphic and the variable length text box can extend in either direction from that position. Then the text background rectangle is drawn, the text over the top of it and finally an outlined rectangle drawn on the top of that.

Back in the setUpScreen function, you make a note of what the correct answer is and what position it is in. You will use that later when it comes to flashing the correct answer.

After setting up the question on the screen you need to check for the answer coming in, see if it is correct and take the appropriate action. All this is done in the checkInput function. This starts with a loop that checks the input and looks for any pygame events such as quit. As soon as a player button press is detected the code works out which player has pressed first by looking at the input bit pattern as a number. Because you have arranged all the buttons for one player to occupy four consecutive bits, this test is easy. If the number is greater or equal to the hex value 0x10, player two has pressed first; otherwise it is player one. The next bit of code initially assumes that the first player to press is correct, and the bit patterns that are going to turn on the red and green LEDs on the two joysticks and enable the Slot Car game are set up. Then the response is evaluated to see if it is correct. This is done by using the list called `single` to convert or look up the four button press bits into a screen answer position, which is then compared to the answer position that was previously noted. If it matches, the initial assumption is correct – that is, the player to respond first got it right; however, if it doesn't match, you need to invert the bits defining the LEDs and relay with an exclusive OR operation ^ using a mask of 0x3f. Also, the results display needs to be changed.

With the results displayed and Slot Car game enabled, the correct function is called. This flashes the correct answer by alternately writing it in the normal text colour, or the alternate text colour. This is done at 0.3 second intervals defined in the last line of the function for ten times as defined in the second line of the function, giving a total of three seconds. Changing any one of these two lines will change this three-second time. When this function returns to the `checkInput` function all the PiFace outputs are turned off. This disables the racing car and turns off the LEDs. Then the correct function is called again. This keeps on flashing the correct answer for a further three seconds.

## Over to You

Well, there you have the game as I wrote it. Now it is over to you to make it better or more suit what you want it to do. You can change the racing car time; three seconds might not seem very long, but I have found it is about right. However, with a bigger track to control you might want it to be longer, or with a smaller track you might want it to be shorter.

Then there are the questions. You can add many more questions to the file, but you might want to have more than one set of questions of differing difficulty or on different subjects. You can arrange that the user types in the name of the question bank file first. Better yet, you can give the user a list of filenames and get him or her to type in the appropriate number. If you use the right sort of file list command, you can list all the .txt files in the directory so that you simply need to add another file to the directory for it to be automatically included in the list.

Finally, think about sound effects. You have seen in many of the programs in previous chapters that there are sound effects, and they are quite easy to add too. How about a car roaring noise when the game is enabled? Or you could add a blip to indicate when a question is up on the screen ready to be answered. Or you could add a correct and incorrect noise of applause and sighs, respectively. The choice is yours. Race away!

# Chapter **15**

# Facebook-Enabled Roto-Sketch

## by Mike Cook

## In This Chapter

- O Learn about rotary shaft encoders
- O Use rotary shaft encoders to control a drawing program
- O See how to make Python draw a picture
- O Discover how to interface to a tilt sensor
- O Learn how to automatically load image files to Flickr and Facebook

HERE IS AN idea I bet nobody has thought of before: Use two rotary controls to steer the path of a point on the screen. Where the point has been, it leaves a trail so you can sketch a picture using two knobs mounted on a box. In a crazy twist, how about if the picture was erased when you turned the box upside down and gave it a shake. Way out? I know, but it might just catch on, especially when you can post your artistic efforts straight to Facebook for all your friends to see.

## The Concept

Well, maybe I have been beaten to a patent on this idea, but it is an interesting project from many angles – not the least of which is the requirement for a rotary control. In the old days of analogue, most rotary controls were *potentiometers*, or *pots* as they are called for short. These were potential dividers where a fixed resistance had a tap off point or wiper, controlled by a rotary knob or a slider control. The rotary type tended to have a travel of somewhere between 180 and 270 degrees; there were some special continuous rotary types, but they were made mainly for servo motor positioning control and were quite expensive. What is more, there was a dead spot where the wiper had to wrap round from one side of the fixed resistor to the other. An extra complication in using this sort of control with a computer is the fact that the pot produced a changing voltage output, and this has to be digitised with an analogue to digital converter (A/D) before a computer could make any use of it.

Although it is perfectly possible to build an A/D, it is often much simpler to keep everything in the digital domain. So, in modern designs where you want a continuously rotating control, a component is used called a *rotary shaft encoder*. These come in many different implementations, but by far the cheapest is the switched type. Another type is an optical encoder where the rotary movement is detected by something interrupting a beam of visible or infrared light. Optical encoders were widely used in the old type of computer mouse, the ones that had a ball in the base. A much newer type of rotary encoder utilises magnetic sensing to detect changes, which is covered in much more detail in the next chapter, "The Pendulum Pi, a Harmonograph".

## Rotary Encoder Types

The switched rotary encoder is at the heart of this project, and you have the choice of several different types. Perhaps the most distinguishing feature is whether the encoder has detents or not. A *detent* is a mechanical stop on a rotary spindle that divides the rotation into a set number of increments. When you twist an encoder with detents you feel multiple clicks as you twist. This is ideal for a control because you get a good positive feedback of its movement and when you release the control it stays where it is.

By far the most common type of encoder is known as the *incremental* type, which gives an indication of the fact that the control has been moved and in what direction it has been moved. Encoders are often classified by how many steps there are in one rotation. For switched encoders this is normally between 8 and 16 clicks per rotation. Some encoders also incorporate a central switch into the rotary control that is activated by pushing down. Applications for these types of controls include menu selection, volume control and switching through a large set of values. The point is that the controls themselves provide very little feedback on the exact angle they are at, leaving it to the application hardware and software to provide it in an appropriate manner.

## The Encoder Output

In order to use an encoder in any project you have to make sense of the signal it produces. There are two signal lines from each encoder and a common line. The signals are either connected to the common line or not by the internal switch, and normally the common line is connected to ground. The signals therefore are simply on and off, but they are phase shifted by 90 degrees from each other; the technical term for the signals is a *quadrature output*. Take a closer look at these in Figure 15-1. The two signals are normally called Ø0 and Ø1 although they are sometimes called A and B. This sort of diagram is called a *timing diagram*, time from left to right, logic level up and down. This shows what happens when you rotate the shaft clockwise. Looking at the two signals you will see there are four different combinations of high and low from the switch; each stable region between the transitions is marked with a letter on the diagram. One very important thing to notice is that only one of the outputs changes at any time; this sort of sequence is known as a *Gray code* after its inventor Frank Gray, and is used so there is never any confusion over what is being indicated, or if there is it is only between adjacent regions. Underneath the timing diagram is a list of each stable state of the output switches for clockwise and anticlockwise rotation. So you will see that you can't tell very much from just looking at the outputs of the switch; you need to know a bit about the history – that is, what state they were in before.

This is all well and good but you have to take another thing into consideration, and that is contact bounce. When any mechanical contact makes or breaks it does not do it cleanly; that is, the transition from on to off is not a nice simple signal as is drawn on timing diagrams. Imagine dropping a table tennis ball onto a hard table; the ball doesn't just hit the table and stop, but it bounces in a sequence of ever shorter bounces. The same thing happens to switches, and if the computer were to look at the switch often enough it would see a series of rapid on/off changes; this is known as *contact bounce* and affects all mechanical switches to a greater or lesser extent. The duration of the bounces might be 20 to 200 mS or even longer in some cases. Most of the time this is not a problem because the rest of the code ensures that the switch is not looked at so frequently, but in some cases it is important, especially ones where the code is doing little between looking at a switch.

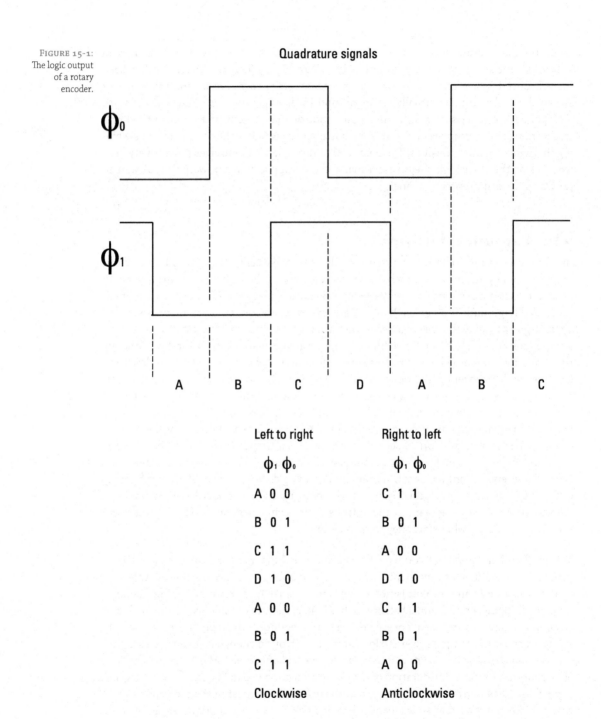

FIGURE 15-1:
The logic output
of a rotary
encoder.

Quadrature signals

$\phi_0$

$\phi_1$

A    B    C    D    A    B    C

| Left to right | | | Right to left | | |
|---|---|---|---|---|---|
| | $\phi_1$ | $\phi_0$ | | $\phi_1$ | $\phi_0$ |
| A | 0 | 0 | C | 1 | 1 |
| B | 0 | 1 | B | 0 | 1 |
| C | 1 | 1 | A | 0 | 0 |
| D | 1 | 0 | D | 1 | 0 |
| A | 0 | 0 | C | 1 | 1 |
| B | 0 | 1 | B | 0 | 1 |
| C | 1 | 1 | A | 0 | 0 |
| Clockwise | | | Anticlockwise | | |

For example, imagine you just want to count how many times a button is pressed; simple code to do this will often fail due to contact bounce. It will appear to record more pushes than you make. The switch needs what is called *debouncing*, reminiscent of Tigger in *Winnie the Pooh*. For the simple example of just counting button pushes, a delay of 20 mS after a push is detected is normally enough to sort things out. However, contact bounce in rotary encoders can lead to problems of adding extra steps or getting the software monitoring it so mixed up that it thinks it is being turned in the opposite direction. As the shaft is sometimes being rotated quite rapidly, using a delay is inappropriate, so you have to consider something else to give a clean output. Fortunately the nature of the Gray code allows you to reject bounces.

For any given state of the outputs of a rotary encoder, there are three possible states it could change to next: one for clockwise rotation, one for anticlockwise rotation and one where it can't possibly go but might due to contact bounce. This last state is an error state. Figure 15-2 summarises each current state of the encoder and the three states that could follow. So when you read an encoder, and knowing the last state, if you come across an error state then all you do is ignore the reading. That is, do not update the last state with the new reading and do not indicate a step movement. Otherwise you can indicate that a clockwise or anticlockwise motion has taken place and update the last state with the new reading.

Well, you would think that covers it all, but there is one last curveball you have to cope with – and that is detents. There are two types of rotary shaft encoders with detents, and this is where the detents are placed in the switch output sequence. Figure 15-3 shows the two methods that are used. The first one has the detent in position A – that is, between the clicks the switch goes through all the transitions available. The order in which these transitions occur tells you if the click was a clockwise or anticlockwise click. The second scheme has a detent in every other position so it comes to rest with either both signals high or both low, but again the transition between these states tells you the direction. I have not seen an encoder with detents in every position, so, if they do exist, they are rare. Encoders made by the company Alps tend to have one detent per sequence, and those made by Bourns tend to have two. In this project I used Bourns encoders although it is simple enough to use Alps.

A rotary encoder needs quite a bit of looking after from the software point of view, and there are two ways to do this: with interrupts or polling. *Interrupts* are where the action of the switch causes the computer to interrupt what it is doing and call a special interrupt service routine which will handle the change. This is by far the best way of doing things, but unfortunately doing this under Linux is tricky and not very effective. It can be done but often the interrupts come too frequently for it to cope. The other way is *polling*, which is looking at the switches as quickly as possible in the code. This is an acceptable solution for this application as the code spends most of its time waiting for movement from the encoder and the visual feedback is such that a missing click or two during rapid rotation is not very important.

FIGURE 15-2:
The logic
sequence of the
rotary encoder.

| | Clockwise<br>Left to right | Anticlockwise<br>Right to left |
|---|---|---|
| | $\phi_1$ $\phi_0$ | $\phi_1$ $\phi_0$ |
| | A 0 0 | C 1 1 |
| | B 0 1 | B 0 1 |
| | C 1 1 | A 0 0 |
| | **D 1 0** | **D 1 0** |
| | A 0 0 | C 1 1 |
| | B 0 1 | B 0 1 |
| | C 1 1 | A 0 0 |

Next state

| Current<br>State | Clockwise | Anticlockwise | Error |
|---|---|---|---|
| $\phi_1$ $\phi_0$ | $\phi_1$ $\phi_0$ | $\phi_1$ $\phi_0$ | $\phi_1$ $\phi_0$ |
| 1 0 | 1 1 | 0 0 | 0 1 |
| 1 1 | 0 1 | 1 0 | 0 0 |
| 0 1 | 0 0 | 1 1 | 1 0 |
| 0 0 | 1 0 | 0 1 | 1 1 |

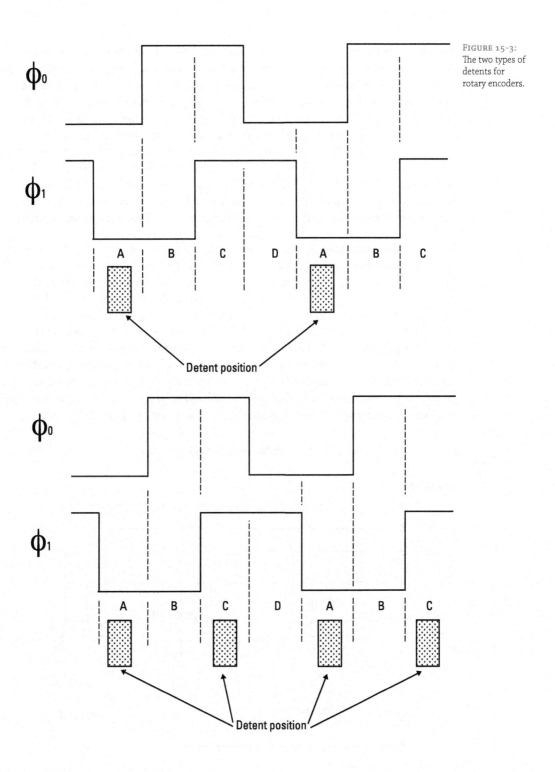

FIGURE 15-3:
The two types of
detents for
rotary encoders.

Just one more thing you need to look at before you can start making your control box, and that is the detector that allows you to erase the drawing when you turn the control box upside down. For this the simplest thing to use is a tilt switch. In the old days this was made with mercury sloshing about in a tube that made an electrical contact with two wires mounted in the end of the tube. Now, however, the use of mercury is frowned upon, and it is even banned in certain classes of electronic equipment although you can still buy mercury tilt switches as a component. Although those are undoubtedly the best form of tilt switch, for this project a low-cost alternative will do quite nicely. This consists of a very small ball bearing sealed in a tube with contacts at one end; as the ball rolls to the end it shorts out the contacts. The problem with this sort of switch is that occasionally sometimes the ball fails to short out the contacts, but all that means in this context is that you need to shake it to bash the ball into the contacts.

Now that you know about all the parts you need, it is time to put them together in a control box. Figure 15-4 shows the schematic of the control box. Basically the two encoders have three connections, and the centre is connected to ground as is one side of the tilt switch. Then all the other wires go to input pins on the PiFace board. Remember the inputs are numbers 0 to 7 – not 1 to 8. The encoders occupy the top four bits with the tilt switch being connected to the next one down, input 3. Note that inputs 2, 1 and 0 are not used in this project. I built this in a low-cost, ready-made black plastic box and wired it up with a length of ribbon cable stripped back to six connectors. I cut a small notch in the wall of the box to allow the ribbon cable to pass through when the lid was screwed on. This is shown in Figure 15-5. Finally the lid was screwed on and became the base of the unit, and four small self-adhesive feet of felt pads were attached and two knobs attached to the shafts. The final unit is shown in Figure 15-6.

FIGURE 15-4:
The schematic
for the
roto-sketch
control box.

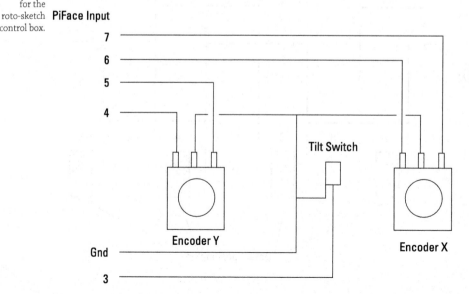

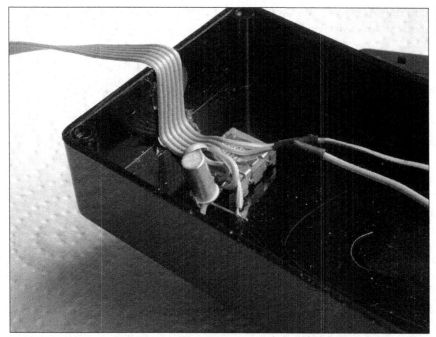

FIGURE 15-5:
The wiring for
the roto-sketch
control box.

FIGURE 15-6:
The finished
roto-sketch
control box!

It is time to test what you have; as usual, a short piece of code whose only function is to test the hardware is given in Listing 15-1.

---

**Listing 15-1**   **Roto-Sketch Control Box Test 1**

```python
#!/usr/bin/env python
"""
Rotary Encoder input test 1 - raw inputs
encoders wired to inputs 6 & 7 and 4 & 5
"""

import piface.pfio as pfio  # piface library
pfio.init()          # initialise piface

print "Single encoder input test  Ctrl C to quit"
print "Displays raw input from encoder"
lastEncoder = -1
display = ["00","01","10","11"]

while True:
        encoder = pfio.read_input() & 0xF8
        if lastEncoder != encoder:
                enc2 = (encoder >> 4) & 0x03
                enc1 = (encoder >> 6)
                print display[enc1]," ",display[enc2],
                if encoder & 0x08 != 0 :
                    print "  box inverted"
                else :
                    print " "
        lastEncoder = encoder
```

---

You can see that this code is a bit fancy in the way it displays the input values. Rather than just have the raw number or even a bit pattern, I have used a list called display to show the bit pattern in a clear way. You can print it out in binary, but you get a 0b before the number, which makes it a bit difficult to read. As it is you will get the bit pattern printed out each time there is a change in the input. You can easily see what sort of detent encoder you have by noting the transitions between clicks. As the tilt switch is activated you will see a message telling you the box is inverted. The first pattern printed out is what you will be using for the X movement.

Next, you'll try to do something with those numbers that are being returned. This is a bit more tricky than you might at first think. The program in Listing 15-2 takes just one of the encoders and keeps track of the clicks.

---

Listing 15-2 **Rotary Encoder Testing**

```python
#!/usr/bin/env python
"""
Rotary Encoder input test 2 - show count
encoder wired to inputs 6 & 7
"""

import piface.pfio as pfio  # piface library
pfio.init()           # initialise piface

print "Single encoder input test  Ctrl C to quit"
print "Displays accumulated count for X control"
lastEncoder = pfio.read_input() & 0xC0
count = 0
while True:
        encoder = pfio.read_input() & 0xC0
        if lastEncoder != encoder and (lastEncoder == 0 or ⤵
lastEncoder == 0xC0):
            if (lastEncoder == 0 and encoder == 0x80) or ⤵
(lastEncoder == 0xC0 and encoder == 0x40) :
                count -=1
            if (lastEncoder == 0xC0 and encoder == 0x80) or ⤵
(lastEncoder == 0 and encoder == 0x40)  :
                count +=1
            print count
        lastEncoder = encoder
```

---

When you study the listing you will see that what happens here is that once the encoder is read, the values are passed into an `if` statement that looks for the condition of the last encoder reading being in one of the two detent positions, and the current reading not being the same as the last reading. In other words the encoder has just moved from its rest position. Now you see in what direction it has turned by looking at the current reading in conjunction with the last reading. There are two possible readings for an anticlockwise motion depending on the previous reading; if either of these two conditions is met then a count is decremented. Similarly for a clockwise movement there are two possible previous and current combinations indicating a click. Notice that the position is printed out independently of either clockwise or anticlockwise rotation being detected. This means that if you see two numbers the same printed out consecutively, then there has been a contact bounce reading that has resulted in an error which has been ignored. You will notice that the values compared with those from the encoder are hard coded. That is, they refer only to that one encoder wired in the top two bits of the input. In order to make things more efficient you can shift the bits you are interested in into the lowest two bits and use the same code for reading both encoders.

## Posting to Facebook

Now you want to be able to post your creations to Facebook, and it is not as easy as you might think. This part has perhaps taken up more hours to get right than anything else in this book. Facebook does allow picture posting to happen remotely, but you have to register with them as a developer and you have to have a server that will run your app. Although this is fine for purveyors of mobile apps and the like, it has a few downsides for the individual. You end up needing to pay for the app hosting and creating a unique name for yourself. Also, the fact that you need to create the app in another language is offputting for beginners. It also would not be good for Facebook to have all of you readers create your own apps just for your own personal use. All in all this is much more complicated than it should be.

## Using Flickr

Whereas Facebook is difficult to post to, Flickr makes it some what easier to upload pictures and, as an added bonus, you can link your Flickr account to Facebook – so two for the price of one. However, it is not all plain sailing, and it is not as simple as it could be. One way to post a picture is to e-mail your pictures to Flickr, to a unique address you can find on your Settings page. This is easy to automate, but unfortunately pictures posted like this never seem to be transferred onto your Facebook timeline. This problem stumped not only the online forum of experts but also Flickr's help desk. It turns out that this is actually a bug in the Flickr web code which might be fixed by the time you read this, but I can't rely on that when writing a book – it has to work now.

Pictures posted from a browser however are linked to Facebook, so what is required is to have some way of doing that automatically from the Pi. The answer I came up with was to use the `folders2flickr` package found at `http://code.google.com/p/folders2flickr/source/checkout`, which is actually a subversion repository for the code. *Subversion* is a revision control software system that is used in professional circles; it keeps track of developers working on a small subset of files for a large project. It maintains a backup system so that any earlier version of code can be reverted to at any time. This is very handy because a common occurrence, when many developers are working on a large program, is that someone will make a change that will break the code in an area he or she is not working on, and therefore will not see. Subversion allows the developers to rapidly backtrack and revert to a previously working project. To get at the source code for the `folders2flickr` package, all you need to do is to use the desktop to go to the directory that you are working with for this chapter; I suggest you name it `sketch` as it will eventually contain the code to drive the roto-sketch hardware. Then from the Tools menu select the Open Current Directory in Terminal option. This will cause a Terminal window to appear. Type this into it:

```
svn checkout http://folders2flickr.googlecode.com/svn/trunk/
folders2flickr-read-only
```

Type the preceding all on one line, and it will download a zip file of the package's source code. Then type

```
unzip folders2flickr-read-only
```

to unzip the source code files. Then go back to the desktop and change the name of the resulting directory to just `folders2flickr`. Now you have to edit a file in this directory called `uploadr.ini` so that it works the way you need it to. Double-click it to open up a text editor and change the line

```
imagedir=d:\pictures
```

to read

```
imagedir=roto-sketch
```

This sets the directory that contains the files to be uploaded to Flickr. Then edit the visibility parameters to read

```
public = 1
friend = 0
family = 0
```

This is needed because only publicly visible files are passed on to Facebook, never family or friends. Save this file in your `sketch` directory – not in the `folders2flickr` directory where it came from. At this stage it is best if you authenticate the package with your Flickr account, so make sure that you have a directory called `roto-sketch` in your `sketch` directory and that it contains a small image. Now make sure that you are connected to the Internet, get a command line in the `sketch` directory and then run the package by typing

```
python folders2flickr/uploadr.py
```

It is important you do this and not get your command line in the `folders2flickr` directory because this package has a bit of an issue with where it puts things and doing it this way will make it work when you get to running the final program. However, this is where things could get tricky because you will be asked if you have authenticated this program yet. Whatever you do at this stage do not answer this question yet. What will happen is that a browser window will pop up. I say "pop", but this rather exaggerates the speed; it will rather ooze up as opposed to pop. When I tried this, the browser Dillo popped up and then refused to do anything. I had to arrange for the browser Midori to pop up instead by deleting the

Dillo browser. When it does you wait and wait, until the window opens and the Flickr login page appears. Even then you have to wait for something to finish. The trick is to keep an eye on the CPU usage block in the bottom right-hand corner; when this stops showing solid green you can then type your username and password and log in. Two more pages will follow asking you if it is correct that you want to authorise the use of this package. Only when the page telling you to close the page has finished loading and you have closed the page can you then go and answer that question on the Python console with an affirmative Y for yes. Then the contents of your `roto-sketch` directory will be transferred to Flickr.

When you look at your `sketch` folder after this you will see that there have been some files created by this process – an error log, a debug log and a file called *history*. This history file is used to make sure only images that were placed in the `roto-sketch` directory since the last upload are uploaded and not all of them again. If you turn on the Show Hidden option in the View menu you will also see a file called `.flickrToken`; this information is used so that you don't have to go through the authorisation process each time you run the uploader. If you are curious, you can double-click the file and see what the token looks like. However don't alter it or delete the file, or you will have to go through the whole authorisation rigmarole again. You should now go to Flickr and check that the image has arrived. At the same time you can go to the Settings page and click the option to connect Flickr to Facebook. You will then have to go to Facebook and set the permissions as to whom you want to see these postings from Yahoo!. (By default it is just you.) This is found in the App Center icon on the left side; click Your Apps, and use the Yahoo one. Click Yahoo to change the settings.

---

**WARNING**    A word of caution: It can take up to an hour after posting on Flickr for the pictures to appear on Facebook. If they still don't appear, Flickr recommends disconnecting the Facebook link, waiting a few minutes and then connecting it again. I have had to do this once.

---

Part of the problem I found with the setup was the poor wording of the instructions that were printed out during the authorisation phase. I think it would be much better if the `getAuthKey` function, in the `uploadr.py` file, were replaced by the code in Listing 15-3.

---

**Listing 15-3   Replacement `getAuthKey` Function**

```
"""
Checks to see if the user has authenticated this application
"""
def getAuthKey( self ):
    d =  {
        api.frob : FLICKR[ api.frob ],
        api.perms : "delete"
        }
    sig = self.signCall( d )
```

```
        url = self.urlGen( api.auth, d, sig )
        ans = ""
        try:
            webbrowser.open( url )
            print "You need to allow this program to access ⊃
your Flickr site."
            print "A web browser should pop open with instructions."
            print "When you have authenticated this application ⊃
type Y"
            print "If you failed or don't want to then type N"
            ans = raw_input("Sucess? (Y/N): ")
        except:
            print str(sys.exc_info())
        if ( ans.lower() == "n" ):
            print "Please try again"
            sys.exit()
```

The action of the function is the same, but the user instructions are much more clear.

## The Final Roto-Sketch Program

With all the pieces of infrastructure in place you now come to the final program which brings this all together. The Roto-Sketch program is shown in Listing 15-4.

**Listing 15-4  The Roto-Sketch Program**

```
#!/usr/bin/env python
"""
Rotary Encoder Roto-sketch
encoder 1 wired to inputs 6 & 7
encoder 2 wired to inputs 4 & 5
Tilt switch wired to input 3
"""

import colorsys
from smbus import SMBus
import os, sys, pygame
from pygame.locals import *
import piface.pfio as pfio  # piface library
import subprocess

pfio.init()          # initialise piface
```

*continued*

**Listing 15-4    continued**

```
pygame.init()          # initialise pygame
pygame.event.set_allowed(None)
pygame.event.set_allowed([pygame.KEYDOWN, pygame.QUIT,⏎
pygame.MOUSEBUTTONDOWN])
os.environ['SDL_VIDEO_WINDOW_POS'] = 'center'
pygame.display.set_caption("Roto-Sketch")
screen = pygame.display.set_mode([512,512],0,32)
lastEncoder = [0,0]
current_reading = [256,256]
last_reading = [256,256,256,256]
# defines initial starting position
col = (0,0,0)
colCursor = (128,128,128)
background = (255, 255, 255)  # screen background colour
picture = 1 # picture number
fileName ="name"
lastPort = -1

def main():
 global current_reading, last_reading
 print "Roto-sketch the keys are:-"
 print "R, G, B, Y, M, P, K (black), W to select colour"
 print "Space bar for wipe screen"
 print "L - for Line to saved point, C for Circle centre on ⏎
save point"
 print "S to save current point for future line and ⏎
circle commands"
 print "Home key to save sketch to file"
 print "# to post on Flickr and Facebook"
 blank_screen()
 while(True): # do forever
      readEncoders()
      pygame.draw.rect(screen,col,(last_reading[0],⏎
last_reading[1],2,2),0)
      pygame.draw.line(screen,col,(last_reading[0],⏎
last_reading[1]),(current_reading[0],current_reading[1]),2)
      pygame.draw.rect(screen,colCursor,(current_reading[0],⏎
current_reading[1],2,2),0)
      last_reading[0] = current_reading[0]
# save this position for drawing from for next time
      last_reading[1] = current_reading[1]
```

```
        pygame.display.update()

#end of main loop

# Function definitions

# read two encoder with alternating 00 11 detent
def readEncoders() : #exit when one has moved
    global current_reading, lastPort
    moved = False
    inc = 8
    while not moved :
        checkForQuit()
        port = pfio.read_input()
        portP = (port & 0xc0) >> 6
        lastPortP = (lastPort & 0xc0) >> 6
        for axis in range(0,2) :
            if lastPortP != portP and (lastPortP == 0 or ⤸
lastPortP == 0x3) :
                if (lastPortP == 0 and portP == 0x2) or ⤸
(lastPortP == 0x3 and portP == 0x1):
                    current_reading[axis] -= inc
                    moved = True
                if (lastPortP == 0x3 and portP == 0x2) or ⤸
(lastPortP == 0 and portP == 0x1):
                    current_reading[axis] += inc
                    moved = True
            portP = (port & 0x30) >> 4
            lastPortP = (lastPort &0x30) >> 4
        if port &0x8 :
            blank_screen()
        lastPort = port

def blank_screen():
    screen.fill(background) # blank screen
    pygame.display.update()

def terminate():
    print "Closing down please wait"
    pfio.deinit()
    pygame.quit()
```

*continued*

**Listing 15-4   continued**

```
    sys.exit()

def checkForQuit():
    global col, picture, last_reading, fileName
    event = pygame.event.poll()
    if event.type == pygame.QUIT :
            terminate()
    elif event.type == pygame.KEYDOWN :
# get a key and do something
        if event.key == pygame.K_ESCAPE :
            terminate()
        if event.key == K_SPACE or event.key == K_DELETE:
            blank_screen()
        if event.key == K_r : # draw in red
            col = (255, 0, 0)
        if event.key == K_g : # draw in green
            col = (0, 255, 0)
        if event.key == K_b : # draw in blue
            col = (0, 0, 255)
        if event.key == K_y : # draw in yellow
            col = (255, 255, 0)
        if event.key == K_m : # draw in magenta
            col = (255, 0, 255)
        if event.key == K_p : # draw in peacock blue
            col = (0, 255, 255)
        if event.key == K_w : # draw in white
            col = (255, 255, 255)
        if event.key == K_k : # draw in blacK
            col = (0, 0, 0)
        if event.key == K_s : # save current point
            last_reading[2] = last_reading[0] # save X
            last_reading[3] = last_reading[1] # save Y
        if event.key == K_l : # draw a line to saved point
            pygame.draw.line(screen,col,(last_reading[2],↵
last_reading[3]),(last_reading[0],last_reading[1]),2)
            pygame.display.update()
        if event.key == K_c : # draw a circle
            try :
                r = ((last_reading[0] - last_reading[2])**2 ↵
+ (last_reading[1] - last_reading[3])**2 ) ** (0.5)
                pygame.draw.circle(screen,col,↵
(last_reading[0],last_reading[1]),int(r),2)
```

```
                pygame.display.update()
            except:
                pass
        if event.key == K_HASH :
#Save folder to Flickr / Facebook
            print "sending folder to Flickr"
            subprocess.check_output("python ⊃
folders2flickr/uploadr.py",shell=True)
            print "done"
        if event.key == K_HOME : # save a picture
            print "save sketch to file"
            if picture == 1 : # first time to save this session
                fileName = raw_input("Enter file name ⊃
for this session ")
            try:
                pygame.image.save(screen,⊃
'roto-sketch/'+fileName+str(picture)+'.png')
            except:
                os.system('mkdir roto-sketch')
                pygame.image.save(screen,⊃
'roto-sketch/'+fileName+str(picture)+'.png')
            print "saving sketch as ",⊃
'roto-sketch/'+fileName+str(picture)+'.png'
            picture +=1;

if __name__ == '__main__':
    main()
```

It is possible that you could get an error on the line

```
from smbus import SMBus
```

If you do then you will need to install smbus, which is easily done by typing

```
apt-get install python-smbus
```

on a command line.

The code might look complex, but it consists of a few simple functions – some of which you have already looked at when you considered the rotary controls. It starts off in the normal fashion by importing the modules it will need, and setting up some global variables. Then it prints out some simple user instructions about the keys. Basically there are a group of keys that will change the colour of the drawing track, a key to wipe the screen in case you have not got a tilt switch fitted, some keys that control what is drawn and finally two keys to save the images and post them to Flickr – and hence to Facebook.

The main function after the instructions are printed out is a simple endless loop of reading the encoders and then drawing the lines when that function returns with an updated reading. The readEncoders function is basically what is in Listing 15-2 only for two encoders. It keeps looking at the input port and makes the decisions based on what it sees. This function can do this for both encoders by using a for loop and shifting the reading for the X encoder into the least two significant bits and then shifting the Y encoder into the least significant bit for the second trip through the loop. When a movement is detected the logic variable move is set to true and the function returns to do the plotting on the screen. The tilt switch is also monitored, and the screen is wiped if it is found to be upside down. The increment value is set at 8; that is, it moves 8 screen pixels per click, but you can make it a smaller value if you want finer control over the movement of the plotting point. When this function returns, the values in the current reading list have been updated, and the program draws a line between the current point and the last point. The current point is replaced with a grey square to allow you to see where you are, in the same way that mechanical versions of this program had a current point that you could just see. This allows you, in theory at least, to retrace over a line to start off somewhere new. So before the program draws a line this cursor square has to be erased and put back in the new position after the line is drawn. That is why there are three drawing commands where you might be expecting only one. The current readings are copied into last-reading variables before the screen is updated.

The checkForQuit function looks at not only quit events but also key events. These drive the settings of the program. For example, the current drawing colour can be changed by pressing a key; all the primary and secondary colours are available as well as black and white. Note that for black you have to press the K key because the B key is already taken with switching to blue. The spacebar or Delete key simply calls the blank_screen function.

The later part of the checkForQuit function performs the neat special effects of the program. First the L key will draw a line between the current point and a previously saved point. Next the C key will draw a circle centred on the current point with a radius given by the distance to the saved point. Finally the S key will save the current point as the set point for those two previous commands. The circle drawing has to be in a try structure to prevent the program from crashing when the current point is the same as the saved point. These circles and lines give the drawings a lot more interest than the random scribblings that is often made with these sorts of toys.

The saving and transfer keys are the Home key and the hash key. The Home key saves the current screen into the roto-sketch folder as a PNG picture file. When you press this for the first time after the program starts you are asked for a name to prefix the picture file. You have to click the Python shell console window to give it the focus and type in a name. The program will then use that name for all subsequent screen saves and append a number on the end of each new file. After you have entered the name, you should click back on the sketch window so that it can process subsequent keys. If there is not a `roto-sketch` directory, one will be created. Now when you press the Home key again, the filename is printed out, but there is no need to enter anything; it uses the name you gave it last time plus an incrementing number. The hash key (#) transfers the new images in the `roto-sketch` folder out to Flickr, which can take from 10 seconds to just over a minute depending on the state of your Internet connection and traffic at the Flickr site.

Many interesting patterns can be drawn with this machine, a few of which are shown in Figure 15-7. You can save the pattern as you go, seeing it get increasingly complex.

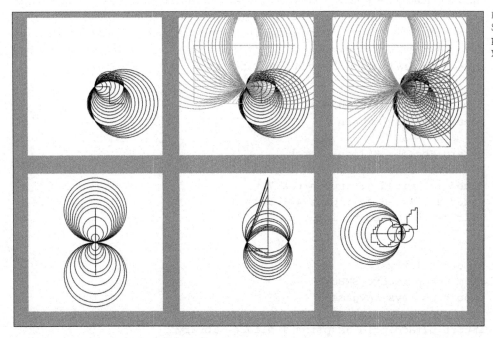

FIGURE 15-7:
Some of the pattern effects you can achieve.

# Creating a Symmetrical Pattern

Consider one extra variant – symmetry. The output can be made more interesting by the use of reflections to generate a symmetrical pattern rather like a kaleidoscope. There are two ways you can do this: The first is by rotation of the points used to draw the pattern, and the second is by copying what is actually drawn and placing it in several places on the screen. At first this might sound like it would produce the same results – and it does for a limited amount of drawing – but the results of the two can look very different. This is because if you draw on a small segment and your drawing extends outside the bounds of the segment, you will not see any lines. However, if you are rotating the drawing points, then drawing outside the segment will be seen in the other segments. This fundamentally changes how things look with regard to reflections. Rotation of a point is easy; you just have to apply the following formula to the X and Y coordinates of the point to get the new point X' and Y':

$$X' = X \cos \theta - Y \sin \theta$$
$$Y' = X \sin \theta + Y \cos \theta$$

$\theta$ is the angle of rotation about the origin. So to get the origin in the centre of the screen, you have to subtract half the width from the reading values. You can use a loop to repeatedly do this for as much repeating as you want. I will leave that with you to do as an exercise. What I will give you here is an example of the second, more interesting, reflection kaleidoscope-style of symmetry. This plots the picture into an off-screen buffer, and then makes up the screen by repeating this buffer in a reflected and inverted manner to give a four-fold symmetrical pattern. This new variant is shown in Listing 15-5.

---

**Listing 15-5   Kilido-Sketch**

```python
#!/usr/bin/env python
"""
Rotary Encoder Kilido-sketch
Four fold symmetry
encoder 1 wired to inputs 6 & 7
encoder 2 wired to inputs 4 & 5
Tilt switch wired to input 3
"""

import colorsys
from smbus import SMBus
import os, sys, pygame
from pygame.locals import *
import piface.pfio as pfio  # piface library
import subprocess

pfio.init()          # initialise piface
pygame.init()        # initialise pygame
pygame.event.set_allowed(None)
pygame.event.set_allowed([pygame.KEYDOWN, pygame.QUIT, ↪
pygame.MOUSEBUTTONDOWN])
```

```
os.environ['SDL_VIDEO_WINDOW_POS'] = 'center'
pygame.display.set_caption("Klido-Sketch")
segSize = 350
screen = pygame.display.set_mode([segSize*2,segSize*2],0,32)
segment = pygame.Surface((segSize,segSize))
lastEncoder = [0,0]
current_reading = [128,128]
last_reading = [128,128,128,128]
# defines initial starting position
col = (0,0,0)
colCursor = (128,128,128)
background = (255, 255, 255)  # screen background colour
picture = 1 # picture number
fileName ="name"
lastPort = -1


def main():
 global current_reading, last_reading
 print "Kilido-sketch the keys are:-"
 print "R, G, B, Y, M, P, K (black), W to select colour"
 print "Space bar for wipe screen"
 print "L - for Line to saved point, C for Circle centre on ⊃
save point"
 print "S to save current point for future line and ⊃
circle commands"
 print "Home key to save sketch to file"
 print "# to post on Flickr and Facebook"
 blank_screen()
 while(True): # do forever
      readEncoders()
      pygame.draw.rect(segment,col,(last_reading[0],⊃
last_reading[1],2,2),0)
      pygame.draw.line(segment,col,(last_reading[0],⊃
last_reading[1]),(current_reading[0],current_reading[1]),2)
      pygame.draw.rect(segment,colCursor,⊃
(current_reading[0],current_reading[1],2,2),0)
      last_reading[0] = current_reading[0]
# save this position for drawing from for next time
      last_reading[1] = current_reading[1]
      screenUpdate()


def screenUpdate():
```

*continued*

**Listing 15-5    continued**

```
        segRect = pygame.Surface.get_rect(segment)
        screen.blit(segment, segRect)
        segRect.topleft = segSize,0
        screen.blit(pygame.transform.flip(segment, True, ⮑
False), segRect)
        segRect.topleft = 0,segSize
        screen.blit(pygame.transform.flip(segment, False, ⮑
True), segRect)
        segRect.topleft = segSize,segSize
        screen.blit(pygame.transform.flip(segment, True, ⮑
True), segRect)
        pygame.display.update()

#end of main loop

# Function definitions

# read two encoder with alternating 00 11 detent
def readEncoders() : #exit when one has moved
    global current_reading, lastPort
    moved = False
    inc = 6
    while not moved :
        checkForQuit()
        port = pfio.read_input()
        portP = (port & 0xc0) >> 6
        lastPortP = (lastPort & 0xc0) >> 6
        for axis in range(0,2) :
           if lastPortP != portP and (lastPortP == 0 or ⮑
lastPortP == 0x3) :
                if (lastPortP == 0 and portP == 0x2) or ⮑
(lastPortP == 0x3 and portP == 0x1):
                    current_reading[axis] -= inc
                    if current_reading[axis] < 0:
# restrain to segment
                        current_reading[axis] += inc
                    moved = True
                if (lastPortP == 0x3 and portP == 0x2) or ⮑
(lastPortP == 0 and portP == 0x1):
                    current_reading[axis] += inc
                    if current_reading[axis] > segSize:
# restrain to segment
                        current_reading[axis] -= inc
```

```
                    moved = True
            portP = (port & 0x30) >> 4
            lastPortP = (lastPort &0x30) >> 4
         if port &0x8 :
             blank_screen()
         lastPort = port

def blank_screen():
    screen.fill(background) # blank screen
    segment.fill(background)
    pygame.display.update()

def terminate():
    print "Closing down please wait"
    pfio.deinit()
    pygame.quit()
    sys.exit()

def checkForQuit():
    global col, picture, last_reading, fileName
    event = pygame.event.poll()
    if event.type == pygame.QUIT :
            terminate()
    elif event.type == pygame.KEYDOWN :
# get a key and do something
        if event.key == pygame.K_ESCAPE :
            terminate()
        if event.key == K_SPACE or event.key == K_DELETE:
            blank_screen()
        if event.key == K_r : # draw in red
           col = (255, 0, 0)
        if event.key == K_g : # draw in green
           col = (0, 255, 0)
        if event.key == K_b : # draw in blue
           col = (0, 0, 255)
        if event.key == K_y : # draw in yellow
           col = (255, 255, 0)
        if event.key == K_m : # draw in magenta
           col = (255, 0, 255)
        if event.key == K_p : # draw in peacock blue
           col = (0, 255, 255)
        if event.key == K_w : # draw in white
           col = (255, 255, 255)
```

*continued*

**Listing 15-5   continued**

```
        if event.key == K_k : # draw in blacK
            col = (0, 0, 0)
        if event.key == K_s : # save current point
            last_reading[2] = last_reading[0] # save X
            last_reading[3] = last_reading[1] # save Y
        if event.key == K_l : # draw a line to saved point
            pygame.draw.line(segment,col,(last_reading[2],
last_reading[3]),(last_reading[0],last_reading[1]),2)
            screenUpdate()
        if event.key == K_c : # draw a circle
            try :
                r = ((last_reading[0] - last_reading[2])
**2 + (last_reading[1] - last_reading[3])**2 ) ** (0.5)
                pygame.draw.circle(segment,col,
(last_reading[0],last_reading[1]),int(r),2)
                screenUpdate()
            except:
                pass
        if event.key == K_HASH :
#Save folder to Flickr / Facebook
            print "sending folder to Flickr"
            subprocess.check_output("python
folders2flickr/uploadr.py",shell=True)
            print "done"
        if event.key == K_HOME : # save a picture
            print "save sketch to file"
            if picture == 1 : # first time to save this session
                fileName = raw_input("Enter file name
for this session ")
            try:
                pygame.image.save(screen,
'roto-sketch/'+fileName+str(picture)+'.png')
            except:
                os.system('mkdir roto-sketch')
                pygame.image.save(screen,
'roto-sketch/'+fileName+str(picture)+'.png')
            print "saving sketch as ",
'roto-sketch/'+fileName+str(picture)+'.png'
            picture +=1;

if __name__ == '__main__':
    main()
```

The bulk of the code is the same. Where it differs is that drawing is done in a memory area called segment. When it comes to updating the screen, this segment is drawn four times on the screen in each quadrant of the screen. Each time it is drawn it is flipped either horizontally or vertically to show mirror symmetry in each quadrant. The variable segSize at the start of the code makes it easy to define any size of square window you like for your system. The results of a few tests are shown in Figure 15-8.

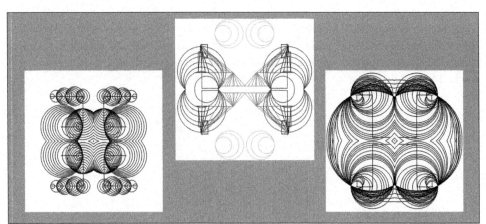

FIGURE 15-8: Some drawings with four-fold symmetry.

# Over to You

Improvements you could make include a stealth mode in which the drawing point is moved without leaving a trail or cutting through existing drawings. For that you have to look at the pixel at the drawing point and redraw the colour over the old grey square. Another thing you could try is to alter the way the circle is drawn with the set point defining the centre and the current point the radius. You can have the two modes available on different keys.

That last program had four-fold symmetry. Consider what it would take to produce five-, six- or any number fold symmetry. Four-fold is easy because the segments you draw in are square, and you just used the flip transformation on the segment for each screen quadrant. However, Pygame has a rotate function that you could apply many times to build up the screen. The point is that the shape of the segment you want to plot is not rectangular but triangular. What you would have to do is to draw in a rectangular segment and then mask it by drawing two triangles on either side of the wanted triangle and filling them with transparent pixels to get a triangular segment. Then you have to rotate that and fill in the screen. This is one of those projects that you will not get right the first time – and serendipity or happy accident might give you something even more interesting that you were trying to create.

If you want to look more at the automatic postings, look at the code at `https://github.com/ept/uploadr.py`. This is an earlier version of the `folders2flickr` code used in this chapter. However, it has some differences you could find useful. You can use the same Flickr secret and API key numbers used in `folders2flickr`; there is no need to apply for your own. This can be set up as a task that runs in the background; every minute it looks at the designated folder to see if there is anything new that needs uploading. This can be a useful computerwide utility.

As to the rotary encoders themselves – see if you can incorporate them as a controller for the games in Chapters 5, "Ping", and 6, "Pie Man". Continuous rotation can be useful in a lot of control situations. The tilt switch also could be used to make a tilting joystick controller if you had four of them.

# Chapter **16**
## The Pendulum Pi, a Harmonograph

**by Mike Cook**

## In This Chapter

- ❍ Learn how to read serial data on the Raspberry Pi
- ❍ See how an Arduino and a Raspberry Pi can work together
- ❍ Discover how to measure angles contactlessly
- ❍ Find the beauty in harmonics

**THIS PROJECT IS** definitely the hardest in the whole book. It will push your mechanical and electronic building skills possibly to the limit. It will also open up a whole new way of getting data to your Raspberry Pi. It is a unique project, at least in the way it has been realised, and best of all – it provokes the reaction "what the . . ." from people seeing it for the first time.

The idea of a harmonograph is not new. It is a mechanical device that started to appear in the mid-nineteenth century and was at the peak of its popularity in the 1890s. It is a mechanical arrangement of pendulums that is used to create complex and detailed patterns by directly drawing them on paper. These things are big, and can be huge, but by using the power of the Raspberry Pi you can make one of a modest size. An example of a pattern produced by this project is shown in Figure 16-1.

FIGURE 16-1:
A harmonograph
pattern from the
Pendulum Pi.

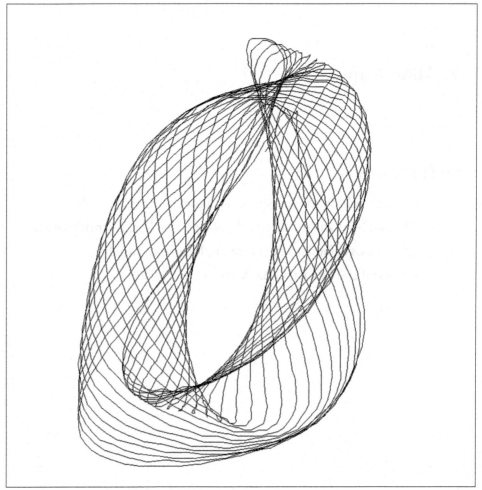

## The Concept

The type of patterns a harmonograph produces are called *Lissajous figures,* which are much beloved of electronic engineers. In fact the first lab I did as an undergraduate student was to apply two signals from separate signal generators to the X and Y deflection circuits of a cathode ray oscilloscope to obtain them. I sneakily got a third signal generator and applied it to the intensity of the beam, a Z axis modulation, and thoroughly confused the supervising lecturer. However, Lissajous figures are only one simple example of the sort of pattern you can get from a harmonograph. In a harmonograph you can have multiple signals defining each axis, and the slow decay of the amplitude of the swing adds greatly to the complexity of the pattern. So how are you going to computerise this mechanical device? Well the secret lies in being able to measure rapidly the angle of a pendulum. In the last chapter, "Facebook-Enabled Roto-Sketch", you saw how the rotary shaft encoder could be used to measure the position of a shaft, but the type used there has detents, and requires a relatively large amount of energy to turn. You can get optical shaft encoders with very little friction, but for any great resolution these are horrendously expensive. To the rescue comes a new chip which offers the possibility of a totally friction-free method of measurement – the Hall effect absolute rotary shaft encoder.

The idea is to use four pendulums to create your drawing, and a shaft encoder on each will measure the angle of each pendulum's swing at any instant of time. Then the Raspberry Pi will plot the information in a window as it comes in, and you will see the picture being plotted in real time. The size of the swing, along with the period of and phase of each pendulum, will alter the picture you produce. You will be able to set the initial swing conditions and alter the length of the pendulums to produce an almost infinite variety of pictures.

## The Hall Effect

A *Hall effect device* is one that uses the influence of a magnetic field on a flow of electrons. It was discovered by Edwin Hall in 1879 but has been widely exploited only in the last 30 years or so with the advent of semiconductors. Basically if current is flowing along a conductor, there will be no potential difference on either side of that conductor. However, if a magnetic field is applied upward through the sample perpendicular to the current flow, then the electrons will initially be deflected by the field toward the side of the conductor. They will build up there, with a corresponding number of holes (positive charge) on the other side. This will continue until they build up an electric field that completely balances the force of the magnetic field. Then the electrons can continue traveling in a straight line through the conductor. This is shown in Figure 16-2. So by measuring this voltage across the conductor you can measure the strength of the magnetic field up through the conductor. This is used in all sorts of devices such as contactless switches, contactless current measurement, the electronic compass and angle measurement.

FIGURE 16-2:
How the Hall
effect works.

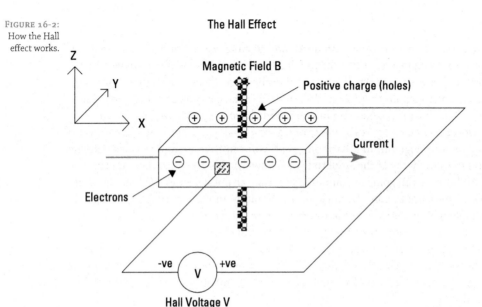

Now an important word in the description "Hall effect absolute rotary shaft encoder" is the word *absolute*. Many rotary encoders, such as the one used in the last chapter, are only relative encoders – that is, you get a signal only to say something has changed by one notch or increment. With an absolute encoder you get multiple output bits to indicate the actual angle. If you thought optical incremental encoders were expensive, then optical absolute encoders are off the scale of expensive. Fortunately the Hall effect version is relatively cheap. The one I have chosen to use is the AS5040, which will operate over the full 360 degrees and return a 10 bit value. That is, it returns a number between 0 and 1023 for one rotation. This means that it produces a resolution of 0.35 of a degree. It does this by having four Hall effect sensors inside the chip and working out the angle from the relative readings they give. It requires a rather special sort of magnet that is cylindrical and diametrically magnetised. Normally a cylindrical magnet will have a north pole at one end and a south pole at the other. However, when it is diametrically magnetised, there is a north and south pole at each end. Think of this as being two bar magnets glued together and shaped into a cylinder. Fortunately, this type of magnet is easy enough to get.

You have to arrange the magnet on the end of the shaft to be just about 1 mm above the chip. The general arrangement of the chip and magnet are shown in Figure 16-3. This chip is capable of all sorts of outputs, but for this project you are simply going to use the access to the internal registers using the SPI interface pins.

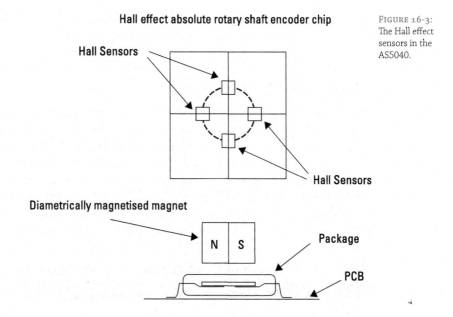

Hall effect absolute rotary shaft encoder chip

Hall Sensors

Hall Sensors

Diametrically magnetised magnet

N | S

Package

PCB

FIGURE 16-3:
The Hall effect
sensors in the
AS5040.

## Enter the Arduino

Now there is one snag with using the Raspberry Pi running Linux with this project, and that is the data from the pendulums is coming out in a constant stream, and, as you know, Linux has a habit of popping out for a cup of tea every now and again. If you were to let this happen, you would have discontinuities in the data, and subsequently, the pattern would look broken up. This is where the Raspberry Pi could do with a little help in reading the data from the sensor, and putting it in a queue or buffer so the Python code can take it out and plot it, without having to worry about when that code is suspended while Linux is doing housekeeping. So here is where the Arduino comes in.

The *Arduino* is a very popular embedded processor, similar in some respects to the one in the Raspberry Pi. However, it is much, much slower, and has a very small amount of memory – but the Arduino has the advantage of not running an operating system at all. This means that if you program it to do one thing it does it without interruption at a regular rate. What you are going to do is use the Arduino to gather the data from the pendulums, do a bit of processing on it and then send it into the USB serial buffer of the Raspberry Pi. Then this buffer is emptied by the Python program, and the points are plotted on the screen.

The Arduino is programmed in C++, but anyone with any experience in C will be able to write a program for it straight off. It is designed to be used by beginners and nontechnical art users, so it is quite easy to use. It comes with its own integrated development environment (IDE) which is a multiplatform program, and you can run it on the Raspberry Pi, on a laptop or on a desktop machine. There are almost a bewildering variety of Arduinos, but the vanilla one at the time of writing is the Arduino Uno, so that is the one I suggest that you use.

## Putting It Together

After you have all the components in place you can start to put them together. The first thing to do is to get the pendulums made. In my version of the harmonograph I have used four pendulums that can be combined in a number of ways to produce the final drawing. In place of the complex arrangement of weights and counterbalances and gimbals used in conventional harmonographs, you just want four simple pendulums of differing lengths. It is the ratio of the pendulum's periods that gives the fundamental class of the pattern, and integer ratios look best. So with that in mind I calculated some pendulum lengths to produce a fundamental frequency of swing along with twice and three times swing harmonics. These are set out in Table 16-1.

### Table 16-1   Length of Pendulum for Various Harmonics

| Harmonic | Normalise Length | Real Length |
| --- | --- | --- |
| Fundamental | 7.96 | 796 mm |
| 2 | 1.91 | 191 mm |
| 3 | 1 | 100 mm |

The practical size of the third harmonic pendulum basically governed the size I needed for the fundamental or longest pendulum. You can make the pendulums covering more harmonics if you like, but you will see that they rapidly get quite big. For example, if you want to cover four harmonics, with the shortest pendulum at 100 mm, then the longest pendulum needs to be 3180 mm. The mass of the pendulum does not affect the frequency of swing, but it will affect how long it will swing. In effect it is the damping factor; in other words, the more the mass, the longer it takes for the friction in the bearings to stop the swinging. Getting sufficient mass into short pendulums is tricky; it is easier for longer ones. In fact the equations assume that all the mass of a pendulum is concentrated at the end of the rod or string. What happens in practice with a distributed mass is that the effective length becomes the centre of mass of the pendulum. This means in practice the pendulums have to be slightly longer than the theoretical length.

A trip around a national chain of DIY stores brought some rectangular metal tubing and solid bar to my attention, and it looked as if that would do the job for the pendulums. So then I had to design a frame to mount them on. For this I used 1 1/2" by 3/4" by 1/8" and 1 1/14" by 1/2" by 1/8" aluminum channels, referred to as the *large channel* and *small channel,* respectively. This has the great advantage that the small channel is a tight fit inside the large one, which makes the design a bit easier. I didn't find that the DIY stores had this size in stock, so I had to order it online. The idea is to make two U-shaped frames and bolt them together with four lengths of aluminum channel. This is shown in Figures 16-4 and 16-5.

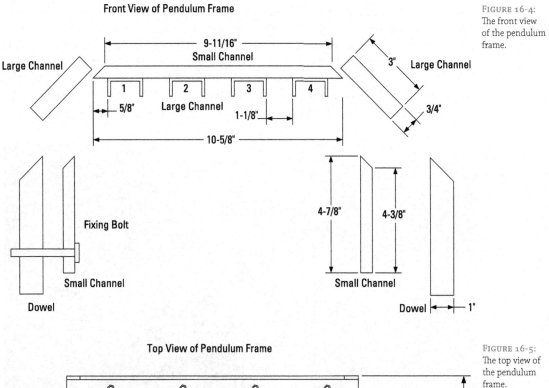

**FIGURE 16-4:**
The front view of the pendulum frame.

**FIGURE 16-5:**
The top view of the pendulum frame.

The angled channel fits flush over the far end of the cross channels, but you need to cut out a small notch out of one side of it as shown in Figure 16-6. The fixings for these angled pieces are not nuts and bolts because there is no room for a nut in the cross channel. Therefore, I had to cut a thread into the hole in the cross channel. For the M3 fixings I used, this meant drilling a 2.5 mm hole and running an M3 tap through it. The aluminum is 1/8" thick, so it takes a thread nicely – but remember that it is only aluminum, so don't tighten it up too much, or you might strip the thread. When cutting thread with a tap, once it is going, always turn it one turn in and then half a turn out. This cuts off the swarf and stops the hole from jamming up. Use a drop of oil when cutting a thread to make the tap last longer. If you are in your local DIY store and ask where the taps are, and are directed to the plumbing section, then find a store that knows what it is selling.

FIGURE 16-6: The notch needed on one side of each angled channel.

Remember when fixing the aluminum channel together you always need two fixing points per side – one is not enough. The bottom channels of each arm of the frame drop onto four 2' 8" dowel rods, which in turn are set into a floor or bench mounting frame shown in Figure 16-7. I bolted the pieces together with M6 nuts and bolts and fixed a 10" by 3" by 1 1/2" block in the middle of the long side with glue and screws from the underside. I drilled in four 1" holes using a saw drill so that the dowels could be slotted in place. Cut off the dowels at 45 degrees at the top so that they slip under the angled aluminum channel, and a hole through the vertical channel and dowel allows a bolt and wing nut to fasten it into place. Study the finished structure shown in Figure 16-8 to get the idea of what you need to build. The frame on the base is approximately 3' by 1' 4", and contrasting bright colours for the paint can give it more of a fun look.

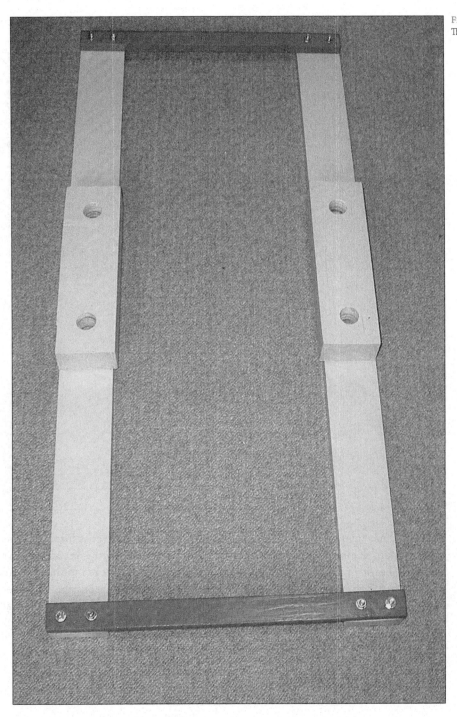

FIGURE 16-7:
The base frame.

FIGURE 16-8:
The whole
pendulum
assembly.

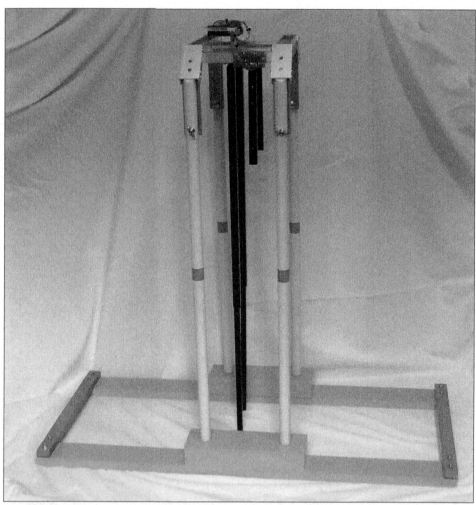

The pendulums themselves are attached to M6 threaded rod, which goes through the sides of the aluminum channel. As shown in Figure 16-9, two lock nuts secure one end; it then passes through a bearing with a nut securing it, and the pendulum is secured to this with another nut. Finally the other end of the channel has a nut on one side of the bearing, with a lock nut on the outside. I drilled out this lock nut's internal nylon washer and glued in the diametrically magnetised magnet. It is vital that this magnet have its face as square as possible to the rod because this will affect the accuracy of readings that you get.

FIGURE 16-9:
Fixing the
pendulum to the
threaded rod
and channel.

The magnets are extremely powerful and can be prone to damage. Never let them fly together, no matter how tempting it is. This is because they come together with such force that they will shatter and small pieces will chip off them. This can happen the very first time they come together. Another thing is that strong magnets can pick up iron filings in a workshop. You need to remove those to get a uniform magnetic field. I have found the best way is to use *blue tack* – the sort of putty used for fixing posters to a wall. Use this to mop up a magnet of filings and then throw the piece away. Better still – do not let filings get onto the magnet in the first place.

**WARNING**

## Smooth Swinging

The bearings I used were the type MR126 sealed, which are quite low cost and are widely used in the construction of 3D printers, inline skates and tools. They have a 6 mm hole for the threaded rod and are 12 mm in diameter. I drilled each side of the channel with a 12 mm drill and used a vice to push the bearings into the hole. This produced a nice interference fit. At first this appeared to work well, but as the threaded rod was tightened up I noticed that there were sections of the rotation that appeared stiff. So in order to exactly align them I filed one hole so that it was slightly larger, allowing a very small amount of slack all around, and then I tightened up the threaded rod and applied epoxy to secure the second bearing (the one not carrying the magnet) in place. In this way I got an exact fit, and the threaded rods would turn on the bearings without any noticeable stiff spots. The pendulum itself is a 12 mm square steel tube, 4" long from the centre of the hole. The area of the tube above the hole needs to be rounded off with a file to prevent it from catching on the top of the aluminum channel. There are two holes at the end of the tube; these should be drilled and tapped with an M3 thread. Although there is not much to thread as the walls of the tube are so thin, this is compensated for by the material being steel; still, overtightening might cause the thread to strip.

I gave two of the four pendulums, numbers 2 and 4, a solid core of steel by filing down two edges of some 12 mm square steel rod so that it slides inside the tube. Then I marked the position of the tapped holes on the solid rod, drilled out 3.5 mm clearance holes and finally applied some epoxy to hold them in place. You could do that with the other two pendulums as well, but there is little point as these are going to eventually be much longer. The idea is that the basic length of the pendulum is the third harmonic; then there are two sizes of extension rod you can use to get the second harmonic and the fundamental. These are shown in Figure 16-10. The short extensions have a solid square completely contained in the tube, whereas the long extension has the solid rod protruding from the end and the choice of a number of holes along the square tube to attach it, giving you some variability on the length of this largest pendulum. Use positions 1 and 3 for the long pendulum extensions and positions 2 and 4 for the short ones.

FIGURE 16-10: The pendulum sections.

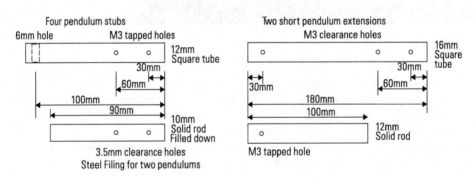

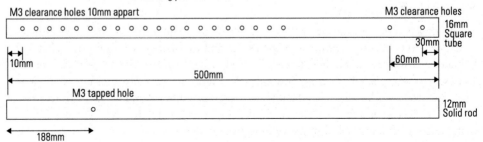

When sliding the rod up the tube it is a bit hard to spot the tapped hole through the clearance hole. So I painted around the tapped hole with white paint so that it could be easily seen through the clearance hole and lined up correctly.

TIP

## Electronics

Next, you come to the electronics, which fortunately are not too complex – just the sensor chip, some decoupling capacitors, two resistors and an LED. The AS5040 rotation sensor can be used from either a 3V3 or 5V supply; I used the 5V supply because that gave the correct voltage level of logic signals for the Arduino I used. A schematic of the sensing board is shown in Figure 16-11. You need to build four of these. The capacitors should be of the ceramic type and mounted as close to the chip as possible. The LED is a red/green common cathode, which will allow you to have three colours: red, green and orange. These are used to indicate if the pendulum is being used to gather data and what axis it is controlling.

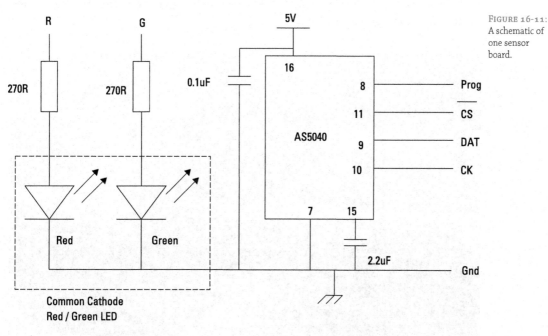

FIGURE 16-11: A schematic of one sensor board.

Sensor Module – build four of these

The only difficulty with this circuit is that the AS5040 is in a 16 pin SSOP package, with a 0.65 mm lead pitch. This is impossible to solder directly onto strip board, but fortunately adaptor boards are available quite cheaply. I used a board designed for an SSOP28 chip, and it converts the fine pitch to normal 0.1" pitch used on strip board. (Its full name is an SSOP28 to DIP28 0.65 mm pitch adapter transfer board, and I got it from Hong Kong through eBay.) It covers more chip leads than you need, so just solder it in the centre with three blank connections on each side. This then should be attached to some strip board by soldering solid copper wires through the holes you want connections to. Make sure that the adaptor board is as close as possible to the strip board. Then mount the strip board on the side of each aluminum channel so that the magnet is exactly over the centre of the chip. Separate the pillars by an odd number of strips on the strip board so that the pillar mounting holes are equally spaced from the centre of the bearing/magnet position. To get the distance between the magnet and sensor correct, I used a 10 mm M3 tapped pillar, a nut and two M3 washers and got the spacing between the magnet and chip to be 1 mm. Fortunately there is an electronic way of telling if the magnetic strength is in the correct range; you will see about this later in the chapter when you look at the data that comes from this sensor. The physical arrangement is shown in Figures 16-12 and 16-13.

FIGURE 16-12:
The mounted
sensor board
showing the
chip.

FIGURE 16-13:
The mounting of
a sensor board.

Now all that remains is to wire up the sensor modules to the Arduino. The wiring for this is shown in Figure 16-14. The sensors are wired up in a daisy chain configuration with the data from the farthest sensor passing through all the others before it gets to the Arduino. It is common to have multiple sensors wired like this, and it eliminates the need for having a data select line for each chip. I placed a single white LED on the Arduino to indicate if there are any problems with the data from the chips. I drew this module wiring to make the wiring clear; however, in practice I wired it up in a star configuration. That means that the wires are taken directly from each sensor module to the Arduino and not chained, from one sensor board to the next. This ensures that any problems with grounding loops and power distribution are minimised.

Mount the Arduino on pillars on top the pendulum frame as shown in Figure 16-15. Solder the wires to small pieces of copper strip board to which you should solder pin connectors for attaching to the pin headers on the Arduino. Mount the white error LED onto one of these strips close to pin A5. The wiring of the whole thing is shown in Figure 16-16. I used cable ties to make the wiring look neat.

FIGURE 16-14:
A schematic of
the sensor
modules' inter-
connections.

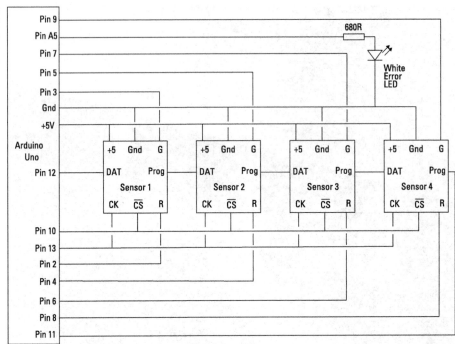

FIGURE 16-15:
The Arduino
mounted on top
of the frame.

FIGURE 16-16:
The complete
system
wired up.

## Programming the Arduino

Next you have to be able to program the Arduino. To do this you need to use the Arduino IDE. You have a choice of either doing this on your laptop or desktop computer or loading a version into the Raspberry Pi. Using a PC or Mac is much faster than using the Pi, but I have successfully used the Raspberry Pi to program the Arduino. I will show you how to use the Raspberry Pi here.

To install it is simple enough: From a command line just type

```
$ sudo apt-get update
$ sudo apt-get install arduino
```

Depending on your Internet access speed this could take 20 minutes or more as you have to download the Java code that supports it. Note that this code might take up more space than you would like; you will be informed of the size before you commit to the download. After it is down-loaded start up the desktop and open the File Manager window. Navigate to /usr/bin and double-click the arduino file. A pop-up window will invite you to do various options; click Execute. Plug in your Arduino Uno directly to one of the Raspberry Pi's USB sockets. I have found that although once programmed the Arduino will work happily through a hub, at the time of writing, the Arduino IDE implementation will not work correctly if it is connected through a hub. Next go to the Tools menu. Choose the Serial Port option and click /dev/ttyACM0. Your Arduino is now connected. Check that the Uno board is selected by clicking Tools ⇨ Board.

Now you need to test that everything is working, so type in Listing 16-1.

---

**Listing 16-1    Arduino Blink**

```
// Blink
void setup(){
  pinMode(13, OUTPUT);
}

void loop(){
  digitalWrite(13, HIGH);
  delay(700);
  digitalWrite(13, LOW);
  delay(700);
}
```

---

Now click the right-pointing arrow to upload the blink program into the Arduino. When it has finished uploading the orange LED with a letter L next to it will steadily blink. Click the down-pointing arrow at the top of the IDE window and save your file under the name blink. This will automatically generate a sketchbook folder in your home directory. In the Arduino world the program that runs on an Arduino is known as a *sketch*.

There are example programs built into the IDE you can look at under File ⇨ Examples. After you have the blink sketch in the sketchbook folder you can start the Arduino IDE at any time by double-clicking any of the .ino files in this folder. For now you have only one called blink.ino.

I would encourage you to download and study the data sheet of the AS5040 encoder – it contains a lot more information than you could ever need – but the point is it shows you the full capability of the chip; you are only using a part of its capabilities here. It talks to the outside world using a protocol known as *serial protocol interface* (SPI), which is a loosely defined protocol that has a lot of subtle differences and variations – so much so that this chip is not quite compatible with the hardware SPI interface of the Arduino, so you will have to write a program to manipulate the SPI lines specifically. This sort of technique is known as *bit banging*. Figure 16-17 shows the way the interface works. Basically a chip select line is brought low, and then the clock line is made to go up and down – and every time it goes up a new bit of data is placed on the chip's output. In order for this data to be stable, the Arduino should read the data bit when it places the clock high. As the data appears one bit at a time on the chip's output the bit banging code must shift it into a variable one bit at a time to make up all

16 bits of the full data. Because you have four of these chips daisy chained together, you must do this four times with a different variable being used to shift the reading each time.

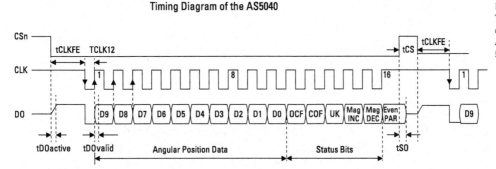

FIGURE 16-17: The timing diagram for the AS5040 interface.

**DO to D9 – The angle data**

**Status Bits**
**OCF – Offset Compensation Finished**
**COF – Cordic Overflow**
**LIN – Linearity Alarm**
**Mag Inc – Magnitude Increase of magnetic field**
**Mag Dec – Magnitude Decrease of magnetic field**
**Even Par – Even parity bit**

This is not a book about C or programming the Arduino, so if you are not familiar with them, just treat this section as a black box, the way you treat Python libraries – that is to say you know they work and how to interact with them but you don't know the details of what they do.

After you install the Arduino IDE and program a flashing LED sketch it is time to test out the sensors and LEDs. It is always good to write something simple to check out the hardware before trying to make it do too much. So type the code in Listing 16-2 into the Arduino IDE.

---

Listing 16-2 **Hardware Test Code**

```
/* Harmonograph reading four rotary encoder
and test out the LEDs
By Mike Cook Feb-April 2013
Bit banging the SPI
*/

// define SPI pins
#define CS_ENC 10
```

*continued*

Listing 16-2   **continued**

```
#define CK_ENC 13
#define MISO_ENC 12
#define MOSI_ENC 11

long int time;
byte npRead = 4; // number of detectors to read
float th [] = {0.0, 0.0, 0.0, 0.0 }; // angle reading
int dig1 [] = { 0, 0, 0, 0};
int dig2 [] = { 0, 0, 0, 0};
byte ledRed [] = {2, 4, 6, 8}; // pins controlling red
byte ledGreen [] = {3, 5, 7, 9}; // pins controlling green
int count =1; // LED test pattern
int error = 1; // error LED test count

void setup(){
   Serial.begin(9600);
   pinMode(CS_ENC, OUTPUT);
   digitalWrite(CS_ENC, HIGH);
   pinMode(CK_ENC, OUTPUT);
   digitalWrite(CK_ENC, HIGH); // set clock high
   pinMode(MOSI_ENC, OUTPUT);
   digitalWrite(MOSI_ENC, LOW);
   pinMode(MISO_ENC, INPUT);
   pinMode(A5, OUTPUT);
   for(int i=0; i<4; i++){ // set up LEDs
     pinMode(ledRed[i], OUTPUT);
     digitalWrite(ledRed[i], LOW);
     pinMode(ledGreen[i], OUTPUT);
     digitalWrite(ledGreen[i], LOW);
    }
 time = millis() + 2000; // reading every 2 seconds
}

void loop(){
  if(millis() > time){ // only take reading every 2 seconds
   time = millis() + 1000;
   encRead(); // read in all sensors
   for(int i =0; i<npRead; i++){ // print them out
   Serial.print(th[i]); // angle
   Serial.print(" -> ");
   Serial.print(dig1[i],HEX);  // ready
   Serial.print(" -> ");
```

```
    Serial.println(dig2[i], HEX); // magnetic strength
    }
    count = count << 1;
    if(count > 0xff) count = 1;
    upDateLEDs(count);
    error++ ;
    digitalWrite(A5, error & 1); // flash error LED
    Serial.println(" ");
  }
}

void upDateLEDs(int n){ // MS nibble red - LS nibble green
  ledsOff();
  for(int i = 0; i<4; i++){
    if( (n & 1) != 0) digitalWrite(ledGreen[i],HIGH);
    n = n >> 1;
  }
    for(int i = 0; i<4; i++){
    if( (n & 1) != 0) digitalWrite(ledRed[i],HIGH);
    n = n >> 1;
  }
}

void ledsOff(){
    for(int i=0; i<4; i++){
    digitalWrite(ledRed[i], LOW);
    digitalWrite(ledGreen[i], LOW);
  }
}

void encRead(){ // reads two bytes from each encoder
    int hallReading; // to hold 16 bits from sensor
    digitalWrite( CS_ENC, LOW);  // enable encoders
    for(int i = 0; i<npRead; i++){ // read in each sensor
        delayMicroseconds(50);
        digitalWrite( CK_ENC, LOW); // clock low
        delayMicroseconds(50);
        for(int i=0;i<16;i++){
// read in all bits for one sensor
            hallReading = hallReading << 1;
            digitalWrite( CK_ENC, HIGH); // clock high
            delayMicroseconds(50);
```

*continued*

Listing 16-2   **continued**

```
            hallReading = hallReading | digitalRead(MISO_ENC);
            digitalWrite( CK_ENC, LOW); // clock low
            delayMicroseconds(50);
        } // all bits in
        digitalWrite( CK_ENC, HIGH); // clock high
        delayMicroseconds(50);
        th[i] = ((hallReading>> 6) & 0x3ff); // the angle data
        dig1[i] = (hallReading & 0x3f) >> 3;
// the magnetic field
        dig2[i] = (hallReading & 0x6)>>1;
// ready and error bits
    }
    digitalWrite( CS_ENC, HIGH); // remove chip enable
}
```

Now before you run this save it under the name Encoder_read. Then click the tick icon to see if it compiles correctly; any simple mistakes will be highlighted. Correct those and save again. When you can get it to compile without errors click the upload icon to transfer it to the Arduino. This could take up to ten minutes. Only when you have done this should you disconnect the Arduino, plug in the sensor hardware and reconnect the Arduino to the Raspberry Pi.

This sketch reads the sensors and flashes the LEDs in turn at a rate of about two seconds. It prints out the results to the serial port. You can see these results on the serial port terminal program built into the Arduino IDE. Simply click the icon that looks like a magnifying glass in the top-right corner. You will see four groups of numbers, each line being one sensor. The first number is the angle data, followed by the conversion error flags and finally the magnetic indicators. The numbers are separated by an ⇔ symbol.

What you are initially looking for is that the second two numbers are 4 and 0, indicating that they are error free, and the first number changes as you move the pendulum. If this is what you see, then it is time to make the adjustments to the pendulums. There is a wraparound point at some place in the rotation where the data goes from 1023 back to zero. You want this point to be outside the permitted swing angle. I adjusted each pendulum's magnet position by putting the pendulum assembly on its back and just having the short stubs on the pendulums. Then I slackened the nut holding the pendulum to the threaded rod and twisted the rod so that the reading was within 64 of 256 for the pendulum horizontal to one side and within 64 of 768 when moved to the other side. This means that when the pendulums are hanging straight down the reading should be close to 512. The exact value does not matter but write down what it is for each pendulum because you are going to use it in the real sketch so that you get a zero angle reading when the pendulum is hanging straight down.

## The Final Arduino Code

Now it is time to program the Arduino for the real job. The `Harmo` Arduino code is designed to send data to the Raspberry Pi only when it is asked to start. The Pi sends commands to the Arduino that consist of just a single letter. These are Start Sending, Stop Sending and instructions on how to process the pendulum data. So type the code in Listing 16-3 into the Arduino IDE and save it under the name `Harmo`.

---

**Listing 16-3  The `Harmo` Arduino Code**

```
/* Harmonograph reading four rotary encoder
By Mike Cook Feb-April 2013
Bit banging the SPI
Sending out to serial port as two 10 bit values split into two
5 bit values with the top two bits used to identify the byte
Serial data flow and configuration control
*/

#define CS_ENC 10
#define CK_ENC 13
#define MISO_ENC 12
#define MOSI_ENC 11

// constants for scaling the output
#define OFFSET 400.0  // centre of the display
#define H_OFFSET 200.0 // half offset
#define RANGE 540.0  // range +/- of co-ordinates
#define H_RANGE 270.0
// half the x range when using two pendulums

long int interval, timeToSample;
float th [] = {0.0, 0.0, 0.0, 0.0 }; // angle reading
// change the line below to your own measurements
int offset[] = {521, 510, 380, 477}; // offsets at zero degrees
int reading[4]; // holding for raw readings
boolean active = false, calabrate = false;
byte np = 2; // number of pendulums to output
byte npRead = 4; // number of detectors to read
byte ledRed [] = {2, 4, 6, 8}; // pins controlling red
byte ledGreen [] = {3, 5, 7, 9}; // pins controlling green

void setup(){
  Serial.begin(115200);
  pinMode(CS_ENC, OUTPUT);
```

*continued*

**Listing 16-3   continued**

```
  digitalWrite(CS_ENC, HIGH);
  pinMode(CK_ENC, OUTPUT);
  digitalWrite(CK_ENC, HIGH); // set clock high
  pinMode(MOSI_ENC, OUTPUT);
  digitalWrite(MOSI_ENC, LOW);
  pinMode(MISO_ENC, INPUT);
  interval = 20; // time between samples
  timeToSample = millis() + interval;
    for(int i = 0; i<4; i++){ // initialise indicator LEDs
    pinMode(ledRed[i], OUTPUT);
    pinMode(ledGreen[i], OUTPUT);
  }
  upDateLEDs(np);
  delay(100); // allow sensor to power up
  pinMode(A5,OUTPUT);
  digitalWrite(A5,LOW);
  if(calabrate){
    encRead(); // get offset
    calabrate = false; // calibration done
    }
}

void loop(){
  if(millis() >= timeToSample && active) {
// send data if we should
    digitalWrite(13, HIGH);
    timeToSample = millis() + interval;
    encRead();
    sendData();
    digitalWrite(13,LOW);
  }
  else {
    if(Serial.available() != 0) {
// switch on / off sample sending
    char rx = Serial.read();
    switch (rx) {
      case'G': // Go - start sending samples
      active = true;
      break;
      case'S': // Stop - stop sending samples
      active = false;
      break;
      case '2':
```

```
// make samples from sensors 1 for X and 3 for Y
        upDateLEDs(0x45);
        np = 2;
        break;
        case '3': // samples from sensors 1 & 2 for X and 3 for Y
        upDateLEDs(0x47);
        np = 3;
        break;
        case '4':
// samples from sensors 1 & 2 for X and 3 & 4 for Y
        upDateLEDs(0xcf);
        np = 4;
        break;
        case '5':
        upDateLEDs(0x8a);
        np = 5;  // make samples from sensors 2 for X and 4 for Y
        break;
        case '6':
// make samples from sensor 1 for X and 3 & 4 for Y
        upDateLEDs(0xCD);
        np = 6;
        break;


    }
  }
 }
}

void encRead(){ // reads two bytes from each encoder
     int hallReading =  0;
   digitalWrite( CS_ENC, LOW);  // enable encoder
   for(int i = 0; i<npRead; i++){
        delayMicroseconds(10);
        digitalWrite( CK_ENC, LOW); // clock low
        delayMicroseconds(10);
        hallReading =  0;
        for(int i=0;i<16;i++){ // read in all four bits
            hallReading = hallReading << 1;
            digitalWrite( CK_ENC, HIGH); // clock high
            delayMicroseconds(10);
            hallReading = hallReading | digitalRead(MISO_ENC);
            digitalWrite( CK_ENC, LOW); // clock low
            delayMicroseconds(10);
```

*continued*

**Listing 16-3  continued**

```
        } // all bits in
        digitalWrite( CK_ENC, HIGH); // clock high
        delayMicroseconds(10);
        reading[i] = hallReading;
    }
  digitalWrite( CS_ENC, HIGH); // remove chip enable
  // all data in now process the data
  int errorLEDs = 0;
  for(int i=0; i<npRead; i++){
      th[i] = ((reading[i] >> 6) & 0x3ff) - offset[i];
//angle data
      th[i] = th[i] * 0.006135; // convert into radians
      if((reading[i] & 0x6) != 0) errorLEDs++;
//  shows an error
   }
  if(errorLEDs != 0) digitalWrite(A5,HIGH);
   else digitalWrite(A5,LOW); // drive error LED
}

void upDateLEDs(int n){ // MS nibble red - LS nibble green
  ledsOff();
  for(int i = 0; i<4; i++){
    if( (n & 1) != 0) digitalWrite(ledGreen[i],HIGH);
    n = n >> 1;
  }
    for(int i = 0; i<4; i++){
    if( (n & 1) != 0) digitalWrite(ledRed[i],HIGH);
    n = n >> 1;
  }
}

void ledsOff(){
    for(int i=0; i<4; i++){
    digitalWrite(ledRed[i], LOW);
    digitalWrite(ledGreen[i], LOW);
  }
}


void sendData() { // send X Y points to plot
  int s1,s2;
  byte t;
  // pendulums 1 and 3 are short and so have a wider range
```

```
  switch(np) {
    case 2: // from two pendulums
      s1 = OFFSET + (RANGE * sin(th[0]));
      s2 = OFFSET + (RANGE * sin(th[2]));
        break;
    case 3: // from three pendulums
      s1 = OFFSET + (H_RANGE * sin(th[0])) + ⤵
(H_OFFSET * sin(th[1]));
        s2 = OFFSET + (RANGE * sin(th[2]));
        break;
    case 4: // from four pendulums
      s1 = OFFSET + (H_RANGE * sin(th[0])) + ⤵
(H_OFFSET * sin(th[1]));
      s2 = OFFSET + (H_RANGE * sin(th[2])) + ⤵
(H_OFFSET * sin(th[3]));
        break;
    case 5: // from other two pendulums
      s1 = OFFSET + (OFFSET * sin(th[1]));
      s2 = OFFSET + (OFFSET * sin(th[3]));
    case 6: // from three pendulums
      s1 = OFFSET + (RANGE * sin(th[0]));
      s2 = OFFSET + (H_RANGE * sin(th[2]) + ⤵
(H_OFFSET * sin(th[3])));
        break;
  }
  // split up the data into 4 bytes, tag top
  // two MS bits and send
  t = (s1 >> 5) & 0x1f; // MSB first
  Serial.write(t);
  t = (s1 & 0x1f) | 0x40; // LSB plus top index bits
  Serial.write(t);
  t = ((s2 >> 5)  & 0x1f)| 0x80; // MSB plus top index bit
  Serial.write(t);
  t = (s2 & 0x1f) | 0xC0; // LSB plus top index bits
  Serial.write(t);
}
```

The first thing to note is that the line

```
int offset[] = {521, 510, 380, 477}; // offsets at zero degrees
```

should be changed to the readings you took with the previous sketch when the pendulums were hanging down. It is impossible that you will have the same readings here for your construction.

One important thing to note is the way the data is sent to the Raspberry Pi. In order to minimise the number of bytes sent, you send only the X and Y coordinates that need to be plotted. However, you can't just send the bytes because you then have no way of knowing which was which at the receiving end. If one was missed, then the whole thing would be out of sequence, and the data would be corrupted. There are two ways around this problem: The first is to send data in packets – send the data and add a header to it. The header should be a unique value that does not appear in the data. The receiving side keeps fishing bytes out of its buffer until it sees this header byte; then it has a good chance of knowing that the next few bytes are in the order they are sent. This is fine especially for larger amounts of data, but you have to ensure a unique value for the start of packet indicator, and that often means restricting the data to something like a string representation, which is inefficient. Here, the approach I have used is to tag each individual byte, which works because you are trying to send two 10-bit data values and there are plenty of spare bits if you divide the data up correctly. Figure 16-18 shows what I have done. Basically each coordinate is split up into two 5-bit fields, and the top two bits of each field have a unique bit pattern to identify them. Therefore the receiving side can identify if the bits come in in the right order and verify that none have been dropped. This was important, especially during development, because initially the Raspberry Pi's buffer was filling up to overflowing and data was being lost. Therefore I knew I had to do something to alleviate the problem; more on that when you see the Python code in the section "Programming the Pi".

FIGURE 16-18: Splitting up the data to tag each byte.

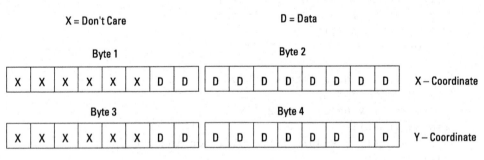

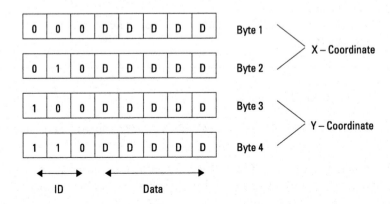

The other main point is the code that looks at the serial port to see if the Raspberry Pi has sent any data back. You will see that all that happens is that variables are set, but these variables affect the program flow later on, specifically in the sendData() function. This function converts the angles you measure from each pendulum into the distance to plot on the screen. Using the simple sin rule of geometry shown in Figure 16-19, you can calculate the distance from the centre of the swing.

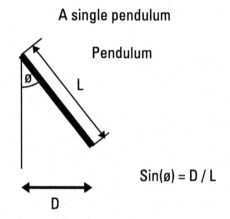

**A single pendulum**

FIGURE 16-19: Generating a displacement from an angle.

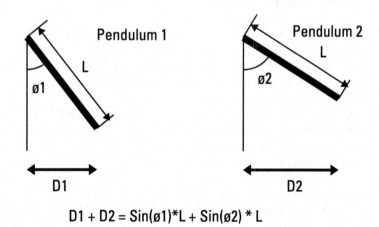

**The combined effect of two pendulums**

The actual length of the pendulum is substituted by a value of half the number of pixels you want to cover, and when you have two pendulums you use half that value and add them up. In the sketch you will see that this is not quite the case with the values of the constant

RANGE; this is because the large pendulums do not swing as much as the small ones, so there is a bit of an amplification factor to make a slightly bigger display. When two pendulums are used, the displacement distance at any time is simply the two pendulum readings added together. As they swing back and forth you need to add a fixed offset so that the swing will be in the centre of the window when you plot it on the Raspberry Pi. You will see in the sendData() function the angle data from each pendulum can be combined in a number of different ways depending on what commands have been received. Then finally the data is split up, tagged and sent out of the serial port to the Raspberry Pi.

## Programming the Pi

Finally you have come to the point where you want to take the data streaming in from the pendulums and plot them onto the screen to see what patterns they make. The first thing a program has to do is to establish communication with the Arduino. When you plug an Arduino into the USB port it can potentially appear on one of two ports, so you have to try both of them. You want to send the data as fast as possible, so use the Arduino's top speed of 115200 baud. Then you have to open a Pygame window and command the Arduino to start sending data by sending it the letter *G* for "go", down the serial port. The full listing of the Python program to do this is shown in Listing 16-4.

**Listing 16-4　The Pendulum Pi Plotting Program**

```python
import piface.pfio as pfio      # piface library
#!/usr/bin/env python
"""

Harmonograph plotter
Data comes from pendulums attached to an arduino and feeding
into the Pi through the USB serial port
version 2 with reduced byte transfer count
"""
import time                     # for delays
import os, pygame, sys
from pygame.locals import *
import serial

try:
    ser = serial.Serial('/dev/ttyACM0',115200, timeout=2)
except:
    ser = serial.Serial('/dev/ttyACM1',115200, timeout=2)

pygame.init()                          # initialise graphics interface
```

```python
os.environ['SDL_VIDEO_WINDOW_POS'] = 'center'
pygame.display.set_caption("Harmonograph")
screen = pygame.display.set_mode([800,800],0,32)
background = pygame.Surface((800,800))

cBackground =(255,255,255)
background.fill(cBackground) # make background colour
col = (0,0,0) # drawing colour
reading = [0, 0, 0, 0]
lastX = 0
lastY = 0
picture = 1 # picture number
nextTime = time.time()
timeInc = 0.2 # update screen every half a second
fileName = "harmo"
running = False

def main():
        openPort()
        getData()
        drawData() # to get the starting positions
        blank_screen()
        while True :
            checkForQuit()
            getData()
            drawData()

def drawData():
        global readings, nextTime, lastX, lastY
        x = reading[0]
        y = reading[1]
        pygame.draw.line(screen,col,(lastX,lastY),(x,y),1)
        lastX = x
        lastY = y
        # see if it is time to update the screen
        if time.time() > nextTime :
            pygame.display.update()
            nextTime = time.time() + timeInc

def openPort():
        global running
```

*continued*

Listing 16-4   **continued**

```
        ser.flushInput()
        # tell the arduino to start sending
        running = True
        ser.write('3')
        ser.write('G')

def checkInput(b):
# see if the bytes have been received in the correct order
        correct = True
        for i in range(0,4):
            #print i," - " # ,hex(ord(b[i]))
            if (ord(b[i]) >> 6) != i :
                correct = False
        return correct

def getData():
    global reading, running
    if running :
        a = ser.read(4)
        if checkInput(a) :
            reading[0] = ((ord(a[0]) & 0x1f)<< 5) | ↩
(ord(a[1]) &0x1f)
            reading[1] = ((ord(a[2]) & 0x1f)<<5) | ↩
(ord(a[3]) &0x1f)
            #print reading[0]," - ",reading[1]
        else:
            correct = False
            while correct == False : # resynchronise
                print "lost sync ",ser.inWaiting()
                b = ser.read(1)
                t = a[1] + a[2] + a[3] + b[0]
                a = t
                correct = checkInput(a)

def blank_screen():
    screen.fill((255,255,255)) # blank screen
    pygame.display.update()

def terminate(): # close down the program
    print ("Closing down please wait")
    # tell the arduino to stop sending
```

```
    ser.write('S')
    ser.close()
    pygame.quit()
    sys.exit()

def checkForQuit():
    global col, picture, fileName, running
    event = pygame.event.poll()
    if event.type == pygame.QUIT :
            terminate()
    elif event.type == pygame.KEYDOWN :
# get a key and do something
        if event.key == pygame.K_ESCAPE :
            terminate()
        if event.key == K_SPACE or event.key == K_DELETE:
            blank_screen()
        if event.key == K_r :
            col = (255, 0, 0)
        if event.key == K_g :
            col = (0, 255, 0)
        if event.key == K_b :
            col = (0, 0, 255)
        if event.key == K_y :
            col = (255, 255, 0)
        if event.key == K_m :
            col = (255, 0, 255)
        if event.key == K_c :
            col = (0, 255, 255)
        if event.key == K_w :
            col = (255, 255, 255)
        if event.key == K_k :
            col = (0, 0, 0)
        if event.key == K_s : # see the size of the buffer
            print ser.inWaiting()
        if event.key == K_2 :
            ser.write('2') # data from two pendulums
        if event.key == K_3 :
            ser.write('3') # data from three pendulums
        if event.key == K_4 :
            ser.write('4') # data from four pendulums
        if event.key == K_5 :
            ser.write('5') # data from alternate two pendulums
```

*continued*

**Listing 16-4   continued**

```
        if event.key == K_6 :
            ser.write('6')
# data from alternate three pendulums
        if event.key == K_h :
            ser.write('S') # stop arduino from sending
            running = False
        if event.key == K_j :
            ser.write('G') # start arduino sending
            running = True
        if event.key == K_HOME :
            ser.write('S') # stop arduino from sending
            print "save sketch to file"
            if picture == 1 : # first time to save this session
                fileName = raw_input("Enter file name ⤶
for this session ")
            try:
                pygame.image.save(screen,'harmo/'+⤶
fileName+str(picture)+'.png')
            except:
                os.system('mkdir harmo')
                pygame.image.save(screen,'harmo/'+⤶
fileName+str(picture)+'.png')
            print "saving sketch as ",'harmo/'+⤶
fileName+str(picture)+'.png'
            picture +=1;
            ser.write('G') # start arduino sending

if __name__ == '__main__':
    main()
```

If you get an error at the line

```
import serial
```

Then you will have to install it by typing

```
sudo apt-get python-serial
```

The main function is quite simple: It opens the serial port and then gets one point of data, plots it and wipes the screen. This primes the last coordinate positions so that the drawing starts at the current point. Then there is a simple infinite loop that checks for any quit or keyboard inputs, and then gets another pair of points and plots them. The getData() function simply reads four bytes from the serial port, and the checkInput() function is called as part of an if statement. This returns true or false depending whether the input bytes have the correct tag bits on them. If they are okay, the bytes are unpacked into a reading variable; if not then a message is printed out, and bytes are read in one at a time in an attempt to resynchronise the data stream.

Drawing the data on the screen is quite simple and handled by the drawData() function. A line is drawn between this new pair of points and the last set. Now at this point you might expect to update the screen. However, when I tried this it took too long, and the data backed up in the buffer leading it to overflow and thus fail. So I came up with the compromise that the actual screen would only be updated every 0.2 of a second. This is done by using the timer module to see if it is time to update the screen. This results in a slightly jerky drawing, but it is not too disturbing to look at. As a result, in normal circumstances, the buffer is nearly always empty. However, when the operating system times out the program, the buffer is big enough to cope, and the display is not disturbed. You can see the display very rapidly catch up when the program returns.

The other main part of the program is the checkForQuit() function. This checks for the Esc key or the window close click as normal, but it also checks to see if any keyboard key has been pressed. These are used for various functions, as summarised in Table 16-2.

**Table 16-2   Keyboard Functions**

| Key | Function |
| --- | --- |
| R | Plot in red |
| G | Plot in green |
| B | Plot in blue |
| C | Plot in cyan |
| Y | Plot in yellow |
| M | Plot in magenta |
| W | Plot in white |
| K | Plot in black |
| Spacebar | Wipe the screen |
| S | See the number of bytes waiting in the buffer |
| H | Halt the sending of data from the Arduino |

*continued*

**Table 16-2    continued**

| Key | Function |
| --- | --- |
| J | Start sending data from the Arduino |
| Home | Save the screen as a PNG file |
| 2 | Data from pendulums 1 for X and 3 for Y |
| 3 | Data from pendulums 1 & 2 for X and 3 for Y |
| 4 | Data from pendulums 1 & 2 for X and 3 & 4 for Y |
| 5 | Data from pendulums 2 for X and 4 for Y |
| 6 | Data from pendulums 1 for X and 3 & 4 for Y |

## Using the Pendulum Pi

To finish off, here are a few notes on using the Pendulum Pi. To get a feel of what is going on, start off with a simple two pendulum by pressing the 2 key. Now swing the two long pendulums at positions 1 and 3 exactly together or as we say, "in phase"; you will see a diagonal line at about 45 degrees being drawn. Now make them swing exactly opposed to each other – that is, 180 degrees apart – and you will see the same diagonal line but drawn in the opposite direction. Finally, get them at 90 degrees apart, let one go and release the second when the first is at the bottom of its swing. What you should then see is a circle. Of course you will not get it exactly spot on so what you will actually see is an elongated ellipse instead of a straight line and a fat ellipse instead of a circle. You might want to try some fine adjustment on the pendulums' length to get them to swing exactly at the same rate. As the two drift out of phase you will see the same shapes being traced slightly shifted. This is where it starts getting interesting as pleasing patterns are built up.

Also as the swing decays, the excursions will get smaller, and the pattern being drawn will slowly get smaller. This also adds interest to the pictures drawn. Now switch to a three pendulum setup, and see how the second pendulum modifies the swing plotted. I have found it best if you release the pendulums from a height rather than pushing them. Also, don't just swing them the maximum amount they will go; often less is more. You will also find some energy is transferring from one pendulum to another, which also adds to the variety of patterns you can get. There are many patterns you can generate from just one setup. Figure 16-20 shows some of the patterns I have managed to generate in a few sessions. To save a picture, press the Home key on the keyboard. You will then be asked for a session name in the Python console. Odds are you will have to click the console window to give it focus while you type in the base name. After you have done this for the first time any further screen saves use the same filename with an increasing number tacked on. These are stored in a folder called harmo, so make sure that you create one first.

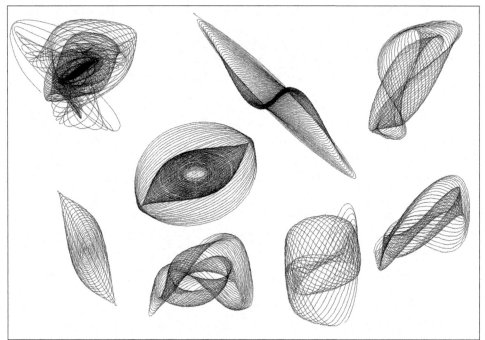

FIGURE 16-20:
Some of the
patterns
generated with
this project.

## Over to You

I think the best patterns are achieved when the long and short pendulums are an integer harmonic of each other, so you might want to change the way the long pendulum's length is adjusted to get a finer degree of control over it. You could write some software to measure the period of the pendulum to allow you to adjust the period even more accurately.

You could make the frame higher so that you could use longer pendulums and get higher ratios of swing. A pendulum of just over three meters might be pushing how much space you have in a domestic environment, however.

You could add the automatic Facebook posting of the pictures as shown in the last chapter.

One enhancement that would involve changing the Arduino software is to use one of the pendulums to send information that changes the colour of the trace in a gradual way. That would produce smoothly changing multicolour traces – although you might want to try that idea purely in the Python software based on the number of samples received. You can explore the difference between RGB colour space and HSV colour space in the colour changing.

One radical change you could do is to generate the swings purely in software using the same algorithm, either in the Arduino or the Raspberry Pi. This will allow you to produce patterns with a high swing ratio that otherwise would require very long pendulums. However, you will have to model the swing decay, and you won't get the energy transfer effects – so in my opinion, it is not nearly as much fun as swinging them and seeing what you get.

# Chapter **17**
# The Techno–Bird Box, a Wildlife Monitor

**by Dr. Andrew Robinson**

**In This Chapter**

- ○ Build a light beam
- ○ Get the current time and format it
- ○ Store data to a file
- ○ Implement a state machine
- ○ Filter out noise
- ○ Draw a graph in Python

**HAVE YOU EVER** wondered what the birds in your garden get up to when you're not watching? Thanks to the Raspberry Pi, with a couple of taps on a smartphone you can monitor the bird activity in your garden from anywhere in the world.

In this project, you will build a "techno–bird box" that will keep an eye on the comings and goings of our feathered friends, recording when they enter and leave a nest box.

You can go on to program your Raspberry Pi to do a range of things when it detects a bird. You might want to make it send a message by SMS, Twitter or e-mail or trigger a camera to take a picture. You could log the activity and use it to draw a graph such as the one shown in Figure 17-1.

FIGURE 17-1: Bird activity shown against temperature.

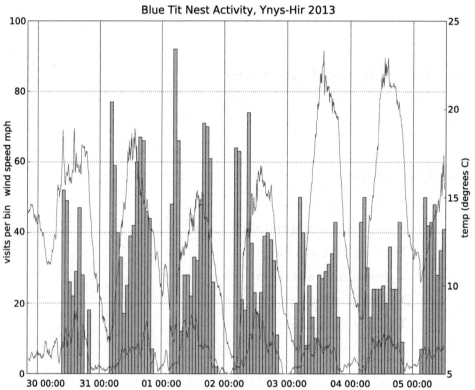

You might want to combine this with other data to find out more about bird behaviour. Are they busier in the evening or early morning? Are your birds more active than your friends' birds? You could store weather data and then see if temperature, rainfall and wind speed make a difference.

## Remote Monitoring

Computers and technology are playing an increasing role in monitoring our wildlife. Zoological Society London (ZSL) is using Raspberry Pis in Africa to save rhinos from poachers. They are using the computational power of the Raspberry Pi to analyse images to detect poacher activity and raise an alert over a satellite data connection. They're also deploying Raspberry Pis in the sea to monitor sharks.

I used a similar setup to the one in this chapter to collect information about blue tits for the BBC Springwatch programme; for details you can go to the blog at www.bbc.co.uk/blogs/natureuk/posts/Raspberry-Pi-bird-box.

Using computers as data loggers to make measurements is not new, but the increase in computing power means monitoring can be more sophisticated. Better digital communications mean that it's easy to collect data from around the world in real time. The falling cost of hardware is opening up the opportunity to gather massive data sets. If more people get involved in citizen science, and collect and contribute data through the Internet, new scientific discoveries can be made. Technology has made it easier for everyone to become a scientist, with the potential to be a part of the next earth-shattering discovery.

Alternatively, you could adapt the sensors to monitor small mammals, and perhaps use it to photograph rodents, or even keep an eye on your pet hamster.

In this project, you will detect bird activity with a pair of infrared light beams that are broken when a bird enters or leaves the nest box. One beam is mounted just inside the nest box, and the other is mounted just outside. You will write code that determines bird direction based on the order the beams are broken and unbroken. This chapter introduces some fairly advanced background information, which will help you understand how you can build your own projects in the future. However, if you just want to build a techno–bird box, you can just follow the steps and type in the complete program listing.

## Building Invisible Light Beam Sensors

The first step is to build the light sensors. Light beam sensors offer a way of detecting objects without making physical contact. You could use them in another project that detects other animals or for one of the suggestions in the "Over to You" section at the end of this chapter.

The light beam sensors are based on of a pair of components – an emitter and a detector. In order to measure the speed or direction an object (in this case a bird) is moving, you will need to build two pairs.

## The Required Parts

It's quite easy to build your own light beam detectors; parts are readily available for less than £1.

There is a range of many different LEDs and phototransistors that all work in a similar way. They're available from the typical electronics suppliers online. Although it's possible to substitute parts, I have tested only the following components. Because you are wiring up electronics to the Raspberry Pi, I suggest that you use PiFace Digital to provide additional protection, and enough current to drive the emitters. You will need

- 2 IR LEDs, such as part number OSRAM - SFH484-2 - INFRARED EMITTER, 5MM, 880NM
- 2 IR photodetectors, such as part number QSE113 - INFRARED PHOTOTRANSISTOR
- 2 1k ohm resistors
- 2 330 ohm resistors
- Wire

## Wiring Up the Emitter

The emitters are made using an infrared LED. Infrared LEDs are much the same as normal LEDs, but they emit infrared light rather than the typical red, yellow, blue and so on LEDs you might see on electronic devices. Here's a reminder of things to consider when using LEDs:

- LEDs work only one way around, so you need to ensure that the correct leg is connected to a +ive (positive) power supply.
- LEDs can be damaged by too much voltage, so you may need a resistor in series.

For most LEDs, the longer lead of the LED (called the *anode*) should be connected to the power supply. However, if you have the SFH484-2 IR LED, the longer lead is the cathode and should be connected to 0V (also sometimes called *ground*, *negative* or *-ive*).

Connect the anode of the LED to the 330 ohm resistor. Connect the other side of the resistor to the power supply as shown in Figure 17-2.

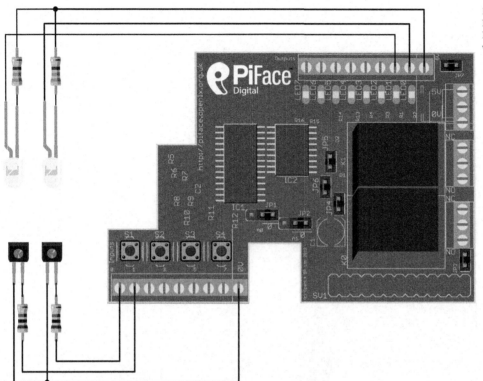

FIGURE 17-2:
IR SFH484-2 IR
LED emitter
wiring.

## Wiring Up the Detector

The detector is made from a phototransistor, which allows current to flow when light falls on it. It must be connected the correct way around, or it may be damaged, and it should also have a resistor in series to limit the current. Phototransistors have pins labelled *emitter* and *collector*. When illuminated, current flows into the collector and out of the emitter.

Take care to identify the legs of the phototransistors. Lay the flat side of the phototransistor on your desk, with its legs facing you. The leg on the left is the emitter, and the leg on the right the collector (see Figure 17-3). If you are not using a QSE113 phototransistor, check the data sheet for your device.

FIGURE 17-3:
Identifying the
emitter (left)
and collector
(right) legs of
the QSE113
phototransistor.

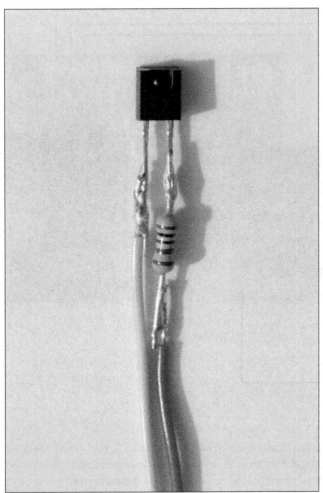

Wire the emitter of the phototransistor to ground. Connect the collector to one side of a 1k ohm resistor. Connect the other side of the resistor to the input pin, as shown in Figure 17-4.

## Testing the Sensors

It's easier to check that your sensors are working before you attach them to the bird box! Start the PiFace Digital emulator (as described in Chapter 9, "Test Your Reactions") and make sure that Update Inputs is selected. Point the IR LED at the phototransistor. The appropriate input should indicate that it is turned on. As you stop the light falling on the detector, you should notice that the corresponding input is no longer turned on.

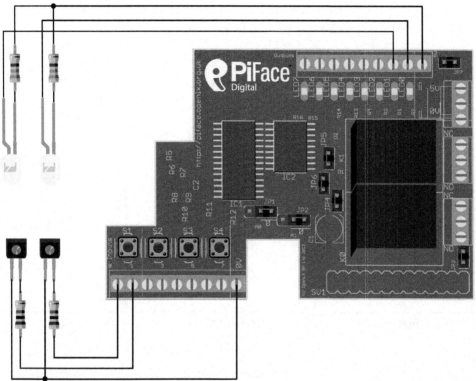

FIGURE 17-4:
IR
phototransistor
detector wiring.

If the circuit doesn't work, check the wiring. Use a multimeter set on resistance to check the resistance of the joints – it should read a few ohms at the most. It's also worth checking that the polarity is correct – that you've connected the IR LED and the phototransistor the right way around. Some digital cameras are sensitive to IR, so you might be able to use one to "see" if the LED is emitting IR light.

After you've checked that your sensors work, it's time to mount them in your bird box.

## Mounting the Sensors

You could build your own bird box from plans (such as those that are available online) or buy a ready-made one from a garden centre or elsewhere. Either way, you will need to mount the emitters and detectors near the entrance hole.

It is important not to create a perch for predators near the entrance to the nest box, or they could attack the birds in your box. With this in mind, so that the front face around the entrance remains flat, and to provide some protection to the electronics, it's best to sand-wich the sensors in layers of plywood.

An example layout of the three different layers of plywood is shown in Figure 17-5. You will need one front piece and a set of beam A and beam B pieces for each beam.

FIGURE 17-5:
Cutting plans
for plywood
sheets.

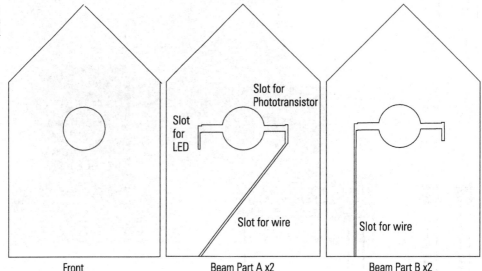

**Front**          **Beam Part A x2**          **Beam Part B x2**

> **TIP** Ensure that you use exterior- or marine-grade plywood, as these grades are suitable for use outside. Other grades may disintegrate, potentially while birds are nesting! Also if you use glue, ensure that it's waterproof, and nontoxic!

To hold the sensors, cut five pieces of plywood the same size as the front of your nest box. Cut a hole in all five, the same size and in the same place as the nest box opening. Check that they all align with the front of your box, and then put one piece of plywood aside. This will become the new front of the box.

You need to cut a slot for the sensors in the four remaining pieces of plywood. Draw a horizontal line across the middle of the entrance hole where the beam will be. Mark out 3 mm above and below the line to define a slot where the light beams will be.

> **TIP** It's better to have the slots horizontal so that they don't fill up with feathers, dirt, muck and such as the birds enter and leave the nest.

With the four pieces of plywood together, cut outward from the entrance hole, 30 mm along the marked-out slots, as shown in Figure 17-6. Check that the IR emitter and IR receiver will fit at the end of the slots. If necessary, enlarge the end of the slots so that they fit.

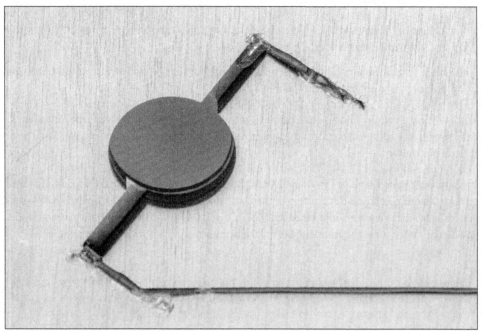

FIGURE 17-6: A closeup of the IR LED emitter and phototransistor receiver in the slot near the hole for the nest entrance.

Decide how you will route your wires and where they will come out from the plywood sandwich. It is usually best that they come out from the bottom to avoid water getting in. If you cut slots going to the emitter and receiver on the same piece of wood, you will end up with a separate piece, which is tricky to align. Instead, cut a narrow slot for cables from the outside to the emitter on two pieces of wood (refer to Figure 17-5, beam part A), and on the other piece of wood cut a slot to the receiver (refer to Figure 17-5, beam part B).

Glue beam part A and beam part B together with the sensors fitted and the wires running down the slots. Repeat this for the second beam. Test that both the beams work and then fasten the two beams together and attach the front piece of plywood.

Check that the entrance to the nest box remains unrestricted by the five pieces of plywood. Also check that there is nothing sharp sticking out that could injure the birds, and then mount the pieces of plywood in place on the front of the nest box with either glue or screws.

## Protecting Your Raspberry Pi from the Elements

Now is a good time to think where you will house the Raspberry Pi. Although the Raspberry Pi is fairly robust, it's better to protect it from extremes of temperature or humidity. You have a couple of options:

○ Mount the Raspberry Pi near the bird box and run a long wire to supply it with power and transmit data back via Wi-Fi or Ethernet.

○ Have your Raspberry Pi inside a building and run long wires from it to the LEDs and phototransistors in your bird box.

You may find a compromise is best, perhaps with your Raspberry Pi in a shed or outbuilding, with medium-length wires running to your nest, and a data connection via Wi-Fi to your broadband router.

If you mount your Raspberry Pi outside, you should use a waterproof box. You can buy these boxes from most electrical distributors or hardware stores. These enclosures typically have a rubber gasket to make a waterproof seal with the lid. If you buy a box that has an IP rating of IP66, you can be pretty sure that your Raspberry Pi will remain dry from water from the outside.

---

**TIP**    Often electronic product packaging contains sachets of silica gel to protect the item from humidity during transit. Put a couple of these sachets in with your Raspberry Pi to keep the humidity in the enclosure under control. You can revitalise silica gel by gently warming it to dry it out.

---

## IP Rating

Enclosures may be given an IP rating that describes how much protection they give to their contents. The IP rating consists of two numbers: The first digit indicates the protection against solid objects, such as tools, fingers and dust, and the second digit describes the protection against liquids. The higher the numbers, the greater the protection offered and the less that can enter the enclosure. For liquids, 1 ranges from protection from vertically dripping water, 5 for protection from jets and 8 for continuous immersion in water.

If the manufacturer wants to provide a rating for only one digit, X is used for the other. For example, an enclosure may be rated IPX6, meaning that it is protected against powerful water jets, but nothing is claimed about the protection from solids.

If you've built a project with your Raspberry Pi and need to protect it, the IP rating is a good way of knowing if a manufacturer's box will be up to the job.

# Recording Activity to a File

Now that you have your Raspberry Pi able to detect when the light beams are broken and unbroken, it is time to write a program to record this information. Ultimately you are interested in the direction that the birds are traveling in, which is deduced from the order the beams are broken and unbroken.

## Real Time or Post-Process?

The Raspberry Pi is more than capable of running a program that can process the beam break information to determine bird direction in *real time* – in other words, as it happens. However, for this application it is better to record the raw sensor readings and process the data later. This approach means that information is not thrown away.

If you processed the beam break information and just recorded if a bird left or entered the nest box, you would limit your options for future analysis. For example, what if you later decided that you were interested in the speed the bird entered and left the nest? If you store the time of every instance of a beam's breaking and unbreaking, you can process it later to determine direction, and you can calculate the speed. If you stored only direction information, this information about speed could not be calculated later.

Furthermore, as you will see later in the "Dealing with Sensor Noise" section, you will need to filter out noise from the sensors, and at a later stage you might develop a more sophisticated filter to process the raw data.

If you wrote a program to process the beam break data in real time and there was an error in it, you would have lost valuable information about your birds. Before deciding to store the unprocessed data, it's worth doing a quick calculation to predict how much data the bird-logging program would produce. If a bird visited every minute, for 18 hours a day there would be 1080 (60*18) events per day. Assuming the nesting period is at most 60 days, this is 64800 (60*1080) events. If each visit results in 10 sensor events (due to noise) and each takes 30 bytes to store, the total storage required is 19440000 (64800*30*10) bytes, or about 20 megabytes. Because there is plenty of low-cost storage available with a Raspberry Pi on a cheap SD card, it is better to write a very simple program to store the raw beam break data that can be analysed offline later.

# Information and Data

When you are considering logging events it's worth thinking about the information you are storing. Sometimes storage space is limited, or the cost of remotely transmitting data is high. The power available to the computer might be limited, or the computer might be in a hostile environment, so the data is at risk of corruption.

When logging data you may need to consider compression, encryption and error detection and correction.

How much information does a piece of data contain? How do you measure information, for example, and how much information does a web page contain? Is there more information on the Internet than contained in the DNA that describes you? How much can you compress a file? *Information theory* is a branch of computer science concerned with storing and processing information and data and provides an answer for many of these questions. It can lead to some deep philosophical discussions and mind-blowing concepts. Do you need to read every page of this book to get all the information from it?

Computing is all about taking data in, processing it and outputting it. As such it follows that information theory, which is all about how data is stored and processed, is important to computer science.

Thinking about information theory leads to some fascinating questions – how much information is contained in an English sentence? Text speak shows that it is possible to communicate without needing all the words and letters in a sentence.

When you are collecting data with computers, maybe in a bird box in your garden, maybe in the middle of Africa or maybe on a satellite in a distant part of the solar system, information theory provides tools and reasoning to ensure that the valuable research information gets back safely.

# Compression and Checksums

Think of the information stored on a CD. If the CD is slightly scratched, it still plays with no loss of sound quality. If it becomes more scratched, there comes a point when it will not play. Effectively, there is an amount of data that can be lost from a CD without mattering; so this data must be redundant in terms of the information the CD contains. Information is useful in calculating the amount of extra data needed for error correction on CDs and in communication links, such as radio, which may be unreliable.

Now think about converting an audio file from a CD to an MP3 file. Most people cannot tell the difference between playing a CD and an MP3 file, yet the MP3 file size (the amount of data) will be typically a tenth of the size. Nine tenths of the data has apparently been thrown away! This is an example of *lossy compression*. It takes advantage of assumptions of how the audio data will be interpreted in our brains – for example, if a quiet and a loud sound are played together, the quiet sound isn't heard, and therefore there is no value to the ear in the data representing it.

If you wanted to record birdsong in your bird box, then without audio compression you would quickly run out of storage space on the SD card. Lossy compression isn't suitable for all applications; for example, you wouldn't want to throw away data about bird visits. Instead, *lossless compression* would be more appropriate.

Lossless compression represents data in a more efficient format. For example, if you had a list of numbers 2,0,0,0,0,0,1, instead of sending each 0 you could encode the list as 2,5x0,1. Zip compression is an example of this form of compression (and is used to make the Raspbian OS download smaller).

If you needed to transfer your bird data remotely, over a mobile phone connection, then you might use zip to make the file smaller, or you might consider doing some other processing (to get rid of noisy readings) to send just the information you need.

In some cases you want to know that the data hasn't been corrupted. In this case you might add redundant data so that you can detect or even correct any errors. MD5 checksums that represent the contents of a long file with a short sequence of characters are an example of this. You came across MD5 checksums in Chapter 1, "Getting Your Raspberry Pi Up and Running", to detect if the Raspbian OS download had been corrupted.

## The Complete Logging Program

The program in Listing 17-1 records the time, which sensor triggered and whether it was broken or unbroken in file.

Listing 17-1   recordBird.py

```
#!/usr/bin/env python
import piface.pfio as p
import datetime
p.init()

#Define the inputs/output pin number that
#the beams are connected to.
INNER_BEAM = 0
OUTER_BEAM = 1

#keeps track of the last state the beam was in
```

*continued*

## Listing 17-1    continued

```
#used to know if a new event has occurred
innerBeamStateWasBroken = False
outerBeamStateWasBroken = False


#function to return the current time, formatted as
# e.g. 13 Jun 2013 16:07:30 572
def getFormattedTime():
    now = datetime.datetime.now()
    return now.strftime("%d %b %Y %H:%M:%S. ") + ⤸
str(int(round(now.microsecond/1000.0)))


#generate and record an event to file
def logEvent(sensor, state):
    logFile.write(str(sensor) + "," + str(state) + ⤸
"," + getFormattedTime() + "\n")


#turn on IR LED emitters
p.digital_write(INNER_BEAM_EMITTER,1)
p.digital_write(OUTER_BEAM_EMITTER,1)


#open a file for appending, do not buffer
logFile = open('birdlog.txt', 'a', 0)

#indicate the point the program started in the log
logFile.write("###starting up at:" + getFormattedTime() + "\n")

#main loop of the code
while (True):
    #read the current state of the beam
    innerBeamIsBroken = (p.digital_read(INNER_BEAM) == 0)
    outerBeamIsBroken = (p.digital_read(OUTER_BEAM) == 0)

    ##handle Inner Beam
    # if the beam has become broken, that is if the beam
    # was not broken before but is now,
    # then record that the beam was broken and log to file
    if (not innerBeamStateWasBroken and innerBeamIsBroken):
        innerBeamStateWasBroken = True
        logEvent(0,1)
        #print  "inner beam has been broken"
```

```
    # this detects when the beam has become un-broken again.
    # That is when the beam was broken and it is not broken
    # any longer. When this occurs, record the new state and
    # log it to file
    if (innerBeamStateWasBroken and not innerBeamIsBroken):
        innerBeamStateWasBroken = False
        logEvent(0,0)
        #print "inner beam has been un-broken"

    ##handle Outer Beam, with same structure as inner
    if (not outerBeamStateWasBroken and outerBeamIsBroken):
        outerBeamStateWasBroken = True
        logEvent(1,1)
        #print "outer beam has been broken"

    if (outerBeamStateWasBroken and not outerBeamIsBroken):
        outerBeamStateWasBroken = False
        logEvent(1,0)
        #print "outer beam has been un-broken"
```

The structure of Python programs should be familiar to you by now, but it is worth considering new concepts introduced and reinforcing others.

## Constants

Some languages (such as C) have constants to hold values that do not change over the lifetime of a program. They allow programmers to define the value of a constant in one place and then refer to it throughout the program. If the programmer updates the program, the value needs to be changed in only one place. This is easier than searching through the code looking for all instances of the value to change. In Listing 17-1 the pin number of the PiFace interface that is connected to the beams is defined in INNER_BEAM and OUTER_BEAM. As such, if the circuit is changed, the value needs to be updated in only one place in the program. This is part of program design for the future. It takes into consideration that the beams may be connected to other pins and so makes it easy for them to be changed in one place at the top of the program.

---

Unlike other programming languages, Python does not really have constants. However, the convention is to use variables with all uppercase names instead.          TIP

---

## Detecting Changes of State

The variables innerBeamStateWasBroken and outerBeamStateWasBroken are initialised to False. These variables are used to detect if the state of the input pin has changed, so the event of a beam changing can be recorded.

### Formatting the Current Time

The function getFormattedTime() is used to get the current time and format it. Looking inside the function, you'll see that the variable now gets a datetime.datetime object containing the current date and time:

```
now = datetime.datetime.now()
```

The method strftime is called with an argument that specifies how the current time is formatted:

```
return now.strftime("%d %b %Y %H:%M:%S. ") + ⤵
str(int(round(now.microsecond/1000.0)))
```

The format argument provides a template of codes in a string. When the program runs, the codes in Table 17-1 are replaced by different parts of the date and time stored by the object.

### Table 17-1   Date-Formatting Codes

| Code | Meaning | English Example |
| --- | --- | --- |
| %a | Shortened weekday name | Mon |
| %A | Full weekday name | Monday |
| %b | Shortened month name | Mar |
| %B | Full month name | March |
| %d | Day of the month | 14 |
| %H | Hour (24-hour clock) as a decimal number | 18 |
| %I | Hour (12-hour clock) as a decimal number | 6 |
| %m | Month as decimal number | 03 |
| %M | Minute | 15 |
| %p | AM or PM (or local equivalent description) | PM |
| %S | Second | 12 |
| %y | Two-digit year | 13 |
| %Y | Four-digit year | 2013 |
| %% | Use to display a single % sign | % |

**TIP**   Different places around the world have different conventions; for example, the 14th of March in the U.K. would be written as 14/03, but in the U.S. as 03/14. Linux locale sets the various settings like these that are unique to a particular place in the world. For example, it also defines the currency used, default paper size and keyboard layout. strftime uses your locale setting to determine what %p displays. It also uses it to make %c format the date and time appropriately for you.

Why not try it yourself in an interactive Python session? Type the following

```
import datetime
datetime.datetime.now().strftime("Today is: %A %d %B %Y. ↵
The time is: %I:%M:%S %p")
```

---

Create a format string to format the time and date so that if now was 6:15 p.m. on the 14th of March, it would be displayed as 1815 2013-03-14.    **YOUR TURN!**

There are other codes too. Find out what %j does.

---

You will notice that there is no code to display the time in milliseconds. As the time between beams breaking and unbreaking can be less than a second, a way to format the time in milliseconds needs to be created by the programmer.

The `datetime.datetime` object has the attribute `microsecond`. Because there are 1000 microseconds in a millisecond, this number is divided by 1000, rounded to the nearest whole number by the `int` and `round` functions and then converted to a string and concatenated to the end of the formatted date/time.

## Writing to a File

The `logEvent` function is called to record an event to a file. You will see later that in the program initialisation a file object called `logFile` is created:

```
#generate and record an event to file
def logEvent(sensor, state):
    logFile.write(str(sensor) + "," + str(state) + ↵
"," + getFormattedTime() + "\n")
```

The `logEvent` function builds the string to be written to the file and then passes it to the `write` function of the `logFile` object. Which beam and how it changed are passed as arguments to the function and stored separated by commas. The end of the string written is an `"\n"`, which is a special character code to create a new line in Linux.

---

The code for a new line varies across operating systems. Files in Microsoft Windows require the code `"\r\n"` instead of just `"\n"`.    **TIP**

---

### Initialisation

After the function definitions come the statements that set things up for the main part of the program. The IR LED emitters are controlled by the outputs of PiFace Digital, so they need to be turned on. This is done with the `digital_write` function that sets a pin to value 1, that is, turn on. `INNER_BEAM` and `OUTER_BEAM` specify the pin numbers the IR LEDs are connected to:

```
#turn on IR LED emitters
p.digital_write(INNER_BEAM,1)
p.digital_write(OUTER_BEAM,1)
```

### Working with Files

Before a Python program (and programs written in most other languages) can write data to a file it needs to open it first. Python does this with the open function, which takes a filename, mode and buffer length as arguments and returns a file object. The file object provides an easy way of keeping track of the file that has been opened.

It is worth studying the open function in more detail, looking at the example in the program:

```
#open a file for appending, do not buffer
logFile = open('birdlog.txt', 'a', 0)
```

The function returns a file object that is stored in the `logFile` variable. This variable is used in your `logEvent` function to identify which file the data about the event is to be written to.

### Opening Files – Filename

The first argument of the function, `'birdlog.txt'`, is the name of the file that will be opened. It is *relative* to where the program was run from. This means that `birdlog.txt` will be opened in the same directory where the command was issued to run your program. If you wanted to create the file somewhere else in the filesystem, you would need to give the appropriate file path.

## Linux File Paths

Linux, like most operating systems, has a hierarchical filesystem; that is, it has a tree type structure with files in directories (sometimes called *folders*), directories within other directories and so on. It provides a means to describe the location of a file within the tree of directories as a *file path*. The top of the tree is the *root,* where it is not possible to have directories above it.

The path to a particular file may be given relative to another location in the filesystem or the full path from the root of the tree.

For example, in a terminal type `pwd` to show the current directory. By default this is usually your home directory. Type `ls` to list the files and directories you have in this directory. To get to know how file paths work in Linux, it's time for a quick tour:

Linux refers to the root of the tree by starting paths with a forward slash (`/`). Change to the root of the tree by typing `cd /`.

Type `ls` to show the contents.

Type `cd etc` to move into the `etc` subdirectory that contains the configuration files for Linux. Type `pwd` to show the path. Linux will print `/etc`, indicating that you are in the `etc` directory under the root of the tree. Now move into the network settings subdirectory by typing `cd network`. Type `pwd` again. Linux will print `/etc/network`, indicating that you are in the `network` subdirectory of the `etc` subdirectory of root.

From this you should be able to see that directories are separated with slashes, and that a path starting with `/` is relative to the root.

Linux users get their own directory to store their files in, which Linux calls a user's *home directory*.

Type `cd ~` to change to your home directory. Type `ls` and you will see your files. Type `pwd` and you will see that your home directory's full path is `/home/pi`.

Type `cd ..` and you will move up into the parent directory. Type `pwd` and you will see you are now at `/home`. Type `cd ../` and you will now be at the root. Type `pwd` and you will see you are at `/`. Type `cd ../` again and you will still be at the root as you can't go any higher!

Here is a summary of what you've just seen:

- `/` – refers to the root, the topmost point of the filesystem, independent of your current position.
- `./` – refers to the current directory, that is the directory you are in.
- `../` – refers to the current parent directory, that is the directory that is containing your current directory.
- `~/` – refers to your home directory.
- `~username` – refers to the home directory of *username*.

After you've mastered file paths you can use them within your programs to specify files anywhere in the filesystem. Remember, `pwd`, `cd` and `ls` are useful commands to run in a terminal when you are moving around the filesystem and to check file paths.

### Opening Files – Mode

The second argument, `'a'`, specifies the mode the file is opened with. In this program you want to *append* to the file – in other words, add to the contents already there. (If the file doesn't exist in the first place, it is created.) If you wanted to replace a file, then you should use the write mode with an argument of `'w'`. In other programs you might want to read from a file without changing it, and in this case you should open a file with a mode of `'r'`.

In summary, files can be opened in three different modes:

- ○ r – read. The file is read only, so you know you will not change the contents.
- ○ w – write. The file is cleared and started from the beginning.
- ○ a – append. The file can be added to.

### Opening Files – Buffer Size

The third argument of the open function is the size of the file buffer – that is, the number of characters that will be grouped together before transferring them from memory onto the computer's permanent storage. For logging birds, it is sensible to have a buffer size of 0 so that the data is written to the SD card as soon as possible. That way, if the power fails before the buffer has been written out to the SD card, the least amount of data is lost.

# Buffering

Buffering is a way to work more efficiently. For example, most people do not put the washing machine on for individual items of clothing; instead they collect their clothes together in batches. This is because it takes about the same amount of time and energy to do a batch of washing as it does for an individual item.

In the case of computers, writing characters to disk is similar; writing a few characters to a file takes about the same time as writing a single character. As such, the computer collects characters together in a buffer in memory, and then writes them out (called *flushing*) when it is full. Of course, if the power is interrupted before the computer has flushed the buffer, the data is lost.

### Writing an Initial Timestamp

The first thing written to the file when the program starts up is a timestamp:

```
#indicate the point the program started in the log
logFile.write("###starting up at:" + getFormattedTime() + "\n")
```

This makes it easier to look at the logs to check when a program started running. If the clock is set incorrectly on the Raspberry Pi and you know the real time you started the program logging, you can use the date recorded in the file to calculate the offset to correct the times recorded for the bird activity.

### The Main Loop

The main part of the program is a `while` loop that repeats forever. On each loop, it looks at the current state of the light beams by reading the PiFace Digital inputs as shown in the following:

```
while (True):
  #read the current state of the beam
    innerBeamIsBroken = (p.digital_read(INNER_BEAM) == 0)
    outerBeamIsBroken = (p.digital_read(OUTER_BEAM) == 0)
```

Next are two pairs of `if` statements, one for each beam. The purpose of these statements is to see if the state of the beam is different from the last time it was checked. This is done by comparing the state of the beam that has been read into the variable `innerBeamIsBroken` with the state previously recorded in the variable `innerBeamStateWasBroken`. If there is a change, `innerBeamStateWasBroken` is updated, and the `logEvent` function is called to record it to the file:

```
if (not innerBeamStateWasBroken and innerBeamIsBroken):
    innerBeamStateWasBroken = True
    logEvent(0,1)
if (innerBeamStateWasBroken and not innerBeamIsBroken):
    innerBeamStateWasBroken = False
    logEvent(0,0)
    #print "inner beam has been un-broken"
```

## Testing the Program

You should be familiar with the notion of testing your programs as you write them. Uncomment the `print` statements in the code to indicate when the beams are broken and unbroken and run the program. Use a Ping-Pong ball or other object to break and unbreak the light beams to check that your program prints the correct corresponding messages.

Press Ctrl + C to exit the program and check the events have been logged to the `birdlog. txt` file. You can quickly look at the contents of a file in Linux by using the `more` command. From the command line, type

```
more birdlog.txt
###starting up at:13 Jun 2013 16:07:29.425
0,1,13 Jun 2013 16:07:30.496
1,1,13 Jun 2013 16:07:30.572
0,0,13 Jun 2013 16:07:30.792
1,0,13 Jun 2013 16:07:30.961
```

Check that your file looks similar to entries shown here. If so, it is time to write another program that will analyse the log file to translate the raw sensor data to bird actions.

You can download a sample log file from `www.wiley.com/go/raspberrypiprojects`.

## Processing the Data

After you have the data of when the sensors break and unbreak it is time to write a program to interpret this to know whether a bird is entering or leaving the nest box. To do so, you will write a program that reads in the log file and processes it with a state machine. You will also see that it is necessary to filter out noise.

Think about a bird entering the box, and how the sensors will record it. Here is the list of events:

1. The outer beam breaks.

2. The inner beam breaks.

3. The outer beam clears.

4. The inner beam clears.

When a bird leaves the nest box, the order will be as follows:

1. The inner beam breaks.

2. The outer beam breaks.

3. The inner beam clears.

4. The outer beam clears.

To interpret the sensor data, you need to write a program that looks for these orders of events. However, birds don't just fly in and out of their nest boxes; they also might pop just their heads out, have a look around and then pop back into the box.

This bobbing out of heads has sensors in this sequence:

1. The inner beam breaks.

2. The outer beam breaks.

3. The outer beam clears.

4. The inner beam clears.

When a mother bird is tending her young, she may stand in the nest box entrance and pop her head into the box. It may be clearer to represent this number of sequences in a diagram, as shown in Figure 17-7. The next task is to write a program to implement this diagram, which you will see is best done with a state machine.

## Building a State Machine

Diagrams similar to Figure 17-7 that show the *transition* (movement) between sequences of states occur frequently in computer science, and as such there are standard techniques to implement one in code. State machines (sometimes called more fully, *finite state machines* or FSMs) consist of states and conditions that govern when there is a change from one state to another.

In the diagram in Figure 17-7, each circle is a state, with the transitions (movement) between states represented by arrows and labelled with the event that causes the transition. The arrow from the block dot shows the starting state.

State machines are implemented in programs with a variable to hold the current state and a loop. The loop contains a series of if statements that determine when there should be a change from one state to the next. On each iteration of the loop, all the conditions that allow the leaving of the current state are tested, and if satisfied the current state is updated, together with any necessary actions required for the transition.

FIGURE 17-7:
A state diagram
for birds
entering, leaving
and bobbing
their heads.

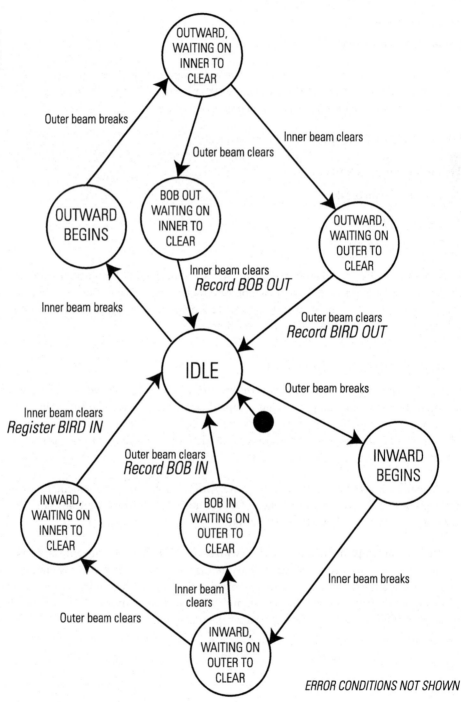

## The Basic Analysis Program

To implement the state machine, enter the Python code in Listing 17-2 into a new file,
analyseBirdDataBasic.py.

Listing 17-2   analyseBirdDataBasic.py

```python
#!/usr/bin/env python
import sys
import datetime

#print a debug message if debugging is turned on
def debug(msg):
    if DEBUG:
        print msg

state="IDLE"
#Constants
INNER_BEAM = 0
OUTER_BEAM = 1

BROKEN = 0
UNBROKEN = 1

DEBUG = True

outwardTimes = []

# loop over every line that is being piped into the program
for line in sys.stdin:

    #ignore lines beginning#
    if line.startswith('#'):continue
    # remove the new line character
    line = line.rstrip('\n')
    #split the text at each comma. This creates
    #the event array, with three items
    event = line.split(',')
    #store the first item in the sensor variable -- this
    #is which beam (inner or outer)
    sensor = int(event[0])
    #store the type of the event in the eventType
    #variable -- this is if the beam broke or unbroke
    eventType = int(event[1])
```

*continued*

Listing 17-2 **continued**

```
    # convert the text representation of the time into
    #a datetime object in eventTime variable
    eventTime = datetime.datetime.strptime(event[2],⤸
"%d %b %Y %H:%M:%S.%f")

    debug ("RawEvent:"+line+", Current STATE:"+state)

    #Main state machine

    #The idle state is waiting for either the outside
    #or inside beam to be broken.
    if (state == "IDLE"):
        # the inside sensor has been broken
        if ((sensor==INNER_BEAM) and (eventType==BROKEN)):
            debug ("on way out")
            state = "OUTWARD_BOUND"
        if ((sensor==OUTER_BEAM) and (eventType==BROKEN)):
            debug ("on way in")
            state = "INWARD_BOUND"

    # the bird has started leaving. Check to see if
    # it bobs back or breaks the next sensor
    elif (state == "OUTWARD_BOUND"):
            # if bird puts head back in box return to IDLE
            if ((sensor==INNER_BEAM) and (eventType==UNBROKEN)):
                debug ("inside bob back")
                state = "IDLE"
            # bird continues and breaks the OUTER_BEAM
            elif ((sensor==OUTER_BEAM) and (eventType==BROKEN)):
                debug ("outward")
            # bird is still going out, wait for the inner
            # beam to clear
                state = "WAITING_OUTWARD_I_CLEAR"

    ##the bird is still in the entrance hole, blocking
    ##both beams
    elif (state == "WAITING_OUTWARD_I_CLEAR"):
        if (diffTime.seconds < 5):
            # bird is very nearly out, waiting for the
            # outside beam to clear now
            if ((sensor==INNER_BEAM) and (eventType==UNBROKEN)):
                debug ("inside cleared, waiting for outside ⤸
to clear")
```

```
                state = "WAITING_OUTWARD_O_CLEAR"
    elif (state == "WAITING_OUTWARD_O_CLEAR"):
        if ((sensor==OUTER_BEAM) and (eventType==UNBROKEN)):
        debug (str(eventTime)+" BIRD has left")
        outwardTimes.append(date2num(eventTime))
        state = "IDLE"
#set of states for bird coming in
    elif (state == "INWARD_BOUND"):
        if ((sensor==OUTER_BEAM) and (eventType==UNBROKEN)):
            debug ("outside bob out")
            state = "IDLE"
        elif ((sensor==INNER_BEAM) and (eventType==BREAK)):
            debug ("inward")
            state = "WAITING_INWARD_O_CLEAR"
    elif (state == "WAITING_INWARD_O_CLEAR"):
        if ((sensor==OUTER_BEAM) and (eventType==UNBROKEN)):
            debug ("outside cleared, waiting for inside to clear")
            state = "WAITING_INWARD_I_CLEAR"
    elif (state == "WAITING_INWARD_I_CLEAR"):
        if ((sensor==INNER_BEAM) and (eventType==UNBROKEN)):
            state == "IDLE"
            debug (str(eventTime)+" BIRD has returned")
    # if we end up in any other state, then we generate an error
    else:
        debug ("error")
        raise ValueError, "unexpected input block state: "+state
```

The main part of the program in Listing 17-2 is performed by the `for` loop which reads `stdin`, line by line:

```
for line in sys.stdin
```

Each loop iteration processes another line of the file. First the line is split at each comma and placed into separate variables. The `datetime.datetime.strptime` function is the opposite of the `strftime` function, converting a string-formatted time into a date object that Python can process.

The variables are tested by the `if` statements in the state machine to determine if a state transition should be made. If it is detected that a bird has left, then the time it left is appended into the `outwardTimes` array. You will use this array to draw a graph of activity.

## Standard Streams

Linux supports *standard streams,* a mechanism to allow the output of one program to be fed into another one. This allows very powerful combinations of programs to be connected together on the command line to process data. There are three standard streams:

○ Standard in (`stdin`) – Used for input.

○ Standard out (`stdout`) – Used for output.

○ Standard error (`stderr`) – Another sort of output, reserved for reporting error messages.

Essentially standard streams can be thought of as special files. One program will write to its `stdout` stream, which can be *piped* (think of the commands as stages in a pipeline) to the `stdin` stream of another. This program reads from its `stdin` to receive the data. If no other program is specified, by default `stdin` will be taken from the keyboard, and `stdout` will be displayed on the screen in the terminal.

The | character is used to indicate that the output of one program should be piped into another. For an example of how pipes work, imagine that you want to sort the list of the files in your home directory in reverse order. The command `ls` lists the contents of a directory to `stdout`. The `sort` command takes input from `stdin`, orders it and sends it to `stdout`. The `-r` argument tells `sort` to reverse the ordering. So, to reverse sort a list of contents of a directory, in a terminal type

```
ls | sort -r
****sort uniq wget cat grep >
```

To test the analysis program, use the `cat` program to pipe the contents of your `birddata.txt` file into your Python program by typing the following in a terminal:

```
cat birddata.txt | python analyseBirdDataBasic.py
```

With `DEBUG=1` set, the program will go through the state machine, process the sensor log entries and print a description of what it thinks the bird is doing.

## Dealing with Sensor Noise

In everyday life, someone may say that an environment is too noisy for him or her to hear properly. *Noise* is the sound that is unwanted and getting in the way of what the listener wants to hear. In computing the term *noise* is used to describe data that is not wanted and gets in the way. Your light beams are noisy sensors, not in that they make a sound, but that they generate data that's not meaningful information. The noise occurs because an object passing through the beam may cause it to break and unbreak a few times. Think of a bird passing through the nest box entrance – as well as its body breaking the beam, its tail may wag up and down, additionally breaking the beam as it leaves.

You could run the program again and test it with your finger. As you move it away from the central beam in the hole it may trigger multiple beam break and unbreak events. If the software considered every time a beam broke to be a bird leaving the nest, it would record a higher number than the actual number of bird visits.

## Filtering Out Noise

You may be familiar with the reduction of audio noise through the use of filters; you might turn the treble down to remove a high-pitched hiss. Similarly, in computing, data can be filtered to remove noise.

Looking at logs, you should notice that the additional beam break events are usually very short. In comparison, the time taken for a bird to leave the nest box, turn around and come back is a lot slower. Because the time that events occurred is recorded, this information can be used to filter out breaks and unbreaks that happen in quick succession.

The world is full of unknowns that computers have to try and make sense of: Did a bird really leave, or did its tail cause a second beam break to be recorded? Has some dirt been caught in the sensor? You can make your analysis program very complicated by modeling as many possible explanations of sensor readings. In industry sensor models may consider probability to best determine what is happening.

## Filtering Contact Bounce

Filtering is used more often than you might think in computers. Inputs from mechanical switches, such as key presses on the keyboard, are filtered to remove contact bounce. *Contact bounce* happens when a switch is opened or closed and the metal contacts of the switch bounce off each other as they leave or come together. This bouncing action causes a number of pulses to be sent to the computer. Because, in the case of a keyboard, a user wouldn't want multiple key presses to be registered, the signal is filtered. Typically, this filtering creates a short period when the signal is ignored, which gives the contacts enough time to settle.

# The Analysis Program with Noise Filtering

Listing 17-3 shows the modified basic analysis program to include the concept of time. It is shown in full here.

---

**Listing 17-3**    analyseBirdDataFiltered.py

```python
#!/usr/bin/env python
import sys
import datetime

#print a debug message on if debugging is turned on
def debug(msg):
    if DEBUG:
        print msg

state="INIT"

#Constants
INNER_BEAM = 0
OUTER_BEAM = 1

BROKEN = 0
UNBROKEN = 1

DEBUG = True

# timestamp of event from previously processed event
lastEventTime = 0

outwardTimes=[]

# loop over every line that is being piped into the program
for line in sys.stdin:

    #ignore lines beginning #
    if line.startswith('#'):continue

    # remove the new line character
    line = line.rstrip('\n')
    #split the text at each comma. This creates the event
    #array, with three items
```

```
    event = line.split(',')
    #store the first item in the sensor variable - this
    #is which beam (inner or outer)
    sensor = int(event[0])
    #store the type of the event in the eventType
    #variable -- this is if the beam broke or unbroke
    eventType = int(event[1])
    # convert the text representation of the time into
    #a datetime object in eventTime variable
    eventTime = datetime.datetime.strptime(event[2], ⤴
"%d %b %Y %H:%M:%S.%f")

    debug ("RawEvent:"+line+", Current STATE:"+state)

    #Main state machine

    #INITIALISATION, runs the first time around the loop
    if (state == "INIT"):
        lastEventTime = eventTime
        state = "IDLE"

    #calculate the time since the last event took place
    diffTime = eventTime - lastEventTime

    #to recover state, if the last event was greater than
    #30 seconds ago, treat it as independent and reset the
    #state machine to IDLE.
    #since the idle state of the box is both sensors
    #unbroken, waiting for an entry or exit to start
    if (diffTime.seconds > 30):
        if (state != "IDLE"):
            debug ("TIMEOUT - statemachine reset")
        state = "IDLE"


    #The idle state is waiting for either the outside or
    #inside beam to be broken.
    if (state == "IDLE"):
        # the inside sensor has been broken
```

*continued*

**Listing 17-3    continued**

```
        if ((sensor==INNER_BEAM) and (eventType==BROKEN)):
            debug ("on way out")
            state = "OUTWARD_BOUND"
            #record when the inner beam was broken
        outTime = eventTime
        if ((sensor==OUTER_BEAM) and (eventType==BROKEN)):
            debug ("on way in")
            state = "INWARD_BOUND"

## the bird has started leaving. Check to see if it
##bobs back or breaks the next sensor
elif (state == "OUTWARD_BOUND"):
    # check that this event is within 5 seconds of the last
    if (diffTime.seconds < 5):
        # if bird puts head back in box return to IDLE
        if ((sensor==INNER_BEAM) and (eventType==UNBROKEN)):
            debug ("inside bob back")
state = "IDLE"
        # bird continues and breaks the OUTER_BEAM
        elif ((sensor==OUTER_BEAM) and (eventType==BROKEN)):
            debug ("outward")
        # bird is still going out, wait for the inner
        # beam to clear
            state = "WAITING_OUTWARD_I_CLEAR"

##the bird is still in the entrance hole, blocking
##both beams
elif (state == "WAITING_OUTWARD_I_CLEAR"):
    if (diffTime.seconds < 5):
        # bird is very nearly out, waiting for the
        # outside beam to clear now
        if ((sensor==INNER_BEAM) and (eventType==UNBROKEN)):
            debug ("inside cleared, waiting for outside⤶
to clear")
            state = "WAITING_OUTWARD_O_CLEAR"
    else:
        debug ("timeout on waiting outward I Clear")
        state= "IDLE"

elif (state == "WAITING_OUTWARD_O_CLEAR"):
```

```
            if (diffTime.seconds < 5):
                if ((sensor==OUTER_BEAM) and (eventType==UNBROKEN)):
                    debug (str(eventTime)+" BIRD has left")
                        outwardTimes.append(date2num(eventTime))
state = "IDLE"
                if ((sensor==INNER_BEAM) and (eventType==BROKEN)):
                    debug ("inside has broken again -- ⤸
waiting for it to clear again")
                    state = "WAITING_OUTWARD_NOISE_CLEAR"
            else:
                debug ("timeout on waiting outward O Clear")
                state= "IDLE"


    elif (state == "WAITING_OUTWARD_NOISE_CLEAR"):
        if (diffTime.seconds < 5):
            if ((sensor==INNER_BEAM) and (eventType==UNBROKEN)):
                debug ("inside cleared again, waiting for⤸
 outside to clear")
                state = "WAITING_OUTWARD_O_CLEAR"
        else:
            debug ("timeout on waiting outward noise Clear")
            state= "IDLE"


#set of states for bird coming in
    elif (state == "INWARD_BOUND"):
        if (diffTime.seconds < 5):
            if ((sensor==OUTER_BEAM) and (eventType==UNBROKEN)):
                debug ("outside bob out")
                state = "IDLE"
            elif ((sensor==INNER_BEAM) and (eventType==BROKEN)):
                debug ("inward")
                state = "WAITING_INWARD_O_CLEAR"


    elif (state == "WAITING_INWARD_O_CLEAR"):
        if (diffTime.seconds < 5):
            if ((sensor==OUTER_BEAM) and (eventType==UNBROKEN)):
                debug ("outside cleared, waiting for inside⤸
 to clear")
```

*continued*

Listing 17-3　continued

```
                state = "WAITING_INWARD_I_CLEAR"
        else:
            debug ("timeout on waiting inward O Clear")
            state= "IDLE"

    elif (state == "WAITING_INWARD_I_CLEAR"):
        if (diffTime.seconds < 5):
            if ((sensor==INNER_BEAM) and (eventType==UNBROKEN)):
                state == "IDLE"
                debug (str(eventTime)+" BIRD has returned")
                state = "IDLE"
        else:
            debug ("timeout on waiting inward I Clear")
            state= "IDLE"


    # if we end up in any other state, then we generate
    # an error
    else:
        debug ("error")
        raise ValueError, "unexpected input block state: "+state

    #independent of state
    #update the lastEventTime to be the value from this loop
    #for next iteration of loop
    lastEventTime = eventTime
```

Ensure that debugging is turned on (check that DEBUG=1 is set) and run the program by typing the following:

```
cat birddata.txt | python analyseBirdDataFiltered.py
```

Python will print the states of the state machine as it processes your bird data. The next step is to visualise this data so that you can see trends about your bird behaviour.

# Drawing a Graph

You may be familiar with using a spreadsheet to draw charts or graphs. LibreOffice is a free office suite that runs on the Raspberry Pi. It contains the spreadsheet program Calc, which is largely compatible with Microsoft Excel and Google Docs Spreadsheets. The most appropriate representation of bird activity is a histogram showing the frequency of bird visits. Although it is possible to produce a histogram with Microsoft Excel using the Data Analysis add-in, it is a manual process with multiple steps.

Python can programmatically create graphs with a module called `matplotlib`. The numpy module is also useful for mathematical and statistical operations. To install the modules, on the command line type the following:

```
sudo apt-get install python-matplotlib python-numpy
```

Create a new Python file called `drawgraph.py` in the same directory as `analyse BirdDataFiltered.py` and enter the code in Listing 17-4.

---

**Listing 17-4**   `drawgraph.py`

```python
import numpy
import matplotlib
import math
matplotlib.use('PDF')
from matplotlib import pyplot
from matplotlib.dates import DateFormatter, DayLocator,⊃
 HourLocator
from matplotlib.dates import date2num, num2date


def plotDatehist(dates, binCount, title=None,⊃
 intervalSize=None ):
    #create histogram
    (hist, bin_edges) = numpy.histogram(dates, binCount)
    #calculate width of each bin
    width = bin_edges[1] - bin_edges[0]

    #initialise chart drawing
    fig = pyplot.figure()

    #create the object for the chart
    ax = fig.add_subplot(111)

    #draw a bar chart, starting at the first data point, data
    #for bars will be held in hist variable.
    #the width of the bars is the width you calculated of the
    #binss. The colour of the bar will be orange
        ax.bar(bin_edges[:-1], hist, width=width,⊃
```

*continued*

**Listing 17-4    continued**

```
 facecolor='orange')

        #label the y axis
    ax.set_ylabel('visit rate per ' + str(intervalSize/60)⤸
+ "mins")
    #label x axis
    ax.set_xlabel('Time')

    #add title if one specified
    if title:
        ax.set_title(title)

    # format the x axis
    # see: http://matplotlib.org/examples/api/date_demo.html
    # for more info
    ax.xaxis.set_major_locator(DayLocator())
    # format major tick boxes as Day of month/Month Hour:Min
    ax.xaxis.set_major_formatter(DateFormatter('%d/%m %H:%M'))
    ax.xaxis.set_minor_formatter(DateFormatter('%H'))
    #uncomment the set_minor_locator function to put minor
    #lines for every hour
    #if the logging has run for some time, then there are
    #too many to display!
    #ax.xaxis.set_minor_locator(HourLocator())

    # format the coords box, which is displayed when mouse
    # is over graph
    ax.format_xdata = DateFormatter('%d %H:%M')
    ax.grid(True)
     fig.autofmt_xdate()
    return fig


def drawGraph(events,filename):
    #determine the number of bins (bars) on the graph by
    #splitting the time the data spans by a time interval.

    #calclulate the time spanned by the data
    latestReading = num2date(max(events))
    earliestReading = num2date(min(events))
    dateRange = latestReading - earliestReading
```

```
    numberOfSeconds = dateRange.seconds + dateRange.days *⤾
24 * 3600

    #chop the data up into roughly 20 min intervals (in seconds)
    intervalSize = 20*60

    #calculate how many intervals are there in numberOfSeconds
    #round up so there is always at least one
    histogramBins = math.ceil(float(numberOfSeconds)/⤾
float(intervalSize))

    #draw the graph
    fig = plotDatehist(events, bins=histogramBins, title=⤾
"Bird Box Activity", intervalSize=intervalSize)

    #save the graph to a file
    pyplot.savefig(filename)
```

The code contains two functions, `drawGraph` and `plotDatehist`. `drawGraph` sets up the parameters for drawing the chart. It calculates the number of *bins* (bars) for the histogram. It then calls the `plotDatehist` function, which actually creates the graph.

`plotDatehist` uses the `histogram` function from the `numpy` library to gather the visits together into time periods which correspond to the bins for the histogram. The `histogram` function takes the array of data (in this case the times when the nest box was visited) and the number of bins it should be split into. It returns both the number of items in each bin and the highest and lowest points for each bin. The function sets up the layout of where the charts will be drawn. In this case `subplot(111)` states that one chart will be drawn. The line

```
ax.bar(bin_edges[:-1], hist, width=width, facecolor='orange')
```

draws the bar chart.

The remainder of `plotDatehist` function sets up the axes – setting labels and grid lines. Finally, the graph is saved to file as a PDF.

To draw graphs from the analysis program, edit the file `analyseBirdDataFiltered.py` and make the following additions:

1. At the start of the file, add

   ```
   import drawgraph
   ```

2. On the last line add the following line, which will call your graph-drawing function:

```
drawgraph.drawGraph(outwardTimes, "birdGraph.pdf")
```

3. Finally, test that your program produces a graph by running it:

```
cat birddata.txt | python analyseBirdDataFiltered.py
```

Your program should produce a PDF with a chart showing bird activity. You can view the PDF on the Raspberry Pi with the command xpdf. If xpdf is not installed, install it with apt-get as follows:

```
apt-get install xpdf
```

To view the chart on the Raspberry Pi with the graphical environment running (type startx if it is not), into a terminal type

```
xpdf birdGraph.pdf
```

## Putting the Nest Box into Service

With all the code written and tested, it is time to get your Raspberry Pi in service gathering real data on wildlife. Before deploying you need to remove the test data by deleting the birddata.txt file. To delete a file from the command line, you can type rm *filename*.

Mount the Raspberry Pi and nest box securely and start the recordBird.py logging program running. You can check for bird activity by looking for entries in the birddata.txt log file with the more command.

Hopefully you'll see some activity, after which you can analyse the data by running the analyseBirdDataFiltered.py program.

## Over to You

With your nest box gathering valuable information about the habits of the birds in your garden, it is worth considering how you can take things further. Some of these suggestions are simple to implement; you can reuse code from other chapters of the book. Others are more involved and will require further research.

You could extend the logging program to send a tweet when one of the sensors was broken so that you knew it was worth watching the box. A good starting point would be to modify the code from Chapter 10, "The Twittering Toy". Look online for further documentation about the Twitter API – the `PostUpdate` function can help. Here's a hint:

```
api.PostUpdate('Bird Activity detected!')
```

A development of this would be to take a photo or short sequence of video when the beam is broken. You can execute `raspistill` or `raspivid` from Python to control the Raspberry Pi camera. Chapter 10 shows how to call an external process. Look on the Raspberry Pi forums or search Google for more information about controlling the camera.

If you don't have a bird nest box, you could fit the sensors to a bird feeder, or to the entrance of a box on the floor containing bait to capture rodents coming in and going out.

## Sharing Your Data with Others

How does your bird data compare with the data collected by other people?

You could share your photos or activity graphs by uploading them to a web server, perhaps over FTP or ssh if you are familiar with these. If you use Google Sites or WordPress, there are APIs available to transfer images. You could look at Chapter 15, "Facebook-Enabled Roto-Sketch" and use that as a basis to publish to Facebook.

You could set your Raspberry Pi up to be a wireless access point, run its own web server and check on your birds from your smartphone.

If you are really feeling adventurous, why not write a web application that stores bird activity data and plots it on a graph, or as an overlay on Google Maps? You would have to design your own API that would allow Raspberry Pis to submit their data.

## Adding More Sensors

You could interface your Raspberry Pi to more sensors. The Raspberry Pi bird box used on Springwatch also recorded data from a weather station. This allowed trends in bird activity to be linked to changes in the weather conditions. You could also add more instrumentation to the nest box, perhaps recording the temperature and humidity inside. Search online for information about interfacing analogue sensors to the Raspberry Pi.

# The Possibilities Are Endless

As you can see, the possibilities for extending this, like the other projects, are endless. The aim of this book is to have put you on the road to discover how exciting computing can be, while building really fun projects. You may not have understood every piece of code at first, but in computing this is not uncommon for experts! Sometimes you may need to spend some time playing with the code, copying bits out, changing it, experimenting to find out how it works. The background information in the chapters will hopefully give an introduction to the basics, which you can use to know how to modify the projects to make them your own. Treat it a bit like a cookbook where you reuse techniques from recipes in your own dishes.

You never stop learning with computing; technology will continue to change, but the underlying principles remain more constant. If you learn these principles, you can apply them to the latest technology and know where to find reference documentation. Sometimes part of the challenge is knowing what the jargon means, hopefully some of which this book has demystified.

Computing touches nearly every part of modern life. You can use it as a springboard into virtually any field. Computing changes the world. And often it starts with an idea and some code written by one or two people. Think how mobile phones, digital cameras, MP3 players, Facebook and Twitter affect millions of people. Anita Borg, Steve Furber, Bill Gates, Steve Jobs, Martha Lane Fox, Sophie Wilson and Mark Zuckerberg – contemporary famous names in the field of computing – all started with an idea. You and your invention can be part of it. It's over to you, what are you going to create? How will you change the world?

# Index

CPSIA information can be obtained
at www.ICGtesting.com
Printed in the USA
LVOW04s1924301217
561334LV00005B/9/P